A Prince of Martial Splendour in the Sixteen Kingdoms

Sinica Leidensia

Edited by

Barend J. ter Haar
Nicolas Standaert

In co-operation with

P.K. Bol, D.R. Knechtges, E.S. Rawski,
W.L. Idema, H.T. Zurndorfer

VOLUME 171

The titles published in this series are listed at *brill.com/sinl*

A Prince of Martial Splendour in the Sixteen Kingdoms

Li Hao (351–417), Ruler of Western Liang

By

Dominik Declercq

BRILL

LEIDEN | BOSTON

Cover illustration: a Northern Wei warrior, 386–535 CE, Private collection. Photograph © New West 2024.

The Library of Congress Cataloging-in-Publication Data is available online at https://catalog.loc.gov
LC record available at https://lccn.loc.gov/2024057385

Typeface for the Latin, Greek, and Cyrillic scripts: "Brill". See and download: brill.com/brill-typeface.

ISSN 0169-9563
ISBN 978-90-04-71643-8 (hardback)
ISBN 978-90-04-72738-0 (e-book)
DOI 10.1163/9789004727380

Copyright 2025 by Dominik Declercq. Published by Koninklijke Brill BV, Plantijnstraat 2, 2321 JC Leiden, The Netherlands.
Koninklijke Brill BV incorporates the imprints Brill, Brill Nijhoff, Brill Schöningh, Brill Fink, Brill mentis, Brill Wageningen Academic, Vandenhoeck & Ruprecht, Böhlau and V&R unipress.
Koninklijke Brill BV reserves the right to protect this publication against unauthorized use. Requests for re-use and/or translations must be addressed to Koninklijke Brill BV via brill.com or copyright.com.
For more information: info@brill.com.

This book is printed on acid-free paper and produced in a sustainable manner.

Contents

Preface VII
Maps VIII

1 Introduction 1

2 The Hexi Corridor 18

3 The Colonisation of Liangzhou, 100 BCE to 300 CE 43

4 Former Liang (320–376): Li Hao's Forebears under the Former Liang 61

5 Former Qin (351–384) and Later Liang (385–403) 76

6 Linked Destinies: Li Hao and Juqu Mengxun 87

7 Building a State, Part 1: Li Hao's Western Liang 105

8 Building a State, Part 2: Juqu Mengxun's Northern Liang 114

9 Relations with Eastern Jin 126

10 Li Hao Moves to Jiuquan 139

11 Li Hao's Last Years 149

12 The Sequel: Li Hao's Son Loses Western Liang 164

13 The Aftermath, and Conclusions 170

Appendix 1: Commandant Protectors of the Qiang 183
Appendix 2: Prefects of Wuwei, Zhangye, Jiuquan and Dunhuang 186
Abbreviations 191
Bibliography 192
Index 202

Preface

This monograph started life as an article drafted in Beijing during weekends when I was not distracted by my day job in the automotive business. Its first aim was to achieve as close as possible an understanding of *Jin shu* 87, the "Life of Li Hao". Li Hao lived on China's periphery, in 4th–5th century Gansu alongside non-Chinese populations, but essential though these facts are for his historical significance, they receive less attention than they deserve in the limits set by traditionally Sinocentric biographical convention. To do the subject justice, I needed to cast my net wider. I was stimulated to do so by the two anonymous peer reviewers of the original draft article, submitted to *Early Medieval China* in 2019, who brought their broader knowledge of the Sixteen Kingdoms to bear on my first effort and thereby showed where (the Chinese text being limpid enough) inchoate realities nevertheless lurk under the polished surface. In expanding the article into this book I tried to probe deeper, adding a range of other historical material on what made the Hexi Corridor special to its Chinese settlers. Evidence emerged of how Li Hao and his ephemeral state on the edge of the desert participated in the influences and exchanges that played out between the steppe and the sown, and for which Gansu was a necessary conduit from and into the Chinese Central Plain. Such evidence, it is true, I have coaxed predominantly from Chinese written sources. How much more material testimony there may be stands magnificently on display in Étienne de la Vaissière's recent work of much wider scope, *Asie centrale 300–850: Des routes et des royaumes* (2024). Here, multilingual voices paired with wide-ranging archaeological finds show these exchanges and influences structuring the Eurasian continent over immense distances and in the *longue durée*. I hope that future field research may add material detail corroborating the role Li Hao's Western Liang fulfilled in actively connecting China with the wider world beyond. I thank Daniel Garrido for creating the maps, and Kristen de Joseph for her meticulous copy-editing. Among those who encouraged my writing, I would like to single out the anonymous collector whose imposing Northern Wei warrior graces the cover of this book.

Antwerp, October 2024

Maps

1   Liangzhou Inspectorate 涼州刺史部, 100 BCE
2   Liangzhou Inspectorate, 50 BCE
3   Liangzhou Inspectorate, 150 CE
4   Liangzhou and Yongzhou 雍州, 200 CE
5   Liangzhou Inspectorate, 250 CE
6   Former Liang 前涼, 300 CE
7   Former Liang, 370 CE
8   Liangzhou under Later Liang 後涼, 390 CE
9   Later, Northern, Western, & Southern Liang, 400 CE
10 Liangzhou in 410 CE

CHAPTER 1

Introduction

The ill-starred succession of the first Western Jin 西晉 (265–316) emperor Sima Yan 司馬炎 (236–290, r. 265–290) by the mentally retarded Sima Zhong 司馬衷 (259–306, r. 290–306) triggered the internecine war known as the "Disturbances of the Eight Princes (*ba wang zhi luan* 八王之亂)," spelling the end of a briefly reconstituted Chinese empire. The war and its aftermath prompted the mostly non-Chinese peoples living in North China's Central Plain to wrest power from their Jin overlords and to launch as many as twenty-two competing states and statelets over a period of one hundred and thirty-six years, the so-called period of the "Sixteen Kingdoms (*shiliu guo* 十六國)" (304–439).[1] Meanwhile, a substantial number of the Jin elite who could afford it crossed the Yangtse River and fled south, gathering around a scion of the imperial house based in Jiankang 建康 (today's Nanjing) and marking the continuation of the dynasty henceforth known as the Eastern Jin 東晉 (317–420). Other refugees, some of whom shall appear prominently in these pages, instead found their way north to present-day Gansu. Only in 439 did the Northern Wei 北魏 dynasty (386–534) prove strong enough to reunify the North, and finally its heirs the Northern Zhou 北周 (557–581) and the Sui 隋 (581–618) succeeded in bringing Jiangnan 江南, i.e. Southern China, into the northern fold as well. Thus did a centrally ruled realm re-emerge in the image of its famed exemplar, the Han 漢 empire (206 BCE–220 CE).[2]

Taking a longer view, the Tang 唐 (618–907) dynasty that followed and indeed unified China as we know it inevitably derives some of its character from the

---

1   The name derives from the *Annals of the Sixteen Kingdoms* (*Shiliu guo chunqiu* 十六國春秋) by Cui Hong 崔鴻 (d. ca. 525), which has been lost as an independent work since Northern Song 北宋 times (960–1127), and since then only partially transmitted inasmuch as other works quote from it — the Northern Song encyclopaedia *Taiping yulan* 太平御覽 (*Imperial Digest for the Taiping* [*xingguo* 興國] *Era*, 976–984, comp. by Li Fang 李昉 [925–996] et al.) in particular. Reconstructed versions by Tu Qiaosun 屠喬孫 (*jinshi* 進士 1606) and Tang Qiu 湯球 (1804–1881) exist in various collectanea, as does a modern edition to which I shall refer: Tang Qiu, ed., *Shiliu guo chunqiu jibu* 輯補, punctuated and collated by Nie Weimeng 聶溦萌, Luo Xin 羅新 and Hua Zhe 華喆, Beijing 2020.

2   For an overview, see now Charles Holcombe, "The Sixteen Kingdoms," Ch. 6 in Albert E. Dien and Keith N. Knapp, eds., *The Cambridge History of China* Volume 2: *The Six Dynasties, 220–589* (Cambridge 2019; hereafter *CHC* 2), pp. 119–144. On using the term "Chinese" to denote the native people who identified as "Han people 漢人" during the Han, "Jin 晉人" during the Jin dynasty, see id. p. 120 n. 4.

© DOMINIK DECLERCQ, 2025 | DOI:10.1163/9789004727380_002

great reshuffling of cards that took place during the Sixteen Kingdoms. Rather than subsuming the bewildering events of the time under the us-versus-them phrase "the five Hu (= northern and northwestern nomads) threw our civilisational heartlands into turmoil (*wu Hu luan Hua* 五胡亂華)," the period, on balance, instead witnessed a general growth in population and a grand fusion of peoples in the North that laid the groundwork for the eras to come.[3] This mutual blending process, as Charles Holcombe says, in the long run "eliminated most of the old ethnic distinctions and generated a new 'Chinese' synthesis," in which, to be sure, the Chinese language emerged triumphant; and in which one may also posit, and with equal certainty, that both in terms of political and economic institutions and in terms of the resulting culture, the Northern invader regimes were the great transforming agent.[4] Keeping this theme of creative interaction between Chinese and non-Chinese in mind, the specific purpose of this study is to take a closer look at one of the more short-lived northern polities of this period of division, namely Western Liang 西涼 (400–421), at the edge of the realm, in the Hexi Corridor of today's Gansu province. The almost exclusive source for this is the biography of its Chinese founder Li Hao 李暠 (351–417), in the official *History of the Jin Dynasty* (*Jin shu* 晉書), edited early in the Tang dynasty by Fang Xuanling 房玄齡 (578–648).[5] The text merits a close re-reading, with all the sidelight that related materials may shine upon it. First, though, a few words on the antecedents of the Sixteen Kingdoms: a story of migrants that turned sour.

• • •

The simplest yardstick for judging a historical period is whether populations grew or shrank in it. By that measure, the Sixteen Kingdoms failed. Chronic warfare, social dislocation and economic collapse took a heavy toll. Though census figures undercount the real population, the Disturbances of the Eight Princes and the Xiongnu (Former Zhao 前趙, 304–329) onslaught that saw the sack of the Western Jin capital Luoyang 洛陽 in 311 and Chang'an 長安 in 316 caused a population drop of nearly 50 per cent. Growth recovered under the initially quite successful Former Qin 前秦 empire (351–384), the population

---

3   The "five Hu" are the Xiongnu 匈奴, Xianbei 鮮卑, Qiang 羌, Di 氐 and Jie 羯.

4   Chen Yinke 陳寅恪 (1890–1969) introduced this insight in his *Sui Tang zhidu yuanyuan lüelun gao* 隋唐制度淵源略論稿 (*A Draft Introduction to the Origins of Institutions of the Sui and Tang Dynasties*), Chongqing 1944. See also Holcombe, op. cit. p. 123.

5   *Jin shu* (*History of the Jin Dynasty*, 266–420; Beijing 1974; hereafter *JS*). All references to the dynastic histories will be to the Beijing Zhonghua shuju 中華書局 editions unless indicated otherwise.

INTRODUCTION   3

in the North *reportedly* increasing from its low of 7 million to 23 million from
the year 329 to 383, until the disastrous collapse of the Qin state in 383 and
384 caused figures to plummet again, to perhaps 10 million. Only by the end
of Northern Wei, in 520, is the population estimated to have exceeded the
20 million level again.[6] Ceaseless violence for often ephemeral gain undeniably marks the period of the Sixteen Kingdoms, but the storm had long been
coming.

• • •

To begin with, the Xiongnu 匈奴 were steppe nomads active in all of modern (Inner and Outer) Mongolia, and bore the brunt of the Qin 秦 empire's
(221–207 BCE) territorial expansion in one of their traditional pasture lands
within the northern bend of the Yellow River (i.e. the Ordos Plateau). Chased
out of the Ordos by the Qin, and moving north, this particular branch or group
of the Xiongnu was then forced to face new enemies: the Eastern Nomads
(*donghu* 東胡) to their east, in eastern Mongolia and western Manchuria, and
the Yuezhi 月氏 to their west, in modern Gansu and further westward into the
Tarim Basin of Xinjiang. Modun 冒頓, the eldest son of the *chanyu* 單于, i.e.
supreme leader of the Xiongnu, was held hostage by the Yuezhi to ensure the
Xiongnus' subservience to them. Modun escaped, managed to unite a host of
Xiongnu tribes into a veritable empire under his leadership (r. 209–174 BCE),
and proceeded to destroy the Eastern Nomads and oust the Yuezhi from Gansu
before retaking all the territories that his father had lost to the Qin general
Meng Tian 蒙恬 (d. 210 BCE), best known to later generations as the builder of
the Great Wall.[7]

---

6   The starting point is the 280 CE census figure of a 16.16 million population, 2/3 of which (sc. 11
    million), it was thought, lived in the North: *JS* 14:415. The figures' "trajectory" may be roughly
    correct, but since the census figures take only registered subjects into account, the figures are
    undercounted "by as much as a quarter or a third, if not more" (see Victor Cunrui Xiong, "The
    Northern Economy," in *CHC* 2, pp. 309–329 at pp. 323–325). However, an increase from 7 to 23
    million over 54 years implies a compound annual growth of 2.22%, which cannot be correct;
    for Europe, the growth rate between 1500 and 1750 was 0.17% (see Fernand Braudel, *Les Jeux
    de l'échange* [Paris 1979], p. 213), which would give an increase from 7 to 7.67 million over
    54 years. Conversely, if 23 million is correct, the initial, Northern, population figure for 280
    should (at a 0.17% compound rate) in reality have been ca. 19 million instead of 11 — hence
    the official figure was undercounted by 72%. I therefore qualify these data with the term
    "reportedly."
7   Sima Qian 司馬遷 (ca. 145–ca. 86 BCE), *Shiji* 史記 (*Records of the Historian*; Beijing 1959),
    107:2885–2890 = Ban Gu 班固 (32–92), *Han shu* 漢書 (*History of the* [*Western, Former*] *Han
    Dynasty*; Beijing 1962; hereafter *HS*), 94A:3748–3750.

After a punitive campaign by the first Han emperor against this Xiongnu empire ended in disaster in 200 BCE, for the next seventy years, the Han resorted to a policy called *heqin* 和親, or seeking "peace through kinship relations," that involved intermarriage between the ruling houses as well as the payment of an annual tribute to buy off further Xiongnu territorial advances.[8] An additional benefit was the opening of border trade, as officially sanctioned by the second Han emperor Wen 漢文帝 (Liu Heng 劉恒, r. 179–157).[9] But the high cost of the *heqin* policy and, as the Han empire strengthened, the increasing perception that a policy of appeasement was an indignity, prompted Emperor Wu 漢武帝 (Liu Che 劉徹, 156–87, r. 141–87 BCE) again to go on the offensive in 134 BCE. In a series of victories, the Han took the Ordos back from the Xiongnu in 127, and in 121 conquered Gansu province to gain access to the Western Regions beyond Dunhuang 敦煌. In the latter campaign, a "viceroy" of the *chanyu*, as one might put it — the Hunye 渾邪 king (d. 116 BCE) — surrendered to the Han general Huo Qubing 霍去病 (ca. 140–117 BCE) with 40,000 (some say 100,000) men. These men were forcibly relocated to five "Dependent States (*shuguo* 屬國)" under Chinese supervision, created for them within the five commanderies on the Ordos Plateau — that is to say, in their own former homelands.[10]

Over the next seventy years, internal power struggles over the succession of the *chanyu* severely weakened the Xiongnu empire and allowed the Han to gain control over the Western Regions. The creation of a Han "Protector-General of the Western Regions" (*xiyu duhu* 西域都護) in 60 BCE — who had his office in Wulei 烏壘 fortress, west of modern Karasahr (Yanqi 焉耆) in Xinjiang[11] — well nigh coincides with the *chanyu* Huhanye 呼韓邪 (r. 58–31 BCE), from a southern faction of the Xiongnu, coming over to pay homage to the Han in 54 BCE. For this, Huhanye was lavishly rewarded by the Han court. His realm

---

8   Nicola Di Cosmo, *Ancient China and Its Enemies: The Rise of Nomadic Power in East Asian History* (Cambridge 2002), in particular Ch. 5; Mark Edward Lewis, *The Early Chinese Empires: Qin and Han* (Cambridge, Mass., 2007), pp. 129–134.

9   *Shiji* 110:2904; *HS* 94B:3831. Emperor Jing 景帝 (Liu Qi 劉啟, r. 157–141) also allowed trade: *HS* 94A:3764; so too, at the beginning of his reign, did Emperor Wu: *Shiji* 110:2904 = *HS* 94A:3765.

10 *Shiji* 110:2909, 111:2933–2934 = *HS* 94A:3769, 53:2482–2483. The five Dependent States were located in the Longxi 隴西, Beidi 北地, Shangjun 上郡, Shuofang 朔方 and Yunzhong 雲中 commanderies. See also Yü Ying-shih, "Han Foreign Relations," in Denis Twitchett and Michael Loewe, eds., *The Cambridge History of China* Volume 1: *The Ch'in and Han Empires, 221 B.C.–A.D. 220* (Cambridge 1986; hereafter *CHC* 1), pp. 377–462 at pp. 383–405.

11 Yü, "Han Foreign Relations," in *CHC* 1, pp. 391–394, 408; A.F.P. Hulsewé, with M.A.N. Loewe, *China in Central Asia. The Early Stage: 125 B.C.–A.D. 23* (Leiden 1979; hereafter *CICA*), pp. 64, 164 n. 514 (Wulei).

INTRODUCTION 5

north of the Han defensive walls remained his to rule as he saw fit, but the status of his realm became that of a Han tributary state.

The coup that brought Wang Mang 王莽 (r. 9–23 CE) briefly to power, as well as the civil war that followed upon the Wang Mang interregnum in order to restore the Han dynasty (Eastern Han, 25–220 CE), put paid to this tributary arrangement. While the new Emperor Guangwu 光武帝 (Liu Xiu 劉秀, 5–57 CE, r. 25–57) had his hands full eliminating political rivals, the Xiongnu regained control over the Western Regions. Xiongnu also raided the Han borders; Chinese farmers were forced to flee inland, and the government as much as gave its blessing to this capitulationism, agreeing to re-register the farmers in designated inland commanderies. Eventually, the Xiongnu reoccupied all the lands they had been forced to vacate more than two centuries earlier, including the "Dependent States," while exercising power over vast areas north of the Chinese *limes* as well.

Internal dissension caused yet another split in the Xiongnu leadership in 49 CE. A northern *chanyu* was pitted against a southern rival, the militarily weaker *chanyu* Bi 比 (r. 48–56). When Bi threw in his lot with the Han, Emperor Guangwu made sure that he was as richly rewarded as his predecessor Huhanye had been; from then on, however, the Southern Xiongnu, as they became known, were regarded as Han subjects, and were instructed to take up residence in eight frontier commanderies in present-day Shanxi, Gansu and Inner Mongolia. There, imperial troops as well as Han Chinese made to move in from the interior settled next to the relocated Xiongnu communities. In hindsight, this was a fatal mistake. Should the emperor have embraced the southern *chanyu*'s tactical submission to the Han and joined forces with him against their common Xiongnu threat further north, perhaps Bi and his people would have displaced the defeated Northern Xiongnu and become a Han vassal state like Huhanye's. As things stood, the uneasy cohabitation of Southern Xiongnu nomads and their Chinese minders led to friction and conflict.[12]

The strategy of using Southern Xiongnu against Northern Xiongnu did however become operative forty years later, when a joint force under the command of Dou Xian 竇憲 (d. 92) succeeded in driving the Northern Xiongnu towards the west and reclaiming a few strongholds for the Han in the Western Regions. This did not put an immediate end to the border trade in cattle and horses,

---

12 Yü, "Han Foreign Relations," in *CHC* 1, pp. 394–403; Hans Bielenstein, "Wang Mang, the Restoration of the Han Dynasty, and Later Han," in *CHC* 1, pp. 223–290 at pp. 265–268; Ying-shih Yü, "The Hsiung-nu," in Denis Sinor, ed., *The Cambridge History of Early Inner Asia* (Cambridge 1990), pp. 118–149 at pp. 138–141; Di Cosmo, *Ancient China and Its Enemies*, in particular Ch. 6; Lewis, *The Early Chinese Empires*, pp. 136–139.

which was beneficial to both sides. Nonetheless, with or without Han enmity, through internal problems the Northern Xiongnu had become a spent force by the end of the first century. The Eastern Nomads re-entered the picture as the Wuhuan 烏桓 and the Xianbei 鮮卑, harassing the Xiongnu from the northeast. Not only did the Southern Xiongnu continue their nomadic life on Han soil; worse, more and more Northern Xiongnu defected and joined them. By 90 CE, the total population of Xiongnu in the south attained 230,730; over the next hundred years, they also moved gradually further south into Shanxi, and by the early Western Jin — acculturation setting hesitantly in — there were about one million semi-nomadic, semi-sedentary Xiongnu farmers/herdsmen living alongside Chinese settlements in the whole of what is now Shanxi province.[13]

•••

Just as the Xiongnu, chased northward by the victorious and expansive Qin, had crushed the Eastern Hu whom they had encountered on their way, two centuries later, when conditions permitted the Xiongnu to descend from the Mongolian Plateau and cross back into Han territory, one of these Eastern Hu peoples — the Wuhuan 烏桓 (or Wuwan 烏丸) — followed southward in the Xiongnu's wake from their ancestral grounds in the Laoha River 老哈河 basin. They were keen hunters, and yurt-dwelling pastoralists who put cattle, horses and goats to graze while also cultivating foxtail millet (*ji* 穄, *Setaria italica*) and sand rice (dongqiang 東牆/薔, *Agriophyllum squarrosum*); their men "thought it spry and practical to shave their head completely bald," and "were adept at fashioning bows and arrows, saddles and bridles, and [forging] weapons out of bronze and iron," while their wives "pierced hides to make patterned embroideries, and wove coarse woollens."[14]

Wuhuan showed up wherever Xiongnu pulled back. In 49 CE, Emperor Guangwu permitted perhaps as many as a hundred thousand Wuhuan to make their way south, to some of the same border commanderies where the Southern Xiongnu were active; in exchange for regular payments of food and

---

13 Yü, "Han Foreign Relations" pp. 403–405; Bielenstein, "Wang Mang ..." pp. 268–269; *JS* 97:2549; Misaki Yoshiaki 三崎良章, *Goko Jūrokkoku: Chūgoku shijō no minzoku dai-idō* 五胡十六国: 中国史上の民族大移動 (2012), transl. by Liu Kewei 劉可維 as Wuhu Shiliuguo: Zhongguo shishang de minzu da qianxi 五胡十六國: 中國史上的民族大遷徙 (Beijing 2019), pp. 6–10.

14 Fan Ye 范曄 (398–446), *Hou Han shu* 後漢書 (*History of the Later [or Eastern] Han Dynasty*, hereinafter *HHS*; Beijing 1965), 90:2979–2980: "烏桓者 [⋯] 俗善騎射，弋獵禽獸為事。[⋯] 以穹廬為舍 [⋯] [男子] 以髡頭為輕便 [⋯] 婦人能刺韋作文繡，織氀毻。男子能作弓矢鞍勒，鍛金鐵為兵器。其土地宜穄及東牆。".

INTRODUCTION

clothing, they were to guard the Han borders against inroads by Northern Xiongnu and to keep an eye on the next wave of nomads advancing from the north: the Xianbei. In fact, the Xianbei tracked the Wuhuan at close remove, having started their long journey from higher up, namely the wooded slopes north of the Xar Moron River 西拉木倫河 in Inner Mongolia. As they did so, gradually occupying lands that had previously been Xiongnu-dominated territory, the Xianbei occasionally came face to face with Xiongnu communities that had been slow to move. "There were still over a hundred thousand encampments of remaining Xiongnu tribes that had stayed on," says the *History of the Later Han*, referring to a time around 100 CE, "and when these began to call themselves Xianbei" for their own safety, "the Xianbei from then on gradually became more formidable."[15] This is a salutary reminder of the fluid boundaries between these peoples. It has even been suggested that the name "Xiongnu" itself means no more than "the alliance," concluded through a mutual give-and-take between perhaps quite disparate groups.[16]

• • •

Linguistically speaking, Xiongnu, Wuhuan and Xianbei all appear to have been Proto-Mongol peoples.[17] In 386 CE, the other formerly Eastern Hu people, the Xianbei — or to be more precise, the Tuoba 拓跋 tribe of the Xianbei — were to found the Northern Wei that proceeded to unify the North and eventually the whole empire. Looking back to that time from the vantage point of a recently reunited empire, the Buddhist author Daoxuan 道宣 (596–667) asks rhetorically: "Are we to reject the illustrious rulers of the Tuoba Wei dynasty merely on account of their original nationality?"[18] But at first, when Xianbei horsemen first made their appearance on the Chinese border, they were but

---

15   *HHS* 90:2986.

16   See William Honeychurch, *Inner Asia and the Spatial Politics of Empire. Archaeology, Mobility, and Culture Contact* (New York 2015), passim.

17   For expert discussion of their "proto-Mongol" language, see now Andrew Shimunek, *Languages of Ancient Southern Mongolia and North China: A Historical-Comparative Study of the Serbi-Mongolic Language Family, with an Analysis of Northeastern Frontier Chinese and Old Tibetan Phonology* (Wiesbaden 2017).

18   Daoxuan, "Liedai wangchen zhihuo jie 列代王臣滯惑解" (664 CE), in his *Guang hongming ji* 廣弘明記 (*Expanded Collection on the Propagation and Clarification [of Buddhism]*). I quote the translation of E. Zürcher, in his *The Buddhist Conquest of China. The Spread and Adaptation of Buddhism in Early Medieval China* (2nd ed., Leiden 1972), p. 266.

the latest manifestation of the permanent threat that steppe nomads posed to the Han empire.

From about 50 CE and for half a century thereafter, the Wuhuan guarding the northern frontier at Emperor Guangwu's behest appear to have been vigilant enough that, in Ningcheng 甯城, northwest of modern Xuanhua District 宣化區 (Zhangjiakou Municipality 張家口市) — or, as it used to be called, Chahar 察哈爾 (Hebei province) — a Han Commandant Protector of the Wuhuan (*hu Wuhuan xiaowei* 護烏桓校尉) was installed to supervise a market for trade that welcomed Xianbei business as well. "Gratified with gifts [that the Xianbei received from the Han] and placing their sons as hostages [with the Han]," the Xianbei in return "engaged in mutual trade there, in every season of the year."[19]

In 109, however, the Wuhuan, colluding with both the Xianbei and Southern Xiongnu, reneged on their allegiance to the Han, and for the next century resorted to pillage and warfare instead. From the Xianbei side — and as we have seen, "Xianbei" may have comprised a sizeable percentage of Xiongnu groups that chose to rally to them — the peril to the Han intensified when their confederation gained an able leader, Tanshihuai 檀石槐 (ca. 136–181), who broke through Han defences from Liaoning in the far east down to Gansu in the northwest. Upon Tanshihuai's death, however, the confederation disintegrated.[20] By the early third century, one finds a number of individual Xianbei tribes (or opportunistic, multi-ethnic alliances named after a Xianbei clan assuming leadership) pursuing their separate ways. Such is the case of the Yuwen 宇文, Duan 段 and Murong 慕容 in Liaoxi, and the Tuoba Xianbei north of the Yin Mountains 陰山 (west of present-day Hohhot): there, in 220, the Tuoba leader Liwei 力微 (d. 277) imposed his authority over a range of tribal groups, and by 258 had built a capital city, Shengle 盛樂, surrounded by a still visible tamped-earth wall 670 by 655 m in length. More westward, the Tufa 禿髮, Qifu 乞伏, Tuyuhun 吐谷渾 and others moved into Hexi 河西 (the area of modern Gansu "west of the Yellow River" and north of Lanzhou) and Longxi 隴西 (the area of modern Gansu south of Lanzhou, as we have seen).[21]

---

19 *HHS* 90:2982: "賞賜質子，歲時互市焉。" On these events, see Wang Chen 王沈 (d. 266), *Wei shu* 魏書 (*History of the [Cao-]Wei* 曹魏 *State*, 220–265), in Pei Songzhi's 裴松之 (372–451) commentary on Chen Shou 陳壽 (233–297), *Sanguo zhi* 三國志 (*Record of the Three States*, 220–265; Beijing 1959; hereafter *SGZ*) 30:837, largely similar to *HHS* 90.2981–2986.

20 See on Tanshihuai, K.H.J. Gardiner and Rafe de Crespigny, "T'an-shih-huai and the Hsien-pi tribes of the second century A.D." (Canberra 1977).

21 Misaki Yoshiaki, op. cit. pp. 12–14. On Shengle: Albert E. Dien, *Six Dynasties Civilization* (New Haven 2007), p. 24; Nancy Shatzman Steinhardt, *Chinese Architecture in an Age of Turmoil, 200–600* (Honolulu/Hong Kong 2014), p. 32.

INTRODUCTION 9

The insurrectionist Wuhuan, meanwhile, eventually found their match in Cao Cao 曹操 (155–220). In 207, having inflicted heavy losses on them, Cao Cao forcibly moved 10,000 *luo* 落 or "encampment groups" of "Wuhuan of the three commanderies 三郡烏桓" into China proper, where they acculturated over time.[22]

• • •

Also deserving of a brief mention here are the Dingling 丁零, a proto-Turkic nomad people from the northern Mongolian Plateau who, being at first subjugated to the Xiongnu, later fell under Xianbei domination (they joined Tanshihuai's confederation), and at least partly moved with them into Northern China. In 212, one finds Dingling soldiers serving in an army commanded by Cao Cao. We also find them in Gansu later on; in 383, they stood up against Former Qin rule as far south as Henan.[23]

Yu Huan 魚豢 (3rd cent.), in his *Wei lüe* 魏略 (*An Outline History of [the State of Cao-]Wei*), mentions two peoples with the name Dingling 丁令. One, which could field a fighting force of 60,000 cavalry, lived as herdsmen and hunters north of Kangju 康居, i.e. north of Samarkand, in southeastern Uzbekistan. They had been subjugated to the Xiongnu in the past, just like the other Dingling that he mentions as roaming around in what is today Gansu, who were a subgroup of what he refers to as the "chattel caitiffs (*zilu* 貲虜)": "The 'chattel caitiffs' originally were [with the] Xiongnu, [for] the Xiongnu called their slaves 'chattel.' At the beginning of the Jianwu 建武 time (25–57 CE), when the Xiongnu were on the wane, they parted with their slaves, [who] then absconded into Jincheng 金城 [Commandery = modern Lanzhou], Wuwei 武威, and to the east and west of the Heishui 黑水 and Xihe 西河 [rivers] north of Jiuquan 酒泉 [Commandery]. Herding their livestock, they moved in pursuit of water and pasture, [but they also] raided and pillaged Liangzhou 涼州. Of distinct encampments (*buluo* 部落) they have, at a rough count, a few tens of thousands, which are not to be equated with [those of] the Xianbei [formerly] of the Eastern Division 東部鮮卑 [in Tanshihuai's confederation]. Not all of them are of the same tribe/clan (*zhong* 種): there are Dahu 大胡, and there are [also] Dingling 丁令, and some of them in quite many aspects look mixed up with the Qiang, for the good reason that originally they were fugitive slaves. During the transition from Han to Wei (= 220), one of their leaders was

---

22 *SGZ* 30:835, *HHS* 90:2984; Misaki Yoshiaki, *op. cit.* pp. 10–11. The "three commanderies" were the Liaodong Dependent State 遼東屬國, Liaoxi 遼西, and Youbeiping 右北平.

23 Misaki Yoshiaki, op. cit. p. 17; Holcombe, op. cit. p. 139.

Tanzhe 檀柘, and after his death, leaders from his collateral branches (*qi zhi daren* 其枝大人) moved south near the confines of Guangwei 廣魏 and Lianju 令居;[24] [one of them,] Tuguilai 禿瑰來, rebelled several times and was killed by [the] Liangzhou [authorities]. At present, there is Shaoti 劭提, who makes as if coming to surrender, then again flees, and at all times is a threat on the roads one travels in [this] western province 西州."[25] The text is unfortunately none too clear. If the Dingling, manumitted by Xiongnu, spread into Liangzhou after "Southern Xiongnu" began to arrive there in ca. 50 CE (*vide supra*), the dating is wrong (this was not at the beginning, but near the end of the Jianwu era of the Eastern Han), and there seems to be no point in comparing the number of their settlements (if that is what *buluo* here means) with that of the "Eastern Xianbei," who may (or may not) have entered Gansu at least 130 years later. Does Yu Huan mean that the Dingling were, in fact, Qiang? Tanzhe, Tuguilai and Shaoti, presumably all Dingling chieftains, are (*errore excepto!*) not mentioned anywhere but here. In spite of this, the precise geography intrigues. "The confines of Guangwei and Lianju" corresponds fairly closely to a ca. 300 km stretch of the present railway link between Yongdeng County 永登縣, 75 km west of Lanzhou (= Lianju), and Linwei District 臨渭區, in the west of Shaanxi province (= Guangwei), which follows the natural lay of the land and runs along the River Wei 渭河 for half of its distance.[26] The way from Jincheng to Wuwei to Jiuquan takes one in a northwesterly direction; between Wuwei and Jiuquan lies Zhangye 張掖, and it is there rather than in the Jiuquan area (ca. 150 km northwest of Zhangye) that most of the runoff water from the Qilian Mountains collects into today's Heihe 黑河 or Black River, the upper section of the Ruo River (Ruoshui 弱水, also known as Etsin Gol). The Ruoshui splits downstream into an Eastern and a Western River (Xihe 西河) that empty into two lakes in the extreme desert north of Gansu province. Heihe and Xihe need not be the same as Yu Huan's Heishui and Xihe rivers; the latter two could just as well have been among the many runoff streams that feed into today's Black River. Because the climate of the area has become progressively drier over the last millennium or so, it is not possible to identify ancient water channels with any certainty. Let us simply conclude that

---

24 For the pronunciation of *ling* 令 as *lian*, see Meng Kang's 孟康 (fl. 180–260) gloss in *HS* 28B:1611 n. 4.

25 Yu Huan, *Wei lüe*, as quoted in the commentary on *SGZ* 30:862 (Dingling north of Kangju) and 859 (Dingling in Liangzhou = Gansu).

26 Guangwei was the name given in Yu Huan's lifetime to Lüeyang Circuit 略陽道 in the Han (*HS* 28B:1612) and Lüeyang Commandery 略陽郡 (Qinzhou 秦州 province) in the Jin, of which present-day Linwei (then also named Lüeyang) served as the administrative seat. See *JS* 14:435.

INTRODUCTION

the Dingling people were one of several non-Chinese pastoralist communities living in present-day Gansu province from the first century of the common era.

• • •

Now, whether or not a dip in the Mongolian climate was a contributing factor to these peoples' southward migration over centuries, in so doing, they certainly moved into milder climes and into "a wide belt of transitional borderland — suitable for both farming and pasturage — that stretches across much of the north of China, approaching surprisingly close in places to the political and population centres of the early Chinese empire."[27] To Cao Cao in the last years of the Han, and later to Sima Yan (Emperor Wu of the Jin 晉武帝) as well, allowing the Xiongnu in — creating a reservoir of mounted warriors relatively close by and easily conscripted, who bred their own supply of horses — was a policy worth following as long as the immigrants were kept under Chinese control. In Shanxi, Cao Cao divided 29,000 Xiongnu camps up into five "divisions (bu 部)," each supervised by a Chinese "major (sima 司馬)"; for the Western Jin, that function appears to have been taken over by a "chief clerk (zhangshi 長史)."[28] Contemporaries also remarked upon the fact that the nineteen separate Xiongnu tribes or branches (buluo 部落) on Chinese soil, much like the Qiang in this respect (vide infra), rather kept to their own and did not bond easily: in other words, that they had not attained an advanced form of statehood.[29] Hence, in spite of the occasional mishap (a chief clerk was assassinated ca. 275), from the years 279 to 287, Emperor Wu proceeded to admit five more Xiongnu chieftains at the head of their tribes. One brought 29,300 people with him, another more than 100,000; a third 11,500 people, not to mention 22,000 head of cattle and 105,000 goats.[30] Moreover, as attendant secretary (shi yushi 侍御史) Guo Qin 郭欽 wrote in a 280 CE memorial to the emperor, after the devastation wrought by the fall of the Han, "there was a dearth of people early

---

27   Holcombe, op. cit. p. 121. I have not seen climate cooling mentioned; the presence of a large stone-built palace-like structure (the Shimao site 石峁遺址) on the territory of Shenmu Municipality 神木市 in the far north of Shaanxi, built ca. 2300 BCE and abandoned ca. 1800 BCE, is suggestive of climate change in an earlier period.

28   JS 97:2548–2549.

29   JS 97:2549–2450. Asked by the Han Emperor Xuan 漢宣帝 (r. 73–49 BCE) about the Qiang, General Zhao Chongguo 趙充國 (ca. 137–51 BCE) replied: "What makes the Qiang people easy to control is that every one of their tribes naturally has its own strongman and that they quite frequently go on the offensive against each other, so that their propensity is not towards unity" (HS 69:2972).

30   JS 3:70, 97:2549.

in the [succeeding Cao 曹-]Wei 魏 state (220–265)," and so even then it was not wrong *per se* that "the northwestern commanderies [were] all inhabited by Rong 戎 barbarians."[31] Besides, while their prime use to the state was military, as a fighting force welded to their horses, under a more temperate sky, the Xiongnu, just like the Xianbei or the Wuhuan, also took up a more sedentary way of life, combining animal husbandry with agriculture.

Nonetheless, not all was well, and not only because the "barbarians'" military prowess might one day turn against their hosts. For Guo Qin, who took care not to criticise the emperor, that eventuality lay far in the future: "Today they may be submissive; but should there be a war alert a hundred years from now, setting out from Pingyang 平陽 and Shangdang 上黨 [commanderies, in Shanxi], the Hu horsemen shall be in Mengjin 孟津 in fewer than three days (where one crosses the Yellow River to reach Luoyang), and Beidi 北地, Xihe 西河, Taiyuan 太原, Pingyi 馮翊, Anding 安定 and Shangjun 上郡 [commanderies in Shaanxi, Gansu and Shanxi] shall all have turned into Di 狄 chiefs' encampments."[32] The Xiongnu would be expelled without delay, and the land they left behind be reoccupied by natives carted in from the interior. Twenty years later, another policy recommendation by Jiang Tong 江統 (d. 310), "On Deporting the Rong Barbarians (*Xi Rong lun* 徙戎論)," sounds even more urgent and ominous. Its immediate background is also more concerning: in 296, a rebellion had broken out quite close to the central part of modern Shaanxi designated as "the land within the passes (*Guanzhong* 關中)," and it involved multiple actors. Hao Duyuan 郝度元, a Xiongnu, mobilised the "Malan Qiang 馬蘭羌" and the "Lushui nomads 盧水胡" and took control of Beidi and Pingyi. Galvanised by this success, "all the Di 氐 and the Qiang in Qin 秦 and Yong 雍 [provinces: Shaanxi, Shanxi and Gansu] rose in revolt, and incited the Di commander Qi Wannian 齊萬年 (d. 299) to arrogate the title of 'emperor (*di* 帝)' to himself" in Jingyang 涇陽, just 50 km away from Chang'an. Qi Wannian was defeated only three years later.[33]

---

31 *JS* 97:2549. Rong, like Di 狄 also, is an archaic and denigratory term for non-Chinese people in the north and west, and as such (or in combination) can refer to Xiongnu, Xianbei, Wuhuan, Dingling ...

32 "Chiefs' encampments": *ting* 庭, as explained by Yue Chan 樂產 (n.d.) in a note to *Shiji* 110:2892: "The *chanyu* 單于 did not have inner or outer walls. They did not understand how these could define a 'capital'. It was the open area in front of their yurts that was just like a court to them, which is why this was called their 'court'." I owe this reference to François Thierry, "Yuezhi et Kouchans: Pièges et dangers des sources chinoises," in Osmund Bopearachchi and Marie-Françoise Boussac, eds., *Afghanistan, Ancien carrefour entre l'est et l'ouest*, Indicopleustoi (Turnhout 2005), pp. 421–539, at p. 464.

33 *JS* 4:94–95.

INTRODUCTION

Jiang Tong's piece has much to say about the irredeemably violent nature of barbarians beyond the pale of Chinese civilisation, opining that the policy of letting them into the country "had been, at best, a calculation arising of expediency, and of no benefit to later generations: for in what we are confronting today we are reaping its ill effects."[34] But he also points a finger at his own compatriots for aggravating a tense situation:

> Guanzhong is a fertile land where all living things abound [...] it is where emperors and kings have taken up residence, while for Rong and Di to stay on this land is quite unheard of. Not being our kith and kin, their hearts and minds are necessarily different. [...] But taking advantage of their being down and out, we relocated them into the heart of our realm, an object of diversion for gentlemen and commoners alike, who made fun of their abject weakness and caused a mood of hatred and resentment to envenom the very marrow of their bones. By the time they had procreated into a teeming multitude, what else could happen but that, sitting idle, they nurtured those sentiments? With their covetous and violent nature, harbouring wrath and fury, they watched out for any chance they could take to turn aggressive and defy us. Moreover, living in our own domains, without barricades or strongholds to keep them segregated from us, they caught our unprepared people by surprise and captured the stacked crops from dispersed fields. That is how it was possible for the harm they perpetrated to spread ever wider, terror and devastation striking unexpectedly — and inevitably all this was bound to happen, as events have all too clearly demonstrated.

For various observers, the areas where Chinese and "barbarians" were bound to clash shared the characteristics of being centrally located and being blessed with particularly fertile soil. "Guanzhong is a fertile land where all living things abound; its farmland is of top-notch quality [...]" The Qiang and Di, who in ca. 40 CE were forcibly relocated there (in Pingyi and Hedong 河東) from southern Gansu (Longxi), preferred to rise up in revolt in 107 CE rather than be drafted to campaign back home in the "Western Regions 西域." They subsequently spread throughout Guanzhong: in ca. 300, Jiang Tong advocates

---

34   The text is from Jiang Tong's biography, *JS* 56:1529–1538, with the quoted sentence on p. 1531 and the next paragraph on p. 1532, which I translate from the abbreviated version in Sima Guang 司馬光 (1019–1096), *Zizhi tongjian* 資治通鑑 (*Comprehensive Mirror for Aid in Government*), annotated by Hu Sanxing 胡三省 (1230–1302), Beijing 1959¹; hereafter *ZZTJ*: 83:2623–2628.

chasing the Qiang out of Anding, Xinping 新平, Beidi and Pingyi (a string of commanderies marking the north of Guanzhong) and the Di out of Fufeng 扶風, Shiping 始平 and Jingzhao 京兆 (a string of commanderies marking the south of Guanzhong, with Chang'an at the centre of Jingzhao Commandery).[35] The other such region was Sizhou 司州, the metropolitan province with Luoyang at its centre: Ji Commandery 汲郡, for instance, "counts thousands of acres of fine farmland [...] once the saline soil [should be drained of water and] becomes plain field, the benefit to all should be very considerable. [...] In such areas in particular could bumper harvests be achieved irrespective even of what the seasons bring." In Sizhou (the north of modern Henan), like in modern Shanxi to its north, Xiongnu had settled in considerable numbers: in Pingyang, Hedong 河東, Hongnong 弘農, Henan 河南 (where Luoyang lay), Henei 河內, Wei Commandery 魏郡, Yangping 陽平 and Dunqiu 頓丘.[36]

In these regions, the Qiang and Di "procreated into a teeming multitude"; the Xiongnu (e.g. in Yangping and Dunqiu) "[had been] thriving and [now] constituted five to six thousand households altogether."[37] For good measure, our source here, Shu Xi, takes pains to underline that "in the ten commanderies administered by the province (= Sizhou), a numerous population lives on limited land; that is particularly the case in the Three Wei 三魏," just east of Dunqiu.[38] Now it appears certain that in these most coveted habitats of the empire, the Qiang, Di and Xiongnu combined pastoral traditions with sedentary farming in a way that strained resources. Shu Xi writes of Sizhou, where "a numerous population lives on limited land," that nevertheless, "pig, goat and horse herding is widespread within this area." He must mean that Xiongnu immigrants put the land to this use, when it could be used more productively for farming:

> This [herding] should be abolished and abandoned altogether so as to provide [land] to those [now] without [farming] occupation,

---

35   *JS* 56:1531–1532.

36   I quote from Shu Xi 束皙 (ca. 264–ca. 303), "A Policy Proposal on Extending Agriculture 廣農議," in *JS* 51:1431–1432; on the commanderies with a Xiongnu presence, see *JS* 97:2549 and *JS* 51:1432. For Shu Xi's dates, see my "The Perils of Orthodoxy: A Western Jin 'Hypothetical Discourse,'" in *T'oung Pao* LXXX (1994), pp. 27–60 at p. 35 n. 15.

37   "蕃育眾盛" (*JS* 56:1532), "今者繁盛，合五六千家" (*JS* 51:1432).

38   *JS* 51:1431. The "Three Wei" is a fancy appellation for Wei Commandery: according to Li Daoyuan 酈道元 (d. 527), *Shuijing zhu* 水經注 (*Itineraries of Rivers, with a Commentary*), ed. collated by Wang Guowei 王國維 (1877–1927) and arranged and punctuated by Yuan Yingguang 袁英光 & Liu Yinsheng 劉寅生 (*Shuijing zhu jiao* 校, Shanghai 1984), 10:349, Wang Mang renamed Ye 鄴, the administrative seat of Wei Commandery 魏郡, "Weicheng 魏城" (see *HS* 28A:1573), and thereafter, when Cao Cao divided the governance of Wei Commandery up between an eastern and a western commandant 東西都尉 (see *SGZ* 1:42), the name "Three(fold) Wei 三魏" took hold.

INTRODUCTION   15

he says. We know who "those" are: a famine had forced "people in many cases
to roam abroad searching for food: they abandon their occupation [as freehold
farmers] so that [the land's] ownership is left vacant, and [the State] goes without the substantial benefit of farmland levies." If registered Chinese farmers
could no longer pay taxes and fled the area, whereas the Xiongnu stayed, the
implication is that the Xiongnu were exempt from taxes, because they were
not full-time farmers. Shu Xi goes on to say that such people should not occupy
this land:

> Although such people for whom a [farming] occupation forms only a
> minor part [of their livelihood] renounce [a fixed abode] in the main and
> are on the move (e.g., in Shanxi and Gansu), there are also many (namely,
> here in Sizhou) who live a sedentary life and till land at the same place
> that they herd for pasturage; for, avarice being all too human, they are not
> keen on the wide steppe. They will say, therefore, that the soil in the north
> is not suitable for cattle herding, when in fact this is not so. [...] All that
> herding should be moved away to fill these lands [in the North], so that
> while horses, cattle, pigs and goats munch grass on empty fields, those
> (= Chinese) who roam abroad in search of food [can] receive an occupa-
> tion [as farmers] extended to them as a gift.[39]

Shu Xi thus proposes to oust the Xiongnu as a prerequisite for inviting the
local farmers back in. Whatever brittle harmony had perhaps once obtained
between the different communities broke down when a natural disaster
plunged the subsistence economy abruptly into famine.[40] Likewise, a few
years earlier in Guanzhong, when man-made disaster struck in the form of Qi
Wannian's revolt, cohabitation turned nasty. The Qiang and Di do not appear
to have been any better off, economically, than the local populace, for they,
too, "are moribund and wander about as vagrants"; it is quite possible that
they weren't accomplished farmers at all, but were goatherds instead, for as we
read earlier, they were expected to "capture the stacked crops from [the native
population's] dispersed fields." But the suppressed uprising of Qi Wannian has

---

39   *JS* 51:1431: "土狹人繁[⋯]而豬羊馬牧，布其境內，宜悉破廢，以供無業。(人多
      游食，廢業占空，無田課之實。) 業少之人，雖頗割徙，在者猶多，田諸菀
      牧，不樂曠野，貪在人間。故謂北土不宜畜牧，此誠不然。[⋯] 可悉徙諸
      牧，以充其地，使馬牛豬羊齕草於空虛之田，游食之人受業於賦給之賜 ⋯"
40   "If but one farmer fails to till the land, the people may be reduced to famine because of
      him; if but one woman fails to weave, the people may suffer cold because of her." So Guan
      Zhong 管仲 (ca. 723–ca. 645 BCE) is made to say of how brittle ancient economy was, in
      Guanzi 管子 (Ma Feibai 馬非百, ed., *Guanzi qingzhong pian xinquan* 管子輕重篇新詮
      [Beijing 1979]) 13:542.

tarred them all with the brush of treason: "every household of Guanzhong natives looks upon them as foes."[41] However, where Jiang Tong would mobilise the locals to expel the Qiang and Di settlers for that reason, his imaginary interlocutor objects that this would be merely a recipe for greater turmoil:

> Right now, the calamity that has hit Guanzhong is to have been exposed to warfare for two years running (296–298); the aggravation of being conscripted for front duty has resulted in an exhausted army of a hundred thousand; the ravages caused by floods and droughts, by successive famines and repeated crop failures, visit [the people] with epidemic diseases that fell them before their appointed time. Now that the vicious insurrectionary (= Qi Wannian) is slain, [his followers,] repenting of the evil that was done, and newly submissive, are in turn being sincere [towards us] and fearful [of us], grateful as well as apprehensive; while [our own] population, anxious and distressed, share the same concern with these aliens [at least in this respect], that they so fervently hope for peace to take hold as during parching dryness they long for rain and dew: and therefore, they really should be kept quiet by having them feel safe, secure and happy. Yet you, on the contrary, would right now put them to hard labour and start them on corvée work, letting these wearied and worn-out masses undertake the task and perform the business of moving away those naturally mistrustful desperadoes. You would have these savages, who lack food, be relocated by people who have no grain themselves. I'm afraid that at the end of their tether, their forces depleted, the enterprise will not succeed; that the Qiang barbarians may be dispersed, but will not be of one mind [in agreeing to leave Guanzhong]; so that a new insurrection might suddenly erupt before the earlier disaster has even been contained.[42]

The Jin government did not act upon Jiang Tong's, Shu Xi's or Guo Qin's recommendation to move the aliens out. Qi Wannian's insurrection was nevertheless a harbinger of things to come.

• • •

Let us note once again that the tinderbox areas were those where the "steppe" and the "sown" lived in closest proximity, in China's heartland — where, as a

---

41 *JS* 56:1533: "迫其死亡散流 ..."; p. 1532: "收散野之積"; p. 1533: "與關中之人，戶皆為讎 ..."

42 *JS* 56:1532.

INTRODUCTION

consequence, the "barbarians" rubbed shoulders with the natives, and were fastest to learn. Numerically this is where they were strongest, too. As Jiang Tong writes — not without a note of hysteria — half of Guanzhong's population was non-Chinese:

> Moreover, of the one million-odd registered inhabitants of Guanzhong, more or less one half are Rong or Di, and their staying or moving out inevitably affects the local food situation. Assuming [the Rong and Di] suffer penury or scarcity, when they don't know when their next bowl of rice gruel may come, perforce we will have to empty the grain stocks in Guanzhong so as to safeguard their means of livelihood, and by all means to keep them from being pushed into the gutter, that they don't cause another disaster by going on the rampage.[43]

Commencing with the creation of five "Dependent States" for capitulated Xiongnu in 116 BCE, passing through the admittance of Wuhuan in early Eastern Han and the condoned or encouraged immigration of Xianbei, Dingling and more Xiongnu to China even into Western Jin times, non-Chinese communities were to be found from the frontier zone ever further inland into today's Shanxi, Shaanxi and Henan provinces. (Not arriving as invaders from the distant north, the Qiang staked their right to the land on age-old occupancy, and will be considered separately hereafter.) A situation resulted that had its parallels elsewhere — ones that less resemble a frontal collision between civilisations than the takeover of the incumbent by the new kid on the block. In 9 CE, in the southeast of England, Cunobelinus (Shakespeare's "Cymbeline"), "strongly influenced by Roman culture, [called] himself *rex* [...]: for when one people begins to assimilate the maturer culture of another, it usually tries to complete the imitation by an attempt at self sufficiency." Or, in the case of the Germanic peoples of the fifth century: "Whenever the barbarian won, it was because he was already more than half civilized. He had spent a long time in an antechamber and knocked not once but ten times before gaining admission to the house. He was, if not completely civilized, at least deeply imbued with the adjacent civilization."[44]

---

43   *JS* 56:1533 ("且關中之人百餘萬口，率其少多，戎狄居半，處之與遷，必須口實。若有窮乏糝粒不繼者，故當傾關中之穀以全生生之計，必無擠於溝壑而不為侵掠之害也。").

44   Arnaldo Momigliano, *Claudius: The Emperor and his Achievement* (Cambridge 1961²), p. 56; Fernand Braudel, *Civilization and Capitalism, 15th–18th Century*, Vol. 1: *The Structures of Everyday Life* (London 1979), p. 94.

CHAPTER 2

The Hexi Corridor

Finding passage through the steep Wushao Range 烏鞘嶺 north of modern Lanzhou City 蘭州市, Gansu, one gains access to the Hexi Corridor 河西走廊, a narrow strip of land nearly 1000 km long, wedged between the Qinghai-Tibet Plateau to its southwest and the Gobi Desert to its northeast. For the first 100 km or so out of Lanzhou, the route is a narrow ribbon of land between towering mountains, giving out on the Hexi Plain upon arriving at the county town of Gulang 古浪 (Changsong 昌松 in the Sixteen Kingdoms period); from there the Wushao Range begins to recede, with its snow-capped summits Maomaoshan 毛毛山 (4070 m) and Lenglongling 冷龍嶺 (4843 m), as one continues on the modern G30 freeway from Lanzhou — the same road one takes to Gulang along the Zhuanglang River's bed 莊浪河, which informs the freeway's trajectory through the mountains. The Hexi Plain is dominated by Wuwei City, inhabited for millennia thanks to irrigation, and surrounded by grasslands most suitable for pastoral nomadism in the pre-modern age. From the southwest corner of this Hexi Plain, an ancient route leads westward via Ledu 樂都 (now Ledu District 區, the administrative centre of Haidong City 海東市) to Xining 西寧, the capital of adjacent Qinghai province on the Tibetan Plateau, and further, south of the Azure Sea 青海 (= Qinghai, Koko Nor), all the way down to Lhasa appr. 2000 km away. From the northeast, that is to say from the Ordos region, travellers for Central Asia would proceed first southward along the Yellow River's bank and then take a turn westward to continue straight to Wuwei. On the ancient trade routes that linked Luoyang and Chang'an on China's Central Plain with Central Asia and the Western world beyond, Wuwei was an important hub. Joining a trade caravan from Wuwei to the Western Regions, one would notice how the plain narrows to a corridor, flanked on the southern side by the forbidding Qilian Mountains 祁連山 (once called the Richthofen Range) — which constitute an abrupt end to the Tibetan Plateau — and delimited on the other, northern side by the equally forbidding Badain Jaran section of the Gobi Desert. The climate of the Hexi Corridor as a whole is arid to semi-arid, but there is no lack of spring runoff water from the mountain snow, which flows in numerous bourns and creeks in a northeasterly direction from the Qilian Mountains and, often collecting underground in gravelly deposits, creates arable and liveable oases. Here a whole string of oasis settlements have sprung up since Western Han 西漢 times (206 BCE–8 CE): from Wuwei in the wide, southeastern end of the corridor, via

© DOMINIK DECLERCQ, 2025 | DOI:10.1163/9789004727380_003

Zhangye and Jiuquan to Dunhuang in the northwest. They served as so many staging posts on this key section of the famed Silk Roads. From the Ming 明 dynasty (1368–1644), where the corridor is at its narrowest beyond Jiuquan, the fortress of Jiayuguan 嘉峪關 guards the double gate in the Great Wall through which all travellers had to pass.

The Hexi Corridor has been open both ways since the earliest times. To Chinese scholars, the Qijia 齊家 culture (ca. 2000 BCE) of eastern Gansu, archaeological research on which has yielded jade artefacts for ritual use, is proof that the Liangzhu 良渚 culture (ca. 3300–ca. 2500 BCE) once centred upon present-day Hangzhou and defined by its jade objects, radiated outwards over the centuries so as to include far-away Gansu within the arc of Chinese civilisation. The Qijia culture's role in shaping the next phase of Chinese civilisation finds further proof in the earliest known examples of bronze casting unearthed from eastern Gansu sites, a technique that would gradually be diffused inland to find its most consummate expression in the bronzes of the Shang 商 (ca. 1600–1045 BC) and Western Zhou (1045–771 BCE) dynasties.[1] Others, however, do not rule out that Gansu was itself on the receiving end of earlier metallurgical know-how originating in Siberia, and that jade-carving in the Qijia culture had reached a stage where it depended on foreign supply of the stone from Hotan (Khotan) 和田 (ancient 于寘) in today's Xinjiang. In fact, the Western Han name "Jade Gateway Pass (*Yumenguan* 玉門關)" for China's final western frontier beyond Dunhuang may refer as much to an indispensable import material as to a profitable export article. If these arguments underline the position of the Qijia culture in Gansu as a vital link and relay between Central Asia and the Chinese world — rather than a distant peripheral satellite of Chinese civilisation — it is a further sobering reality that we cannot put any label (ethnic or cultural) on the people who fashioned these jade and bronze artefacts. The most one can say is that Gansu was home to "a distinctive metallurgical culture."[2]

Moreover, an important feature of the Qijia culture is the presence of numerous domesticated horses, and subsequent sites of the Xindian 新店 (ca. 1500 BCE), Siwa 寺洼 (ca. 1500–1000 BCE) and Kayue 卡約 (early Shang into Han) cultures testify to a steady transition from an agriculture-based to

---

1   Liu Gang 劉剛 & Li Dongjun 李冬君, *Wenhua de jiangshan* 文化的江山, 01: *Wenhua Zhongguo de laiyuan* 文化中國的來源 (Beijing 2019), pp. 225–228; Robert Bagley, "Shang Archaeology," in Michael Loewe and Edward L. Shaughnessy, eds., *The Cambridge History of Ancient China: From the Origins of Civilization to 221 B.C.* (Cambridge 1999), pp. 124–231 at pp. 139–141.

2   Nicola Di Cosmo, "The Northern Frontier in Pre-Imperial China,'" in *The Cambridge History of Early China*, pp. 885–966 at pp. 905–906; Liu Gang & Li Dongjun, op. cit., p. 235 (Yumenguan).

a pastoral-based economy. That is to say, in the area covered by these cultures from southeastern Gansu to western Qinghai (the valleys of the Yellow River 黃河 and the River Huang 湟水 at around the longitude of Xining) over a width of some 500 km, cattle, sheep and horse breeding became dominant. Such animal husbandry necessitated moving in search of pasture; hence, to a certain extent, farmers became nomads, and not the other way round. This evolution in peoples' livelihood was greatly advanced, from the seventh century BCE onwards, by the introduction of horse-riding technology, such as the horse bit (the stirrup would appear much later, in the 4th century CE).[3] Concomitant with horsemanship, as well as with developments in metalworking, came a further specialisation — mounted warfare.

As it happens, the early fourth-century BCE *Remnant Zhou Documents* (*Yi Zhou shu* 逸周書) contain a laconic reference to a "Yuzhi 禺氏" people somewhere northeast of the Zhou capital (sc. modern Luoyang), who possessed or could offer *taotu* 騊駼 horses in tribute to the court.[4] Also vague in geographical terms is the fourth-century BCE account of the marvellous travels of King Mu of Zhou 周穆王 (r. 956–918 BCE), which says that, having crossed the "pass-like stairway of Yu 隃之關隥" (identified as Mount Yanmen 雁門山, just west of Dai County 代縣 in today's Shanxi) and heading west, "Mu the Son of Heaven" arrived six days later on the plain of the Yanju 焉居 and the Yuzhi 禺知: is one to understand this as the alluvial plain of the Sanggan River 桑干河 (northern Shanxi)?[5] The next reference takes one almost 1000 km southwest. In Anding Commandery 安定郡 (now Guyuan 固原 in southern Ningxia, but then part of Liangzhou 涼州, i.e. roughly modern Gansu), a non-Chinese "chief herdsman (*muzhang* 牧長)" and trader by the name of Luo 倮, either hailing from Wuzhi 烏氏 (a county in Anding) or belonging to a Wuzhi clan or tribe, caught the attention of the First Emperor Qin Shi Huangdi 秦始皇帝 (r. first as king, then as emperor, 246–210 BC) for his enormous wealth: he "raised herds, and when they became numerous, he would take them out to sell them; the rare silk goods he sought [in exchange for them] he privately offered as a present to the king of the Rong 戎王. The king of the Rong compensated him tenfold, giving him livestock — so much livestock, horses and cattle, that it took a whole valley to hold them all."[6] That Luo traded "privately" means that he managed to

---

3 N. Di Cosmo, op. cit., pp. 891–892, 900–902.

4 *Yi Zhou shu* 59 ("Wang hui jie 王會解"): "On the dais on the northern side, due east [...] the Yuzhi, with *taotu* horses [for tribute] 北方臺正東 [...] 禺氏騊駼."

5 *Mu Tianzi zhuan* 穆天子傳 (*The Tradition of Mu, Son of Heaven*), SBCK ed. 1.4b; Guo Pu's 郭璞 (276–324) commentary identifies Yu with Mount Yanmen (still so named).

6 *Shiji* 129:3260: "烏氏倮畜牧，及衆，斥賣，求奇繪物，閒獻遺戎王。戎王十倍其償，與之畜，畜至用谷量馬牛。" = *HS* 91:3685, where the individual in question is called

circumvent the regulated border trade and still conduct his business with the Western Regions (of the Rong).[7]

These ethnonyms could well have sounded much the same as that of the Yuezhi 月氏 who at one time lived in Gansu, though this sinicised rendering of their name dates from somewhat later. Bernhard Karlgren's (1889–1978) phonetic reconstructions of Archaic and Ancient Chinese yield *ngiu-'tiĕg/*ngiu-tśię for Yuzhi 禺氏; *ngiu-ti̯ĕg/*ngiu-'ti̯ę for Yuzhi 禺知; *'o-'ti̯ĕg/*'uo-tśię for Wuzhi 烏氏; *ngiŭg-'ti̯ĕg/*ngi̯əu-'ti̯ę for Niuzhi; and *ngiwăt-'ti̯ĕg/*ngiwDt-tśię for Yuezhi 月氏.[8] The version "Niuzhi" occurs (next to "Yuzhi") in the curious chapters 68 to 86 of the composite text *Guanzi* 管子, the authors of which, writing most probably under the Wang Mang 王莽 (r. 9–23 CE) interregnum between the Western and Eastern Han, made the ancient statesman Guan Zhong 管仲 (ca. 723–ca. 645 BCE) the spokesman for a long list of interventionist economic policies that they wished to see enacted in their own time. In this deliberately archaising setting, Guan Zhong mentions the Yuzhi/Niuzhi a few times as sitting on white jade reserves "at a distance of 7800 *li* 里 (some 3100 km) from the Zhou, by long and very arduous roads," a people as yet unabsorbed, but important as a source of jade currency.[9] Amongst these names, Wuzhi seems the odd one out phonetically; in the same Anding Commandery with which it is associated, however, a county-level Yuezhi Circuit 月氏道 was created at

---

Ying 嬴 (one would expect Luo 贏, as a *var. lect.* of Luo 倮). Wuzhi was a county in Anding Commandery established in the reign of King Huiwen of Qin 秦惠文王 (r. 337–311): see Li Tai 李泰, comp., *Kuodi zhi* 括地志 (*Records Spanning the Earth*), as quoted in Zhang Shoujie's 張守節 (fl. ca. 737) Zhengyi 正義 commentary on *Shiji* 110:2884 n. 9; and *HS* 28B:1615.

7   In *Shiji* 110:2905 = *HS* 94A:3765, another individual in Han times "clandestinely (*jianlan* 奸蘭/間闌) took goods outside to trade with the Xiongnu": another expression for the same reality.

8   Bernhard Karlgren, *Grammata Serica*, reprint from *BMFEA* 12 (Stockholm 1940), Taipei 1966.

9   Among others, *Guanzi* 6:255 ("Jade is extracted by the Yuzhi 玉起於禺氏"), 14:569 ("Now, jade is extracted from the frontier mountains of the Niuzhi [...] all of them at a distance of 7800 *li* from the Zhou, by long and very arduous roads 夫玉起於牛氏邊山 [...] 此皆距周 七千八百里，其涂遠而至難"), 11:460 ("Jade from the frontier mountains of the Yuzhi is one form [*ce* 筴, namely, of currency, *bi* 幣] 禺氏邊山之玉，一筴也") and 13:560 ("Lord Huan [of Qi 齊桓公, r. 685–643 BCE] said, 'The four barbarians have not submitted.' [...] Guanzi replied, [...] 'If the Yuzhi fail to appear at court audiences, let them know that white jade discs shall be deemed [acceptable] currency' 桓公曰，四夷不服 [...] 管子對曰 [...] 禺氏不朝，請以白璧為幣乎.") On the dating of different parts of the *Guanzi*, see Michael Loewe, ed., *Early Chinese Texts: A Bibliographical Guide* (Berkeley, Calif. 1993), p. 244; on "Qingzhong 輕重" chapters 68 to 86 ("Striking the Balance"), I am convinced by Ma Feibai's arguments, "Lun Guanzi qingzhong 論管子輕重," on pp. 3–114 of his 1979 *Guanzi qingzhong pian* edition.

22   CHAPTER 2

an unspecified date prior to 2 CE.[10] This by no means proves, but does somewhat comfort the notion that "Luo of the Wuzhi" was actually a Yuezhi: "For the Snark was a Boojum, you see."

Of the Yuezhi themselves, our sources begin to speak only after they had vanished from the scene. When, in 133 BCE, as is likely, the Han Emperor Wu sent Zhang Qian 張騫 (ca. 164–113 BCE) to the Western Regions and, starting from Chang'an, he travelled through the Wushao Range and along the Hexi Corridor past Dunhuang and the Jade Gateway Pass, he did not meet with any Yuezhi there. Zhang Qian did eventually encounter the Yuezhi, but years later (ca. 126 BCE) and north of the Oxus River (the Gui River 媯水, or Amur Darya), in today's Tajikistan or Uzbekistan. There he was informed that, until as little as fifty years earlier (ca. 176 BCE), the Yuezhi had been the predominant "nation on the move (xingguo 行國)" in Gansu, "making light of the Xiongnu," and sharing the entire corridor "between Dunhuang and Qilian" with the Wusun 烏孫, who lived on an eastern edge of it, and whom the Yuezhi treated as subordinates.[11] Since this comes verbatim from Zhang Qian's report to the throne after his return — probably in 125 BCE, which predates the establishment of Dunhuang as a commandery between 101 and (at the latest) 91 BCE — it has been argued that the original report, before Sima Qian anachronistically corrected it, must have read "between the Dunhong 敦薨 (Mountains, i.e. the Richthofen Range) and the Qilian (Mountains)," the latter of which, according to a gloss by Yan Shigu 顏師古 (581–645), would have indicated the Tianshan 天山 Mountains. This very broad area would certainly include Gansu and theoretically all of the Tarim Basin in today's Xinjiang as well, including Hotan with its jade deposits.[12] But, as Zhang Qian was told, a wave of attacks by the

---

10   HS 28B:1615. Ban Gu's "Geographical Treatise 地理志," HS 28A–B, presents the administrative geography of the Han empire as it stood in a census from 2 CE (see Hans Bielenstein, "The Census of China during the Period 2–742 A.D." [1947]). By the Later Han, "Yuezhi Circuit" did not exist anymore, and Wuzhi is written Wuzhi 烏枝; see HHS, "Treatises 志" 23 ("Junguo 郡國"), p. 3519.

11   See the account of Zhang Qian in Shiji 123 ("Da Yuan liezhuan 大宛列傳": "An Account of Da Yuan [= Ferghana]"), at pp. 3157–3172, and the corresponding text in HS 61:2687–2698, translated in CICA pp. 207–238. Zhang Qian probably left China in (or perhaps even after) 133 BCE; he is thought to have arrived back in 126 or 125 (CICA p. 210 n. 774). The story that early on his journey, he was detained by the Xiongnu for over ten years (Shiji 123:3157 = HS 61:2687) must therefore be exaggerated. "Ca. 126 BCE" is a bit of a stretch for Zhang Qian's stay with the Yuezhi, but not impossible. On the year of Zhang Qian's death, see CICA p. 218 n. 819. "Making light of the Xiongnu": Shiji 123:3161 = HS 96B:3890. "Nation on the move": HS 96B:3890.

12   "Verbatim report": in HS 61:2691 ("祁連、燉煌間"), transl. CICA p. 214; from there in Shiji 123:3162 ("敦煌、祁連間"), HS 96A:2890 (idem), transl. CICA p. 120. CICA does not pick up on Sima Qian's "anachronism"; see instead Yu Taishan 余太山, "Daxia he Da Yuezhi

THE HEXI CORRIDOR

Xiongnu under Modun, the latest of which would have taken place in 176 BCE, expelled the Yuezhi from Gansu and forced them to trek ever further westward to where Zhang Qian eventually found them. This version of events gains corroboration from Modun's famous 174 BCE letter to the Han emperor, in which he boasts that "with Heaven's blessing, and due to the excellence of my officers and soldiers and the strength of my horses, I have wiped out the Yuezhi, killing and subjugating them to the last man."[13]

Sima Qian then continues: "A remaining small group [of Yuezhi], who were unable to leave, sought protection amongst the Qiang of the Southern Mountains 南山羌中 (that is to say, today's Wushao Range), and were termed the 'Lesser Yuezhi 小月氏.'"[14] That is probably the source of the statement by Kan Yin 闞駰 (d. ca. 440), who lived in Zhangye, that "between Xiping 西平 (modern Xining) and Zhangye, after their split from the Greater Yuezhi, lay the kingdom of the Lesser Yuezhi." He does not seem to have met them. And Li Tai 李泰 too, writing in the Tang dynasty, sounds like an antiquarian when he says that "all the land of Liangzhou, Ganzhou 甘州, Suzhou 肅州, Yanzhou 延州 and Shazhou 沙州 was originally the Yuezhi state."[15] That is to say, all of present-day Gansu, including the southern tongue of Ningxia province (Guyuan = ancient Anding) in its southeast and extending further east to include Yanzhou (modern Yan'an 延安) in the north of Shaanxi; and extending in its northwest beyond Dunhuang to include at least part of southern Xinjiang (= Shazhou). What we have here, in fact, is a Yuezhi state comprising both Zhang Qian's definition of it "between the Dunhong and the Qilian (Mountains)" and the presumed loci of ancient Yuzhi/Wuzhi activity as well. It is this nation of the "Greater Yuezhi" that would have been driven out of their habitat by the Xiongnu under Modun. The "Lesser Yuezhi" absconded "into the inaccessible mountains to the south, settling down near to and relying on the various Qiang and then intermarrying with them."[16]

What occasioned Zhang Qian's voyage in the first place was intelligence gathered from Xiongnu deserters that, after Modun's victories, the displaced Yuezhi dreamt of revenge. Seeing in these Yuezhi a potential ally in his wars against the Xiongnu, Emperor Wu sent Zhang Qian to sound them out. The

---

zongkao 大夏和大月氏綜考," in *Zhong Ya xuekan* 中亞學刊 III (Beijing 1990), pp. 17–46, summarised in François Thierry, op. cit. p. 452. Yan Shigu's gloss is at *HS* 55:2481 n. 2.

13   *Shiji* 110:2896.

14   *Shiji* 123:3162 = *HS* 96A:3891, transl. *CICA* p. 121.

15   Kan Yin, *Shisan zhou zhi* 十三州志 (*Treatise on the Thirteen Provinces*), quoted in *Shuijing zhu* 2 (*Shuijing zhu jiao* 2:59; alternatively, in Chen Qiaoyi 陳橋驛, ed., *Shuijing zhu jiaozheng* 校證 [Beijing 2007], 2:48); Li Tai, *Kuodi zhi*, quoted in the commentary to *Shiji* 110:2888 n. 1.

16   *HHS* 87:2899.

Greater Yuezhi, however, showed no interest in such an alliance. They had redirected their ambition westward to Daxia 大夏 in the west (i.e. the Scyths, or Śakas, in Bactria), which they subjected; later, having become known in Chinese sources as the Kuṣāṇas (*Guishuang* 貴霜), they founded the Buddhist Kushan Empire (30–375 CE) in present-day northeast Afghanistan, centred on modern Balkh.

As one tries to account for the rather shadowy "Lesser Yuezhi," an idea formulated by Shiratori Kurakichi 白鳥庫吉 (1865–1942) as long ago as 1928 may provide some light."It has been noticed," Shiratori wrote, "how the old Chinese authors seem to have been addicted to the practice of tracing the origin of a foreign country to something native to their own country or some name found in their own literature"; in the same vein, Nicola Di Cosmo writes: "[K]inship closeness and cultural distance [were] established at the outset as the two chief principles adopted to explicate both the continuity of the relationship between the Hsiung-nu and the Chinese and the tension generated by their presence."[17] If cooperation with the (Greater) Yuezhi was to be sought, the opening gambit, so to speak, was to posit a bond on which to construct it. This was easier established if, closer to the Chinese world, there were the "Lesser Yuezhi," a stranded remnant of the fugitive Greater, and having the same ancestry. So, perhaps, the "Lesser Yuezhi" came into being so as to fit a preconception that was hardwired into Han foreign policy. Whether or not Zhang Qian's appeal to the Greater Yuezhi started with something along these lines, in any case it failed. Besides, we do not know which Yuezhi word (in the "Tocharian" language?) the Chinese characters *yuezhi* were meant to transcribe. It could be that Zhang Qian hit upon the name Yuezhi because it had some previous currency in China, as one finds attested by its possible cognates Yuzhi/Wuzhi in Longxi and Anding Commanderies in Han-time Liangzhou — and indeed by the Western Han establishment of a Yuezhi Circuit in Anding Commandery.[18]

• • •

The Yuezhi having been disposed of, the Hexi Corridor — from 176 BCE and for as long as the Han *heqin* policy lasted (134 BCE) — was undisputedly

---

17 Shiratori Kurakichi, "A Study on Su-t'ê (粟特) or Sogdiana," in *Memoirs of the Research Department of the Toyo Bunko* 2 (1928), pp. 81–145 at p. 103; Nicola Di Cosmo, *Ancient China and Its Enemies*, p. 301.

18 The account of the displaced Greater Yuezhi and their remnant in Gansu, i.e. the Lesser Yuezhi, is universally accepted by the Chinese scholarly tradition, also, e.g., in *The Cambridge History of Early Inner Asia* (1990), passim. Dissenting views are mentioned, e.g., in Valerie Hansen, *The Silk Road: A New History* (Oxford 2012), Ch. 1 n. 19 (with references).

THE HEXI CORRIDOR   25

under Xiongnu control. Their *chanyu* placed its western half, in the area of
later Zhangye, under the supervision of the Hunye king, a lesser Xiongnu
noble, and its eastern half in the area of later Wuwei, under the supervision
of the Hunye king's counterpart the Xiuchu 休屠 king (d. 121 BCE).[19] In Wuwei,
the Xiuchu king had an oblong walled enclosure built, seven *li* from north
to south by three *li* from east to west (i.e., 3 km by 1.2 km), called Reclining
Dragon City (*Wolongcheng* 臥龍城). It was an enclosure for horses as well as
a royal encampment, and on its foundations Guzang 姑臧, the capital city of
Liangzhou, would later be erected.[20] During these decennia, wherever markets
existed on the border crossings between the Han and Xiongnu empires, these
were open to mutual trade.[21]

But then, as we have seen, the Xiongnu came under attack from Huo Qubing
in 121 BCE: *en passant*, he "opened Huangzhong 湟中," i.e. the central segment
of the Huang River basin in Qinghai, south of modern Xining, where "seven
major clans of Lesser Yuezhi with a combined force of 9000 fighters" now lived
amongst the Qiang,[22] before killing the Xiuchu king and taking the Hunye king
captive. While Xiongnu were moved out of the Hexi Corridor, several hundred households of "Lesser Yuezhi" reportedly moved back in, to the Zhangye
region — but the late, fifth-century source that tells us this is in fact relating
what a first-century CE army regiment made up of various ethnic elements,
known as the "Yicong hu 義從胡" or "Loyal Nomad Auxiliary," believed about
its own historic origins. By the time this group took centre stage in Liangzhou's
historical record in 184 CE, as instigators of the "Liangzhou Rebellion," the predominant element in its ethnic make-up was doubtless Qiang.[23]

• • •

Closely involved in Huo Qubing's campaigns was the "flying general" Li Guang
李廣 (d. 119 BCE), a famous personage in his own right. Li Guang is said to have
been Li Hao's sixteenth-generation ancestor. Even today, every schoolchild

---

19   *HS* 28B:1644 (writing Kunye 昆邪 for Hunye: the two renderings are interchangeable).
20   Wang Yin 王隱 (4th cent.), *Jin shu* 晉書 (*History of the Jin*), quoted in *Shuijing zhu jiao*
     40:1275; *JS* 86:2222 is based on the same source. Shatzman Steinhardt, op. cit. pp. 23–26
     describes the fourth-century construction works that gave Guzang its lay-out in five "clus-
     ters 攢聚" of buildings, each with a palace.
21   *Shiji* 110:2904: "通關市."
22   *HHS* 87:2899: "開湟中 […] [小月氏] 大種有七，勝兵合九千餘人，分在湟中及
     令居。"
23   *HHS* 87:2899, 8:350. In fact, the "Yicong hu" are referred to as "Yicong *Qiang* hu" in *HHS*
     16:610, 23:814, and as "the Yicong *Qiang* from Huangzhong" in *HHS* 65:2146, 2152.

in China knows that Li Guang, "seeing a rock in the grass that he took for a tiger, shot an arrow at it, that pierced the rock and left the arrowhead embedded inside." Li Guang's grandson Li Ling 李陵 fell victim to another bout of Han-Xiongnu hostilities. In 99 BCE, Li Ling was forced to surrender to a Xiongnu *chanyu* in Juyan 居延 (Edsin Gol, Inner Mongolia), becoming a captive for the rest of his life; it was for imprudently speaking out at court in Li Ling's defence that Grand Historian Sima Qian 司馬遷 (ca. 145–ca. 86 BCE) was punished with castration. The Li clan in question hailed from Longxi 隴西, the area of modern Gansu south of Lanzhou, where the rivers Tao 洮河 and Wei 渭河 have their source. After Li Ling's surrender, writes Sima Qian with bitter irony, "the Li clan's reputation was finished, and Longxi 隴西 notables — at least, such as occupied a social position inferior to the Li clan — all invoked it as a byword for infamy."[24] But this is jumping ahead of our main story.

•••

From very early times, as the graph by which they were designated (meaning "sheep men") is already found on Shang oracle bones, a people known as the Qiang 羌 were found west of the Chinese heartland, from Gansu down to Yunnan.[25] When one plots on a map the places where Qiang were said to live in the Han, the result is an area at its densest to the southwest of the Hexi Corridor, especially in present-day Qinghai province, around its capital Xining. The inference that the Qijia, Xindian, Siwa and Kayue cultures (from ca. 3000 BCE to the Han) were in fact Qiang cultures is more than plausible. From there, a number of them descended into modern Sichuan, and if the original language of a trio of solemn songs transmitted to us in the *History of the Later Han* and composed there ca. 65 CE actually is Qiang (the Chinese translation is accompanied by a contemporary phonetic transcription of the songs' original language), then its similarity to Tibetan makes the Qiang proto-Tibetans, hence the progenitors of the Tibetan speakers of today.[26] If the same people also spread out beyond Dunhuang along the northern foothills of the Kunlun

---

24   The biographies of Li Guang and Li Ling are in *Shiji* 109:2867–2878; I quote from pp. 2871, 2878 ("[李] 廣出獵，見草中石，以為虎而射之，中石沒鏃"; "自是之後，李氏名敗，而隴西之士居門下者皆用為恥焉。").

25   Helmut Hoffman, "Early and Medieval Tibet," in *The Cambridge History of Early Inner Asia*, pp. 371–399 at p. 372. For everything that follows, see also Yü, "Han Foreign Relations," at pp. 422–435: "The Ch'iang."

26   *CICA* p. 80 n. 68; *HS* 7:230 (Qiang nobles fighting on the Han side in Yizhou 益州, i.e. Sichuan, 107 BCE); *HHS* 86:2843 (Qiang entering Yizhou in large numbers, 148 CE), 86:2855–2856 (the three songs with transcription).

THE HEXI CORRIDOR

27

mountain range — that is to say, if the 450 "Chuoqiang 婼羌" households that Zhang Qian visited ca. 800 km southwest of Dunhuang were indeed related to the Qiang in Qinghai — then the Qiang left a footprint along the southern route of the Silk Roads almost parallel to that of the Greater Yuezhi.[27] We will however limit our concern here to the Qiang in their area of greatest concentration, in what corresponded to today's Qinghai and Gansu.[28]

There, the Western Han Longxi Commandery was home to a Di 氐, a Di 狄 and a Qiang Circuit, a "circuit (*dao* 道)," as explained by Fu Qian 服虔 (ca. 125–195), being a county (*xian* 縣), but where aliens (*yiman* 夷蠻) live; and the earliest mention of Qiang Circuit 羌道, in 184 BCE, suggests that the local Qiang population had been incorporated into the Han administrative structure from this early date.[29] In fact, at around this time, a nineteenth-generation ancestor of the subject of this monograph, Li Hao, a certain Li Zhongxiang 李仲翔 (fl. ca. 200 BCE), had had to contend with "rebellious" Qiang marauders in precisely this region. Or so we are told: it is more than likely that the Qiang in question tried to resist Han occupation of lands they had long considered their own. The same is probably the case with the adjacent commandery of Tianshui 天水 (est. 114 BCE), where one finds a "Circuit for Rong Settlements (Rongyi Dao 戎邑道)" as well as a county named for its inhabitants from the Han 罕 and Jian 幵 clans of the Qiang.[30] (Given that there were 154 "kinds [*zhong* 種]" of Qiang, "clans" appears a more realistic meaning for *zhong* than "tribes.")[31] Again, neighbouring Tianshui on the east, Anding Commandery (est. 114 BCE) would have been an early abode of non-Chinese groups — witness Wuzhi County 烏氏縣 and the Yuezhi Circuit mentioned earlier. This area as a whole corresponds to the southern part of Gansu province, under Lanzhou. The Qiang

---

27 *HS* 96A:3875, *CICA* pp. 80–81. "Chuoqiang" is also read Erqiang or, in the toponym instated in 1903 to rekindle the memory of this ancient group of people, Ruoqiang 婼羌 (from 1959 written Ruoqiang 若羌), a county in Bayingolin Mongol Autonomous Prefecture 巴音郭楞蒙古自治州, Xinjiang.

28 For what follows, I have made grateful use of Rachel Meakin, "Qiang 羌 References in the Book of Han 漢書, Part 1 (Chapter 1 to Chapter 78)," pp. 1–34 (2013); "Qiang 羌 References in the Book of Han 漢書, Part 2 (Chapter 79 to Chapter 99)," pp. 1–51 (2013); "Qiang 羌 References in the Book of the Later Han 後漢書," pp. 1–48 (2011); "Qiang 羌 References in the Book of the Later Han 後漢書 Chapter 117: The Biography of the Western Qiang," pp. 1–29 (2011): all uploaded to the website www.qianghistory.co.uk as well as accessible through academia.edu.

29 *HS* 28B:1609, 3:96–97 with Fu Qian's gloss p. 97 n. 13.

30 *HS* 28B:1612 (Hanjian County 罕幵縣), 69:2974 n. 14.

31 *HHS* 1B:62, n. 1. *HHS* 87:2898 says "150," being "the branches of sons and grandsons" into which the Qiang had split over time after the death of their mythical ancestor Yuanjian 爰劍 (on whom *vide infra*).

who lived in this area are sometimes labelled "Eastern Qiang" to distinguish them from the unassimilated "Western Qiang" from Qinghai.[32]

The Qiang are described as "without constancy in where they dwell, their hearth contingent upon water and grass": pastoralists, indeed sheep breeders by name. The race of sheep they bred apparently had a preference for heights, which could explain the Qiang way of life in which, mounted on small horses, they would "venture out a little, seeking water and pasture, and then enter their mountain forests" again. They were organised in small groups with relatively little cohesion (as compared to the horse-breeding Xiongnu, for example), because shepherding small flocks of sheep puts looser demands on tribal organisation than managing herds of horses. "When waging war, it was in mountain valleys they had the advantage, while on level ground they were at a disadvantage, nor could they hold out very long; but when in fact they struck, they thought it a stroke of good luck to die in battle, and bad luck to be felled down by illness." The distances they covered with their flocks were no doubt modest. The Qiang, like the Di, also wove and practised agriculture, hence their annual transhumance had to allow for a permanent return base where they could harvest their autumn barley.[33]

Having decided to turn against the Xiongnu, the Han Emperor Wu first attacked them in the north (modern Hebei), then again in 121 BCE, after Zhang Qian had returned with a trove of information about the Western Regions, also in the northwest, i.e. in Gansu and through the Hexi Corridor. As a long-term effort not only to deal decisively with the Xiongnu but also to open up the Tarim basin to Han influence or direct rule, the Xiongnu wars that lasted for nearly a century (133–54 BCE: the surrender of Huhanye) required provisioning for the armies sent over long distances on lengthy campaigns. For that reason, in 126 BC, the province-level administrative unit of Liangzhou 涼州 (modern Gansu above the Wushao Range) was created, with Guzang 姑臧 (today's Wuwei City) as its administrative seat. The choice of Guzang as the embryonic provincial capital was in the first place strategic, not economic: Guzang was situated "on advantageous terrain, although its soil is poor," according to one description.[34] Lianju 令居 county, established in 115 BCE, was equally strategic. For the Western Qiang of Qinghai to invade Han-held Liangzhou, the best way in was to follow the current of the River Huang 湟水, which empties into the

---

32 "Eastern Qiang 東羌": *HHS* 8:330, 65:2153.

33 *HHS* 87:2869 ("所居無常，依隨水草"); Wolfram Eberhard, *Conquerors and Rulers: Social Forces in Medieval China* (Leiden 1970), pp. 114–115 ("the Ch'iang tribes' *Tibetan* form of organization"); *HS* 69:2978 ("稍引去，逐水屮，入山林"); *HHS* 87:2869 ("其兵長在山谷，短於平地，不能持久，而果於觸突，以戰死為吉利，病終為不祥"); *HS* 69: 2979, *HHS* 87:2883 (barley 麥 harvest).

34 *JS* 126:3149.

THE HEXI CORRIDOR

Yellow River in Jincheng (mod. Lanzhou); for them to make contact with the Xiongnu holding the Hexi Corridor, the best way was, just before Jincheng, to turn north at "Zheng Bo's Ford 鄭伯津," where the River Huang is joined by the River Jian 澗水. Upstream of the River Jian, though, and as if designed to block access to the Xiongnu further north, Lianju was established "by several tens of thousands of men [sent by Emperor Wu] to cross the [Yellow] River [in Jincheng] and build [it]."[35] It seems by no means impossible that Lianju was from 115 BCE the base of a "Commandant Protector of the Qiang 護羌校尉," who was to keep an eye on Qiang movements.[36] The establishment of commanderies followed: Jiuquan in 104 BCE (at the latest) to separate Xiongnu from Qiang to the south,[37] Zhangye in the same year (also at the latest) so as "to impress upon the Qiang and Di 狄 that [the Han now] extended (*zhang* 張) the country, supporting it (*ye* 掖) with its strong arm."[38] Dunhuang Commandery was founded before 91 BC, a 10,000 km² northern split-off of Jiuquan, and Wuwei followed between 81 and 67 BC. In each case, the commandery prefect (*taishou* 太守) was aided by a commandant (*duwei* 都尉); the *taishou* administered the Han colonist-soldiers brought in to farm the land in agricultural garrisons, the produce of which supported the *duwei*'s soldier-colonist armed force.[39] One global figure for the number of agricultural colonists involved is 600,000, though they were deployed over a larger area: "Zhangye and Jiuquan Commanderies were for the first time established (104 BCE), and there and in Shangjun, Shuofang and Xihe [commanderies in the adjacent province of Shuofang], 600,000 men, officials charged with opening up agricultural land as well as soldiers dismissed from border [duty] both guarded and farmed it."[40]

Indeed, the Han had evidence that Qiang and Xiongnu sought to join forces against Han encroachment,[41] but once the Xiongnu had been driven out of

---

35 *HS* 28B:1611; *Shuijing zhu jiao* 2:64 (where the river Jian is called Run 潤); *HS* 24:1173.

36 Hans Bielenstein, *The Bureaucracy of Han Times* (Cambridge 1980), p. 110, says that the Han Emperor Wu had already established the office of *Hu Qiang xiaowei* 護羌校尉, according to Ying Shao's 應劭 (ca. 140 to before 204) *Hanguan yi* 漢官儀 (quoted in *HHS* 1B:55–56; see Bielenstein, p. 191 n. 151). However, no incumbent is named until Xin Tang 辛湯 ca. 6 BCE.

37 *HS* 28B:1614; Ying-shih Yü, "The Hsiung-nu," p. 130; Di Cosmo, *Ancient China and Its Enemies*, p. 246.

38 *HS* 28B:1613; I quote Ying Shao, *Notes on the Patterns of the Earth and Popular Customs* 地理風俗記 (a variant title for his *Fengsu tongyi* 風俗通義?), quoted in *Shuijing zhu jiaozheng* 2:41.

39 Di Cosmo, *Ancient China and Its Enemies*, p. 246.

40 *HS* 24:1173: "初置張掖、酒泉郡、而上郡、朔方、西河、河西開田官、斥塞卒六十萬人戍田之。" "Hexi 河西," not the name of a commandery, has I think crept into this sentence by mistake.

41 Thus in 112 BCE (*HS* 6:188) and again in 90 BCE (*HS* 69:2973).

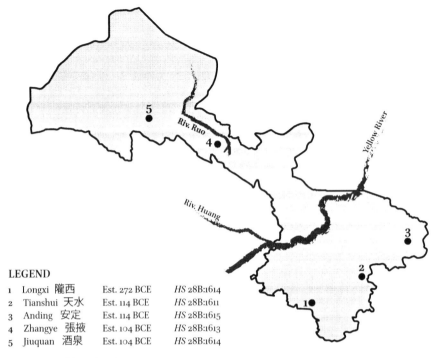

LEGEND
1 Longxi 隴西   Est. 272 BCE   HS 28B:1614
2 Tianshui 天水 Est. 114 BCE   HS 28B:1611
3 Anding 安定   Est. 114 BCE   HS 28B:1615
4 Zhangye 張掖   Est. 104 BCE   HS 28B:1613
5 Jiuquan 酒泉   Est. 104 BCE   HS 28B:1614

MAP 1   Liangzhou Inspectorate 100 BCE

the Hexi Corridor, the Western Qiang were still bellicose enough on their own to put Han resources under serious strain. Sometime around 70 BCE, "grandees from the Xianlian 先零 [clan of the Western Qiang] said [to a visiting Han envoy] that they wished at certain times to cross the Huang River northward [into Han territory] to seek out, for the purpose of pasturing their flocks, such areas as were not under cultivation by the [registered Han] population." When this request was met with a refusal, in the year 63, the Xianlian allied with the leaders of "200 more" Qiang clans, including the Eastern Qiang Han 罕 and Jian 开, and went on a rampage in Liangzhou. It took the combined forces of the local commanderies together with an army sent from Chang'an three years to restore control; after a final battle near Jincheng in 60 BCE, 31,200 Qiang surrendered and were resettled in a newly-created "Jincheng Dependent State" west of the commandery seat.[42] From now on, the historical record names several men appointed Commandant Protector of the Qiang: in 62 BC, in quick

---

42 See HS 69:2972 and 69:2972–2993 on the military strategy executed by General Zhao Chongguo, who consulted frequently with the Emperor about which tactics to adopt; see also HS 8:260–262. For the pronunciation of Xianling 先零 as Xianlian, see HS 69:2973

THE HEXI CORRIDOR   31

succession, two brothers belonging to the Xin 辛 clan of Han settlers in the
region, followed by another brother, Xin Wuxian 辛武賢, who was Prefect of
Jiuquan when appointed and who eventually died in Dunhuang. Xin Wuxian's
son Xin Qingji 辛慶忌 (d. 18 BCE) occupied posts in Jincheng, Zhangye and
Jiuquan, and his grandson, Xin Tong 辛通, in his turn became Commandant
Protector of the Qiang until 3 CE, when the Xin clan fell victim to Wang Mang's
machinations.[43]

Shortly before Wang Mang's interregnum, a group of Qiang volunteered to
become Han subjects, and in 4 CE, Wang Mang created a Xihai Commandery
西海郡 to administer them, just east of the lake that gives the modern province of Qinghai its name (Qinghai = Koko Nor); however, as he proceeded to
send large numbers of criminals there for banishment, the Qiang rebelled, and
the Commandant Protector of the Qiang at that time, Dou Kuang 竇況, had to
pacify them in 7 CE. It is likely that this Dou Kuang was the great-uncle of Dou
Rong 竇融 (15 BCE–62 CE).[44]

Dou Rong's career foreshadows that of several others — notably also that
of Li Hao — who managed to carve out Liangzhou and the Hexi Corridor as
their personal power base while remaining nominally loyal to the central government. His forebears had "for many generations established a presence in
Hexi," hence Dou Rong "was aware of its local customs"; and in 24 CE — after
Wang Mang's fall, when the restoration of the Han dynasty was as yet by no
means assured — Dou Rong, who by this time was a 40-year-old military officer of good repute, requested and obtained the post of Commandant of the
Dependent State of Zhangye (*Zhangye shuguo duwei* 張掖屬國都尉).[45] "Upon
his arrival, he humoured the more prominent [local] notables and attached
them to himself, and by showing that he cared, assembled the Qiang savages
around him; in this way he successfully gained the sympathy of all of them, so

---

n. 2 (by "Master Zheng 鄭氏," Western Jin or earlier: see Yan Shigu's "Preface 敘例" to
the *HS*, p. 4).

43   *HS* 69:2992–2998.

44   *HS* 99A:4077–4078, 4087; *HHS* 23:795 (stating that Dou Rong's unnamed great-uncle had
been Commandant Protector of the Qiang). Wang Mang's Xihai Commandery is not identical with the Xihai Commandery, which in 195 CE became the new name of Zhangye and
the Zhangye Juyan Dependent States, on which see *JS* 14:434.

45   Only once is this position mentioned in Western Han: Guo Zhong 郭忠 (d. 71 BCE) held
it in 78 BCE (*HS* 17:668). The "Dependent State of Zhangye" was not, it seems, a unit in
administrative geography in W. Han (it goes unmentioned at *HS* 28B:1613), but by implication, it was in 24 CE and explicitly in 74 (*HHS* 2:122, where it is listed next to and
independently of Zhangye Commandery); thus, too, in the treatise on geography, *HHS*
"Treatises" 23:3521. Feng Zong 馮宗 was commandant ca. 60, Zhang Fang 張魴 ca. 70
(*HHS* 26:911, 79A:2553).

that all of Hexi rapidly pledged him their allegiance."[46] As Dou Rong realised, "Hexi lies isolated in the midst of Qiang nomads," and that made it imperative to join forces with them; on the other hand, united under a strong leader, Hexi could also be a safe beacon within natural frontiers, "girt [to its south] by the Yellow River for its security" while the Central Plain beyond was in turmoil.[47] So it was that Dou Rong found himself propelled, by his fellow local officials, into the position of Chief General of all Five Commanderies West of the River (*Hexi wujun da jiangjun* 河西五郡大將軍). "Thereafter," under his unquestioned authority, "the Xiongnu were chastened into submission so that they only rarely invaded to plunder again; while the Qiang nomads occupying the borders were all subjected through sheer fear and sought to become allies, and fugitives from Anding, Beidi and Shangjun fleeing famine flocked to him in endless numbers."[48] In 32 CE, it is reported, "the whole empire was in turmoil; only Hexi was safe, and Guzang became known as a wealthy town. Trade with the Qiang nomads flourished; markets were held four times a day. Residents of [Guzang] county often achieved opulence in less than a few months."[49] Dou Rong, meanwhile, was ready to accept the suzerainty of the new Emperor Guangwu, but on his own terms. He surrendered his office, and was received with full honours in Luoyang in 36 CE, where he died a respected elder statesman at the age of 78.

The office of Commandant Protector of the Qiang was discontinued during Wang Mang's reign, and reinstated, apparently in 33 CE, on the recommendation of Ban Biao 班彪 (3–54 CE) so as to "deal with pent-up resentment (*li yuanjie* 理冤結)" amongst the Qiang. The commandant had his base in Lianju.[50] The move had the opposite effect, however. Ban Biao explains a problem that must have grown more acute as Han migrants arrived in Liangzhou in ever greater numbers:

---

46   *HHS* 23 (Dou Rong's biography), p. 796: "既到，撫結雄傑，懷輯羌虜，甚得其歡心，河西翕然歸之。"

47   *HHS* 23:797 ("河西斗絕在羌胡中"), 796 ("帶河為固").

48   *HHS* 23:797: "其後匈奴懲义，稀復侵寇，而保塞羌胡皆震服親附，安定、北地、上郡流人避凶飢者，歸之不絕。"

49   *HHS* 31:1098: "時天下擾亂，唯河西獨安，而姑臧稱為富邑，通貨羌胡，市日四合。每居縣者，不盈數月輒致豐積。"

50   *HHS* 1B:55 dates the reinstatement of the post to 33 CE; Ban Biao's proposal of the same year is in *HHS* 87:2878. The first incumbent, in 33, is said there as well as in *Hanguan yi* (quoted in *HHS* 1B:55 n. 2) to have been Niu Han 牛邯, but *HHS* 81:2672–2673 mentions an earlier holder of the office (Wen Xu 溫序, in 30 CE) who died before reaching his destination. After Niu Han's death in 34, no successor was appointed until 58: *HHS* 87:2878.

THE HEXI CORRIDOR   33

now in every part of Liangzhou there are surrendered Qiang who still wear their hair unbound and button their lapels on the left but live mixed with our Han people. Since their customs are different and languages unintelligible, they are frequently robbed by minor officials and scheming people. Thoroughly enraged and yet helpless, they rebel. All barbarian disturbances are like this.[51]

And indeed, almost immediately, the Xianlian Qiang did rebel. It is no exaggeration to say that the Qiang caused the Eastern Han as much trouble as the Xiongnu had brought to the Western Han. From 34 CE onwards, there was hardly a year without hostilities. As Commandant Niu Han 牛邯 died that year, it fell to the prefect of Longxi, Ma Yuan 馬援 (14 BCE–49 CE), to put down the Xianlian Qiang in a series of violent encounters in Jincheng and Longxi commanderies over the next few years.[52] Frightened Chinese colonists fled the area, and for a moment the court even considered abandoning the western half of Jincheng (which included Lianju) to the Qiang; one hears of protracted battles in which the Qiang "made trenches to protect themselves" against Han "siege engines fabricated on a large scale"; after a single attack in 35 CE, several hundred Qiang were beheaded and over 8000 gave themselves up, while more than 10,000 livestock were taken. One tactic Ma Yuan adopted to bring peace to the region was to relocate such captives further inland, where they could settle as farmers, a move that relieved external pressure on the frontier but sowed the seeds for the jeremiads of Jiang Tong and Shu Xi two centuries later. Already in 168, a later Commandant Protector of the Qiang rued the decision "to move them into the Three Bulwarks (sanfu 三輔, i.e., the metropolitan commanderies of Jingzhao, [Zuo]pingyi 左馮翊 and [You]fufeng 右扶風 in Guanzhong, centred upon Chang'an), where initially they were submissive but in the end proved rebellious, sticking like a fishbone in our throats until this very day." To bring the Han colonists back, Ma Yuan supervised the reconstruction of Jincheng's inner and outer city walls, the erection of fortresses and watch towers, as well as irrigation works.[53]

By appointing the son of a cousin of Dou Rong as the next Commandant Protector of the Qiang in 58, the court appears to have given more heed to Ban

---

51   Lewis, *The Early Chinese Empires*, pp. 147–148, from whom I borrow this translation of *HHS* 87:2878.

52   *HHS* 1B:56–58, 60 (34–36 CE), 24:836 (37 CE).

53   *HHS* 24:835–836 (abandoning Jincheng), 15:588 ("皆營壍自守 … 乃大修攻具"), 24:835 (casualty numbers), 836 (peace established in Longxi, 37 CE), 1B:58 (relocation of Qiang captives inland into Tianshui, Longxi and Youfufeng), 65:2131 (Duan Jiong's 段熲 [d. 179] complaint: "馬援遷之三輔，始服終叛，至今為鯁"), 24:836 (construction works).

Biao's message. Dou Lin 竇林 (d. 59) set up office not in Lianju, but in Didao 狄道, Longxi Commandery, an extra 150 km to the southeast, where he scored a diplomatic victory by convincing the chief of the Shaodang 燒當 Qiang clan to come over to the Han.[54] It must be added, however, that this was just as much the result of a prolonged campaign against the Shaodang Qiang led by a general sent by the central government, ending in 4600 Qiang being killed and 1600 captured; further, to complicate the picture, Ma Wu's 馬武 (d. 61) 40,000-strong army is said to have consisted of "Wuhuan, conscripted men from the Liyang battalion (in Guanzhong) and from the Three Bulwarks, as well as Qiang nomads from the various commanderies of Liangzhou and convicts released into military service."[55] What is more, the Qiang who surrendered were made to resettle on Han territory away from their ancestral lands and were "pressed into corvée service by minor officials and local strongmen"; this explains why one of the Shaodang chief's sons, Miwu 迷吾 (d. 87), upended the agreement and rose up in arms in the year 77, seeking to return to the Qiang's own pasture grounds.[56] On the Han side, this new insurrection prompted a change of policy. Lulled into complacency by nearly twenty years of relative calm (no Commandant Protector of the Qiang was appointed between 59 and 76), from that point on, new holders of the office received the mission to control the Qiang by military means. In 76, Wu Tang 吳棠 (fl. 65–77) took up the office in Anyi 安夷 ("Pacifying the Barbarians"; modern Ping'an County 平安縣, Qinghai); he was replaced the next year by Fu Yu 傅育 (d. 87), who operated from Linqiang 臨羌 ("Overseeing the Qiang"; west of Xining).[57] As these toponyms suggest, these bases were situated right in the middle of contested territory, further away from modern Lanzhou and closer to modern Xining. Fu Yu died on the battlefield, ambushed by Miwu. His successor Zhang Yu 張紆 (fl. 86–88; also in Linqiang), with 10,000 troops at his disposal, forced Miwu to surrender his arms, but then treacherously killed him together with 800 of his tribal grandees (*qiuhao* 酋豪) when he came to discuss peace terms. Miwu's son Mitang 迷唐 (d. ca. 105) vowed revenge, and by the year 88 had assembled such a multitude under his command that the Han court had to disavow Zhang Yu, replacing him with the craftier Deng Xun 鄧訓 (36–92), who "for a little while, by means of rewards and bribes, sowed discord amongst them."[58]

---

54   *HHS* 23:808, 87:2880.

55   *HHS* 22:786 ("烏桓、黎陽營、三輔募士、涼州諸郡羌胡兵及弛刑").

56   *HHS* 87:2886 ("諸降羌 ⋯ 皆為吏人豪右所徭役").

57   *HHS* 87:2881. I also quote freely from the syntheses in Rafe de Crespigny, *A Biographical Dictionary of Later Han to the Three Kingdoms (23–220 AD)* (Leiden 2007).

58   *HHS* 87:2882–2883. *HHS* 3:157 mentions a Liu Xu 劉旴 as Commandant Protector of the Qiang in 87, but this must be a mistake (for Zhang Yu).

Like his predecessor, Deng Xun was based in Linqiang, north of the Yellow River; this appears from the fact that Mitang's Shaodang people's home was the area called the Greater and Smaller Yu Valleys 大、小榆谷 just south of the upper Yellow River near present-day Guide County 貴德縣 in Qinghai (south of Xining), where "with an army of over 40,000 men, [Mitang] waited until the ice froze over to cross the river [northward], and to attack [Deng] Xun."[59] Mitang moreover counted upon Qiang clans 種羌 who lived further up north, in Wuwei Commandery, to descend to Linqiang at the appointed time, as Mitang's forces ascended from the south. A potential obstacle to this pincer movement's success, however, was the Lesser Yuezhi living in between, from Koko Nor to Wuwei, who were no friends of the Qiang and who had even, "although a shilly-shally lot, occasionally also made themselves useful to the Han."[60] Deng Xun proved his wile again by offering the Yuezhi sanctuary in the face of the Qiang menace, thereby binding them more closely to the Han side; he subsequently trained several hundred of their young men to become — as we have seen before — the Loyal Nomad Auxiliary 義從胡, soon augmented to 4000 through the addition of Chinese as well as Qiang recruits.[61] With his Loyal Auxiliary force, Deng Xun turned the tide; crossing the Yellow River, he drove Mitang out of his base and the Qiang coalition collapsed as a result. Although the following years saw further unrest, the building of a pontoon bridge over the Yellow River by a new commandant protector (Guan You 貫友, 93–96) gave the Han easy access to the Greater and Lesser Yu Valleys south of it and allowed for the establishment of Han military colonies; a son of Mitang formally surrendered possibly in 105, and the Han remained in control of this part of today's Qinghai province until 107.[62]

Worse was to come, however, with a major rebellion by the Xianlian Qiang (107–117) under their chief Dianlian 滇零 (d. 112), who at the peak of his fortunes adopted the title "Son of Heaven" in defiance of the Han. Dianlian was

---

59   I quote *HHS* 16:609 ("期冰合度河攻訓"). In *HHS* 87:2883–2884, both Commandant Protector Nie Shang 聶尚 in the year 93 as well as Emperor He 和帝 (r. 89–105) in an audience with Mitang in the year 98 (see also 4:185) tell Mitang — whether to placate him or belatedly to grant his late father Miwu's request — to return home "to the Greater and Smaller Yu Valleys." Their location is further clear from *Shuijing zhu jiao* 2:46 and from Cao Feng's 曹鳳 101 CE description of it (*HHS* 87:2885 = *Shuijing zhu jiao* 2:47). The last time the Yellow River froze over in this area (Lanzhou) was in 1968, but it was apparently a yearly occurrence in the past: "between December and January, the enormous volume of the Hwang-ho is frozen so solidly across that you can take carts from one side to the other," writes Reginald Farrer in *The Geographical Journal* Vol. LI (1918) No. 6, p. 341.

60   *HHS* 16:609 ("雖首施兩端，漢亦時收其用").

61   *HHS* 16:609–610, 87:2899.

62   *HHS* 87:2883–2885.

emboldened to take to the field by the decision of the government, dominated by the regent Empress Dowager Deng 鄧太后 (Deng Sui 鄧綏, 81–121) in 107, to abandon the Han footholds in the Western Regions that general Ban Chao 班超 (32–102) had painstakingly and almost single-handedly secured there over a period of thirty years.[63] The withdrawal, of which the immediate cause was the inept conduct of Ban Chao's successor Ren Shang 任尚 (d. 118) as Protector-General of the Western Regions (*xiyu duhu* 西域都護), in itself necessitated levying new troops, including Qiang recruits from Liangzhou, so as to escort Han colonists from the region back home; the resentment this caused amongst the Eastern Qiang (of which the Xianlian), not to mention the weakness of the empire that was suddenly on display, triggered this Eastern Qiang rebellion. Soon all of Liangzhou was in turmoil and the Chinese fled to escape a massacre. In 108, the Qiang defeated a major army sent against them in Longxi; a few months later, they inflicted 8000 casualties upon troops in Tianshui Commandery placed under Ren Shang's command.[64] They proceeded to "raid the Three Bulwarks, to violate Zhao 趙 and Wei 魏 in the east (roughly, the modern provinces of Hebei and Shanxi), and to enter Yizhou (modern Sichuan) in the south," reaching Hedong and Henei (north of Luoyang) in 111. At that point, local administrators evacuated Liangzhou: "all the commanderies of Liangzhou were temporarily governed from Pingyi and Fufeng (in the vicinity of Chang'an)."[65] But then Dianlian died, and the revolt lost momentum. The Han regained initiative, and Ren Shang, together with Commandant Protector Ma Xian 馬賢 (d. 141), eventually ended all resistance to Han rule by 118. Although the roads connecting the Central Plain to the far west were re-opened, still the campaign had cost the central government the enormous

---

63 As in Xianlian and in Lianju, *ling* in the name Dianlian is pronounced *lian*: see De Crespigny, *Biographical Dictionary* p. 139. *HHS* 5:211, 87:2886 ("Son of Heaven"), 47:1571–1586 (Ban Chao's career), 88:2911 (Western Regions abandoned).

64 *HHS* 47:1586 (Ren Shang's conduct: "[Ren] Shang had but been in his post for a few years when the Western Regions rose up in revolt and he was summoned [back to Luoyang] due to his wrongful conduct, just as [Ban] Chao had forewarned 尚至數年，而西域反亂，以罪被徵，如超所戒。"); 87:2886 ("several hundred if not thousands of horsemen levied from the Qiang in Jincheng, Longxi and Hanyang 漢陽" in 107, causing discontent); 5:209, 211, 87:2886 (Han defeats in 108, 8000 casualties).

65 *HHS* 5:211, 216. I quote *HHS*, "Treatises" 14 ("Wuxing 五行" B), p. 3293 ("涼州諸郡寄治馮翊、扶風界"); 5:216 is more precise. The administrative seat of Longxi (mod. Lintao County 臨洮縣) had its local officials evacuated to Xiangwu 襄武 (mod. Longxi County 隴西縣), 100 km east; Anding (mod. Guyuan) evacuated to Meiyang 美陽 (mod. Fufeng; in Fufeng Commandery), 100 km south; Beidi (mod. Yaoxian 耀縣) evacuated to Chiyang 池陽 (mod. Dali 大荔; in Pingyi Comm.), and Shangjun to Yaxian 衙縣 (mod. Baishui 白水縣; also in Pingyi Comm.), 80 km south. See also *ZZTJ* 89:1587 with Hu Sanxing's note.

THE HEXI CORRIDOR

sum of 24,000 million cash and left Liangzhou with a population loss from which it did not recover.[66] As Wang Fu 王符 (85–165), a contemporary witness, noted, "These commanderies on our borders, now, are a thousand *li* wide, yet on that whole sweep of land, each one consists of just a couple of counties, where but a few hundred homesteads still stand; and should their prefects go on a circuit of ten thousand *li* in these jurisdictions of theirs, all they will find is emptiness, with not a soul alive, the rich farmlands abandoned with no one to cultivate or develop them."[67]

Only in 129 were the worst-affected commanderies of Liangzhou, i.e. Anding, Beidi and Shangjun in the south, deemed safe enough for local prefects to be stationed there again. Their garrisons were beefed up; to the west, in Lintao in Longxi Commandery, the post of Commandant for the Southern Division (of Liangzhou; *nanbu duwei* 南部都尉) was resuscitated (it had been created in 125 BCE, but remained unfilled for more than a century); the wisdom of building three hundred garrisoned fortresses along the military highway out of Chang'an to Jincheng was demonstrated when, as if on cue, the Judong clan of the Qiang 且凍羌 set fire to the barbican on the Longguan 隴關 pass, the road's entry point into Liangzhou.[68] How volatile the region still was showed again in 140, when a prefect and two commandant protectors, "hard and unkind" men, instead of keeping the peace amongst the Qiang, pushed them too far with their intransigence; in Jincheng Commandery, which is presumably where the protectors still exercised their function (i.e. in Lianju), the Judong and Funan clans 傅難種 of the Qiang went on a rampage, and were soon joined by Western Qiang from the Xining area in carrying out raids on the Three Bulwarks, i.e. Chang'an and environs.[69] The protectors were "condemned as accountable (*zuo zheng* 坐徵)" for what had happened. The prefect

---

66 The roads that had been blocked (*HHS* 5:207 ["斷隴道"]), still in 115 (5:221 ["絕隴道"]), re-opened later that year (51:1689 ["通河西路"]); Longyou is pacified (5:227–228), but at enormous cost (65:2148).

67 Wang Fu (a native of Anding), *Qianfu lun* 潛夫論 (*A Hermit's Disquisitions*): Wang Jipei 汪繼培 (1751–1819) & Peng Duo 彭鐸 (1913–1985), eds., *Qianfu lun jian jiaozheng* 潛夫論箋校正 (Beijing 1985), 24:285 ("今邊郡千里，地各有兩縣，戶財 (*sic*) 置數百，而太守周迴萬里，空無人民，美田棄而莫墾發。").

68 *HHS* 6:256, 257 ("An edict ordered that all convicts condemned to the death penalty, incarcerated in either the commanderies or princedoms or in central government agencies, have their punishment reduced by one level and be rendered to the garrisons of Beidi, Shangjun and Anding 詔郡國中都官死罪繫囚皆減罪一等，詣北地、上郡、安定戍。"); 262 (*nanbu duwei*); 269–270 = 87:2895 (fortresses, Longguan pass).

69 *HHS* 87:2895: Ma Xian, Lai Ji 來機 and Liu Bing 劉秉 were "hard and unkind (虐刻)," and in their "intransigence (疾惡)" failed to heed Confucius' warning (*Analects* 8.10) not to "push too hard (疾之已甚)."

(Ma Xian), given a general's sweeping powers and 100,000 men, was killed in battle in 141. Then the Prefect of Wuwei, Zhao Chong 趙沖 (d. 144), "having received instructions to supervise all troops from the four commanderies (in the northwest) of Hexi," confronted Han 罕 Qiang in Beidi and Shaohe 燒何 Qiang in Anding with mixed success, resulting in 30,000 of them surrendering to Han rule, but at the price of abandoning Beidi and Anding: their prefects were once more evacuated to Pingyi and Fufeng in the vain hope that they would return to their yamens in time.[70] A Gentleman of the Palace had indeed warned that "once you give up Liangzhou, the Three Bulwarks [will] become the new frontier *de facto* and our imperial mausolea will lie exposed — which is out of the question!" Efforts had been made, upon retaking Anding, Beidi and Shangjun in 129, to consolidate these possessions by "repairing inner and outer walls, establishing observation and relay posts and, once rivers were dammed up and canals dredged, by creating agricultural garrisons, economising in the hundreds of millions of cash per year on inland commanderies' expenses";[71] now these endeavours were wasted. What made the loss of this eastern part of Liangzhou (corresponding roughly to the southern half of today's Ningxia, from the provincial capital Yinchuan down to Guyuan) far more dramatic was that to its east, in the northern swathe of Bingzhou 幷州 (i.e., in today's Inner Mongolia, the northern bend of the Yellow River known as the Ordos Loop), a Southern Xiongnu tribe had also risen in revolt. Besides dispatching an army to quell the uprising, the Han court also sent an emissary to the elderly *chanyu* (Xiuli 休利, r. 128–140) to demand that he rein in his subjects; yet Xiuli was sadly powerless to do so, and rather than admit it, he preferred to commit suicide, as did his brother and designated heir. In the ensuing leadership vacuum amongst the Xiongnu, the rebel chiefs hastily claimed the *chanyu* title for one of their own and, safety lying in numbers, "reached out to the Wuhuan

---

70   *HHS* 87:2895–2896 (with the phrase "督河西四郡兵為節度").

71   This Gentleman of the Palace (*langzhong* 郎中) was Yu Xu 虞詡 (d. 137), in *HHS* 58:1866 ("涼州既弃，即以三輔為塞，則園陵單外") = 87:2893, with the resulting action: "繕城郭，置候驛，既而激河浚渠為屯田，省内郡費歲一億計". Wang Fu, in his *Qianfu lun*, echoes Yu Xu: "Therefore, if Liangzhou were to be lost, then the metropolitan area would become the frontier [...]" (22:258), and explains (p. 267) why "inland commanderies" had to bear heavy expenses: "In several provinces and commanderies, more than a hundred thousand soldiers are now being quartered, all of them receiving food rations from the state to the tune of millions of bushels a year, and in addition, there is their monthly pay. Already those costs per head are more than what they can come up with; not only that, one fears their out-of-pocket expenses, too, are entirely out of control. 今數州 [郡] 屯兵十餘萬人，皆廩食縣官，歲費百萬斛，又有月直。但此人耗，不可勝供，而反憚暫出之費，甚非計也。" Cf. transl. Ivan P. Kamenarović: Wang Fu, *Propos d'un hermite* (Paris 1992), p. 156.

THE HEXI CORRIDOR   39

to their east, and to their west took in myriad Qiang barbarians and other nomad people, with whom they assailed and utterly destroyed Tiger Tooth Camp in Jingzhao, murdered the commandant and his major in Shangjun, and went on to plunder the four provinces of Bing[zhou], Liang[zhou], You[zhou] 幽州 and Ji[zhou] 冀州. There was no choice but to move the administrative seat of Xihe [Commandery] to Lishi 離石 [County], the administrative seat of Shangjun to Xiayang 夏陽, and the administrative seat of Shuofang 朔方 to Wuyuan 五原 [Commandery]."[72] The dire outcome of these near-simultaneous Qiang and Xiongnu rebellions in Liangzhou and Bingzhou provinces was that the Eastern Han permanently lost control over a huge chunk of land above Guanzhong. Let it be added for clarity's sake that a territorially diminished western Liangzhou, including the Hexi Corridor above modern Lanzhou, remained in Chinese hands.

The last spate of trouble in Liangzhou involving the Qiang, in Han times, was the so-called Liangzhou Rebellion of 184 to 220.[73] "In the winter (of 184), the Xianlian Qiang in Beidi revolted, together with bands of marauders in Fuhan 枹罕 (county, now Linxia City 臨夏市, Gansu) and Heguan 河關 (county, near Guide County in Qinghai; both in Longxi Commandery, appr. 200 km west of Beidi)." Beidi had been abandoned, while Fuhan and Heguan were both situated on the western border of Longxi, where Han suzerainty ended and Qiang control began; hence, where the writ of the Han did not run, there can be no question of a revolt. Instead, more probably, these Qiang invaded Han-held Liangzhou. The text goes on: "Next, they jointly set up Beigong Boyu 北宮伯玉 and Li Wenhou 李文侯, of the Loyal Nomad Auxiliary of Huangzhong, to be their generals." The Huangzhong Loyal Nomad Auxiliary was stationed in Linqiang; Beigong Boyu (d. 186) may have been a Yuezhi or a Qiang, Li Wenhou (d. 186) may have been Chinese (we have seen that the Loyal Auxiliaries were a multi-ethnic force), and (if and when this force came to stand eye to eye with the Qiang "rebels") they manifestly mutinied, as did two other Chinese members

---

72   *HHS* 89:2960–2961. In Xihe, the commandery seat moved from Pingding County 平定縣 to Lishi County (both still so named; Lishi County is now a district of Lüliang City 呂梁市, Shanxi), appr. 150 km south; in Shangjun, the seat moved from Fushi County 膚施縣 (south of today's Yulin City 榆林市, Shaanxi) to Xiayang County (today's Hancheng City 韓城市, Shaanxi), appr. 220 km south; and by saying that the administrative seat of Shuofang Commandery (most of which is today's Kubuqi Desert 庫布齊沙漠, with the ancient seat at today's Dengkou County 磴口縣, Bayannur League 巴彥淖爾盟, Inner Mongolia) moved appr. 180 km east to Wuyuan, its neighbouring commandery, with its administrative seat near today's Baotou City 包頭市, Inner Mongolia, the author means that the two commanderies merged into one.

73   On which, see Gustav Haloun, "The Liang-chou Rebellion, 184–221 A.D.," in *Asia Major*, NS 1:1 (1949), pp. 119–132; and Yü Ying-shih, "Han Foreign Relations," pp. 432–435.

of the force identified by name, Song Jian 宋建 (d. 214) and Wang Guo 王國 (d. 189).[74] Accounts differ on what happened next, but in any case the Qiang quite disappear from the scene. The most circumstantial narrative says that Song Jian and Wang Guo, perhaps at the head of a vanguard for the main body of rebels, arrived at the administrative seat of Jincheng Commandery in Qianya 允吾 (sic!) and, "pretending that [all the rest of] Jincheng Commandery had surrendered, demanded to see the now retired Magistrate (ling 令) of Xin'an 新安 Bian Yun 邊允, a notable figure in Liangzhou, and [the commandery's] Assistant Officer (congshi 從事) Han Yue 韓約."[75] This is interesting, since both the retired Bian Yun (a.k.a. Bian Zhang 邊章, d. 186) and Han Yue (a.k.a. Han Sui 韓遂, d. 215) were partisans of the "righteous protest (qingyi 清議)" movement against the abuse of power by court eunuchs in the reign of Emperor Ling 靈帝 (Liu Hong 劉宏, 157–189, r. 168–189); in fact, on an official mission to Luoyang only months before, Assistant Officer Han had urged General-in-Chief He Jin 何進 (d. 189) to exterminate the eunuchs.[76] The Great Proscription (danggu 黨錮) of 169 to 184, engineered by the eunuchs, had blighted the careers of countless officials and created a generation of disaffected men of education; it was held to be the direct cause of the Yellow Turban 黃巾 rebellion (184–185), whose leader, Zhang Jue 張角 (d. 184), had set his sights on supplanting the Han dynasty.[77] Was this also the objective of the Liangzhou mutineers? Perhaps not initially. The text continues: "When [Han] Yue failed to show up, the prefect, Chen Yi 陳懿, urged him on and let him betake himself [to the meeting venue], where [Wang] Guo and his associates then promptly seized [Han] Yue and others, several tens of men, as hostages." The Hou Han shu version of events says that the Commandant Protector of the Qiang, Ling Zheng 泠徵, had at this point already been murdered by the insurgents. His office may have been

---

74 I quote HHS 72:2320; the name of Song Jian associated with that of Beigong Boyu as ringleaders of a mutiny appears in Yu Huan's third-century Dian lüe 典略, quoted in the commentary on SGZ 1:45; that of Wang Guo, in Xiandi chunqiu 獻帝春秋, quoted in HHS 72:2321. Neither of these two mentions a Qiang revolt; one understands instead that the mutinying Loyal Auxiliary started the disturbance.

75 For the pronunciation Qianya instead of Yunwu, see HS 28B:1611 n. 2 (by Ying Shao). Xin'an was a county in Hongnong Commandery 弘農郡, close to Luoyang (HHS, "Treatises" 19:3401).

76 Bian Zhang and Han Sui were "equally renowned 俱著名" (Dian lüe in the comm. on SGZ 1:45), and jointly (together with a third official who goes unmentioned in HHS) sponsored the carving of a stele in memory of a former Prefect of Jincheng, Yin Hua 殷華 (d. 178): the text is extant, a paean to Confucian virtues. I assume Han Yue/Sui met He Jin (see Dian lüe, ibid.) when the latter had just become General-in-Chief (early 184) and was powerful enough in theory to accede to Han Yue's plea: HHS 69:2246.

77 See B.J. Mansvelt Beck, "The Fall of Han," in CHC 1, pp. 317–376 at pp. 328–329.

THE HEXI CORRIDOR 41

in Qianya, too. Now "Jincheng (read: Qianya) erupted in turmoil; [Chen] Yi vacated [the city,] and [Wang] Guo and the others took him along to make it to the camp of the [Commandant] Protector of the Qiang, where they killed him and released [Han] Yue and [Bian] Yun."[78] By siding with their captors, Han and Bian became outlaws and changed their names to Bian Zhang and Han Sui, according to this source.[79] At once they also took the lead of a politically motivated armed band that "in the spring of the following year, with several ten thousand horsemen, invaded the Three Bulwarks and trampled the imperial mausolea on the pretext that they had come to punish the eunuchs." Han commanders Dong Zhuo 董卓 (d. 192) and Huangfu Song 皇甫嵩 (d. ca. 195) at first failed to stop them, but Bian Zhang and Han Sui's ascendance did not last: from Meiyang 美陽, west of Chang'an, where they probably intended to loot the imperial tombs, they were beaten back and fled back to Jincheng. In what looks like a separate development, with 30,000 troops, Dong Zhuo unsuccessfully "chastised" Xianlian Qiang in Wangyuan 望垣, 200 km southwest of Bian Zhang and Han Sui's refuge.[80] Two years later, in the winter of 186, there was a falling-out in which Han Sui killed Bian Zhang, Beigong Boyu and Li Wenhou, and remained alone in charge of "over 100,000 soldiers" marching upon Didao (now Lintao), where the prefect of Longxi Commandery had his office. Rather than resist, the prefect joined Han Sui with his local troops, as did two subordinate officers, again together with the troops under their command, who had deserted from a provincial army detachment sent out to confront Han Sui. One of these officers was, confusingly, Wang Guo. This Wang Guo now found himself cast in the role of "general of all troops combined (*hezhong jiangjun* 合衆將軍)"; with these troops, he entered the Three Bulwarks again and invested the walled city of Chencang 陳倉 (near modern Baoji 寶雞市, Shaanxi). In early 189, giving up after a fruitless eighty-day siege, Wang Guo's army retreated and was attacked in the rear by Huangfu Song: more than 10,000 prisoners were taken and beheaded, and though Wang Guo managed

---

78 *Xiandi chunqiu* in *HHS* 72:2321: "約不見，太守陳懿勸之使往，國等便劫質約等數十人。金城亂，懿出，國等扶以到護羌營，殺之，而釋約、允等。" Cf. *HHS* 8:350 for a terse summary.

79 *Xiandi chunqiu*, ibid. Once the civil and military administrators of Jincheng commandery were eliminated, it was the prefect of neighbouring Longxi commandery, apparently, who then spoke for Liangzhou province as a whole: "Longxi publicly proclaimed whose side it took, by branding [Han] Yue and [Bian] Yun by name as outlaws; the province placed a bounty on their heads [worth the tax revenue of] a thousand-household marquisate for either [Han] Yue or [Bian] Yun" ("隴西以愛憎露布，冠約、允名以為賊，州購約、允各千戶侯。").

80 *HHS* 72:2320.

to escape, he died soon afterwards.[81] As a result of this setback, the "combined troops" split up again under their various chiefs; one source speaks of as many as thirty-six battalions. One of these, under the command of Ma Teng 馬騰 (d. 212), whose mother was a Qiang, went over to the government side to fight "rebellious Qiang and insurgent Di" and then pledged allegiance to Dong Zhuo. Han Sui, politically the most outspoken of the Liangzhou Rebellion leaders in his hatred of the eunuchs, did the same. And indeed, Dong Zhuo presented himself as a restorer of the greatness of the Han; what is more, he hailed from Longxi. Unfortunately, once the eunuchs had been disposed of, Dong Zhuo kidnapped the young emperor Liu Bian 劉辯 (173/174–190; r. as Emperor Shao 少帝, 189) and his brother Liu Xie 劉協 (181–234, r. as Emperor Xian 獻帝, 189–220) and, entering Luoyang (189), set up his own regime. Open civil war ensued; Dong Zhuo was assassinated, and Cao Cao eventually emerged victorious. The final battalion commander whose fate is known was Song Jian, ostensibly one of the original Loyal Auxiliaries. In his native county of Fuhan, Song Jian set up a statelet that he ruled for thirty years as self-proclaimed "King of the Sources of the Yellow River Who Will Pacify the Han (*Heshou ping Han wang* 河首平漢王)"; in 214, Cao Cao's general Xiahou Yuan 夏侯淵 (d. 219) destroyed it, and also subjugated all the Qiang he found in nearby Huangzhong and who, one must assume, lived in peace with Song Jian.[82] Yet concluding from this presumed cohabitation (as from the Liangzhou Rebellion as a whole) that this frontier province, because of the predominant Qiang element in its population, had "barbarize[d] the frontier Chinese rather than sinicize[d] the Ch'iang," or that the rebellion "illustrates the extent to which frontier peoples in the region, both Chinese and non-Chinese, had developed a common geographical identity of their own" (since it was a "joint rebellion of Ch'iang, Hsiung-nu, and Yüeh-chih peoples, as well as Chinese") seems to get things the wrong way round.[83] Although it is entirely possible that a sizeable number of the rebellion's troops were Qiang, Xiongnu and Yuezhi, and although Dong Zhuo — who in the end absorbed the remnant of these troops under his own banner — was passably uncouth, as a typical product of a less than civilised northwest, what nonetheless drove the rebel leaders was antithetical to Qiang interests: it was to revive the glory of the Han.

---

81   *HHS* 72:2321, 71:2305.

82   "Thirty-six battalions": *Yingxiong ji* 英雄記, quoted in *HHS* 72:2322 n. 2. Ma Teng's mother (*Xiandi zhuan* 獻帝傳, quoted in *HHS* 72:2335 n. 1); Ma Teng fighting "rebellious Qiang and insurgent Di 反羌叛氐" (*SGZ* 18:545); Ma Teng and Han Sui join Dong Zhuo (*HHS* 72:2335). On Dong Zhuo, see Mansvelt Beck, "The Fall of Han"; on Song Jian's fate, *SGZ* 9:271.

83   Yü Ying-shih, "Han Foreign Relations," pp. 433–434.

CHAPTER 3

The Colonisation of Liangzhou, 100 BCE to 300 CE

The Western Han's greatest geopolitical rival was the Xiongnu, and in order to gain the better of them, the Han had to assimilate Xiongnu military know-how, obtain a steady supply of horses, and learn how to conduct lengthy campaigns far from the metropolitan heartland of the empire. Agricultural colonies needed to be established in forward areas close to the battle lines to make military colonists self-sufficient and to provision armies sent out into the field. We now make abstraction of the immense northeastern frontier area constituted by the Yellow River's Ordos Loop (in modern Ningxia and Inner Mongolia) and of contested areas even further east (in modern Hebei and Liaoning) up to North Korea. Instead, we concentrate on the Hexi Corridor, flanked by the Mongolian Plateau (with the Gobi Desert) to its east, and by the Tibetan Plateau to its west and southwest. It was to implant and administer military colonies there that, in 126 BCE, the province-level administrative unit of Liangzhou was created, a province not much different in its geographical outline from modern Gansu (appr. 450,000 square km), with Guzang (today's Wuwei City) as its administrative seat. Around today's provincial capital, Lanzhou (then Jincheng), and in the southern third of the province, Han settlers had to contend with mostly Qiang natives of the region, as we have just described; north, one should perhaps say, of the strategic post of Lianju (established in 115 BCE), the Hexi Corridor extended towards the northwest and the Tarim Basin, and the Taklamakan Desert beyond. In the process of driving the Xiongnu out of this area, the Han Emperor Wu established Zhangye and Jiuquan Commanderies at the latest in 104 BCE: Zhangye was to serve as the administrative centre of an immense territory circumscribed by the Yellow River to the southeast and the Ruo River to the northeast, while Jiuquan, with the Heli Mountains 合黎山 in its northeast, presided over the Badain Jaran Desert, stretching out nearly 50,000 square km to its north. Dunhuang Commandery was founded between 101 and 94, certainly before 91 BCE, as a northern split-off from Jiuquan that formed an ill-defined, open passage into the deserts of the west, and Wuwei followed between 81 and 67 BCE, a southern split-off from Zhangye that created a slightly more manageable administrative unit in the south of the corridor.[1]

---

1 Zhangye and Jiuquan in 111 BCE, according to *Shiji* 37:1439 n. 2 (by Sima Zhen 司馬貞 [fl. 713–742]); in 104 BCE, according to *HS* 28B:1613 as well as *CICA* p. 76 n. 40. See *CICA*, ibid., on Dunhuang and Wuwei. Cf. also Di Cosmo, *Ancient China and Its Enemies*, p. 246. On the early

© DOMINIK DECLERCQ, 2025 | DOI:10.1163/9789004727380_004

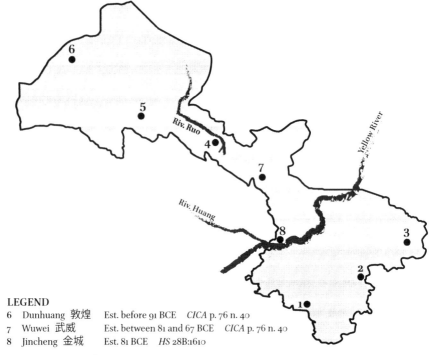

LEGEND
6   Dunhuang 敦煌   Est. before 91 BCE   *CICA* p. 76 n. 40
7   Wuwei 武威   Est. between 81 and 67 BCE   *CICA* p. 76 n. 40
8   Jincheng 金城   Est. 81 BCE   *HS* 28B:1610

MAP 2   Liangzhou Inspectorate 50 BCE

Zhang Qian had informed Emperor Wu that fabulous horses were to be had in Ershi 貳師 (today's Osh in Kyrgyzstan), in the Ferghana Valley, and the Han offered to buy them against a thousand catties of gold; however, rebuffed by its king, the emperor substituted war for trade. Li Guangli 李廣利 (d. 89 BCE), appointed "Ershi General 貳師將軍" after the goal of his expedition, failed in his first attempt, but, departing from Dunhuang with 60,000 men, "100,000 head of cattle, 3000 horse and asses and camels by the ten thousand," successfully vanquished the place and took possession of the horses on his second try in 101 BCE. Not only that, but as further logistic back-up, the counties of Juyan in Zhangye and Xiuchu in Wuwei were created in 102 BCE and peopled with 180,000 conscripts especially to till the land and bring its crop, as well as their own extra manpower, if and when required.[2] Caravans set out from

---

colonisation of Liangzhou, see also Arnaud Bertrand, "Conquête et occupation de la frontière nord-ouest au temps des Han occidentaux (206 av. J.-C.–9 apr. J.-C.)," in Jean Baechler & Jérôme de Lespinois, eds., *La Guerre et les Eléments* (Paris 2019), pp. 211–246.

2   *HS* 96A:3895, 61:2700 = *Shiji* 123:3176; see *CICA* pp. 132–135 and 228–231 with n. 880, explaining how the *HS* and *Shiji* texts are in need of reconstruction here. On Juyan and Xiuchu counties, see *HS* 28B:1612, 1613.

Chang'an on a regular basis with surplus Chinese products, mostly silk, to bring back woollens, furs and luxury goods. Once Lianju, Zhangye and Jiuquan were operational as staging posts, "more missions, as a result, were sent out and reached Anxi 安息 (= Arsacid Persia, 247 BCE–224 CE), Yancai 奄蔡 (= Yanqi 焉耆, i.e. Karasahr in Xinjiang), Ligan 黎軒/犂軒 (= Nabataean 'Raqēmō,' i.e. Petra, in Jordan?) and Tiaozhi 條枝 (= Tawwağ, near the Iranian port city of Bushehr on the Persian Gulf), as well as the states of Shendu 身毒國 (= Northern India). These envoys were in sight of each other on the roads. A single mission comprised several hundred members if large, and a hundred or so if small [...] Later, [the despatch of missions] became more a matter of routine, and they were reduced to smaller numbers. Each year, the number of Han missions amounted to over ten, if many, and five or six, if few; those that went on long distances returned after eight or nine years, those on shorter distances after a few years."[3] Perhaps a note of caution is in order, however, since these "missions" may have been more about projecting Han power and expanding Han influence than about trade. Government-sponsored trade, in any case, involved prestige, and prestige came at a price. In the *Discussions on Salt and Iron* (*Yantie lun* 鹽鐵論), the "counsellor (*dafu* 大夫)" who stands for Imperial Counsellor (*yushi dafu* 御史大夫) Sang Hongyang 桑弘羊 (152–80 BCE) has this to say in praise of trade:

> By means of gold from our Ru and Han rivers, the slenderest of tributary gifts, do we entice outer states and draw in treasure from the Hu and Qiang. With a single length of poplin silk from our Central States do we obtain from the Xiongnu goods worth their weight in gold, and nibble away at the riches of that enemy state. And so it is that mules, asses and camels in a single file come pacing over our frontiers, and khulans and takhis make up all our livestock;[4] squirrel, marten, fox and raccoon furs,[5] colourful felts and patterned cashmeres pile up in the imperial

---

3 *Shiji* 123:3170 ("因益發使抵安息、奄蔡、黎軒、條枝、身毒國。使者相望於道。一輩大者數百，少者百餘人　[…]　其後益習而率少焉。漢率一歲中使多者十餘，少者五六輩，遠者八九歲，近者數歲而反。") = *HS* 61:2694; *CICA* pp. 219–220, with the proposed emendation to the *Shiji*/*HS* text that I reproduce here.

4 For the rendering "khulan" (*Equus hemionus hemionus*) for *dianxi* 驒騱, I am indebted to David R. Knechtges's note in his translation of the *Wen xuan, or Selections of Refined Literature*, Volume Two (Princeton 1987), p. 88 n. L. 165–166, referring to Egami Namio 江上波夫, *Yūrashia kodai hoppō bunka: Kyōdo bunka ronkō* ユーラシア古代北方文化: 匈奴文化論考 (Tokyo 1948), pp. 203–216. *Yuanma* 驥馬 is explained as a bay horse with a pale ("pangaré") underside; the takhi or Przewalski's horse (*Equus ferus przewalskii*) might fit.

5 *Hun* 鼲, the Daurian ground squirrel (*Spermophilus dauricus ramosus*); *he* 貉, the raccoon dog (*Nyctereutes procyonoides*).

46 CHAPTER 3

storehouse; and their worked jade, coral and glass have become our own national treasure. That is to say, the riches of outer states find their way towards us, and are purely of benefit to us, not causing any deficit. Importing exotic goods procures wealth for the nation, and since there is benefit without deficit, the people remains well provided for.

To which his critic, the "man of learning (*wenxue* 文學)," objects that these outer states

are a myriad leagues and more distant from the Han. When tabulating the effort spent ploughing and cultivating mulberry [for silk] as well as the expense in capital and goods [employed in trade missions], it transpires that we buy any of these baubles at a hundred times its price, and that a mere armful costs us ten thousand bushels of grain. And no sooner does high society acquire a taste for luxury and extravagance than their excess corrupts the lower classes too. By attaching such high value to goods coming from afar, our specie and riches go plenish foreign coffers. For that reason, a true king does not cherish useless things, and makes his people frugal as a consequence; he is not partial to exotic goods, and makes his nation rich as a consequence.[6]

This is the voice of Confucian moderation, or of disillusioned hubris, asserting itself against the overweening early Han state of which the Legalist Sang Hongyang was a proud representative. Sang Hongyang, although himself the son of a rich merchant of Luoyang, had established state monopolies on salt and iron; in his view, as that of like-minded colleagues, it was the historical mission of the state to expand ever further and to tower over the economy. To that end, he advocated extending direct Han rule over the Western Regions by sending conscripts and long-term civilian migrants as far as Luntai 輪臺 (southeast of present Kuqa 庫車, Aksu Prefecture 阿克蘇地區, Xinjiang) to set up agricultural colonies. Yet the Xiongnu wars, as well as the disastrous

---

6　Huan Kuan 桓寬 (2nd half 1st cent. BCE), ed., *Yantie lun* (Shanghai 1974), 2:5–6: "汝、漢之金，纖微之貢，所以誘外國而釣胡、羌之寶也。夫中國一端之縵，得匈奴累金之物，而損敵國之用。是以騾驢馲駝，銜尾入塞，馯騠駃騠，盡為我畜，鼲貂狐貉，采旃文罽，充於內府，而璧玉珊瑚琉璃，咸為國之寶。是則外國之物內流，而利不外泄也。異物內流則國用饒，利不外泄則民用給矣。[⋯] 此距漢萬有餘里。計耕桑之功，資財之費，是一物而售百倍其價也，一捪而中萬鍾之粟也。夫上好珍怪，則淫服下流，貴遠方之物，則貨財外充。是以王者不珍無用以節其民，不愛奇貨以富其國。" Cf. translation Jean Levi, *La Dispute sur le sel et le fer* (Paris 2010), pp. 14–15.

THE COLONISATION OF LIANGZHOU, 100 BCE TO 300 CE 47

flooding of the Yellow River in 136 BCE that inundated the most fertile plains of Northern China for two decades, so depleted the treasury that it eventually prompted the Han state to reconsider its proper aims and limitations. Emperor Wu vetoed the colonies of Luntai, long-distance trade missions were discontinued, and by the time the (historic, 86–80 BCE) court discussions on the salt and iron monopolies were written up, from original notes, by Huan Kuan twenty years after the event, Confucian restraint had become, of necessity, mainstream, and the "men of learning" had won the day.[7]

· · ·

In order to turn Wuwei, Zhangye, Jiuquan and Dunhuang from lines drawn on a map into dependable possessions, from 111 BCE, Emperor Wu began to "move people there, to fill the places (or 'give them substance')."[8] As previously mentioned, in the year 102, a contingent of 180,000 "conscripts engaged on garrison and agricultural duties (*shutian zu* 戍田卒)" was despatched to the northwest.[9] One wonders how, at this same time, the hapless commander Li Ling managed to induce 5000 "Chu natives from Danyang 丹陽楚人," in China's balmy south, to sign up for archery practice in Jiuquan and Zhangye and remain garrisoned there as a protection against the nomads.[10] The new jurisdictions suffered a constant barrage of attacks; thus, in 88 BCE, before Xiongnu power in the region was definitely broken, their *chanyu* let it be known to the Qiang people further south, through the intermediary of the Lesser Yuezhi, that "Zhangye and Jiuquan have always been part of these lands of ours, its soil being lush and

---

7 For the colonies at Luntai see *CICA* pp. 165–174; for the policy debates that lie behind the *Yantie lun*, see Michael Loewe, *Crisis and Conflict in Han China, 104 BC to AD 9* (London 1974), esp. Ch. 3.

8 *HS* 6:189 ("徙民以實之").

9 *HS* 61:2700 = *Shiji* 123:3176; *CICA* p. 230. Conscripts, and also peasants subject to corvée duty: "Currently (= ca. 80 BCE), men are made to serve their corvée duty at extreme distances from home, in the coldest and most hostile regions, of greatest peril and hardship. Having set foot in Hu or Yue territory (= in the far northwest, or in the far southeast), where they arrive in one year to return home the coming year, their parents crane their neck peering westward or, if man and wife, they miss one another, chafing at their separation. For those left behind in Chu in the east, their only thought is with the one beyond the Yellow River in the west; therefore when one man leaves, his entire hamlet pines for him, and when one man dies, ten thousand people grieve. 若今則繇役極遠，盡寒苦之地，危難之處，涉胡、越之域，今茲往而來歲旋，父母延頸而西望，男女怨曠而相思，身在東楚，志在西河，故一人行而鄉曲恨，一人死而萬人悲。" (*Yantie lun* 39:86, cfr. transl. Levi p. 212.)

10 *Shiji* 109:2877 = *HS* 54:2451.

fertile; let us then all together strike at them and settle there!"[11] Little wonder that one hears of few Han volunteers willing to move to the Hexi Corridor. In 108, Di 氏 troublemakers from Wudu 武都 (in Sichuan) were brought to heel and deported to Jiuquan. In 91 BCE, after a riot in Chang'an, lower officials who had looted government property were banished to Dunhuang; so were a few individuals who had fallen from the emperor's grace.[12] In 73 CE, an edict ordered that

> convicts condemned to the death penalty, incarcerated in either the commanderies or princedoms or in central government agencies, have their punishment reduced by one level, be exempt from the bastinado, and be rendered to the army garrisons quartered in Shuofang and Dunhuang; their spouses and children follow, as a matter of course; [and] parents as well as uterine siblings of the aforementioned be granted full permission to proceed likewise, if so desired; but no woman claiming to be wed as spouse to any of the aforementioned may be allowed to join.[13]

Qiang bands pillaged Wuwei, Zhangye and Jiuquan, sometimes even Dunhuang, in 120, 141, 160, 162, 163 ("Liangzhou was almost lost!"), 166, 167, etc. — and one reads of those who were tasked with these fortified cities' defence that, having previously been conveyed to their barracks as felons with shaven heads, the state sometimes eventually acknowledged their services by nullifying their outstanding punishment.[14] In spite of Li Guangli's or Huo Qubing's exploits, therefore, the state's hold on the corridor was rather tenuous. Further, on several occasions, the state had to make loans of grain to alleviate the poorest in Dunhuang, Zhangye and elsewhere, and to waive tax payments.[15] Understandably, the commandery prefects singled out for praise were those who, though firm in government, went out of their way to keep relations with non-Chinese groups as uneventful as possible (officials with local background and valued local knowledge were often promoted to the next post in the same

---

11   HS 69:2973 ("張掖、酒泉本我地，地肥美，可共擊居之").
12   HS 6:194 = HHS 86:2859 (Di from Wudu), HS 66:2882 ("吏士劫略者皆徙敦煌郡"), HS 70:
      3027 (Chen Tang 陳湯 and Xie Wannian 解萬年), HS 83:3396 (Xue Kuang 薛況).
13   HHS 2:121 ("詔令郡國中都官死罪繫囚減罪一等，勿笞，詣軍營、屯朔方、敦
      煌；妻子自隨，父母同產欲求從者，恣聽之；女子嫁為人妻，勿與俱。").
14   HHS 87:2892 (120), 6:271 (141), 7:306 = 65:2146 (160), 7:311 = 65:2147 = 87:2897 (162), 65:2147
      ("涼州幾亡！") = 87:2898 (163), 7:317 = 65:2139 (166), 7:318 (167); 47:1591 ("髡輸," conveyed
      there with their heads shaven), 2:122 ("皆一切勿治其罪," all punishments remitted; this
      in 74 CE).
15   HHS 4:187 (in 100 CE), 4:190 (in 102), 4:191 (in 103).

province), and who personally invested themselves in local irrigation works, careful husbandry and the always uncertain time of harvest. Such an exemplar was Diwu Fang 第五訪 (d. 159):

> He was transferred to become Prefect of Zhangye. There was a famine that year, and barley cost several thousand cash a bushel; and Fang, without hesitation, threw open the public granary to meet the most urgent needs, and rescue the most downtrodden. His subordinate officers, afraid, blamed him for what he had done and insisted upon first informing higher authority. But Fang told them, "If you must report first, you abandon the people! As your prefect, I'm more than happy to risk my one life in order to save the lives of many!" And right away he had the grain brought out to give to the people. Emperor Shun 順帝 (Liu Bao 劉保, 115–144, r. 125–144) sent a letter of commendation. In this way, the whole commandery was saved. Before the year was out, officials and populace both knew plenty, and from across the borders, brigands did not even come to steal.[16]

The little that one hears about trade through the corridor suggests that commandery prefects levied a substantial tax on goods in transit. That might well have been justifiable, given the hazards of the journey and the relative safety of the Han walled cities on the way through troubled Liangzhou. However that may be, the point of an edifying anecdote about another model official, Li Xun 李恂 (prefect of Zhangye and later also prefect of Wuwei, sometime between 85 and 100 CE), who refused "slaves, horses from Ferghana, gold and silver, perfumes and cashmeres" offered to him by merchants and their princely backers in the Western Regions, can only be that the regular Han levy was more onerous than was this kind of material lobbying to wave a caravan through unhindered.[17]

Also and emphatically held up as a model were local administrators who carried Chinese civilisation to the barbarians. Ren Yan 任延 (5–68), Prefect of Wuwei ca. 40–50 (?), had this and other pertinent qualities:

> [Wuwei] commandery faced the Xiongnu to its north, and to its south abutted a tribe of Qiang: fearing their incursions and raids, many of its people had given up taking care of their fields. When [Ren] Yan arrived at his post, he selected and gathered together a force of a thousand men

---

16   *HHS* 76:2475.
17   *HHS* 51:1683.

50   CHAPTER 3

with martial nous, [and trained them so that they became an efficient militia ...]

As Hexi was perennially short of rain and moisture, he purposely named subordinate officers to a Water Bureau to deal with this, and as they set about mending and repairing the canals, everybody enjoyed the benefit. He further set up a Tuition Office (*xiaoguan* 校官) and ordered everybody, from the sons and grandsons of his own staff officers and below, to go to the school and receive instruction there, [to which end] he remitted their corvée duties. All those who became proficient in [the Classics with their] chapter-and-verse [commentaries, *zhangju* 章句] he singled out for honours and advancement, so that by and by, the commandery came to boast men of learning and culture.[18]

To put the Han drive to colonise the Hexi Corridor into perspective, a look at the census figures for the duly registered, tax-paying population is instructive; no doubt the households counted here were almost exclusively Chinese. The figures to the left are from the *History of the (Former) Han* and date from 2 CE; those on the right come from the *History of the Later Han* and date from 140 CE. *Tantae molis erat ...*

2 CE	Households	Individuals	140 CE	Households	Individuals
Wuwei	17,581	76,419	Wuwei	10,042	34,226
Zhangye	24,352	88,731	Zhangye	6,552	26,040
			Zhangye Dep. State	4,656	16,952
			Zhangye Juyan Dep. State	1,560	4,733
Jiuquan	18,137	76,726	Jiuquan	12,706	N/A
Dunhuang	11,200	38,335	Dunhuang	748 (?)	29,170

The totals come to 280,211 individuals in 2 CE and, assuming 3.7 individuals per household (to account for the missing Jiuquan data), 157,833 individuals in 140 CE, i.e. a drop of 56% over 138 years. These two totals correspond to 0.05% and 0.03%, respectively, of the registered national population in

---

18   *HHS* 76:2463.

these two census years. Of course, these four Western Han commanderies, six in Later Han (since Zhangye Dependent State 張掖屬國 [est. 24 CE?] and Zhangye Juyan Dependent State 張掖居延屬國 [split off from Zhangye proper ca. 110–120] had themselves the status of commanderies),[19] do not equal the whole of Liangzhou, which in Later Han further included the six commanderies Longxi, Hanyang 漢陽 (the Tianshui of Former Han), Wudu (on the Sichuan border), Jincheng, Anding and Beidi. Yet there is some justification for isolating the Hexi Corridor commanderies, and not only the circumstance that the career of Li Hao Prince of Western Liang played out in this particular arena. In the interesting typologies — a set of cameo pieces depicting the human geography of every region of the realm — with which Ban Gu concludes his "Geographical Treatise," he writes about this corner of the Chinese world:

> From Wuwei towards the west, there used to be the Xiongnu lands of the Hunye and the Xiuchu Kings. After they were expelled in the time of Emperor Wu, four commanderies were established there to ensure communication with the Western Regions as well as to keep the Qiang, in the south, and the Xiongnu well separated from one another. The population was partly from the very poorest area east of the Passes (= modern Henan, Shandong), partly from among those who overstepped the proper bounds when avenging wrongs, and partly from among the insubordinate and reprobate, conveyed thither together with their relatives. The local customs are quite unique. As the land is extensive and people are few, and the presence of water and grass lends itself well to livestock herding, Liangzhou counts more cattle than anywhere else in the empire. Of defending the fortresses on the frontier, a two thousand bushel [official, i.e. of the highest salary level] is put in charge, who is wholly devoted to his soldiery and horses; and on every social occasion that is marked by raising mutual toasts of wine, superiors and their subordinates are like each others' equals, [while] officials and populace behave as one family. To this it can be credited that their mores, come wind or rain, remain equanimous, and that the grain at all times is bought cheaply; that thieves and brigands are rare; that one is greeted with an affability greater than in inland commanderies. That is what can be achieved when government is well intentioned and officials are not abusive.[20]

19   For reasons given above (see n. 45 on p. 31 above), it cannot be the case (as stated in R. de Crespigny, *Biographical Dictionary* ..., pp. 1208–1209) that both the Dependent States of Zhangye and of Juyan in Zhangye were divided off from Zhangye Commandery only in the period "*c.*110–120."

20   *HS* 28B:1644–1645: "自武威以西，本匈奴昆邪王地，武帝時攘之，初置四郡，以通西域，鬲絕南羌、匈奴。其民或以關東下貧，或以報怨過當，或以訞逆亡

This is a pleasing picture of Hexi in Ban Gu's first century CE, when all kinds of riffraff flocked to its vast expanses and founded precarious communities behind defensive installations on constant alert. It reminds one of René Grousset (1885–1952), who remarked that "however paradoxical it may seem, if one should compare China's history to that of any other collective humanity, it is the history of Canada or of the United States that springs to mind [...:] the conquest of immense virgin territories by a people of labourers who found only poor nomad populations before them."[21] The early settlers stuck together, and even the highest-ranking Han government representative found himself socialising with them of a bleak evening.

...

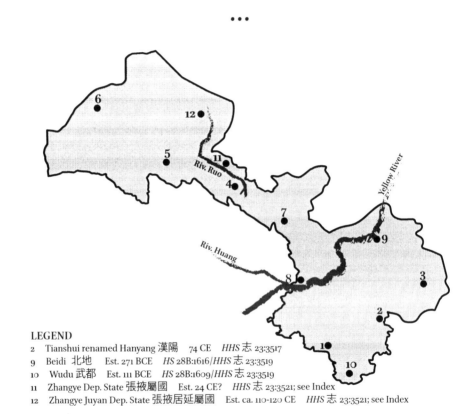

LEGEND
2   Tianshui renamed Hanyang 漢陽   74 CE   *HHS* 志 23:3517
9   Beidi 北地   Est. 271 BCE   *HS* 28B:1616/*HHS* 志 23:3519
10 Wudu 武都   Est. 111 BCE   *HS* 28B:1609/*HHS* 志 23:3519
11 Zhangye Dep. State 張掖屬國   Est. 24 CE?   *HHS* 志 23:3521; see Index
12 Zhangye Juyan Dep. State 張掖居延屬國   Est. ca. 110-120 CE   *HHS* 志 23:3521; see Index

MAP 3   Liangzhou Inspectorate 150 CE

道，家屬徙焉。習俗頗殊，地廣民稀，水屮宜畜牧，故涼州之畜為天下饒。保邊塞，二千石治之，咸以兵馬為務；酒禮之會，上下通焉，吏民相親。是以其俗風雨時節，穀糴常賤，有和氣之應，賢於內郡。此政寬厚，吏不苛刻之所致也。"

21   René Grousset, *Histoire de la Chine* (Paris 1942), p. 23.

THE COLONISATION OF LIANGZHOU, 100 BCE TO 300 CE

In the war-torn final decades of the Han, after Dong Zhuo had seized the young Emperor Shao and his brother, the future Emperor Xian, and was revealed as a usurper, order broke down everywhere and the idea of national unity proved unable to withstand velleities at regional autonomy — aided, of course, by natural barriers that from mythical antiquity have made one think of China as being divided into "Nine Provinces (*jiuzhou* 九州)." In the eastern half of the empire, Dong Zhuo's sworn enemy, Yuan Shao 袁紹 (d. 202), had Jizhou 冀州 for his base (roughly: Hebei), and controlled Qingzhou 青州 (roughly: Shandong) and Bingzhou 并州 (roughly: Shanxi); south of him, Cao Cao held sway in Yanzhou 兗州 (roughly: southern Hebei with part of Henan), with the city of Xu 許 (modern Xuchang 許昌市, Henan); due south of Luoyang, Yuan Shu 袁術 (d. 199) rivalled with Liu Biao 劉表 (144–208) in Yangzhou 揚州 (roughly: Jiangsu and Anhui) and Jingzhou 荊州 (roughly: Hubei); and the as yet barely colonised southeast ("Wu and Yue 吳越," otherwise known as Jiangnan) was controlled by the young warlord Sun Ce 孫策 (175–200). In the empire's western half, there was, to the south, modern Sichuan (Yizhou) ruled by Liu Zhang 劉章 (d. ca. 223); above Yizhou and northwest of another independently-run territory centred on Hanzhong 漢中 (still so named: southern Shaanxi), ruled by the religious leader Zhang Lu 張魯 (fl. 190–215), lay Liangzhou. Liangzhou had been the first rebellious province in the Liangzhou Rebellion of 184 to 220 (which we have read as an essentially loyalist rebellion against the eunuch faction under Emperor Ling, subverted — if that is the word — by Dong Zhuo). The rebellion raged mainly in the south of Liangzhou, roughly between Jincheng (Lanzhou) and the Three Bulwarks and Chang'an; as a consequence, the four northwestern commanderies making up the Hexi Corridor were cut off from the provincial capital. This situation led a local official to petition the emperor to create a separate province — precisely the Hexi region as described by Ban Gu above — consisting of Wuwei, Zhangye, Jiuquan and Dunhuang commanderies: thus, in 194, Yongzhou 雝州 was created.[22] Yet this entity did not last long: in 213, the commanderies east of the Yellow River (the southeastern half of Liangzhou) up to and including Chang'an were merged into Yongzhou, so that "from the Three Bulwarks up to the Western Regions, everything belonged to Yongzhou."[23]

---

22 On Zhang Meng's 張猛 (d. 210?) petition, see *Dian lüe* in *SGZ* 18:547–548; on the creation of Yongzhou, *HHS* 9:376 (where the archaising character 雝 is used instead of the more usual 雍). Li Xian 李賢 (651–684) (note on *HHS* 9:376) is wrong to say that the four commanderies constituting Yongzhou were Jincheng, Jiuquan, Dunhuang and Zhangye; the turmoil in Jincheng was the reason for creating Yongzhou in the first place, and Zhang Meng himself was sent to become Governor of Wuwei in the new province (*Dian lüe, ibid.*).

23 *HHS* 9:387 (Liangzhou abolished); *SGZ* 15:474 ("是時不置涼州，自三輔拒西域，皆屬雍州。").

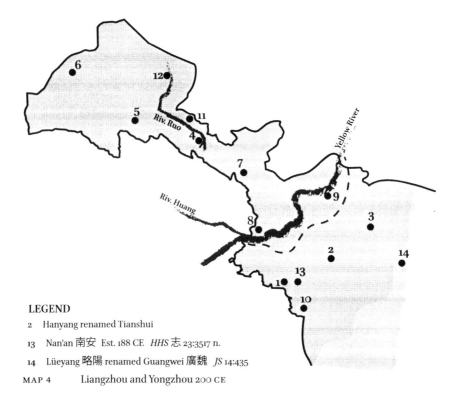

LEGEND
2   Hanyang renamed Tianshui
13 Nan'an 南安 Est. 188 CE *HHS* 志 23:3517 n.
14 Lüeyang 略陽 renamed Guangwei 廣魏 *JS* 14:435
MAP 4   Liangzhou and Yongzhou 200 CE

• • •

When the mighty Han empire finally came crashing down in 220 and the civil wars over the succession subsided, leaving the three states of Wei 魏, Wu 吳 and Shu 蜀 "standing like the three feet of a tripod" over a divided China, this Yong province, like adjacent Liangzhou, lay in the territory or at least in the sphere of influence of the Wei state of Cao Cao's son, Cao Pi 曹丕 (Emperor Wen 魏文帝, 187–226, r. 220–226). In 220, Cao Pi revived the province-level entity of Liangzhou by splitting it off from Yongzhou, with the Yellow River as the boundary between Liangzhou west of it and Yongzhou east of it.[24] A new Inspector (*cishi* 刺史) was appointed for the resuscitated Liangzhou province; he made his way into Hexi, but found himself blocked by self-proclaimed Chinese "generals" who had ousted the governors of Wuwei, Zhangye and Jiuquan and evidently wished for autonomy from Wei rule. This will likewise have been the objective of "Lushui nomads" Yijian Jiqie 伊健妓妾 and Zhiyuanduo 治元多, who also rose in revolt, "creating major disturbance in Hexi." It is unfortunate that the only further information related about this tribe and its leaders is that, when they met defeat on December 6, 221, 50,000

---

24   *SGZ* 15:474.

of them were either slain or taken prisoner and then beheaded, and the victorious Wei army carried away 1,110,000 head of sheep and 80,000 head of cattle.[25] We can at least infer that they were sheep breeders. Also to be noted is that these nomadic or semi-nomadic "Lushui" people had a manifestly important presence in the Hexi Corridor, in contrast to the overwhelming presence of Qiang people in the southern part of Liangzhou.

The next Inspector and an able Commandant Protector of the Qiang restored order to the province, putting down these insurgencies as well as another revolt of Jiuquan Chinese settlers in league with Qiang and Dingling; whereupon "the construction of palisades and stockades, the placing of beacons, watchtowers and public granaries" deterred other, Western Qiang from attempting further inroads from the south.[26]

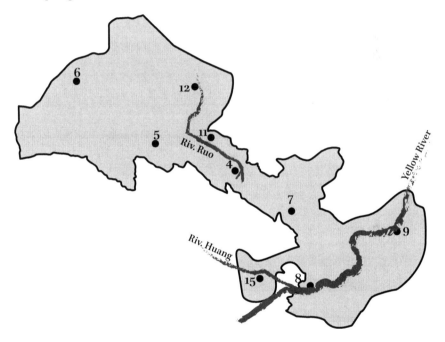

LEGEND
11-12 Xihai 西海 replaces Zhangye Dep. State in 195 CE *JS* 14:434
15   Xiping Est. E. Han? *JS* 14:433
MAP 5 Liangzhou Inspectorate 250 CE

25   *SGZ* 15:474 (Inspector Zou Qi 鄒岐, the Lushui nomads' revolt, "河西大擾"); a (possibly Wang Chen's?) *Wei shu* quoted in *SGZ* 2:79 (where the "rebellious nomads to be chastised and destroyed," "叛胡治元多、盧水、封賞等," should read "盧水叛胡治元多、封賞等," as noted by Wu Jinhua 吳金華, *Gu wenxian yanjiu conggao* 古文獻研究叢稿 [Nanjing 1995], p. 147). Nothing more is known about the third chieftain Feng Shang 封賞 either.
26   Zhang Ji 張既 (d. 223) the inspector, and Su Ze 蘇則 (d. 223) the commandant protector; see *SGZ* 15:476 on the Jiuquan riots and subsequent measures: "築鄣塞，置烽候、邸閣以備胡：西羌恐 …".

56 CHAPTER 3

One reason for the energetic reconquest of Liangzhou will have been to restore access from the Central Plain to the Western Regions, hence to revaluate the role of trade in the state's economy. As Emperor Wen asked an adviser: "Now that we have not long ago defeated [rebels in] Jiuquan and Zhangye, we are exchanging envoys again with the Western Regions, and from Dunhuang we were presented with an enormous pearl an inch across in diameter: do you think it will be possible once more to pursue gains from trade?"[27] Remarkably, in this imperial query — which sounds authentic, being expressed in the vernacular — Cao Pi straightforwardly asks about trade (*shi* 市) rather than its usual Sino-centric euphemism, "tribute-offering." Indeed, in 221, a "Wu and Ji Colonel (*wuji xiaowei* 戊己校尉)" was despatched to take up office, overseeing agricultural colonies on the northern route of the Silk Roads from the crenellated oasis city of Gaochang 高昌 (Karakhoja, 800 km northwest of Dunhuang).[28] As in the Han, agriculture had to be encouraged along the routes taken by traders as well as by envoys and military personnel. In Dunhuang, we read,

> [people] were not very familiar with agriculture. Usually when irrigating they let the water accumulate and allowed [the soil] to become totally soaked through before they would start ploughing it. They also did not know how to make a seed drill (*louli* 耬犁). They watered [the soil instead,] and by the time they began sowing, the men's forces, like their oxen, were already all spent, and the grain they [eventually] harvested was correspondingly less. When [Huangfu] Long 皇甫隆 arrived (as the new governor, in 252?), he taught them how to make a seed drill as well as [the method of] irrigation by overflowing (*yan'gai* 衍溉), and when they made their year-end accounts, these showed that they had saved more than half on labour for five times as much grain.[29]

Again, around 230, "in the reign of the Wei Emperor Ming 魏明帝 (Cao Rui 曹叡, 204–239, r. 227–239), Xu Miao 徐邈 (172–249) was [the Inspector] in charge of Liangzhou, where the soil sees little precipitation and which constantly suffers from a lack of grain. [Xu] Miao submitted [a proposal?] to restore the salt-winning basins lakes in Wuwei and Jiuquan so that the grain from the (Lushui? Qiang?) savages could be collected. He also opened up large tracts of irrigated farmland and recruited poor people to cultivate it. Every

---

27   *SGZ* 16:492 ("前破酒泉、張掖，西域通使，燉煌獻徑寸大珠，可復求市益得不?").
28   *SGZ* 18:551; *Wei lüe Xirong zhuan* 魏略西戎傳 in *SGZ* 30:859 (Gaochang).
29   *Wei lüe* in *SGZ* 16:513 = *JS* 26:785.

THE COLONISATION OF LIANGZHOU, 100 BCE TO 300 CE

household then knew abundance and the granaries were full to overflowing, to the point that he could allocate the surplus [tax income] that remained, after covering the province's military expenditure, to trade in gold and brocade (from China), dogs and horses (from the Western Regions), and defray all fees [levied by?] the Central States 中國 [on these trade movements]. People from the Western Regions brought in tribute; money and goods circulated freely: this was all thanks to [Xu] Miao."[30] The merchants from Central Asia who found their way to Liangzhou more easily as its settlements became more viable staging points included, to a prominent extent, Sogdians (from Sogdiana, centred upon Samarkand in modern Uzbekistan): "[Sogdian 粟特國] merchants came to the land of Liang[-zhou] in great numbers to engage in trade."[31] By 270, Liangzhou had resident Sogdian as well as Kushan (a.k.a. Yuezhi) communities, the latter composed of descendants of the "Yuezhi" who founded the Buddhist Kushan Empire that ruled today's Afghanistan.[32] To Sogdian merchants we owe the only extant first-hand documents attesting to this trade. The early fourth-century Sogdian letters found by Sir Aurel Stein (1862–1943) in an abandoned watchtower 90 km northwest of Dunhuang in 1907 reveal, first of all, that by that time, there was a commercial network comprised of financial sponsors of the trade activity in Samarkand, the actual itinerant traders and their guides, and middlemen and local agents all the way down to Luoyang. That indicates a division of tasks to which a categorisation of trade goods will have corresponded. The letters show that the amounts of goods traded (wool and linen, pepper, camphor, musk, silver etc.) were small and easily carried by a few beasts of burden. Taking it for granted, after some of the evidence that we have seen, that duties were imposed on goods in transit,[33] it is a matter of common sense to deduce that only luxury products could withstand the imposition of repeated taxation on the way and still find a market in the Chinese capital. "More than six months were employed in the tranquil journey of a

---

30   *SGZ* 27:739-740 = *JS* 26:784-785: "魏明帝世徐邈為涼州，土地少雨，常苦乏穀。邈上修武威、酒泉鹽池，以收虜穀。又廣開水田，募貧民佃之，家家豐足，倉庫盈溢。及度支州界軍用之餘，以巿金錦犬馬，通供中國之費。西域人入貢，財貨流通，皆邈之功也。"

31   Wei Shou 魏收 (505–572), ed., *Wei shu* 魏書 (*History of the [Northern] Wei* [386–534], Beijing 1974), 102:2270.

32   Étienne de la Vaissière, *Histoire des marchands sogdiens* (3rd ed., Paris 2016), pp. 62, 66, 134, referring to *SGZ* 33:895 (an edict of 257 quoted in Pei Songzhi's commentary).

33   *HS* 96B:3929 says that the Han Emperor Wu "extended the scope of the levies to wagons and boats 算至車船" (cf. *CICA* p. 201); idem in *Yantie lun* 42:89, "[the State] puts a levy on wagons and boats 算車舡" (cf. transl. Levi p. 222).

caravan from Samarcand to Pekin," writes Gibbon.[34] Most trade, by contrast, would be conducted within much smaller areas of commercial activity: a typical merchant might operate in a circuit roughly 250 km in area. Within such an area, business consisted largely of exchanging one locally produced item for another. The article most frequently transported from China to the Western Regions was silk, primarily sent westward to pay military outposts of the empire as far as Gaochang, and then no doubt continuing its economic life by being traded, within a far smaller geographic radius, for other merchandise. Then there were products better produced locally than traded: the Sogdian letters speak of local workshops they set up (in Jiuquan, for instance) for textile manufacturing. One can easily imagine the calculation by which levies on silk floss would be prohibitive, while the export to Central Asia of finished silk bolts, made in China, was viable by comparison. Finally, one also has to allow room for the luxuries that made their way from east to west and from west to east as prestigious gifts between communities in what could be an unpredictable, prolonged series of diplomatic exchanges. It is tempting to imagine that the famous Hejiacun 何家村 cornelian rhyton (from Gandhara?) reached Tang dynasty Chang'an in just this haphazard fashion. There might therefore well be circumstances in which trade and tribute were hard to distinguish.[35]

A last snapshot of trade activity in the Hexi Corridor comes from the biography of an exemplary Governor of Dunhuang in the Taihe 太和 era (227–233), Cang Ci 倉慈:

> Also, on any day there might be barbarians of various description who, from the Western Regions, wanted to come tribute-offering, yet the leading families frequently and perfidiously stopped them on their way and, having offered to traffic the goods for them, next swindled and bullied them in such a way that no one could still make out the rights and wrongs of either party. Invariably the barbarians resented this, and to all of them [Cang] Ci manifested sympathy. For those who wanted nevertheless to proceed to Luo[-yang], he sealed their laissez-passer; for those who preferred to return by way of the commandery, his office took [their merchandise] from them on mutually agreeable terms, each time using goods readily available from the [commandery's] storehouse to make a trade deal with their whole group. He caused his subordinate officers as

---

34 Edward Gibbon (1737–1794), *The Decline and Fall of the Roman Empire* (New York n.d.), Chap. LXVI, p. 675.

35 É. de la Vaissière, op. cit.; Hansen, *The Silk Road*, ch. 4, 8; Honeychurch, *Inner Asia and the Spatial Politics of Empire*, e.g. 4.2, 9.5.

well as the people [even] to escort [the merchants] on their way, for their protection. After this, natives no less than aliens were united in praising his benevolence and kindness.[36]

In this fashion, the Hexi Corridor developed and survived the change of dynasty when the Jin succeeded the Wei in 265, with little bloodshed. The twin objectives that an inspector of the province or a prefect of one of its commanderies pursued are admirably summed up in the eulogy of Fan Can 范粲, Prefect of Wuwei ca. 240, that "the commandery's soil was rich in produce, and valuables filled it to capacity," thus juxtaposing good husbandry of the land with the boons of lively trade.[37] In fact, however, the population figures show no growth at all between the 140 CE census (*History of the Later Han*) and the 280 CE census (*History of the Jin*). The Western Jin province of Liangzhou was larger than the short-lived late Han province of Yongzhou (with its four commanderies and two "dependent states"), since it comprised eight commanderies (the aforementioned four, plus three newly-created commanderies as well as Jincheng Commandery) with the Yellow River as its natural southern border. Even so, between 140 and 280, the number of registered households in this Western Jin Liangzhou Province actually dropped by half, from 62,401 to 30,700. For all the havoc caused by Qiang and Lushui nomads, this decrease is nonetheless puzzling[38] — unless, perhaps, the appearance of Xianbei hordes in Liangzhou in the period 270 to 280 proved particularly murderous? Yet this appears to be contradicted by the central government's decision, in 295, to create at least three new county-level administrative units in Dunhuang Commandery and to split Jiuquan Commandery into two (Jiuquan and a new Jinchang Commandery 晉昌郡).[39] Such a move, it seems, could only be

---

36   *SGZ* 16:512 ("又常日西域雜胡欲來貢獻，而諸豪族多逆斷絕；既與貿遷，欺詐侮易，多不得分明。胡常怨望，慈皆勞之。欲詣洛者，為封過所，欲從郡還者，官為平取，輒以府見物與共交市，使吏民護送道路。由是民夷翕然稱其德惠。"). Transl. Arakawa Masaharu, "The Transit Permit System System of the Tang Empire and the Passage of Merchants" (2001), pp. 1–2, *adiuvante*.

37   *JS* 94:2431 ("又郡壤富實，珍玩充積").

38   The comparison is between *HHS* "Treatises" 23, pp. 3518–3521 and *JS* 14:433. *JS* gives only numbers of households, not individuals. In order to compare household numbers, the *HHS*'s problematic figure of 748 households in Dunhuang is hypothetically corrected by dividing the number of individuals (29,170) by the average number of persons per household, i.e. 3.7.

39   *JS* 14:434 says — in one of the "postscripts" of the 280 CE administrative geography overview that it essentially reproduces — that in 295, Emperor Hui 惠帝 (Sima Zhong) divided Dunhuang up to create five new counties; of these five, *HHS* "Treatises" 23:3521 already names two (Ming'an 冥安 and Guangzhi 廣至). Nonetheless, there is an increase,

motivated by a substantial population increase in these counties and commanderies. We are thus left with a question mark.

to which an increase in registered farmers is likely to correspond (6 counties in 140, 10 counties in 280 [the original version of the *js* "Geographical Treatise"], and 11 counties in 295 [as per this "postscript"]). Note that Xinxiang 新鄉, which formed part of Dunhuang in 280, was apparently re-assigned to the territory of the new Jinchang Commandery in 295, together with the newly created county of Kuaiji 會稽 (*js*, ibid.). Hence I do not include Xinxiang among the counties (11 in number) that constituted Dunhuang in 295. Of the 9 counties in Jiuquan Commandery in 140 (*HHS*, ibid.), unchanged in number in 280, it is unclear which ones were re-assigned to Jinchang (that from 295 is said to have been made up of Xinxiang, Kuaiji and 6 other counties), because the *js* "Geographical Treatise," as we have it — shoddily (one assumes) updated according to 295 CE information when it comes to Dunhuang Commandery (because Xinxiang has been left in) — has at any rate not been updated to list Jiuquan and Jinchang Commanderies as separate entities: Jinchang is not a listed item at all.

CHAPTER 4

Former Liang (320–376): Li Hao's Forebears under the Former Liang

Liangzhou in the Western Jin, girt by the Yellow River to its south and shielded by an inhospitable desert to its northeast and a mountain range to its southwest, was to some extent naturally protected. By the same token, Liangzhou was separated from the metropolitan heartland by the Yellow River and was thereby sometimes tempted to secede from central control. Examples of this tendency occurred under the Cao-Wei regime; under the Western Jin as well, a prefect of Dunhuang declared himself independent from the government in 272 and was briefly succeeded as *de facto* ruler of Dunhuang by his son before the provincial governor could reassert Jin power.[1]

Simultaneously (in 270), the Tufa tribe or lineage of the Xianbei rose up in arms under their chieftain Tufa Shujineng 禿髮樹機能 (d. 279). It would appear that his people already lived in Liangzhou; under the Wei, General Deng Ai 鄧艾 (ca. 197–264) had suppressed several Xianbei attacks and relocated "several tens of thousands of surrendered Xianbei, whom he had taken to the areas of Yong[zhou] and Liang[zhou] to settle amidst the local populace,"[2] and these captives, it seems, then rebelled. Three governors of Liangzhou in succession perished fighting against the Xianbei; in 278, Shujineng could claim to be "in full possession of all of Liangzhou." Moreover, in 271, at an early stage in the hostilities, the Qiang and other "nomads" joined forces with the Xianbei. Eventually, "after years and years of punitive expeditions in which [Liangzhou] could but barely be stabilised," a new Prefect of Wuwei, Ma Long 馬隆 (in office 278–281?) managed to defeat and slay Shujineng and to restore peace.[3] Soon afterwards, the Sushen 肅慎 people from the far north (in present-day Manchuria) came to offer the Jin court tribute consisting of "stone-tipped arrows with shafts of *hu* wood," which, as Confucius himself attests, they had been doing since the time

---

1 *JS* 3:66 (prefects Linghu Feng 令狐豐 and his son Hong 宏, both d. 276; governor Yang Xin 楊欣).

2 *JS* 126:3141, *ZZTJ* 79:2508.

3 Three governors: Su Yu 蘇愉 (d. 270?; *JS* 126:3141), Qian Hong 牽弘 (d. 271; *JS* 35:1036) and Yang Xin (d. 278; *JS* 3:69). *JS* 126:3141 ("盡有涼州之地"); "Qiang and other 'nomads' joined forces ...": "北地胡寇金城，涼州刺史牽弘討之。衆胡皆內叛，與樹機能共圍弘於青山，弘軍敗而死" (*ZZTJ* ch. 79 under 271 CE); *JS* 35:1036 ("征討連歲，僅而得定"). Ma Long: *JS* 57:1555.

© DOMINIK DECLERCQ, 2025 | DOI:10.1163/9789004727380_005

of King Wu of the Zhou 周武王 (r. 1049/1045–1043 BCE) as a pledge of their allegiance. It will have been a comforting reminder of better days for Emperor Wu who, at the height of the crisis, reportedly "had to postpone his meals" in his distress.[4]

A decade later, though, Emperor Wu was dead and the Disturbances of the Eight Princes began (291–306). The ensuing chaos made Qiang and other non-Chinese rebellions against Chinese overlordship a thing of the past; amidst the free-for-all, one choice open to the Qiang, as for others with a cavalry detachment for hire, was to join one or another of the Sima princes' private armies, such mercenary service bringing more lucre than the raids of old. Another was to strike out on their own. As we saw in another context (see p. 12, *supra*), a rebellion that began in 295 with a Xiongnu attack on Shangdang 上黨 (modern Zhangzi County 長子縣 in southeast Shanxi, in what is still called the Shangdang Basin 上黨盆地) proved but the overture to a larger uprising that threw the whole Central Plain into chaos, with Qiang and Lushui nomads joining the fray, culminating with Qi Wannian — who was in fact a Qiang — proclaiming himself emperor (296–299).[5] Another ambitious Qiang leader was Yao Yizhong 姚弋仲 (280–352), in Liangzhou. From their original roaming lands west of the Yellow River's bend, upstream of where the river turns eastward in today's Guide County, Qinghai,[6] Yao Yizhong's Shaodang Qiang ancestors had started making incursions into Liangzhou from ca. 145 BCE until, three generations later, Yizhong's great-great-great-grandfather submitted to the Han, resettled in Longxi Commandery, and was given real or honorific charges (including that of Commandant of the Western Qiang [*Xi Qiang xiaowei* 西羌校尉]), which, over time, were hereditarily transmitted to Yao Yizhong himself. Yao Yizhong proved himself "brave and indomitable when young; he did not engage in any work for profit, occupying himself only with providing shelter and relief [to the needy]. His people all acknowledged his authority and held him in affection. During the troubles of the Yongjia 永嘉

---

4   *JS* 3:70 ("枯矢石砮"), already recognised by Confucius: e.g. in an anecdote in Liu Xiang 劉向 (79–8 BCE), *Shuoyuan* 說苑 (*Garden of Eloquence*) 18.19, transl. Eric Henry, *Garden of Eloquence*. Shuoyuan (Seattle 2021), pp. 1083–1084.

5   *JS* 97:2550, 4:94–95.

6   This is Sima Biao's 司馬彪 (ca. 240–ca. 306) location for the Western Qiang (hence also Shaodang Qiang) homeland, in his (lost) *Xu Han shu* 續漢書 (*Continuation of the History of the Han*), quoted in *Shuijing zhu jiao* 2:44–45, and also in *Taiping yulan* 165:4a (p. 804b). One learns there, from Sima Biao, that the term Cizhi 賜支 or Xizhi 析支 — already used as a name of a Qiang tribe as early as in the "Tribute of Yu 禹貢" chapter of the *Book of Documents* (*Shujing* 書經), and elsewhere also as the name of a river — is in fact a Qiang word meaning the "river bend" west of which they mainly lived.

FORMER LIANG (320–376)

era (= in 312), he moved east to Yumei 楡眉 (mod. Qianyang County 千陽縣, Shaanxi), and non-Chinese as well as Chinese, carrying all their belongings with them, went along with him in their tens of thousands. Once there, he proclaimed himself Commandant Protector of the Western Qiang, Inspector of Yongzhou and Duke of Fufeng."[7] One of his sons proceeded to found the state of Later Qin 後秦 (384–417), which had Chang'an as its capital. This was not chronologically the first of the Sixteen Kingdoms, but it was the first (and perhaps only) one established by the Qiang people.

•••

In 301, a well-connected court official, Cavalier Regular Attendant (*sanqi changshi* 散騎常侍) Zhang Gui 張軌 (255–314), whose family hailed from Wuzhi in Anding — which, as we have seen, was quite probably named after a long-departed community of Yuezhi people — was appointed Governor of Liangzhou and concurrently Commandant Protector of the Qiang. He had lobbied hard to win his appointment to this relatively sheltered region, where the man in charge could enjoy a certain latitude of movement. Almost at once upon his arrival, Zhang Gui's biography avers, he quelled an outbreak of Xianbei who had been "pillaging and thieving with impunity," and "had more than 10,000 of them beheaded," so that "from that moment on, his authority imposed itself on this western province, and his civilising influence gained traction in this area west of the Yellow River."[8] That such a feat should escape the attention of the court annalist in Luoyang, whereas Ma Long's did not, is somewhat surprising — but less so, for sure, when one reads what is in fact found in the imperial annals of the *History of the Jin* for the year 301:

> In the first year of the Yongning 永寧 era, spring, on the day *yichou* 乙丑 of the first month (= February 3, 301), [Sima] Lun the Prince of Zhao 趙王倫 (d. 301) usurped the imperial throne. The day *bingyin* 丙寅 (= Feb. 4), the emperor (= Emp. Hui 惠帝, Sima Zhong 司馬衷, 259–306, r. 290–306) was removed to Metal Wall Fortress and given the title "Emperor Emeritus," Metal Wall being renamed the "Palace of Perpetual

---

7 *JS* 116:2959 ("少英毅，不營產業，唯以收恤為務，衆皆畏而親之。永嘉之亂，東徙楡眉，戎夏繈負隨之者數萬，自稱護西羌校尉、雍州刺史、扶風公。"). For the events leading up to the founding of Later Qin by Yao Yizhong's son Yao Chang, see *JS* 116, translated by Rachel Meakin: "The Founding of the Qiang state of Later Qin: An Annotated Translation of *Jin shu* Chapter 116" (2012).

8 *JS* 86:2221–2222 ("于時鮮卑反叛，寇盜從橫，軌到官，即討破之，斬首萬餘級，遂威著西州，化行河右。").

Prosperity." [Sima] Zang 臧 (297–301), son and designated heir to the crown prince, was deposed and created Prince of Puyang 濮陽王. The five planets criss-crossed capriciously through the sky. The day *guiyou* 癸酉 (= Feb. 11), [Sima] Lun murdered [Sima] Zang the Prince of Puyang. Li Te 李特 (ca. 250–303), a vagrant from Lüeyang, [at the head of perhaps as many as 300,000 famished migrants making their way into Yizhou, sc. today's Sichuan] killed Zhao Xin 趙廞 [the provincial governor, d. 301, who walked out on his duties] and had his severed head sent to the capital.[9] In the third month, [Sima] Jiong, Prince of Qi 齊王冏 (d. 302) and General-in-Chief Holding the East, levied troops so as to punish [Sima] Lun; he had a call to arms put out in the provinces and commanderies and set up camp in Yangdi 陽翟 (today's Yuzhou 禹州, in Henan).[10] [Sima] Ying, Prince of Chengdu 成都王穎 (279–306) and General-in-Chief Campaigning in the North; [Sima] Yong, Prince of Hejian 河間王顒 (d. 307) and General-in-Chief Campaigning in the West; [Sima] Yi Prince of Changshan 常山王乂 (277–304); Li Yi 李毅 the Inspector of Jizhou 冀州 (d. 306); Wang Yan 王彥 the Inspector of Yanzhou 兗州 (n.d.); and [Sima] Xin, Duke of Xinye 新野公歆 (d. 303) and General of the Southern Household, all raised troops rallying to his call, his men now totalling several hundred thousand.[11]

Meanwhile, Zhang Gui made sure both that he had the important local clans on his side and that the influential people of the capital never doubted his loyalty to the Jin dynasty. The first policy meant that he could count on the local clans' private militia to bolster his provincial army regiment, resulting, in 305, in the capture of more than a hundred thousand Xianbei; the second policy showed in the token military assistance Zhang Gui rendered to the capital, as well as in the gifts he dutifully sent to the court. As a consequence, Liangzhou's reputation as a remote but well-run corner of the empire grew; Zhang Gui graciously allowed the prophecy to spread that the province was, under his aegis, now guaranteed a lasting peace; and migrants heard the call and came. Especially after the sack of Luoyang in 311, Liangzhou took in new streams of

---

9   On this incident, see Terry F. Kleeman, "Cheng-Han State," in CHC 2, pp. 145–154 at p. 149, and for background, Kleeman, *Great Perfection. Religion and Ethnicity in a Chinese Millennial Kingdom* (Honolulu 1998), esp. pp. 122–129.

10   On the title (*zhendong da jiangjun* 鎮東大將軍 instead of the *JS*'s *pingdong jiangjun* 平東將軍), see *JS* 4:110 n. 11.

11   *JS* 4:97, with n. 12 p. 110 substituting Jizhou for the received text's Yuzhou 豫州.

FORMER LIANG (320–376) 65

refugees, and the population increase alone gave prosperity and peace a more secure footing. For the purpose of administering this influx of people, Zhang Gui created two new commanderies, Wuxing 武興 and Jinxing 晉興,[12] and — in a sign that this went hand in hand with heightened economic activity — he introduced bronze coinage. The argument that an adviser proffered for doing so is not without intrinsic interest:

> Until well into the Taishi 泰始 era (= ca. 270), as the region west of the Yellow River (= Liangzhou) was uncultivated wasteland, no coinage was used there; bolts of silk were rent apart into any multiple of [currency] units. Yet, once damaged in this way, the silk fabric was difficult to trade with as a result, and great harm was done by so wasting women's handiwork as not to let it be used for clothing. Today, though, with the Central Land 中州 (= modern Henan) in turmoil, this place by contrast is safe and secure enough to bring the [Han] *wuzhu* 五銖 [bronze coin of 3.25 g] back into circulation, to help our conjuncture along by its all-purpose versatility.[13]

Though towards the end of his life, intrigues were afoot to dislodge the Zhang family from the provincial capital Guzang in Wuwei Commandery, still it elicits little wonder that Sima Ye 司馬鄴, the last, "Hapless Emperor 愍帝" of Western Jin (300–318, r. 313–317), opted for continuity when, upon Zhang Gui's death in 314, he formally recognised his son Zhang Shi 張寔 (271–320, r. 314–320) as successor to his father. Thus was official recognition given to a dynasty of *de facto* independent rulers of Liangzhou, known to history as the "Former Liang 前涼" (301–376). Zhang Shi took care to send local tribute from the various commanderies of Liangzhou to Chang'an — the precariously-held new capital of Sima Ye — together with the commanderies' yearly financial accounts, as well as presenting the court with "noble steeds, locally-made objects of value, scriptures and histories [by local authors], maps and population data."[14] When Chang'an fell in 316, and much of the Jin elite, crossing the Yangtse towards the south, rallied around Sima Rui 司馬睿 (276–323,

---

12 Wuxing consisting of no less than eight new counties, Jinxing of ten: *js* 14:434.

13 For the foregoing paragraph, see *js* 86:2221–2226; the argument by the Adviser of Zhang Gui's Governor's Office (*taifu canjun* 太府參軍) Suo Fu 索輔 runs (*js* 86:2226): "泰始中，河西荒廢，遂不用錢，裂匹以為段數。縑布既壞，市易又難，徒壞女工，不任衣用，弊之甚也。今中州雖亂，此方安全，宜復五銖以濟通變之會。"

14 *js* 86:2227 ("[張寔] 送諸郡貢計，獻名馬方珍、經史圖籍于京師。").

r. 318–323) — who thus became the first emperor of Eastern Jin (Emperor Yuan 元帝) — Zhang Shi naturally doubted what to do, since quite close to Liangzhou, in Shanggui County 上邽縣 (Tianshui Commandery, Qinzhou province; today's Qingshui County 清水縣 in southern Gansu), another member of the imperial house, Sima Bao Prince of Nanyang 南陽王保 (296–320), also claimed to be the rightful successor to Sima Ye. Constant attacks by the new Xiongnu rulers of "Former Zhao" (304–329) made Sima Bao's position untenable, though, and Zhang Shi then decided to withhold his support for what had obviously become a lost cause. Nevertheless, like his successors Zhang Mao 張茂 (278–325, r. 320–325) and Zhang Jun 張駿 (307–346, r. 324–346), he continued to use the last era title of Western Jin, Jianxing 建興 (313–316), for calendar purposes, so that when diplomatic relations with the Eastern Jin court were established in 333, Zhang Jun (while humbly calling himself the Jin emperor's "subject") still dated his formal missive to the "twenty-first year of the Jianxing era."

• • •

Undeniably, Former Liang was quite a successful political entity at this point in time. Under Zhang Shi and his successors, its attractiveness as a safe haven continued to feed the need for new administrative units in which to register the new arrivals. Without rivalling Jiangnan as a refuge destination (the numbers of migrants involved, whether southward or northward bound, are in any case not well known),[15] one effect of the influx, and one that may also have contributed to it, is that Qiang, Xianbei, Lushui, Di and Xiongnu insurrections in Liangzhou virtually disappear from the historical record, because Chinese immigrants now outnumbered them. Hence, Zhang Shi split up Jincheng Commandery, the southern part of the province and therefore every migrant's obligatory first destination after crossing the Yellow River, into two commanderies, Jincheng and Guangwu 廣武. For the same reason, Zhang Mao saw a need for a new provincial-level administrative structure that, named Dingzhou 定州, assumed jurisdiction over the existing southern commanderies Jincheng and Xiping, Wuxing (created by Zhang Gui), and a fourth, newly-established Angu Commandery 安故郡. This led to a redrawing of the provincial borders of Liangzhou under Zhang Mao's successor Zhang Jun: Dingzhou, the

---

15   It has been estimated that the number of Western Jin who moved south from 307 to 323 amounted to some 900,000 people, i.e. the North lost about one-eighth of its population. Liu Shufen, "The Southern Economy," in *CHC* 2, pp. 330–354 at p. 331.

FORMER LIANG (320–376)

southern part, received the new name Hezhou 河州 and, while losing Wuxing Commandery, gained six others besides Jincheng and Xiping; the name Liangzhou became reserved for the central part of the Hexi Corridor from Wuwei northwest via Zhangye and Jiuquan up to Xihai 西海 Commandery (this last commandery counting one county only: Juyan i.e. Edsin Gol, Inner Mongolia). Dunhuang became the southeastern starting point for a third constituent part of the Former Liang state, namely Shazhou 沙州. Shazhou comprised "Dunhuang, Jinchang (created by Zhang Gui) and Gaochang (Karakhoja), and these three commanderies' three garrisons: those of the Wu and Ji Colonel (in Gaochang), the Protector-General of the Western Regions (in Jinchang), and the Jade Gateway Great Protecting Army (in Dunhuang)."[16] Zhang Jun, in other words, asserted his satrapy's authority over the northern Silk Roads up to 800 km northwest of Dunhuang.

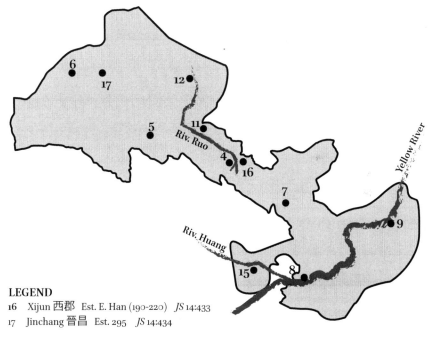

LEGEND
16 Xijun 西郡   Est. E. Han (190–220)   *JS* 14:433
17 Jinchang 晉昌   Est. 295   *JS* 14:434

MAP 6   Former Liang 300 BCE

---

16 *JS* 14:434. Zhang Gong 張恭, the Wu and Ji Colonel 戊己校尉 221–230?, was based in Gaochang (*SGZ* 18:551, 30:859); so was Zhao Zhen 趙貞 (in office ca. 315–327?; *JS* 86:2238). Can one deduce from this that the Protector-General of the Western Regions 西域都護 was based in Jinchang, and the Yumen Great Protecting Army 玉門大護軍 in Dunhuang (on the territory of which the Jade Gateway was located: *SGZ* 30:859)? I believe so.

Another tangible sign of success was that the Western Regions' oasis states responded by offering what can only be interpreted as tribute gifts from state to state: "blood-sweating horses" from Ferghana, asbestos cloth from Sasanian Persia (224–651), zebu perhaps from Kashmir, and peacocks and "huge elephants" no doubt from as far as India, not to mention two hundred more preciosa and mirabilia of every possible description.[17] Success fuelled its own dynamic. "His officials urged Zhang Jun to call himself Prince of Liang," and to announce that his son was officially next in line to succeed him. "From early in the Jianxing era, when the former king (= Sima Ye) occupied the throne," observed one of his courtiers, "Your Excellency governed here with rightful status; the more so today, now that our altars to the soil and grain never before looked so proud. And when [Sima Ye's, the 'Hapless Emperor's'] divine person stood forsaken, our great undertaking burgeoned instead — and should now lack a heritor? I, your subject, venture to believe that our state is still in a highly precarious situation, and that should Your Excellency think of crossing Mount Tai as if it were nothing, You could not be more mistaken."[18] In order to protect and safeguard the gains of the present, there is no alternative but to think ever bigger, to secure the future, to ambition an empire, until the time when perchance Heaven itself shall bless the undertaking by accepting the imperial *feng* and *shan* 封禪 sacrifices on Mount Tai.[19] A saying of Mencius also comes to mind, as it will do to the historian Fang Xuanling when reflecting on the fate of Li Hao. To the question of what the lord of the vulnerable little state of Teng 滕 should do to protect his dominion, Mencius replies:

> In antiquity, Tai Wang 大王 was in Bin 邠 (= the cradle of the Zhou realm, under Tai Wang, its first pre-dynastic ruler). The Di 狄 tribes invaded Bin and he left and went to settle at the foot of Mount Qi 岐山. He did not do this by choice, but out of necessity. Now if you, too, do the right thing, then amongst your sons and grandsons in future generations, there will definitely emerge a true king. For a superior man who initiates an undertaking and transmits its governance to his descendants makes cause for them to follow in his footsteps. Yet as for the time when his merit will see

---

17   *JS* 86:2235 ("西域諸國獻汗血馬、火浣布、犛牛、孔雀、巨象及諸珍異二百餘品。").

18   *JS* 86:2235 ("羣僚勸駿稱涼王 […] 《…建興之初，先王在位，殿下正名統，況今社稷彌崇，聖躬介立，大業遂殷，繼貳闕然哉！臣竊以為國有累卵之危，而殿下以為安踰泰山，非所謂也。》").

19   For these highly prestigious sacrifices, see Édouard Chavannes, *Le T'ai Chan: Essai de monographie d'un culte chinois* (Paris 1910).

FORMER LIANG (320–376) 69

its full accomplishment, that lies with Heaven. So what should you do about it, my lord? Just do the best you can; more I cannot say.[20]

Zhang Jun named Zhang Zhonghua 張重華 (327–353, r. 346–353) his heir; "he kept a troupe of six rows of six dancers (as behoves a feudal lord) and set up a leopard-tail standard (to mark out his carriage); and the bureaucratic apparatus that he established was modelled after that of a prince or king, with (prudently) slight variations in its nomenclature." Miraculously, a jade seal was fished up from the Yellow River bearing the inscription "Thou shalt hold a myriad states and build [an empire?] without limits."[21] These gradual but inexorable steps towards the mystification of power helped to consolidate the state, which was useful for its geopolitical stature towards Central Asia or towards its southern neighbour, the Taoist kingdom of Cheng-Han 成漢 (302–347) in modern-day Sichuan — instrumental, too, in steeling the resistance against the fairly constant harassment of the rival Former Zhao, then Later Zhao 後趙 (319–351) to its east — but not without its problems for maintaining vassal relations with the still-held-to-be legitimate empire of Eastern Jin.

The seventh Zhang ruler, Zhang Zuo 張祚 (d. 355, r. 353–355), took the ultimate step in this process by proclaiming himself "Emperor" and inaugurating his own era title, Heping 和平 (353–355). He issued a document stating that the House of Jin's tutelary element of metal had run its course and that, while he could as yet hardly claim to rule "all under Heaven (*tianxia* 天下)," his vocation was first to unite all hearts and minds as the necessary prerequisite to national reunification. "Today the Central Plain is thrown in turmoil, China's progeniture is without a sovereign; at this juncture, when the collective hopes in the Nine Provinces have nowhere to turn, when gods and spirits of the earth, [divinities of] marchmounts and waterways have no one to depend on [for their sacrifices], all you men of worth, indeed my mainstay, are forcing me — in an acting capacity — to set in motion our great reunification by uniting all hearts and minds between the four seas."[22] But despite Zhang Zuo's hint that he was "acting" and might yet step aside, the mismatch between Former Liang's raw power and its political pretensions was too great: "I make bold to say," remonstrated one of Zhang Zuo's mainstays in Guzang, "that I fail to see how you can possibly proceed with this business of changing the mandate."

---

20 *Mencius* 1B.14 ("昔者大王居邠。狄人侵之，去之岐山之下居焉。非擇而取之，不得已也。苟為善，後世子孫必有王者。君子創業垂統，為可繼也。若夫成功則天也。君如彼何哉。強為善而已矣。"), cf. transl. D.C. Lau, *Mencius* p. 71.

21 *JS* 86:2237 ("舞六佾，建豹尾，所至官僚府寺擬於王者，而微異其名" and "得玉璽於河，其文曰《執萬國，建無極》").

22 *JS* 86:2246 ("今中原喪亂，華裔無主，羣后僉以九州之望無所依歸，神祇嶽瀆罔所憑係，逼孤攝行大統，以一四海之心。").

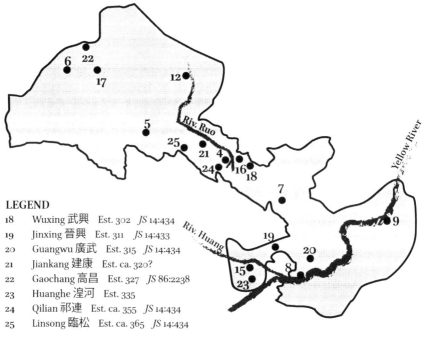

MAP 7   Former Liang 370

Family discord eventually cost Zhang Zuo his life, and his successor, Zhang Xuanjing 張玄靚 (350–363, r. 355–363), put an end to the imperial venture; a few years later (359), he also discontinued the title "Prince of Liang."[23] By then, Former Liang had a new and far more formidable neighbour to its east, the Di 氐 state of Former Qin 前秦 (351–384).

• • •

The forebears of Li Hao 李暠, future Prince of Western Liang 西涼, lived in Chengji County 成紀縣, Tianshui Commandery, Liangzhou.[24]

In one of Ban Gu's vignettes on human geography, he characterises Tianshui, together with neighbouring Longxi, as a fairly wild environment where "the

---

23   JS 86 is the *Jin shu* chapter devoted to this "Zhang dynasty"; for a summary, see Wang Zhongluo 王仲犖, *Wei Jin Nanbeichao shi* 魏晉南北朝史 (Shanghai 1979), pp. 269–272. See also Wicky W.K. Tse, "Fabricating Legitimacy in a Peripheral Regime: Imperial Loyalism and Regionalism in the Northwestern Borderlands Under the Rule of the Former Liang (301–376)," in *Early Medieval China* 24 (2018), pp. 108–130.

24   HS 28B:1612. (In the Jin, Tianshui formed part of Qinzhou 秦州, not Liangzhou: JS 14:435.) Chengji corresponds to modern Jingning County 靜寧縣, appr. 150 km north of Tianshui City, Gansu.

FORMER LIANG (320–376)

mountains are mostly covered with forest; people make their houses with wooden planks. [...] And so in these commanderies people tend to be hard-grained and rigid, and not beneath some banditry and brigandage." That was what tended to happen when people were at the mercy of their ruling element, Wood. But looking back at Li Hao's sixteenth-generation ancestor, General Li Guang, and at other ancient local clans such as the Xin 辛 clan of Didao, Longxi (into which Li Hao would marry, and which also provided the wife of Former Liang's seventh ruler, Zhang Zuo), Ban Gu was more sanguine. For, after all, the Li clan of Chengji, like the Xin clan of Didao, had

> won signal renown for their fearlessness and valour [...] And why so? Because, to the west of Mount [Hua 華山], Tianshui, Longxi, Anding and Beidi [Commanderies] are situated in close proximity to the Qiang barbarians, so that people are well prepared and battle-ready from long habit, and esteem those most who, manful and strong, shoot their arrows astride their horse. About the likes of them, says the Ode from Qin 秦詩:

> The king is raising an army,
> I have made ready both armour and arms;
> You shall share them with me on the march —

> Such a reputation and mettle as is theirs has been in evidence since antiquity, and if their songs nowadays still sound so impassioned, it is because their swashbuckling remains very much in evidence.[25]

* * *

As Li Hao's biography in the *Jin shu* says: "His great-great-grandfather Yong 雍 and great-grandfather Rou 柔 both served the Jin and made it to the position of commandery prefect. His grandfather Yan 弈 served Zhang Gui as General

---

25   *HS* 28B:1644 ("天水、隴西，山多林木，民以板為室屋。[…] 故此數郡，民俗質木，不恥寇盜。"), 69:2998 ("[李廣、辛武賢等] 皆以勇武顯聞 [...] 何則？山西天水、隴西、安定、北地處勢迫近羌胡，民俗修習戰備，高上勇力鞍馬騎射。故秦詩曰：《王于興師，修我甲兵，與子皆行。》其風聲氣俗自古而然，今之歌謠慷慨，風流猶存耳。") The fragment of the Ode is from #133 (Wu yi 無衣) in the *Shijing* 詩經 (see *Mao Shi zhengyi* 毛詩正義 [*The Mao Heng 毛亨 Version of the Book of Odes, with Orthodox Exegesis*] ch. 20B, in Ruan Yuan 阮元 [1764–1849], ed., *Shisan jing zhushu (fu jiaokan ji)* 十三經注疏附校勘記 [*The Thirteen Classics, with Commentaries and Subcommentaries, and Appended Collation Notes* (1817); reprint in 2 vols., Beijing 1935¹; hereafter: *SSJ*], p. 374a), in the transl. of Arthur Waley, *The Book of Songs* (London 1937¹), p. 153.

of the Martial Guard (*wuwei jiangjun* 武衛將軍) and Marquis of Anshi Precinct 安世亭侯."[26] On Li Yong, Li Hao, in a memorial to the Eastern Jin court, indicates that his last post was Prefect of Dongguan 東莞, in modern-day Shandong Province; in chapter 100 of the *History of the Northern Dynasties* 北史 (386–618) — an important reference, because it traces the genealogy of its editor, Li Yanshou 李延壽 (fl. ca. 659), who was a descendant of Li Hao — adds that Li Yong had earlier been Secretarial Court Gentleman (*shangshu lang* 尚書郎) and Prefect of Jibei 濟北 (now Tai'an City 泰安市, also in modern Shandong).[27] These successive rungs in Li Yong's career took him relatively far away from home, to the central government in Luoyang (as Secretarial Court Gentleman) and then to Shandong; as Western Jin descended into chaos, one sees his son Li Rou employed much closer to the family's own power base. Li Hao gives Li Rou's last office as "Prefect of Beidi 北地" (which corresponds to modern-day Fuping County 富平縣, Shaanxi);[28] both the *History of the (Northern) Wei* (386–534) and the *History of the Northern Dynasties* add: "[Li Hao's] great-grandfather Rou was Attendant Gentleman of the Household of the Chancellor of State (*xiangguo congshi zhonglang* 相國從事中郎) during the Jin, and Prefect of Beidi."[29] The chancellor in question, we are told, was Sima Bao, the Jin prince who — in vain — attempted to resuscitate Western Jin from its ashes, clinging on to Qinzhou (with his base in Shanggui) between 311 and 320 with token support from his neighbour, Former Liang's second governor, Zhang Shi. There, he appointed local notables like Li Rou to local offices such as Prefect of Beidi. Sima Bao was given the honorific title of Chancellor of State in 315 by the "Hapless Emperor" Sima Ye, and presumably kept it after Sima Rui ascended the throne as first emperor of Eastern Jin in Jiankang in 318 — a political act that Sima Bao did not recognise.[30] Li Rou will thus have occupied his two last offices between 315 and 320.

As for Li Hao's grandfather Yan, the *Jin shu* is manifestly mistaken in dating his final and highest-ranking post, General of the Martial Guard, to the governorship of Zhang Gui, from 301 to 331. The *Bei shi* states:

> [Li] Rou engendered Yan, byname Xiuzi 秀子, a man of high loyalty and resolute principle, wise as well as broad-minded. When, near the end of the [Western] Jin, havoc struck, he sought protection together with

---

26 *JS* 87:2257.
27 *JS* 87:2260, 15:452 (Dongguan), 14:419 (Jibei); *Bei shi* (Beijing 1974) 100:3314.
28 *JS* 14:431.
29 *Wei shu* 99:2202.
30 *JS* 37:1098–1099.

FORMER LIANG (320–376)

his nephew Zhuo 卓 under Chancellor [Sima] Bao, Prince of Jin. Zhuo's position was Attendant Gentleman of the Household of the Chancellor of State, but when [Sima] Bao failed to pay due attention to matters of government or criminal justice, Zhuo, at the head of his clan, threw in his lot with Zhang Shi, and [Li] Yan also followed him there. Hence [Li Yan] came to serve the House of Zhang as Senior Director of Gallant Cavalry (*xiaoqi zuojian* 驍騎左監). Yan's name had originally been Liang 良, while his wife was *née* Liang 梁. [The fourth Governor of Liangzhou,] Zhang Jun, said to Yan: 'You're called Liang while your wife has Liang for her surname; how do you imagine your sons and grandsons will call their maternal uncles?[31] In the past, Geng Yan 耿弇 (3–58 CE) had established merit in spite of his young age when he helped to usher in the [Eastern Han] Restoration; the confidence I place in you is not unlike [Emperor Guangwu relying on] Geng Yan.' And so he made [Li Liang] take Yan for his personal name. [Li Yan] was successively Prefect of Tianshui and General of the Guard (*wei jiangjun* 衛將軍), and was enfeoffed as Marquis of Anxi Precinct 安西亭侯. After he died aged 56 [*sui* 歲], the title of General of the Martial Guard was bestowed upon him, and in the middle of the Jianchu 建初 era (of the Western Liang, ca. 416), he was given the posthumous name the Effulgent Duke 景公.[32]

Given this information, Li Yan cannot have been much older than twenty when Zhang Jun became Governor of Liangzhou (324).[33] Tianshui, which lies south of the Yellow River, formed part of Former Liang for a very brief period, from 323 to ca. 327, which fits Li Yan's tenure as prefect to a nicety.[34] The *Wei shu* misnames Li Yan at this point (calling him "Li Tai 太"), and assigns the culmination of Li Yan's career to the reign of the seventh governor, Zhang Zuo (354–355).[35] This is plausible: Li Yan's dates would then be 299/300–354/355. Note that, in the middle of the Jianchu era (of Western Liang, i.e. ca. 416), it was Li Yan's grandson Li Hao who gave his deceased grandfather the title of "Effulgent Duke."

---

31 These maternal uncles would have had to be called by their surname Liang 梁, but that word would have had to be avoided due to the taboo against the homophonous personal name of the "sons and grandsons'" father and grandfather, Li Liang 良.

32 *Bei shi* 100:3314.

33 Geng Yan entered Liu Xiu's service at the age of 20: *HHS* 19:704.

34 "In the first year of the Taining 泰寧 era (= 323)," Zhang Jun "regained the area south of the Yellow River," and "early in the Xianhe 咸和 era (326–334)," he "lost the area south of the Yellow River" (*JS* 86:2234).

35 *Wei shu* 99:2202.

"[Li] Zhuo at the head of his clan threw in his lot with Zhang Shi": the decision by Li Hao's grand-uncle to move into northwestern Liangzhou some time before 320 was not fortuitous. We have mentioned that untold numbers of people did the same. For people in the Central Plain, crossing the Yellow River by boat, raft, pontoon or rope bridge in Jincheng or Aowei 媼圍 and seeking refuge in the Hexi Corridor was a well-tried escape path and an alternative option to fleeing to Jiankang south of the Yangtse River.[36] About the Western Jin migrants into Liangzhou, Hu Sanxing says in a note to the *Comprehensive Mirror for Aid in Government*: "During the troubles of the Yongjia era, many gentlemen from the Central Land (= Henan) escaped from there to Hexi to find employ with the Zhang [governors], who treated them with deference; their sons and grandsons continued in their footsteps, never shedding the robes and caps [of office], so that Liangzhou became reputed for its many gentleman-officials."[37] An obvious reason why they found their way there was that many colonists had preceded them since Han times. They might have had relatives there ready to welcome them. This was doubtless the case of the Li clan, with their roots in Didao in Longxi Commandery, who ended up in the Hexi Corridor across the Yellow River after (as their genealogy has it) living in Chengji, Tianshui, adjacent to Longxi and southeast of the Yellow River during intervening generations. For where they were headed in this northwestern part of Liangzhou, the Li refugees reconnected with the Xin clan, who had resided there far longer, and by virtue of that connection, they became related to the Zhang ruling family.

Li Hao's grandfather Li Yan was a member of the gentlemen class described by Hu Sanxing, who upon arrival in Former Liang naturally joined the local elite. That is clear from his career under Zhang Jun, as from the matrimonial alliance that Li Yan's grandson Li Hao contracted with the elite Xin clan. "Li Hao's former (i.e. first) wife was a daughter of Xin Na's 辛納, from the same commandery," we are told in his biography:[38] indeed the Longxi Lis and the Longxi Xins had the same ancestral commandery of Longxi, but most important is what we have already seen of the Xin clan's official record in Liangzhou, beginning in Western Han. For, as one may recall, the first two Commandants Protector of the Qiang to be named one after another in 62 BCE were two Xin

---

36   Aowei (*HS* 28B:1612) corresponds to the old fortress of Maiwo 麥窩古城, in today's Diaogou Village 弔溝村, Luyang Township 蘆陽鎮, Jingtai County 景泰縣, Gansu. *Shuijing zhu jiao* 2:52 is silent about Aowei's significance, but *ZZTJ* 114:3603 mentions how convenient Aowei is for crossing the Yellow River to the north.

37   *ZZTJ* 123:3877.

38   *JS* 87:2268.

FORMER LIANG (320–376)

scions; their brother Xin Wuxian was Prefect of Jiuquan and died in Dunhuang; the latter's son, Xin Qingji, occupied posts in Jincheng, Zhangye and Jiuquan, and his son, Xin Tong, was again Commandant Protector of the Qiang, until 3 CE when "the Xin clan was brought to an end."[39] There is obviously a large hiatus between these appointments and Li Hao's ca. 370 marriage with a daughter of the otherwise unknown Xin Na, and, just as with Li Hao himself, a family genealogy stretching back nearly 400 years into the past perhaps beggars belief.[40] However, seeing that Zhang Zuo also married a woman of the Xin clan, one can be fairly certain that he moved in elite circles.

Li Hao was born in 351. (His father, Li Chang 昶, died young, aged 18 *sui*, says the *Bei shi*: hence, most probably 334–351.) The main sources for his life are: (1) the biography of Li Hao in the *Record of Western Liang* 西涼錄, in Cui Hong's *Annals of the Sixteen States*, based on original Western Liang material; lost as an independent work since Northern Song times, but reconstructed from passages quoted in other works. (2) The biographical notice on Li Hao and his offspring in Wei Shou's *History of the (Northern) Wei*, chapter 99; Wei Shou's *Wei shu*, completed in 554, is the end product of successive draft versions prepared in the course of the Northern Wei dynasty, with the notice on Li Hao clearly indebted to Cui Hong's *Record*. (3) Chapter 87, translated here in full, of the *History of the Jin Dynasty*: also based on Cui Hong's *Record of Western Liang*, but given a light editorial polish by the *Jin shu*'s editor-in-chief Fang Xuanling. Fang Xuanling was Prime Minister at the time, to the Tang 唐 (618–907) founding emperor Li Shimin 李世民 (598–649, Taizong 太宗, r. 626–649), who counted Li Hao amongst his ancestors. That circumstance undoubtedly partly explains a number of (mostly detectable) editorial decisions.[41]

---

39 *HS* 69:2992–2998.

40 The more so as (as we have seen) Li Ling threw the clan into social disrepute in 99 BCE, and Wang Mang did his best to exterminate the Xin clan with the execution of the sons of Xin Qingji in 3 CE (*HS* 69:2998). Nonetheless, the "extreme stability of Chinese gentry society" over centuries struck Wolfram Eberhard (*Conquerors and Rulers: Social Forces in Medieval China* [Leiden 1970], p. 46), and Nicolas Tackett also thinks that, concubinage producing more sons per generation and more genetic material to keep a patriline going, Tang genealogies of aristocratic families going back twenty or thirty generations may well be accurate: *The Destruction of the Medieval Chinese Aristocracy* (Cambridge, Mass., 2014), p. 41.

41 For a comparison of the three sources, see Chen Jihong 陳繼宏, "'*Wei shu* Li Hao zhuan', '*Jin shu* Li Xuansheng zhuan', '*Shiliuguo chunqiu* Xi Liang lu' duidu zhaji 魏書李暠傳、晉書李玄盛傳、十六國春秋西涼錄對讀札記," in *Mingzuo xinshang* 名作欣賞 (Taiyuan, 2016.4), pp. 39–41.

CHAPTER 5

Former Qin (351–384) and Later Liang (385–403)

By 351, the year of Li Hao's birth, successive members of the Zhang clan had ruled Liangzhou for half a century. The vast majority of people alive at the time had never known otherwise but that a scion of the Sima House occupied the imperial throne, although the Jin emperor was now far away, entrenched in Jiankang south of the Yangtse since the year 318. On China's Central Plain, the Xiongnu states of Former and of Later Zhao (whose rulers are more specifically designated as Jie 羯 people) had succeeded one another and, of late, all of Northern China east of the Yellow River and above the River Huai 淮河 had come under the sway of the Xianbei (Murong 慕容 clan) state of Former Yan 前燕 (349–370); meanwhile, Sichuan, having broken away as the Taoist state of Cheng-Han, had recently been reconquered by Eastern Jin.

Right next to the Li clan's ancestral Tianshui, Lüeyang Commandery (now Qin'an 秦安 County), in Gansu, on the border with Shaanxi province, had been home to settlers of the proto-Tibetan Di 氐 ethnicity for several generations when one of their chieftains, Fu Hong 苻洪 (285–350), forced Former and Later Zhao to take notice of him. During the Disturbances of the Eight Princes, he had confederated his community, was elected chief of their tribal alliance, and had started to finance his political aspirations: "ever ready with gifts," Fu Hong "showered money on inviting famous and eminent men, to inquire of them how best to adjust to peace and peril in his own advantage."[1] That entailed, at first, serving the masters of the hour, and leading his fellow Di in waging battles on their behalf; yet as Former Zhao fell and Later Zhao disintegrated, Fu Hong found himself with over 100,000 troops under his own command. In 351, his son Fu Jian 苻健 (317–355, r. 351–355) proclaimed himself first "Heaven-favoured King 天王," then Emperor (*huangdi* 皇帝) of (Former) Qin, in Chang'an.[2]

During the forty-four years of its existence, this Qin empire expanded prodigiously, especially under the long reign of its third ruler, Fu Jian 苻堅 (338–385, r. 357–385). Initially, Qin comprised modern Shaanxi and a central section of

---

1 *JS* 112:2867.

2 According to Sanping Chen, *Multicultural China*, pp. 140–142, *tianwang* 天王 as a formal title was exclusively adopted by "barbarian" rulers, starting from the Later Zhao ruler Shi Le 石勒 (274–333, r. 319–333; see *JS* 105:2746), since *tian* here is the Chinese rendering of Tängri, the heaven god of steppe peoples. Later Zhao's third ruler, Shi Hu 石虎 (295–349, r. 334–349), emphasises in *JS* 106:2762 that *tianwang* is not the same as the Chinese title *huangdi* 皇帝.

© DOMINIK DECLERCQ, 2025 | DOI:10.1163/9789004727380_006

FORMER QIN (351–384) AND LATER LIANG (385–403)

Inner Mongolia. By 370, Fu Jian had conquered the Xianbei state of Former Yan. Three years later, Sichuan was overrun and Chengdu taken from the Eastern Jin. In 376, it was the turn of Former Liang, under its last governor, Zhang Tianxi 張天錫 (346–406, r. 363–376).[3] Already for some years, Zhang Tianxi had hardly been his own master. The south of Liangzhou, the area around modern Lanzhou City to which Zhang Jun had given provincial status as "Hezhou," was already lost in ca. 327, at first to the Later Zhao, then to the Former Qin from 351. In 371, Zhang Tianxi formally declared himself a vassal of Fu Jian, who then recognised Zhang Tianxi as "his" Governor of Liangzhou, but ordered him to move his office to Jincheng, i.e. modern Lanzhou. Zhang Tianxi now called upon the Eastern Jin general Huan Wen 桓溫 (312–373), in Jiankang, for help, but that never materialised. Nor did Zhang Tianxi move. In 376, Fu Jian took action: a huge army invaded Liangzhou, Zhang Tianxi was captured in Guzang (sent to Chang'an, and well treated there), and a new governor was installed. Former Liang had lasted for seventy-six years.[4] Li Hao was twenty-six at the time; much later, in a memorial addressed to the Eastern Jin court, he evoked the event as follows:

> Area Commander-in-Chief (*da dudu* 大都督) and General-in-Chief (*da jiangjun* 大將軍) [Zhang] Tianxi was possessed of a noble bearing and inherited a vocation of seven generations' standing [viz., to rule]. He aspired to be of succour in the troubles of his time, and to outdo his meritorious predecessors in glorious achievements; but in mid-age, disaster struck, armed raiders invaded the borders, and however long [the Zhang clan's] awesome might had lasted, [Zhang Tianxi] was finally unable to equal the praise that his forebears had earned. Withstanding troops from seven provinces with an army raised from just one, his soldiers found themselves defenceless, their force spent, and his state was consequently lost.[5]

• • •

Fu Jian's appointee as Governor of Liangzhou was Liang Xi 梁熙 (d. 385), "a frugal man of integrity, who cared for the people — who, west of the Yellow

---

3 Zhang Tianxi, "Zhang the Heaven-given," is the first recorded theophoric name, i.e. name containing the name of a god, in the Chinese historical record (Sanping Chen, op. cit., p. 147). Combined with his curious three-character byname (see *JS* 86:2250), Gongchungu, Zhang Tianxi's name forms a verse of Ode #300 in the *Shijing*: *SSJ* p. 617c, transl. Waley, *The Book of Songs*, p. 273: "Heaven gives the duke its deepest blessings 天錫公純嘏." The name points not to Buddhist but to (Sasanian) Iranian influence, as the Dunhuang region was a frontier area in Sino-Iranian exchanges (Sanping Chen, op. cit., ibid.).

4 *JS* 86:2250–2252, 113:2897–2898.

5 *JS* 87:2260.

River (i.e. in Liangzhou), felt contented" under his rule.[6] That positive judgement needs to be tempered by other statements, namely that Liang Xi had a redoubtable armed force of 100,000 men at his disposal, and that to keep these soldiers fed, he mercilessly taxed the local population. Nonetheless, when Liang Xi met his end ten years later, one of his commandery governors who had also served under Zhang Tianxi — Suo Pan 索泮 of Dunhuang, from a clan with a long tradition of government service — willingly went to the stake "to requite his lord and father" Liang Xi: weighty praise indeed.[7] Support for their regime seems also to have been, by and large, what Fu Jian's other subjects felt, in what was now the most powerful state in East Asia. Although his military might relied heavily on non-Chinese horsemen — Di, Lushui *hu*, Qiang, Xiongnu, Dingling, and the Murong and Tuoba lineages of the Xianbei — Fu Jian and his relatives were thoroughly sinicised, and certainly as long as Wang Meng 王猛 (325–375) was his chief minister, the programme of government, as the *Jin shu* presents it, invited universal assent: "[Fu] Jian promoted people of signal talent, restored offices that had fallen into disuse, levied taxes on agriculture and sericulture, extended charity to the poor and distressed, paid proper reverence to all gods, established schools, rewarded people of exemplary conduct and instated a successor when a branch of a family became extinct [so that ancestral sacrifices were continued]; the people of Qin were overjoyed."[8] Fu Jian's fellow nobles amongst the Di were given no particular privileges; like other ethnic communities, such as Qiang, Xianbei etc., they interacted only intermittently with the majority Chinese population on the Central Plain. That changed, however, after Wang Meng's death, when (in 380) Fu Jian filled important regional commands with Di nobles, whom he sent to their various posts together with contingents of their tribespeople. From living in a concentrated area on the Gansu-Shaanxi border, 150,000 Di households now found themselves dispersed in a set of garrisons, ostensibly as military colonists but, like their Di commanders, inevitably trying to make the most of their social advancement. Relations with Han as well as other ethnic groups soured rapidly as a result.[9]

The Central Plain now being reunified under one rule, the south beckoned, and in 379, Xiangyang 襄陽 (still so named, in Hubei on the River Han 漢江)

---

6 *ZZTJ* 104:3276.

7 *JS* 126:3150 ("梁熙據全州之地，擁十萬之衆"); "he raked in a maximum of taxes 內多聚斂," one reads elsewhere (*JS* 87:2269). Cf. also *JS* 115:2954 (Suo Pan "以報君父之讎 ⋯ 乃就刑于市，神色不變").

8 *ZZTJ* 100:3167, which conflates statements in *JS* 113:2885, 2888, 2895 and 114:2932.

9 Wang Zhongluo, op. cit. pp. 266, 274–276.

FORMER QIN (351–384) AND LATER LIANG (385–403)

surrendered after a siege of one year. The road to Jiankang now seemingly lay open. In 383, Fu Jian launched the long-awaited offensive against Eastern Jin, with four armies (one of them starting out from Liangzhou) totalling over a million cavalry and infantry, advancing by different routes towards the south. At the River Fei 淝水, a tributary of the Huai, the Qin army was checked by a mere 80,000 Jin troops commanded by Xie Xuan 謝玄 (343–388), standing on the opposite bank. Incredibly, Fu Jian agreed to a sly request by Xie Xuan, that the Qin army step back far enough for his soldiers to cross the river and engage in battle. A stampede ensued; the Qin forces were routed; Fu Jian himself was wounded by an arrow, and barely managed to make his way out of the carnage.[10]

After this catastrophic defeat, Former Qin fell apart very rapidly. Erstwhile commanders deserted Fu Jian. Murong Chui 慕容垂 (326–396, r. 384–396), of the Murong clan of the Xianbei, proclaimed himself King of (Later) Yan 後燕 (384–409), and in 386, in his capital Zhongshan 中山 (now Dingzhou 定州, Hebei), took the imperial title for himself.[11] Yao Chang 姚萇 (329–393, r. 384–393) of the Qiang people likewise defected; in 384, he proclaimed himself "King of Qin Forever 萬年秦王" in Gansu, then descended upon Fu Jian's capital Chang'an, had Fu Jian strangled (385), and ascended his own imperial throne of (Later) Qin (384–417) in 386.[12] Fu Jian had three ephemeral successors, ruling over a much-diminished Former Qin state, first from Jinyang 晉陽 (modern Taiyuan, Shanxi), then from Fuhan (Linxia City, Gansu), not far from modern Lanzhou, and consequently in the then province of Hezhou. There, the fifth Former Qin ruler, Fu Deng 符登 (343–394, r. 386–394), whom Di colonists in Hezhou had hoisted onto the throne, formally took a distant relative of Li Hao's, "*née* of the Longxi Lis," as a concubine, and in 392 made her his empress.[13]

---

10   *ZZTJ* 105:3309, 105:3311–3313. "Incredibly," because it didn't quite happen like this. The battle acquired mythical significance, so much so that Michael C. Rogers argued that it never happened: "The Myth of the Fei River," in *T'oung Pao* LIV (1968), pp. 50–72. In reality, "Fu Jian, with 8000 light cavalry, hurried to Shouyang 壽陽 at the double, but left the bulk of the army behind in Xiangcheng 項城 (still so named, in Henan). After his defeat at the River Fei, Fu Jian fled to the north, but one hears nothing about his army at Xiangcheng attempting to come to his aid, or of any action by Former Qin troops staged along the road. The collapse of the frontline at the River Fei actually was no more than a failed campaign, yet it caused the total disintegration of the entire military system in the rear [... of an army which in fact] was little more than a disorderly band" (Tian Yuqing 田餘慶, *Dong Jin menfa zhengzhi* 東晉門閥政治 [Beijing 2005], p. 224.) For Fu Jian's biography, see also Michael Rogers, *The Chronicle of Fu Chien: A Case of Exemplar History* (Berkeley, Calif., 1968).

11   *JS* 123:3082, 3086; *ZZTJ* 105:3320, 3323; 106:3357, 3358.

12   *JS* 116:2965, 114:2928–2929, 116:2967; *ZZTJ* 105:3328; 106:3348, 3364.

13   *ZZTJ* 108:3404.

80

Cornered by Yao Xing 姚興 (366–416, r. 394–416) — Yao Chang's successor as second Emperor of Later Qin — and Qifu Qiangui's Western Qin (see hereunder), a son and a grandson of Fu Deng's sought refuge with another offshoot of the Di people, the little state of (Later) Chouchi 後仇池 (386–442), named after Mount Chouchi in southeast Gansu, but that need not concern us here. Former Qin came to an end in 394.

•••

Amongst the components of Fu Jian's armed forces was a contingent of horsemen from another Xianbei lineage, the Qifu 乞伏. Originally roaming the frontier between the steppe and the sown, in Liaodong, their ancestors had moved south into Ningxia and Gansu in the third century and had settled around a permanent encampment called "Hero Fort" (Yongshicheng 勇士城) in Yuanchuan 苑川 (Yuzhong County 榆中縣, Gansu), near Lanzhou. The area was fertile and eminently well suited for breeding horses, as the *Shuijing zhu* 水經注 (*Itineraries of Rivers, with a Commentary*) observes; by the late fourth century, the Qifu community may have counted as many as 500,000 people.[14] Their leader at the time, Qifu Sifan 乞伏司繁 (d. 376), accepted the title "Southern *chanyu* 南單于" from Fu Jian and became one of his vassals. After the battle at the River Fei, his successor Qifu Guoren 乞伏國仁 (d. 388) proclaimed himself Great *Chanyu* 大單于 and Governor of Qinzhou and Hezhou 秦河二州牧 in 385, thus inaugurating a new state, "Western Qin 西秦" (385–431), with its first own era title Jianyi 建義. Yet Qifu Guoren was surrounded, first of all, by what remained of Former Qin under Fu Jian's successors in Jinyang and subsequently in the province of Hezhou. (Hezhou was ruled by a succession of Qin governors from 376 to 386, until Fu Deng became governor through a coup in the seventh month of 386 and Emperor of Former Qin four months later.)[15] Next, to Qifu Guoren's east lay the newly-created Later Qin empire of

---

14   The Yongshicheng site still exists: now known as the "upper stronghold 上堡子" in Xiaguanying Town 夏官營鎮, Yuzhong County. Still today, the Yuanchuan River 苑川河 flows through Yuzhong and empties in the Yellow River east of Lanzhou. According to *Shuijing zhu jiao* 2:52, "the Yuanchuan river area made fertile pasturage for the [Eastern Han] imperial stud 龍馬; hence Ma Yuan 馬援 (14 BC–AD 49) requested that it be split up evenly with the military colonists' households 田戶 so as to let them provide [their own horses]. There are two fortresses, one east and one west, on this preserve, 70 *li* apart; the western one is where Qifu 乞佛 made his capital." For the estimated population, see Zhou Weizhou 周偉洲, *Nan Liang yu Xi Qin* 南涼與西秦 (Beijing 2021), pp. 138–142.

15   Peng Yue 彭越 in 376 (named "Governor of Liangzhou," stationed in Fuhan, i.e. in Hezhou: *ZZTJ* 101:3205); Li Bian 李辯 from 376 to 380? (104:3274); Mao Xing 毛興 from 380 to 386

FORMER QIN (351–384) AND LATER LIANG (385–403)

Yao Chang; to his west lay Liangzhou,[16] still a Former Qin province in 385, but about to shake off Qin overlordship a year later. Given the lay of the land, Qifu Guoren did not cut links with Former Qin entirely, but accepted enfeoffment as "Prince of Yuanchuan 苑川王" from Fu Deng.[17]

It has been remarked previously that non-Chinese people at the time were probably best characterised as being "of mixed origin (*zahu* 雜胡)," a term frequently encountered in the sources, rather than as ethnoculturally homogeneous. This was definitely the case with the Xiongnu and the Xianbei, the Yuezhi, the "Loyal Nomad Auxiliary" etc. — and it is instructive to return to this notion here, as it is reflected in some "barbarians'" narratives about themselves. One such instance is Yao Chang's Shaodang group of Qiang, who (as we have seen) had lived in Longxi Commandery for more than 300 years. Certainly, when Yao Chang (taking his father Yao Yizhong's secessionist initiative to its logical consequence) established his own imperial state apparatus in 386, he was well aware that he ruled a mixed population and that this would call for a unifying narrative, amongst other things, if his "Later Qin" was to last. How far the Shaodang Qiang's acculturation with things Chinese may already have come by that time then finds an illustration in the fact that they claimed to descend from the ancient sage-king Shun 舜 (trad. r. 2255–2206 BCE).[18]

Another instance is furnished by the Qifu lineage of the Xianbei, for whom Chinese cultural heritage would have been still too alien to be adopted. The Qifu origin myth, as reported in the *Jin shu*, is an instructive example of the kind of bonding narrative that would have achieved such a purpose. It "explains," in a suitably supernatural way, how and why the Qifu came to Ningxia and Gansu; it extols warrior-like prowess as a central virtue; and in particular, it ignores birthright and heredity, making the hero of the tale a foundling adopted by a Qifu elder. One imagines how a tribal coalition dominated by Xianbei (Qifu,

---

(104:3296, 106:3359); and Wei Ping 衛平 in 386, who was deposed in favour of Fu Deng in the autumn of that year (106:3364, 106:3366–3367). On Fu Deng as emperor, see 106:3371.

16 Former Liang, under its Zhang family rulers, consisted of three province-level administrative units: Hezhou, Liangzhou and Shazhou. Under the Former Qin, Shazhou likely did not exist anymore. In 378, Liang Xi (Governor of Liangzhou) "dispatched envoys into the Western Regions to extol the majestic power of Qin," envoys who returned with "blood-sweating horses from Ferghana 大宛汗血馬" (*JS* 113:2900 = *ZZTJ* 104:3287); if there had been a Qin governor of Shazhou (stationed in Dunhuang), such a mission would have been organised from there.

17 *JS* 125:3113–3115.

18 *JS* 116:2959.

Tuyuhun etc.), but incorporating also Turkic-speaking elements, could unite around this common myth.[19] Upon migrating southward from the steppe,

> as the tribes emerged from the Yinshan 陰山 mountains, they encountered a huge reptile on their way that had the shape of a divine turtle but was as big as a mound or hillock. They proceeded to slaughter a horse in sacrifice to it and prayed, "If you are a good spirit, then open up the way to let us through; if an evil spirit, then keep it blocked, that we pass not through." Suddenly the creature was gone, and in its place appeared a little boy. There was at the time a childless elder in the Qifu tribe, and he asked if he could adopt the boy as his son. The throng unanimously approved this. Happy to have found someone to rely upon, the elder named the boy Hegan 紇干, which in our Xia 夏 tongue means "support." By the age of ten, he was so gallant and manful that he excelled at shooting arrows while riding a horse, and could bend a five-hundred-pound bow. Tribes from all over were impressed by his courage and valour and deferred to him as ruler of their union, giving him the title "Qaghan of the Qifu, Tuoduo Mohe 乞伏可汗託鐸莫何," "Tuoduo" meaning "demi-god" (and "Mohe" meaning "prince").[20]

Qifu Guoren's successor, Qifu Qiangui 乾歸 (d. 412, r. 388–412), maintained the link with the Former Qin, accepting, against a promise of mutual aid, the title "Prince of Henan" from Fu Deng as late as 394. But when Fu Deng died in battle against Yao Xing in that same year, Qifu Qiangui swiftly occupied Hezhou and proclaimed himself Prince of Qin 秦王. Over time, his "Western Qin" would acquire some of the trappings of a state: Xianbei with a Han veneer.[21] Meanwhile, Liangzhou had become an independent and far larger state known to history as "Later Liang," ruled by one of Fu Jian's renegade generals. Qifu Qiangui sent his son to the Later Liang capital Guzang as a hostage to buy peace.

---

19   *JS* 125:3113; see also Scott Pearce, Audrey Spiro and Patricia Ebrey, eds., *Culture and Power in the Reconstitution of the Chinese Realm, 200–600* (Cambridge, Mass., 2001), "Introduction," pp. 1–32 at pp. 6–7.

20   On "Mohe" meaning "prince," see Sanping Chen, *Multicultural China*, pp. 134–137.

21   E.g. *JS* 125:3118: in 409, in a rather un-Chinese way, Qifu Qiangui appointed his son Qifu Chipan as prime minister 領尚書令 (*ZZTJ* 115:3620 writes 錄尚書事), but with the "famous scholar 名儒" Jiao Yi 焦遺, as his tutor and policy adviser (says *ZZTJ* 115:3621; not in *JS*), as well as five ministers 尚書; in 412 (*JS* 3122:3123), Qifu Chipan set up a central administration with a counselor-in-chief 相國 and a censor-in-chief 御史大夫, but abolished all six ministries 尚書六卿.

FORMER QIN (351–384) AND LATER LIANG (385–403)   83

•••

In 382, when Fu Jian was at the zenith of his fortunes in Chang'an, he dispatched his fellow Di, General Lü Guang 呂光 (338–399, r. 385/389–399), to the Western Regions to subdue any nation that had as yet failed to submit.[22] Lü Guang, who "found no enjoyment in reading and was fond only of hawks and horses,"[23] set out from Chang'an early in 383 and, twelve months later, had conquered the oasis city-states of Yanqi (Karasahr) and Kuqa (Qiuci 龜茲, now written Kuche 庫車), in the Tarim Basin, as well as Gaochang (Karakhoja). Kuqa, it seems, boasted palaces as splendid as anything that Chang'an had to offer; but Lü Guang's soldiers became restless, and in the spring of 385, with all his looted treasure strapped onto 20,000 camels, he started on his return journey (in the light of history, Lü Guang's most valuable acquisition in Kuqa was no doubt the Buddhist master [ācārya 阿祇梨] Kumārajīva 鳩摩羅什 (350–409), who was later to become, in Chang'an, a prolific translator of Mahāyāna sūtras).[24] He reached Jiuquan in autumn; Lü Guang did not know that his emperor Fu Jian had died (just two months earlier), but he certainly did know what had happened at the River Fei (almost two years earlier). Liang Xi, the Governor of Liangzhou for the last ten years — which made him a local satrap in his own right — suspected Lü Guang of eyeing his own walled stronghold of Guzang as a base to occupy, rather than moving further into the unsettled jigsaw that the Former Qin lands had turned into. He therefore attempted to check Lü Guang's advance. However, confronted with Lü Guang's army, the commandery prefects of Dunhuang and Jinchang preferred to surrender without a fight, and by the time Lü Guang reached Guzang, the Commandery Prefect of Wuwei (who was based in Guzang) had put Liang Xi (who had his office there as well) under arrest and delivered him, together with the city, up to Lü Guang.[25] Lü Guang then proceeded to proclaim himself Governor of Liangzhou (385), and for the next eighteen years, Liangzhou would be ruled mainly by him (Later Liang 後涼, 385–403).[26]

---

22   *ZZTJ* 104:3298, 3300; 105:3307. Lü Guang's biography in *JS* 122 is the subject of a translation and study by Richard B. Mather: *Biography of Lü Kuang* (Berkeley and Los Angeles, 1959).
23   *JS* 122:3053.
24   *ZZTJ* 105:3332, 106:3343; E. Zürcher, *Buddhist Conquest*, p. 226; Hansen, *The Silk Road*, ch. 2.
25   *JS* 115:2942–2943 = *ZZTJ* 106:3352–3353.
26   The dates for Lü Guang's reign are usually given as 386 to 399. Lü Guang proclaimed himself governor in late 385 (*ZZTJ* 106:3353); then, in the ninth month of 386 (106:3369), he was informed of the death of Fu Jian, and must have heard at the same time that Fu Jian's successor Fu Pi 苻丕 (354–386, r. 385–386) had, upon his accession in the eighth month of 385, initiated the new era title Da'an 大安 or Tai'an 太安 (106:3349). This era title Lü

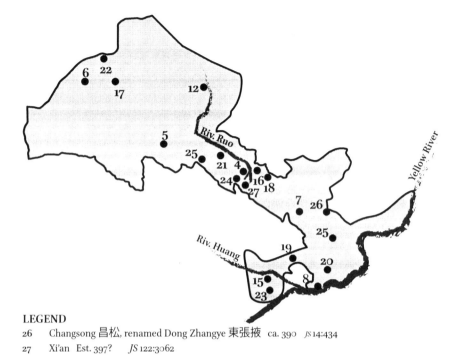

LEGEND
26 Changsong 昌松, renamed Dong Zhangye 東張掖 ca. 390   *JS* 14:434
27 Xi'an Est. 397?   *JS* 122:3062

MAP 8   Liangzhou under Later Liang, 390 CE

Lü Guang's rule did not go unchallenged, nor did the future augur well for Later Liang. The early appointment of a man whom Zhang Tianxi had dismissed from office, the "wily, insinuating, subversive and mean" Wei You 尉祐, brought about the execution (on charges of slander) of ten notable gentlemen whom he bore an old grudge against, and "on this account, others both far and near became much alienated" from Lü's regime. Furthermore "[Lü Guang's] sons (Zuan 纂, Hong 弘, Shao 紹 and Fu 覆) were rapacious and depraved, his three nephews (the name of only one of which, Shi Cong 石聰, is on record)

Guang then adopted; he did not, as the *Jin shu* erroneously says (*JS* 122:3057, also implicitly at 101:2644; cf. also *ZZTJ* 106:3369), launch his own era title Tai'an in 386, even though, unbeknownst to him, the era title Tai'an (or Da'an) would be abandoned by the Former Qin at about the same time as Lü Guang adopted it. Indeed, Fu Pi was killed in the ninth or tenth month of 386 (*ZZTJ* 106:3369), and the new emperor Fu Deng declared a new era title, Taichu 太初, in the eleventh month of the same year (106:3371). Only in 389 did Lü Guang begin his own era title Linjia 麟嘉 and proclaim himself Prince of the Three Rivers 三河王 (107:3387). In other words, Lü Guang took power in 385, and remained formally loyal to Former Qin (386 was therefore a year of no significance) until he declared independence in 389. Two sons and a cousin succeeded in the period 399 to 403.

FORMER QIN (351–384) AND LATER LIANG (385–403)   85

unscrupulous and prone to violence, and should the ground start giving way beneath his feet in his commanderies and counties, [Lü Guang] would not find anyone down there to entrust his life to."[27]

Early in 386, the son of the last Former Liang ruler, Zhang Tianxi, appeared before the walls of Guzang. Zhang Dayu 張大豫 (d. 386) had been spirited away as a child in 376 and brought up incognito; now he was produced as the figurehead of an insurrection against Lü Guang by a group of notables in Wei'an 魏安 (ca. 50 km southeast of Guzang)[28] who duly proclaimed him Governor of Liangzhou (with his own era title: Fenghuang 鳳凰). This group of long-established Chinese settler families was well aware, however, that such a proclamation needed the backup of military force, which in all of the North now meant mounted contingents that the nomadic immigrant peoples had in abundance. Hence an alliance was sought with the semi-nomadic settlers closest to Guzang, who were the Tufa clan of the Xianbei. Earlier, in Western Jin, Tufa invaders had raided all of Liangzhou unchecked in the 270s under an ambitious chieftain (Tufa Shujineng 禿髮樹機能, d. 280), regrouping after his death in and around a Lianchuan Fort 廉川堡 they built on the Gansu-Qinghai border.[29] There, no untoward event is told of the Tufa under the Zhang family's Former Liang — explaining, perhaps, why Zhang family loyalists sought them out as allies against Lü Guang. However, though Zhang Dayu managed to mobilise a force 30,000 strong, and the Tufa leader Sifujian 禿髮思復鞬 (d. ca. 390) brought equally many troops afield, Lü Guang was able to rout Zhang Dayu's army and put it to flight. Zhang Dayu was captured and executed in Guzang.[30]

By 389, Lü Guang proclaimed himself "Prince of the Three Rivers" (era title Linjia),[31] and in 396 he "assumed the position of Heaven-favoured King

---

27   *JS* 122:3056 ("[尉祐]　姦佞傾薄人也　[⋯]　遠近頗以此離貳"); Mather, *Lü Kuang* pp. 16, 37; *JS* 126:3142 ("諸子貪淫，三甥肆暴，郡縣土崩，下無生賴").

28   Wei'an was one of two counties (the other being Cangsong 倉松, renamed Changsong by Lü Guang) constituting Changsong Commandery 昌松郡. The latter he briefly renamed East Zhangye Commandery 東張掖郡; Changsong Commandery corresponds to modern Gulang County 古浪縣, on the territory of Wuwei Municipality, Gansu.

29   In today's Shina Village 史納村, Minhe (Hui and Tu Autonomous) County 民和 (回族土族自治) 縣, Qinghai; between Ledu District 樂都區 in Qinghai and Yongdeng County in Gansu.

30   *JS* 122:3057, *ZZTJ* 106:3359–3360, 3364.

31   The "Three Rivers" are the Yellow River 黃河, the Huang River 湟河 and the Cizhi River 賜支河 (also 析支河). "Cizhi" is explained as an old name for the Xia River, flowing northeast into the Yellow River at a point 60 miles west of Lanzhou (R. Mather, *Lü Kuang*, pp. 99–100 n. 184) or as the Qiang word for a bend of the Yellow River itself; see n. 173 *supra*.

of Great Liang" (new era title Longfei 龍飛). At this point, the territory under his control comprised all of the Hexi Corridor, stretching northwestward from Lanzhou and Linxia midway in modern Gansu, all the way past Dunhuang into the eastern part of modern Xinjiang. Having by now abandoned all pretence of loyalty to the Former Qin, Lü Guang named an heir apparent and created a bureaucratic apparatus modelled on a central, not a local government: with the equivalent of a prime minister (*shangshu zuo puye* 尚書左僕射, "Left [= Senior] Vice Director of the Department of State Affairs") and five Ministers 尚書 including Duan Ye 段業 (d. 401) and Juqu Luochou 沮渠羅仇 (d. 397), whom we will meet again.[32] Meanwhile, southwest of Guzang, Lü Guang made efforts to bind the chastened Tufa tribe to his Later Liang state by offering civil and military titles to their new leader (from ca. 390?), Tufa Wugu 禿髮烏孤 (d. 399, r. 397–399). By this time, however, the Tufa had lived in the area around Lianchuan Fort for nearly 130 years, in which they had "engaged in agriculture and sericulture 務農桑" and made themselves acceptable to Chinese and Qiang neighbours.[33] Already in 395, Tufa Wugu took steps to set up an administration, proudly instituting the office of Senior Major (*zuo sima* 左司馬) for a Chinese notable who had rallied to his leadership.[34] As Tufa Wugu gradually brought more land and people under his control, he also began to arrogate to himself a series of ever grander titles that increasingly made it impossible to consider him a vassal of Lü Guang: as Great *Chanyu* 大單于 and Prince of Xiping 西平王 (397), he even claimed Lü Guang's Jincheng Commandery for his own in 397. From Lianchuan, and with a first era title, Taichu 太初, Tufa Wugu proceeded to found his own state of "Southern Liang 南涼" (397–414). Twelve Xianbei lineages living south of the Yellow River within the bounds of Jincheng Commandery pledged their allegiance to the new polity.[35]

---

32 *JS* 122:3059–3061. Charles O. Hucker, *A Dictionary of Official Titles in Imperial China* (Stanford 1985), #4826, #5042, #5052, #6949.

33 *JS* 126:3141.

34 This was Zhao Zhen 趙振; see *ZZTJ* 108:3422. "[F]rom a clan from Qin-Yong (= central Shaanxi) that had been powerful for successive generations 秦雍之世門," says *JS* 126:3143.

35 *JS* 126:3141–3144; Misaki, *Wuhu shiliu guo* pp. 161–163; Zhou Weizhou, op. cit. pp. 32–43.

CHAPTER 6

Linked Destinies: Li Hao and Juqu Mengxun

The scene is now finally set for the biography of Li Hao. Li Hao "was from Chengji in Longxi," but for two generations before him, his family had lived in Liangzhou, where he spent his youth. As mentioned previously, his father died young. His mother, *née* Yin 尹 (d. 365), subsequently remarried, becoming the wife of Song Liao 宋繇 (d. 361), hence the appearance hereunder of Li Hao's ten years younger half-brother, Song You 宋繇 (361–439?).[1] The *Jin shu* biography begins:

> The Prince of Martial Splendour 武昭王 had the personal name Hao 暠, the byname Xuansheng 玄盛, and the childhood byname Changsheng 長生. He was from Chengji in Longxi [Commandery], and his surname was that of the Li clan; he was a descendant in the sixteenth generation of the General of the Van 前將軍 of Han times, Li Guang. Li Guang's great-grandfather Zhongxiang had been a general early in the Han, sent to chastise rebellious Qiang in Suchang 素昌 — Suchang being the present Didao 狄道 [County] — and, his forces being unequal to theirs, he perished in battle. Zhongxiang's son Bokao 伯考 hurried over to attend to the mourning rites, and so Zhongxiang was buried in Dongchuan 東川,

---

1   Song You has a biography of his own in *Wei shu* 52:1152–1153. There one learns the name of his father, Song Liao, who was from a Dunhuang family notable since the time of Zhang Gui. On the date of Song Liao's death, see *js* 29:883 and *Wei shu* 52:1152. A woman's remarriage would of course be unheard of in post-Song dynasty China ("A virtuous woman shall no more give herself to two successive husbands than a loyal minister shall serve two sovereigns," writes Sima Guang, *zztj* 291:9511), but it was manifestly socially acceptable at this time and in this region of Early Medieval China, as well as, it is worth keeping in mind, between the most prominent clans in this region. Li Hao's and Song You's mother died in 365 (*Wei shu*, ibid.), but her name goes unmentioned; one infers it from the name of Li Hao's maternal grandfather Yin Wen 尹文 at *js* 87:2263. A clue to better understanding the social reasons for remarriage is provided by Yan Zhitui 顏之推 (531–591), *Yanshi jiaxun* 顏氏家訓 (ed. Wang Liqi 王利器, *Yanshi jiaxun jijie* 集解 [Shanghai 1980]) 4:47, transl. Teng Ssu-yü 鄧嗣禹, *Family Instructions for the Yan Clan* (Leiden 1968), pp. 12–13: "In the regions north of the (Yellow) River people despised the children of concubines so strongly that they were given no standing in society. Hence, remarriage was necessary, sometimes three or four times." Li Hao himself, after his first wife's death, remarried a widow of the same Yin clan (vide infra). Jen-der Lee, "Women, Families, and Gendered Society," in *chc* 2 pp. 443–459, also concludes (p. 450) that "widow remarriage was a common practice in this period," at least in the North.

© DOMINIK DECLERCQ, 2025 | DOI:10.1163/9789004727380_007

Didao, and Bokao subsequently set up home there.[2] For generations [the Li clan of Longxi] ranked as one of the most notable clans in the western provinces. [Li Hao's] great-great-grandfather Yong (fl. ca. 290?) and great-grandfather Rou (fl. ca. 310–320) both served the Jin and made it to the position of commandery prefect. His grandfather Yan (299/300–354/355) served Zhang Gui as General of the Martial Guard and Marquis of Anshi Precinct. His father Chang (334–351) had a commanding reputation even as a youth, but died early, so that his mother was a widow when she gave birth to Hao. Li Hao was fond of studying as a child, of a thoughtful and generous disposition and a pleasing personality. He read through the classics and the histories, and was particularly adept at interpreting literary texts. By the time he grew up, he had devoted much practice to the martial arts and could recite Sun [Wu] 孫武 (ca. 545–ca. 470 BC) and Wu [Qi's] (440–381 BC) 吳起 *Arts of War*. When he once stayed overnight with Lü Guang's Grand Astrologer 太史令, Guo Nun 郭黁 (363?–403),[3] and his younger brother by the same mother, Song You, Nun stood up and said to Song You: "Your official career will peak as a minister to someone else, while Master Li is destined for a state; when at home a black-muzzled sandy mare shall give birth to a foal with a white forehead, that will be the sign."[4]

Guo Nun's prediction falls somewhere between Lü Guang's taking possession of Guzang in 385, and 397, when, as we shall see presently, Guo Nun plotted a coup against him. What had Li Hao been up to before 385 (when he was 34 years old), or even into his 40s (he was 46 in 397)? It is most improbable that he had not yet embarked on any military or civil career, and indeed, Guo Nun's words imply that his career, like Song You's, had already begun. It is true

---

2   "Rules on hurrying to mourning rites 奔喪" are the subject of Book 34 of the *Record of Ritual*; see *Liji zhengyi* 禮記正義 ch. 56, *SSJ* pp. 1653b–1657b; Book XXXI in the translation of James Legge, *The Lǐ Kī* (Oxford 1885¹, reprint Delhi 1964¹), pp. 365–374. The burial ground of Li Zhongxiang and his descendants has been found in Nianpu Village 廿鋪村, Longmen Town 龍門鎮, Lintao County 臨洮縣, Gansu, and protected as a cultural relic since 1954: this, then, is the Didao County of old, in Longxi Commandery. Li Bokao's son Li Shang 李尚 moved to Chengji County, Tianshui Commandery (*HS* 28B:1612; *JS* 14:435; and thus not Longxi Commandery, as in the text), and to this branch of the Li clan also belonged the Han general Li Guang and, sixteen generations later, Li Hao: see *Shiji* 109:2867 (Li Guang's biography), *Bei shi* 100:3313–3314; Liu Wen 劉雯, "Longxi Lishi jiazu yanjiu 隴西李氏家族研究," in *Dunhuangxue jikan* 敦煌學輯刊 (Lanzhou, 1996.2), p. 88. Chengji is situated appr. 200 km east of Lintao.

3   *ZZTJ* 113:3550 places Guo Nun's death in 403.

4   *JS* 87:2257.

LINKED DESTINIES

89

that Li Hao — in a *fu* on his lifetime aspirations that he composed ca. 415 — claims that he lived his early life as a bookish recluse, detached from the fray and bustle of the world:

> I despised dark official caps at vermilion gates,
> And envied [Zhuangzi in his] Lacquer Garden, disdaining ordinary mortals.
> I exalted the fisherman in his watchet waves,[5]
> And approved of Chang Ju and Jie Ni tilling the fields, yoked together as a team.[6]

Yet Li Hao must be referring to previous postings himself when he says, in 399, "I have reached my present position just by climbing the official ladder."[7] Conceivably, Li Hao served under Zhang Tianxi, under Liang Xi, and possibly under Lü Guang as well, but we are not told as much, so that we cannot affirm that Li Hao served multiple masters. Whatever the reality may have been, the *Jin shu* is silent on any official position of Li Hao prior to 397, the final year of Lü Guang's rule.

As for Guo Nun, he was one of a breed of men typical in the Northern Dynasties, who served their political masters as court diviners and wonder-workers and have a *Jin shu* chapter devoted to them (ch. 95, "[Men of] Artful Skills 藝術"). They could be Taoists like Wang Jia 王嘉 (d. ca. 390), whom Fu Jian of Former Qin "installed, together with the *śramaṇa* Dao'an 道安 (312–385),

---

5   Zhuangzi 莊子 (ca. 360–ca. 300 BCE), author of the eponymous work the *Zhuangzi*, would have worked as a clerk in the Lacquer Garden in Meng 蒙. Minquan County 民權縣, Henan (on the border with Shandong), upholds the tradition of being the original location of Zhuangzi's Lacquer Garden. In a Taoist parable included in the *Elegies of Chu* (*Chuci* 楚辭; transl. David Hawkes, *The Songs of the South* [Harmondsworth 1985], pp. 206–207), a fisherman advises Qu Yuan 屈原 (d. ca. 315 BCE), the disgraced minister, to adapt to the times rather than to suffer for unattainable ideals in a "muddy" world; his "song of the watchet waves" appears there and also in *Mencius* IVA.8 (transl. D.C. Lau, p. 121): "If the blue water is clear/ It is fit to wash my chinstrap./ If the blue water is muddy/ It is only fit to wash my feet."

6   See *Lunyu* 論語 18.6, transl. D.C. Lau (*Confucius: The Analects* [Harmondsworth 1979]) p. 150: "Ch'ang Chü 長沮 and Chieh Ni 桀溺 were ploughing together yoked as a team. Confucius went past them and sent Tzu-lu to ask them where the ford was. Ch'ang Chü said, 'Who is that taking charge of the carriage?' Tzu-lu said, 'It is K'ung Ch'iu.' 'Then, he must be the K'ung Ch'iu of Lu.' 'He is.' 'Then, he doesn't have to ask where the ford is.' [...] Chieh Ni said, '[...] Throughout the Empire men are all the same. Who is there for you to change places with? Moreover, for your own sake, would it not be better if, instead of following a Gentleman (= Confucius) who keeps running away from men, you followed one who runs away from the world altogether?' [...]"

7   *JS* 87:2258: "吾 ⋯ 因官至此."

in an outer palace hall to consult them on every possible occasion,"[8] or Buddhists, like the Dao'an just mentioned; like Fotudeng 佛圖澄 (d. 349) the court chaplain of Later Zhao; or like Kumārajīva, who advised Lü Guang during his sixteen-year stay in Guzang, and whom thereafter, in Chang'an, Yao Xing of Later Qin "revered as if he was a god."[9] Guo Nun's forte was the *Yijing* 易經 or *Book of Changes* as an aid to divination, as well as "astronomy (*tianwen* 天文) and the numerological arts (*shushu* 數術); people in the capital (*guoren* 國人) put their faith in him and respected him." "[Lü] Guang compared him to [the famous diviners] Jing [Fang 京房, 77–36 BCE] and Guan [Lu 管輅, 209–262], and he often participated in his behind-the-curtain, secret councils." This is precisely why his prediction is recorded in Li Hao's biography.

In 397, Guo Nun, together with Lü Guang's prime minister Wang Xiang 王詳, mounted a coup against him. The coup failed; Wang Xiang lost his life, but Guo Nun barricaded himself in one of the two walled enclosures that made up the city of Guzang (called the "Eastern" and the "Western Park"). In line with his superhuman reputation, "the people all said that a sage (*shengren* 聖人) had risen up in arms, and that nothing of what he undertook could ever fail; and there were very many who followed him." So did three thousand men in Guo Nun's "Eastern Park" redoubt, who chose one of Lü Guang's Di generals, Yang Gui 楊軌 (d. 400), to be their new Liangzhou Governor and Duke of Xiping 西平公. Guo Nun meanwhile sent word to Tufa Wugu asking him for help, and an army did indeed show up within sight of Guzang. Yet Later Liang forces under the command of Lü Guang's son Lü Zuan broke this failed uprising in mid-398. Guo Nun could escape, to Qifu Qiangui's Western Qin; Yang Gui ended up seeking shelter with Tufa Wugu's Southern Liang.[10] The turmoil nonetheless enabled Tufa Wugu to swallow more territory from Lü Guang: thus Ledu Commandery was taken, as well as the commanderies of Guangwu 廣武, Huanghe 湟河, Jiaohe 澆河[11] and Xiping. In that same year, he proclaimed himself Prince of Wuwei 武威王; he moved his base from Lianchuan to Ledu 樂都

---

8   *ZZTJ* 105:3337.

9   *JS* 95:2496–2497 (Wang Jia), 2484–2490 (Fotudeng), 2497–2499 (Guo Nun, with the quote that follows: "光比之京管，常參帷幄密謀"), 2499–2502 (Kumārajīva, with the quote on p. 2501: "興奉之若神"). "Court chaplain" is from Zürcher, op. cit. p. 181.

10   *ZZTJ* 109:3456–3457, 110:3471.

11   Guangwu corresponds to modern Yongdeng County, Gansu. Huanghe Commandery lay south of modern Xining, Qinghai, and corresponds to the "old walled town of Rilan 日蘭 古城," in Qunke Township 群科鎮, Hualong Hui Autonomous County 化隆回自治縣. Jiaohe corresponds to modern Guide County, Qinghai, south of Xining.

LINKED DESTINIES

(appr. modern Ledu District, Qinghai) on the Huang River;[12] and the *Jin shu* names a stellar team of twenty-three Han and non-Han advisers keen to help Tufa Wugu achieve his next aim, to conquer Guzang. From this eventuality, Lü Guang (d. 399) and his sons Shao (d. 399; murdered less than a year after his accession) and Zuan (the next in line: d. 401, r. 399–401) were given an unexpected reprieve when Tufa Wugu made a fatal fall from his horse.[13]

• • •

It is useful at this point to pause and ask, about Li Hao, to what extent do the conventions of the biographical genre predetermine how his life will be told? Guo Nun's prediction, in a way, sets the tone: "Master Li is destined for a state." His *zhuan* 傳, or "biography," in the *Jin shu* will of course bear this out. In this sense, it will be a model biography, meeting the high standard that the Tang theoretician of historiography Liu Zhiji 劉知幾 (661–721), in his *Anatomy of Histories* (*Shi tong* 史通), championed for the genre as against the many unworthy "biographies" that fell short of it. As examples of the latter, Liu Zhiji mentions *zhuan* of personages that may have been invented: the Warring States (481–221 BCE) freelance diplomats Su Qin 蘇秦 (d. 284 BCE?) and Zhang Yi 張儀 (d. 309 BCE?) come to mind. He could also have mentioned the group biographies of sycophants (*Shiji* ch. 125) or harsh officials (*Han shu* ch. 90) that aim to warn rather than to inspire. Li Hao, on the contrary, is a hero and an exemplar of what the "ancients" held up for admiration:

> Alas! Ever since Ban [Gu] and [Si]ma [Qian], far too many individuals have received written notice in the histories of our nation. There are those amongst them who in their lifetime earned no commanding reputation whatsoever and in death left no trace behind of any remarkable achievement. In this way peripatetic policy advisers with not a shred of evidence that they even existed, and [scholars] engaged in talk and study of whom not a soul can remember the names, are given a vain parade in the histories' "Biographies" [section] 史傳, and are made irresponsibly to occupy [precious] paper space. As if such individuals were at all worth recording! What the ancients held to be truly difficult was to die and yet

---

12 The exact location of Tufa Wugu's fortress (of which a knoll remains visible today) is the village of Dagucheng 大古城, 2 km west of Ledu District. Zhou Weizhou, op. cit. pp. 129–130.

13 *JS* 126:3142–3143; Zhou Weizhou, op. cit. pp. 42–46.

to be immortal, and [to illustrate this] has to be the purpose [of a biography in the official histories].[14]

At the end of Li Hao's *zhuan*, the historian sums up what made him memorable:

As the eulogy has it:

> [The Prince of] Martial Splendour, brilliant and farsighted,
> Loyal and courageous, held the world in thrall.
> As the Royal House [of Jin] hung in the balance
> He yet remained faithful, never remiss.
> His stricken people drank his bounty,
> Upon their cut-off land he showered kindness.
> Blessings he laid up, upon a solid base,
> That shall cause his coming descendants to prosper.[15]

Someone whose political career also took off under Lü Guang's rule, but whose life has received a very different treatment in the *Jin shu*, is Juqu Mengxun 沮渠蒙遜 (368–433, r. 401–433), who founded the state of Northern Liang 北涼 (397–439). His official *parcours* ran parallel to Li Hao's for a short while before he became the latter's rival and nemesis. The sources for his life are about the same as those for Li Hao: fragments from Cui Hong's *Record of Northern Liang* 北涼錄 in the *Annals of the Sixteen States*; a biographical notice in Shen Yue's 沈約 (441–513) *Song shu* 宋書 (History of the [Liu 劉] Song Dynasty, 420–479) ch. 98; a notice in *Wei shu* ch. 99 (adjoining the notice on Li Hao in the same chapter) and *Bei shi* ch. 93; and last but not least, a chapter in the *Jin shu*.

Quite possibly, early accounts of Juqu Mengxun were indistinguishable in tone from Li Hao's biography. Just as Guo Nun prophesied Li Hao's success, so too did a *śramaṇa* promise Juqu Mengxun an extraordinary future in a fragment that his *Jin shu* biography pointedly does *not* include. The long-lost *Sanshi guo chunqiu* 三十國春秋 (*Annals of the Thirty States*), by Xiao Fangdeng 蕭方等

---

14 Liu Zhiji, *Shi tong*, Inner Chapters 內篇 6 (Liezhuan 列傳), ed. Pu Qilong 浦起龍 (1679–1762), *Shitong tongshi* 通釋 (Shanghai 1978), 2:48: "嗟乎！自班、馬以來，獲書於國史者多矣。其間則有生無令聞，死無異迹，用使游談者靡微其事，講習者罕記其名，而虛班史傅，妄占篇目。若斯人者，可勝紀哉！古人以沒而不朽為難，蓋為此也。" The last sentence alludes to *Laozi* 老子 33 (cf. transl. D.C. Lau, *Lao tzu: Tao te ching* [Harmondsworth 1963] p. 92): "[Real] longevity consists in dying yet not disappearing (*varia lectio*: yet not being forgotten). 死而不亡 (alt. 忘) 者壽也。"

15 *JS* 87:2271: "贊曰：武昭英叡，忠勇霸世。王室雖微，乃誠無替。遺黎飲德，絕壤霑惠。積祉丕基，克昌來裔。"

of the Southern Liang 南梁 (502–557) — who reminds one how arbitrary the traditional name "The Sixteen Kingdoms" is for this historical period — contains the following anecdote: "Once, as a youth, when Mengxun lay resting on the border of a field after grazing his sheep, a śramaṇa suddenly appeared, and with his hand touched [Mengxun's] head and said: 'You shall later be king: this land shall not suffer much longer.' And having spoken, he vanished."[16]

Chapter 129 of the *Jin shu*, devoted to Juqu Mengxun, stands in a category of its own: it is the twenty-ninth of thirty so-called "Documentary Records" that close the *History of the Jin Dynasty*. The technical term *zaiji* 載記 had been used before, but Liu Zhiji, in his *Anatomy of Histories*, observes that "in the new (= Fang Xuanling's) edition of the *Jin* [*shu*] 新晉, the label 'Documentary Records' is used for the first time for the rulers of the Sixteen States, which is indeed the best practice to adopt and more apposite than if [the editors] had followed ancient usage."[17] What Liu Zhiji means is that these rulers, being considered illegitimate, should have the right neither to orthodox "Annals (*ji* 紀)" (year-by-year reign accounts of legitimate emperors), nor to exemplary "Biographies (*zhuan*)" such as Li Hao deserved. Why exactly the *zaiji* format was so apposite for rulers of the Sixteen States is further explained by the *Jin shu* editors themselves in their prefatory remarks on the "Documentary Records":[18]

> In antiquity, it did happen that an emperor or king engendered unequal issue: hence, the descendants of Chunwei 純維 (the ancestor of the Xiongnu) and those of Elder Yu 伯禹 (the people of the Central Plain) cannot really be regarded as alien in kind.[19] Yet for ages back into the past have [the Xiongnu,] their hair dishevelled, dressed in leather, dining on rank mutton and quaffing mare's milk, set our central realm trembling with alarm. Before Heaven had even repented of this calamity visited upon us, their tribal stock had spread and multiplied. They are treacherous and mistrustful by disposition and restless and fitful by nature, as

---

16 Quoted in *Taiping yulan* ch. 833, fols. 7a–b (p. 3719a): "少牧羊臥息田畔，忽見沙門以手摩其頭，曰：尔後當王，此土不久苦焉。言終而滅。"

17 *Shi tong*, Inner Chapters 11 (Timu 題目), 4:93 ("逮新晉，始以十六國主持載記表名，可謂擇善而行，巧於師古者矣。").

18 *JS* 101:2643.

19 "The ancestor of the Xiongnu was a descendant of the ruling clan of the Xia dynasty, named Chunwei" (*Shiji* 100:2879), whereas "Elder Yu," i.e. Yu the Great (so named e.g. in the *Book of Documents, Shujing* 書經; ed. *Shangshu zhengyi* 尚書正義, Yu 虞 2 [Shun dian 舜典], *SSJ* p. 130b) was himself the founder of the Xia. For the notion that barbarians are distant and degenerate relatives of the Chinese and therefore can be amenable to friendly relations (but also liable to be judged), see p. 24 supra.

earlier histories have documented in passably great detail. Troubled that they should transgress his principles, Xuan[yuan] the [Yellow] Emperor 軒帝 therefore proceeded on a punitive campaign; in banishing them to barren dependencies, King Wu 武王 (of the Zhou) assimilated them with birds and beasts.[20] And yet on their wastelands, exposed to the cold, they keep watch of the moon and observe the winds, spying for an opening to set the dust flying [under their horses' hoofs], seizing any pretext to unleash their violence, so that the walled towns on our frontiers can at no time lower their guard and none of our people can be sure of a home. Confucius said: "Had it not been for Guan Zhong, we might well be wearing our hair down and folding our robes to the left."[21] That this saying may serve as a lesson to our troops to keep their chariots and armour in good order, for only if [the barbarians] remain subdued on the battlefields on the frontier can peace prevail within our borders. Still, [the state of] Yan built [walls] on the outlands of Zaoyang 造陽 and [the state of] Qin dug [trenches] in the defiles of Lintao,[22] up sky-high mountains and cutting through the veins of the earth, encircling Xuantu 玄菟 and abutting the Yellow River — such are the precautions needed to keep the Yi and Di barbarians from throwing our precious land 中華 into turmoil!

Then follows a listing of the Sixteen States that "made us a country at war for 136 years" (Li Hao's Western Liang does not form part of this list); as the foregoing introduction has made clear in no uncertain terms, their history, although too important to be ignored, is that of barbarians beyond the pale of civilisation, and that is why it is relegated to the "Documentary Records" — i.e. documented, lest one should forget — at the very end of the *Jin shu*.

---

20 Xuanyuan 軒轅, the Yellow Emperor 黃帝, subdued Chiyou 蚩尤, who "created havoc and did not heed the Emperor's command" (*Shiji* 1:3); if Chiyou was not a Xiongnu, he may certainly pass for the archetypal "Other." Of King Wu of Zhou, *Shiji* 100:2881 relates that he "pushed the Rong and Yi to the north of the Jing 涇 and Luo 洛 rivers; they brought tribute to the court at appointed times, and [their land] was named 'the barren dependencies 荒服.'"

21 *Lunyu* 14.17, transl. Lau pp. 126–127. Guan Zhong, that is to say, "helped ... to save the realm from collapse 一匡天下," so that Chinese were not forced to adopt barbarian custom.

22 In the late fourth century BCE, "[the state of] Yan also built extended ramparts from Zaoyang up to Xiangping 襄平" (*Shiji* 100:2886), that is to say from today's Zhangjiakou 張家口 (Hebei) to Liaoyang 遼陽 (Liaoning Province). Qin "laid [a straight road for its army] in whatever way it was most practical to do so by clinging to mountain defiles on its borders or digging out narrow gorges, over a distance of more than ten thousand *li* from Lintao up to Liaodong 遼東" (*Shiji*, ibid.). Xuantu Commandery was created in 107 BCE and corresponds roughly to the North Korean province of Hamgyŏng-Bukto 咸鏡北道.

LINKED DESTINIES

...

Juqu Mengxun's "Documentary Record" begins:

> Juqu Mengxun was a Lu River nomad 盧水胡 from Linsong 臨松. One of his forebears had been *Juqu* of the Left 左沮渠 with the Xiongnu, and subsequently, they took the name of the office for the name of the clan.[23]

Linsong Commandery (now Nangu Township 南古鎮, Minle County 民樂縣) was created by the ninth and last ruler of Former Liang, Zhang Tianxi (r. 363–376), at about the time of Juqu Mengxun's birth. It lay some 130 *li* south of Zhangye, and about 500 *li* west of Guzang.

Juqu Mengxun's clan name was a Xiongnu official title, but that does not make Juqu Mengxun a Xiongnu. On the contrary, he was a "Lu River nomad," and "Lu River nomads" are elsewhere identified with a Qiang tribe originally from the vicinity of modern Xining in Qinghai.[24] We know they were sheep breeders. We also know that Lushui nomads were responsible for a major outbreak of ethnic unrest in Liangzhou, in 220 (see p. 54 above). A century and a half later, though, it is not this that Juqu Mengxun's biography remembers (nor that Liangzhou was their land, or that it "suffered" under Chinese domination), but instead how from early times, their lot had been interwoven with that of the Han. Addressing the "various branches of his clan and of their relatives by marriage (*zongyin zhubu*) 宗姻諸部," Juqu Mengxun says that "in the past, when the celestial favour extended to the Han [imperial house] gave out in mid-course, my and your ancestors flanked and supported Dou Rong when he maintained the peace to the right (= west) of the Yellow River (= in Ningxia and Gansu)."[25] We have met Dou Rong, the *de facto* satrap of Liangzhou between 24 and 36 CE, on pp. 31–32 above. Confirmed in his titles

---

23   The division of Xiongnu official posts into two halves (left and right, corresponding to east and west) is attested for several offices mentioned in *Shiji* 100:2890–2891, including that of *juqu* 且渠 (*sic*). These posts' responsibilities were primarily military, in that "the most important ones [commanded] ten thousand horsemen, the least important a few thousand" (*Shiji*, ibid.; Di Cosmo, *Ancient China and its Enemies* p. 177). *Song shu* 98:2412 and *Bei shi* 93:3082 confirm that the term *juqu* had lost its original meaning in Juqu Mengxun's name, since he is there called "Chief 大 Juqu Mengxun," "chief" being explained as the title of Qiang tribal grandees 酋豪.

24   *HHS* 23:810 (73 CE), where they are called "Lushui Qiang nomads 盧水羌胡"; on p. 811, n. 6, Li Xian identifies this Lu River with the Lu Bourn 盧溪 ("Blackbourn") mentioned in *Shuijing zhu jiao* 2:48 as an affluent of the Huang River 湟水.

25   *JS* 129:3189 ("昔漢祚中微，吾之乃祖翼獎竇融，保寧河右。").

(and appointed Governor 牧 of Liangzhou) by Liu Xiu, Emperor Guangwu, in 29, Dou Rong decided to support the new emperor in his bid to consolidate the restored Han dynasty, and in 32, "at the head of several ten thousand infantry and cavalry composed of [the armies of] the five commanderies, as well as of Lesser Yuezhi from amongst the Qiang savages," he joined the imperial army in battle against one of the emperor's last rivals, Wei Ao 隗囂 (d. 33). As we know that the "Lu River nomads" were named after a tributary of the Huang River, and as we are informed elsewhere that the Lesser Yuezhi — after they had "sought protection amongst the Qiang of the Southern Mountains" in the second century BCE — subsequently found a refuge "in the bend of the Huang River,"[26] there must be an affiliation between them, if indeed the "Lu River nomads" and "Lesser Yuezhi" were distinguishable at all. However, the Xiongnu connection cannot be minimised either; Juqu ancestors would have been enlisted in Xiongnu fighting units, and in 296, for instance, one finds Xiongnu, Lushui nomads and Qiang jointly rising in revolt in Beidi (Shaanxi).[27] Although predominantly Qiang, "Lu River nomads" were probably an ethnic mix, of different composition (*zahu* 雜胡).[28]

In any case, Juqu Mengxun's biography tends rather to highlight the tribe's acculturation. His grandfather Qifuyan 沮復延, who may have flourished in ca. 340 to 370, was enfeoffed as Prince of Beidi, possibly by the seventh Former Liang ruler Zhang Zuo (r. 354–355), who had imperial pretensions.[29] Interestingly, Mengxun's mother bore the surname or rather ethnonym Ju 車, which probably means that her family originated from the oasis state of Jushi 車師 near modern Turpan.[30] His father, Fahong 法弘, succeeded to the title of prince,

---

26 *HHS* 87:2899.

27 *JS* 4:94.

28 Both Zhou Yiliang 周一良 and, after him, Tang Zhangru 唐長孺 conjectured that the Lesser Yuezhi were in fact identical to the Lu River nomads. Zhou Yiliang, "Beichao de minzu wenti yu minzu zhengce 北朝的民族問題與民族政策" (1948), reprinted in *Zhou Yiliang ji* 集 (Shenyang 1998), Vol. 1 pp. 149–223 at pp. 197–199; Tang Zhangru, "Wei Jin zahu kao 魏晉雜胡考" (1955), reprinted in *Tang Zhangru wenji* 文集 (Beijing 2011) pp. 369–435 at pp. 398–399. But if so, why the separate moniker "Lu River nomads"? Holcombe, "The Sixteen Kingdoms," p. 134, remarks on "the proliferation of ethnic identities in this period." Surely Nicola Di Cosmo is relevant here: "It is difficult to say whether political leaders based any specific claim on their ethnicity, other than they most likely employed it to mark their own 'brand' as different from other leaders or to express territorial claims based on ancestral rights" ("The Relations between China and the Steppe," in Nicola Di Cosmo & Michael Maas, eds., *Empires and Exchanges in Eurasian Late Antiquity: Rome, China, Iran, and the Steppe, ca. 250–750* (Cambridge 2018), pp. 35–53 at p. 45).

29 *Song shu* 98:2412 gives "Prince of Didi 狄地王," clearly a mistake.

30 *JS* 129:3196; Tang Zhangru, "Wei Jin zahu kao," p. 399. The ruins of the city-state of Nearer, or "Cismontane" Jushi (see *HS* 96B:3921: 車師前國), the "ancient city of Yar 交河古城,"

LINKED DESTINIES

and when Fu Jian conquered Liangzhou in 376 and incorporated it into Former Qin, Juqu Fahong was appointed to the military office of Vice Commandant of Zhongtian (Zhongtian *hujun* 中田護軍). Upon his death (shortly before 400?), Juqu Mengxun took over the command of his militia (*buqu* 部曲).[31] He had, however, received at least a smattering of Chinese education:

> Mengxun was broadly conversant with the histories and had a fair knowledge of astronomy; he was an outstanding strategist, glib-tongued and with a knack for adapting to every change. Both Liang Xi and Lü Guang thought him special but were wary of him, so that he often went on drinking sprees to dissimulate who he really was.[32]

He was thus evidently a frequent visitor to Guzang, from which both Liang Xi (in office 376–385) and, after him, Lü Guang (governor 385–389; r. 389–399) ruled the region. Perhaps in 396, and on the strength of his private militia, Lü Guang gave Juqu Mengxun, then twenty-eight years old, his first appointment. "He was made on his own to take command of the men of a garrison and keep them provided with grain rations (*xiangzhi* 箱直). [Lü Guang] further made Mengxun's uncle Luochou Prefect of Xiping 西平 (= present-day Xining), and [Luo]chou's younger brother Quzhou 麴粥 Prefect of Sanhe 三河 (= present-day Minhe County, also in Qinghai)."[33] But things turned out badly.

---

occupy 680 ha on a natural terrace above the floor of the Yarnaiz Ravine 牙爾乃孜溝, 10 km west of Turpan 吐魯番, on the Silk Roads itinerary that passes north of the Taklamakan Desert; they have been declared a UNESCO World Heritage site.

31 *Bei Liang lu* 1, in *Shiliu guo chunqiu* 95:1053; idem in *Song shu* 98:2412.

32 *JS* 129:3189. Guzang's nightlife was notorious. As a young man, the governor, Zhang Jun, "when it came to debauchery, pulled out all the stops: often at night he would roam the town's wards incognito, and everyone who was anyone in the capital imitated his example 淫縱過度，常夜微行于邑里，國中化之" (*JS* 86:2233). If at this time Guzang already had the equivalent of the *tabernae* excavated in Pompeii, perhaps served by *Hu* barmaids and enlivened by "fashionable Sogdian swirl dancers" (to quote Shing Müller, "Northern material culture," in *CHC* 2, pp. 384–417 at p. 417), things became even livelier after Lü Guang brought "expert entertainers and marvellous actors 奇伎異戲" with him from Kuqa (*JS* 122:3056), as well as its exotic music (Wei Zheng 魏徵 [580–643], Linghu Defen 令狐德芬 [583–661] et al., *Sui shu* 隋書 [*History of the Sui Dynasty*, 581–618, Beijing 1973], 15:378). This music was still all the rage in Luoyang under the Northern Wei a century later, where ca. 500 a dissolute character named Zhen Kan 甄侃 "passed the night with wine and women in an establishment by the River Luo, and in a brawl hit the proprietor ... 以酒色夜宿洛水停舍，毆擊主人" (*Wei shu* 68:1517), of course with the opposite effect of what Juqu Mengxun was after. See also Bo Lawergren, "Music," in *CHC* 2, pp. 698–720 at p. 699.

33 *Shiliu guo chunqiu* 95:1053; *Song shu* 98:2412 is similar. Not in *JS*.

Mobilised into Lü Guang's service with their own horsemen and their new dignities, Juqu Mengxun's two uncles had the misfortune of being on the losing side in a 397 campaign against the Western Qin, and being condemned to death for it.

Juqu Mengxun summarily incited the tribe to take revenge. In front of "more than ten thousand" of his people, he reminded them of the righteous fight their distant forefathers had engaged in against the false pretender Wei Ao, and urged them to repeat this exploit against "'the Lü king, [who is but] a dim-witted old man, resorting to random brutality and devoid of moral sense; we must not fail to pursue our forebears' aspiration to make their mark on our times, lest our two forefathers (Quzhou and Luochou) should bear us rancour, from the Yellow Springs!' The throng unanimously professed their acclamation."[34] They proceeded by beheading their Chinese "minders" in Linsong, the magistrate and the vice commandant, "as a token of their covenant"; and, after being very nearly annihilated by a force under Lü Guang's son, Lü Zuan, Juqu Mengxun nonetheless won a victory of sorts when a cousin (*congxiong* 從兄) who commanded a tribal militia of his own in the Jiuquan area came to Mengxun's rescue. They took Jiankang Commandery (between Jiuquan and Zhangye)[35] and pushed its prefect, Duan Ye, to the fore as

> Area Commander-in-chief, Commissioned with the Staff of Authority, General-in-Chief of Dragon-like Prancing [Cavalry] (*longxiang da jiangjun* 龍驤大將軍), Governor of Liangzhou and Duke of Jiankang. They changed Lü Guang's era title and year count, "the second year of the Longfei 龍飛 era," into "the first year of the Shenxi 神璽 era."[36]

This year (397) is taken as the first of Juqu Mengxun's Northern Liang state, although it was the figurehead Duan Ye who assumed rulership on behalf of Juqu Mengxun, in Jiankang, during its initial four years.

• • •

34   *JS* 129:3189 ("呂王昏耄，荒虐無道，豈可不上繼先祖安時之志，使二父有恨黃泉！衆咸稱萬葳。").

35   The ruins of Jiankang (modern Gaotai County 高台縣, between Jiuquan and Zhangye), now called Camel Fortress 駱駝城, are today a tourist destination. This Jiankang obviously has nothing to do with the Eastern Jin capital Jiankang, i.e. modern Nanjing.

36   *JS* 125:3190; *Shiliu guo chunqiu* 95:1054; *Song shu* 98:2412 is similar but dates these events wrongly to 399.

LINKED DESTINIES   99

Duan Ye was from Chang'an; as a subordinate officer, he had taken part in Lü Guang's expedition to Kuqa; after Lü Guang, on his way back, had taken possession of Guzang, Duan Ye's literary skill earned him an appointment there as Editorial Director (*zhuzuolang* 著作郎) and, in 396, as a Minister (*shangshu* 尚書).[37] In 397, having fallen out with the "Senior Vice Director of the Secretariat (*shangshu zuopuye* 尚書左僕射)" (in effect, the prime minister) Wang Xiang, Duan Ye had distanced himself from Guzang, and was serving as Prefect of Jiankang when Juqu Nancheng and Juqu Mengxun rebelled. Nancheng's troops appeared before Jiankang; after twenty days of siege, in which no relief force was sighted, Duan Ye finally surrendered and accepted the usurping titles that were urged upon him — because, after only twelve years in Liangzhou, "alone and tossed about, living in an alien land," he had little choice but to throw in his lot with the Juqus.[38] Naturally, Duan Ye's first act of state was to anoint Juqu Nancheng as "Bulwark-general of the State (*fuguo jiangjun* 輔國將軍)," "entrusting him with the charge of the military and of the state," while Juqu Mengxun was appointed Prefect of Zhangye: this was initially a notional appointment, since Zhangye still belonged to Lü Guang's "Later Liang." But there were or soon would be other, civil appointments to make, and it is plausible to think that in order to persuade Chinese candidates to accept office under the upstart regime, someone like Duan Ye, "a paragon of Confucian probity," who "had a way with bureaucratese,"[39] could be useful. As we take up Li Hao's biography again:

> At the end of Lü Guang's time in power (= in 397), Duan Ye, from the capital municipality 京兆 (Chang'an), proclaimed himself Governor of Liangzhou. He made the Prefect of Dunhuang, Meng Min 孟敏 of Zhao Commandery 趙郡, Governor of Shazhou,[40] and appointed Li Hao Magistrate of Xiaogu 效穀令.[41]

---

37 Duan Ye wrote a *fu* on the palaces of Kuqa 龜茲宮賦, poems on the model of the "Nine Laments 九歎" of the *Chuci*, and a "sevens 七" (on which see, e.g., Victor H. Mair, *Mei Cherng's "Seven Stimuli" and Wang Bor's "Pavilion of King Terng"* [Lewiston/Queenston 1988]) or the "Seven Remonstrances 七諷" (*JS* 122:3055, 3059). None of these are extant. On his appointments, see *JS* 122:3059–3060.

38 *JS* 122:3061, *ZZTJ* 109:3454–3455, *JS* 129:3191 (Juqu Nancheng's words: "業羈旅孤飄 …").

39 *JS* 129:3192 ("儒素長者," "有尺牘之才").

40 This is the first time since Former Liang times that one hears again of Shazhou, and of a governor appointed over it.

41 *JS* 872257. Xiaogu was one of the counties comprising Dunhuang Commandery (*JS* 14:434), located west of the modern county town of Guazhou 瓜州縣. The name, one reads in *HS* 28B:1615, comes from a constable of this ancient frontier outpost who, having taught

100   CHAPTER 6

It is significant that the first two appointments mentioned went to men with
little or no native roots, Meng Min from Zhao Commandery (in today's Henan)
and Li Hao, a third-generation immigrant. Let us also recall that in 397, Li Hao
was 46 years old and had had no official career, inasmuch as our sources tell
us. Duan Ye himself was a newcomer. Very possibly the established clans of
Liangzhou would have spurned him.

• • •

The year 397 was a tumultuous one. Juqu Mengxun, with the figurehead
Governor of Liangzhou, Duan Ye, as the Chinese face of the new breakaway
state of Northern Liang, at once embarked on territorial aggrandisement to
the detriment of Lü Guang's Later Liang. All of Liangzhou to the northwest
of Jiankang surrendered to Northern Liang, while to the southeast, i.e. in the
direction of Lü Guang's capital Guzang, Juqu Mengxun extended his domain
beyond Zhangye to Xijun Commandery, appr. 100 km before Guzang.[42] In 398,
Northern Liang moved its own capital from Jiankang to Zhangye. In one fell
move, Lü Guang had lost at least two thirds of his state. Yet Juqu Mengxun's (or
Duan Ye's) grip on the new possessions was weak. In Dunhuang, where Meng
Min, the just-appointed Governor of Shazhou, was stationed, the notable local
clans did not welcome the new dispensation any more than they had liked Lü
Guang's rule; and when Meng Min, after only a few months into his new job,
unexpectedly came to die, the local notables took swift action to pre-empt any
meddlesome outsider from being sent by Duan Ye to replace him:

> When [Meng] Min came to die soon after, the Vice Commandant of
> Dunhuang, Guo Qian 郭謙 from Pingyi 馮翊, as well as the Vice-Governor
> (*zhizhong* 治中) of Shazhou, Suo Xian 索仙 from Dunhuang, and sev-
> eral others, proposed that Li Hao become General Pacifying the North
> (*ningshuo jiangjun* 寧朔將軍) and Prefect of Dunhuang on account of his
> moderate, yet principled, mild style of government. Li Hao objected to
> this at first, but it so happened that Song You, serving as an official under
> Duan Ye and on temporary leave in Dunhuang, said to Li Hao: "Have you

---

      the local populace to apply themselves to farming, demonstrated that proper industry
      can indeed "yield grain 效穀."

42   *JS* 129:3190. Xijun Commandery 西郡, est. (see *HHS* "Treatises" 23:3520) under the Han
    emperor Xian's reign (190–220), corresponds to modern Yongchang 永昌縣 and Shandan
    Counties 山丹縣 in Gansu, wedged between Zhangye Commandery to its northwest and
    Wuwei Commandery to its southeast.

LINKED DESTINIES 101

forgotten what Guo Nun said? We did actually get a foal with a white
forehead, don't you know?" Li Hao then decided to go along with the
move. Soon afterwards, his title was raised to Army Commander and he
declared himself a vassal to Duan Ye. [Duan] Ye made Li Hao General
Pacifying the West (*anxi jiangjun* 安西將軍) and Prefect of Dunhuang,
concurrently Commandant Protector of the Western Nomads (*hu xi Hu
xiaowei* 護西胡校尉).[43]

The next year, 399, Duan Ye inaugurated his second era title (the Tianxi 天璽
era), and took the title of Prince of Liang. This initiative triggered an unsuc-
cessful punitive campaign by Lü Guang;[44] at the same time, it emboldened
Duan Ye to try to wrest control over Dunhuang back from Li Hao by appointing a new prefect. The *Jin shu* portrays Duan Ye's candidate for the Prefect of
Dunhuang, Suo Si 索嗣, as little more than a villain. But Duan Ye's choice was
a clever one, since the Suo clan was one of the leading families of Dunhuang.[45]
In fact, that the notable families of Dunhuang put forward Li Hao, who was
a newcomer in their midst, as their leader, both suggests that they could not
agree on one of their own for the position, and that they believed Li Hao would
be amenable to their pressure. The situation was very much as an earlier prefect had found it almost two centuries earlier:

In the Taihe era (227–233), [Cang Ci] was transferred to the post of
Prefect of Dunhuang. Situated on the western border, the commandery
had been cut off by all the turmoil and, thus neglected, had been without
a governor for twenty years, giving powerful local clans a free hand to
do as they pleased, so that, by and by, that had become like the normal

---

43   *JS* 87:2257–2258. Instead of "General Pacifying the West," *Wei shu* 99:2201 gives Li Hao's
      appointment by Duan Ye as "General Defending the West 鎮西將軍."

44   *JS* 129:3190–3191; *ZZTJ* 111:3488, 3491–3492.

45   The Suo clan settled in Dunhuang in the 2nd century CE and remained prominent well
      into the Tang: Paul Demiéville, *Le concile de Lhasa* (Paris 1952), p. 275, who refers to Shi
      Ai 史岩 (sic), *Dunhuang shishi huaxiang tishi* 敦煌石室畫象題識 (*Chinese Inscriptions
      in the Caves of Tun-huang*; Chengdu 1947), Preface, fol. 17a. In 119 CE, Suo Ban 索班, Chief
      Clerk 長史 of the Prefect of Dunhuang, led 1000 men to establish a military colony in
      Yiwu 伊吾, 400 km up north (*HHS* 47:1587); at an uncertain date (mid 3rd cent.?), Suo
      Mai 索勱, also from Dunhuang, and also with 1000 troops, set up an agricultural colony
      in Loulan 樓蘭 (now Qarkilik/Ruoqiang 若羌), some 600 km to the southwest (*Shuijing
      zhu jiao* 2:37). Suo Si's most famous forebear was Suo Jing 索靖 (239–303), a scholar
      and calligrapher who had a glorious official career in the Western Jin capital Luoyang and
      elsewhere, including a stint as Chief Clerk to the Wu and Ji Colonel of the Western
      Regions. Suo Jing's biography is in *JS* 60:1648–1650.

state of affairs. Previous governors, such as Yin Feng 尹奉, for one, did no more than submit to the order of the day and undertook nothing to correct or change it. When [Cang] Ci arrived, he reined in and frustrated the mighty and overbearing, and comforted and provided for the needy and the weak, very much as it should be.[46]

At this crucial juncture, Li Hao managed both to keep Suo Si out — indeed, to eliminate him — and to maintain a facade of subservience towards Duan Ye, the "Prince of Liang." In an anecdote that the *Jin shu* pointedly omits from its biography, Li Hao, recalling how he thwarted Suo Si's appointment, asked a subordinate, sometime after 402: "How would you compare me with Suo Si?" "I find that hard to assess," his interlocutor, Liang Zhongyong 梁中庸 — a local notable in his own right — prudently replied. Li Hao continued: "Should Suo Si's abilities have been a match for me, how would I have been capable of doing him in, and at such a distance?"[47] Liang Zhongyong answered: "Some are wiser than others, some have more luck than others. I really am unable to make out which factor it was, in Your Highness's dealings with Suo Si, that gave you the upper hand. Does the mere fact that he's dead mean that he lost, while the successful outcome of your plot means that you won? [...]" Li Hao was silent.[48] He was aware that his own position in Dunhuang society was that of an arriviste, as he cautions his sons in 406, when he had been ruling for six years and began involving them in the work of government: "The functionaries on your staff were born and raised here: be courteous to them in everything, make them feel respected, banquet and feast them, and be attentive and solicitous for them in every respect."[49]

> When Duan Ye arrogated the title of Prince of Liang to himself, his General of the Right Section of the Guard (*youwei jiangjun* 右衛將軍), Suo Si, made false charges against Li Hao to Ye, who consequently made Suo Si the [new] Prefect of Dunhuang. He set out to the west at the head of five hundred horsemen, and twenty *li* before he arrived, sent a dispatch to Li Hao to have him organise a welcoming ceremony for himself. Li Hao was both startled and suspicious, but was about to go out to

---

46 *SGZ* 16:512 ("太和中，遷燉煌太守。郡在西陲，以亂隔絕，曠無太守二十歲，大姓雄張，遂以為俗。前太守尹奉等，循故而已，無所匡革。慈到，抑挫權右，撫恤貧贏，甚得其理。").

47 Literally, "how could I have strangled him at a distance of a thousand miles?"

48 *ZZTJ* 112:3546.

49 *JS* 87:2262 ("僚佐邑宿，盡禮承敬，讌饗饌食，事事留懷").

welcome him when Zhang Miao 張邈, the Magistrate of Xiaogu, as well as Song You stopped him, saying: "With the Lü government on its last legs, and Duan Ye weak and clueless, this is the day for bold and brilliant men to take action. General, you occupy a land that has the capability to be self-sufficient; why should your hands be tied by others? Suo Si himself, merely because he was born here, says people's sympathies will naturally turn towards him; he does not anticipate that you could instead fend him off, and that's why, for sure, you could capture him in just a single battle." Song You also said: "My lord, you have already been put forward by [the people of] this age; you will become the world's laughing stock if today you capitulate to Suo Si! You impose by your noble bearing, brother; you look every inch the strong leader: even to continue the cause of the Zhang princes (of Former Liang) would be beneath you." Li Hao replied: "I never had an appetite for heroism, and have reached my present position just by climbing the official ladder. I never planned upon being so suddenly pushed forward by the gentlemen of this commandery. When I said earlier that I was going out to welcome him, I had not fully understood what you worthy gentlemen had in mind." Then he sent Song You to observe Suo Si. Song You blandished him with sweet talk, and upon his return, said to Li Hao: "Suo Si is quite self-assured, but his troops are weak. He'll be the easiest of prey." Thereupon Li Hao dispatched his two sons, Li Xin 歆[50] and Li Rang 讓, together with Zhang Miao and Song You, as well as his Assistant (*sima* 司馬) Yin Jianxing 尹建興, to confront Suo Si in battle; they beat him, and Suo Si fled back to Zhangye. Li Hao had always been on good terms with Suo Si, the two being as close as blood brothers; now, on the contrary, having been framed by him, Li Hao has come to resent him deeply and denounced Suo Si to Duan Ye for criminal conduct. Ye's commander Juqu Nan[cheng] also detested Si, and took the occasion, at this juncture, to urge Duan Ye to get rid of him. Ye had Si killed as a result, and sent an envoy to apologise to Li Hao. He separated the three counties of Liangxing 涼興, Wuze 烏澤 (both in Dunhuang) and Yihe 宜禾 (in Jinchang) to form the [new] Liangxing Commandery, and promoted Li Hao to Commander-in-chief of all Military Affairs West of Liangxing, Bearing the Staff of Authority (*chijie* 持節), General Garrisoned in the West (*zhenxi jiangjun* 鎮西將軍), and concurrently 領 Commandant Protector of the Western Yi (*hu xi Yi xiaowei* 護西夷校尉).

---

50   Shiye 士業 in the text, i.e. Li Xin's byname.

At the time, a reddish vapour rose from Li Hao's back garden, and dragon paw traces appeared in the small enclosure.[51]

•••

It is rare to read about a wife's role in a man's career in the dynastic histories. We are therefore fortunate to have a modicum of information about Li Hao's second wife, *née* Yin. Her full name has not been transmitted. Yet, "keen on studying as a girl, clear-headed and articulate, she had aspirations of her own, as well as high principles. She had had a first marriage to Ma Yuanzheng 馬元正 of Fufeng, and when Yuanzheng died, she was married to Li Hao, who had become a widower. Having been given away in marriage twice, for three years she did not speak. She cared for the son(s) of [Li Hao's] first wife (*née* Xin) more than her own. When Li Hao embarked on his undertaking, she assisted and supported him in many ways in devising and planning his grand project. Hence in the Western Province (of Liangzhou) there was the saying, 'Li and Yin lord it in Dunhuang.'"[52]

•••

Thus, less than a year after Juqu Mengxun had broken away from Lü Guang's Later Liang to set up Northern Liang with Duan Ye as its nominal prince, Li Hao went along with the leading citizens of Dunhuang in asserting the oasis city's quasi-independence from Northern Liang. Juqu Mengxun had not yet removed Duan Ye, nor had Li Hao as yet repudiated Duan Ye's overlordship. It was however in the air that it would come to this, and that Li Hao and Juqu Mengxun would come to confront each other.

---

51 *JS* 87:2258. Tan Qixiang 譚其驤, *Zhongguo lishi ditu ji* 中國歷史地圖集 (*The Historical Atlas of China*), Vol. IV (Shanghai 1982), map 13–14 ② 1, places Liangxing Commandery between Dunhuang and Jinchang.

52 *JS* 96:2526 (chapter on "Exemplary Women 列女"). Adding Mme Yin to the total, eight of the 31 "exemplary women" in this chapter are praised for educational attainments: from writing skills to classical learning. Of Mme Yin's first husband Ma Yuanzheng nothing further is known.

CHAPTER 7

Building a State, Part 1: Li Hao's Western Liang

As relations between Duan Ye and Juqu Mengxun began to sour in Northern Liang — with Duan Ye "fearing Mengxun's warlike prowess [...] and believing that Mengxun had outsized ambitions," and Juqu Mengxun accusing Duan Ye of "[putting] his trust in slanderers and [being] partial to flatterers, to the point where he has lost the intelligence to discern and judge things"[1] — in Dunhuang, Li Hao received a boost when the Prefect of Jinchang defected to Li Hao and called upon other commandery prefects to follow his example. This was a decisive moment. Tang Yao 唐瑤, the prefect, belonged to a well-established notable clan. Five generations back, an ancestor of his had married a daughter of Zhang Gui's;[2] once he had persuaded his colleagues and social equals in Dunhuang, Jiuquan, Liangxing, Jiankang and Qilian 祁連 Commanderies to throw their weight behind Li Hao, Western Liang all of a sudden became a larger state than Juqu Mengxun's Northern Liang. Li Hao's biography states:

> In the fourth year of the Long'an 隆安 era (of Eastern Jin: 400), the Prefect of Jinchang, Tang Yao, dispatched an exhortation to six commanderies urging them to publicly recognise Li Hao as Area Commander-in-chief, General-in-chief, Duke of Liang and concurrently governor of the two provinces of Qin and Liang (Qin Liang *erzhou mu* 秦涼二州牧), as well as Commandant Protector of the Qiang. Li Hao then declared an amnesty within his domain, established the era title Gengzi 庚子,[3] and posthumously honoured his grandfather Yan as the Effulgent Duke of Liang 涼景公 and his father Chang as the Frugal Duke of Liang 涼簡公. He made

---

1 *JS* 129:3191 ("業憚蒙遜雄武 [⋯] 業亦以蒙遜有大志"; "[段業] 信讒愛佞，無鑒斷之明").

2 For Tang Yao's ancestry and Tang Xi's 唐熙 marriage to Zhang Gui's daughter, see Ouyang Xiu 歐陽修 (1007–1072) and Song Qi 宋祁 (998–1061), eds., *Xin Tang shu* 新唐書 (*New History of the Tang Dynasty*, Beijing 1975), 74B:3202. The six commanderies are identified by name in the passage corresponding to this one (*JS* 87:2259) in *ZZTJ*. Qilian Commandery, roughly occupying the territory of today's Minle County in Gansu and Qilian County 祁連縣 in Qinghai, was established by Zhang Xuanjing of Former Liang, r. 355–363 (*JS* 14:434).

3 The fourth year of the Long'an era of Eastern Jin was a *gengzi* 庚子 year. Li Hao did not adopt the Eastern Jin era title Long'an, but used the cyclical appellation of the year 400, *gengzi*, as his own first era name. One is to understand that 401 was Gengzi 2, and up to 404, Gengzi 5 (followed by Jianchu 1 in 405).

Ⓒ DOMINIK DECLERCQ, 2025 | DOI:10.1163/9789004727380_008

Tang Yao General of the Eastern Expeditionary Force 征東將軍; Guo Qian, Libationer of the Military Council (*junzi jijiu* 軍諮祭酒); Suo Xian, Senior Chief Clerk (*zuo zhangshi* 左長史); Zhang Miao, Junior Chief Clerk (*you zhangshi* 右長史); Yin Jianxing, Senior Major (*zuo sima* 左司馬); Zhang Tishun 張體順, Junior Major (*you sima* 右司馬); Zhang Tiao 張條, Senior Chief Clerk of the Governor's Bureau (*mufu* 牧府); Linghu Yi 令狐溢, Junior Chief Clerk; Zhang Lin 張林, Recorder (*zhubu* 主簿) of the Grand Bureau (*taifu* 太府); Song You and Zhang Su 張謖, Gentleman Retainers (*congshi zhonglang* 從事中郎); [Song] You in addition Assault-resisting General and [Zhang] Su in addition General Flaunting Martial Prowess. He [further] made Suo Chengming 索承明 Junior Major to the Governor's Bureau; Linghu Qian 令狐遷, General of the Martial Guard and Prefect of Jinxing; Fan Deyu 氾德瑜, General Pacifying Distant Regions and Prefect of Xijun; Zhang Jing 張靖, Assault-resisting General and Prefect of Huanghe 湟河;[4] Suo Xun 索訓, General Daunting the Distant and Prefect of Xiping; Zhao Kai 趙開, Vice Commandant of Xingma 騂馬護軍 and Prefect of Daxia 大夏; Suo Ci 索慈, Prefect of Guangwu 廣武; Yin Liang 陰亮, Prefect of Xi'an 西安;[5] Linghu He 令狐赫, Prefect of Wuwei; and Suo Shu 索術, Prefect of Wuxing, so as to conciliate the Eastern Heartland 東夏 (= Eastern Jin). Song You was next sent to attack Liangxing in the east, and at the same time to assail the forts west of Yumen; he razed them all, and subsequently set up military colonies in Yumen and Yangguan 陽關,[6] where he extended the lands under cultivation and stored up grain to serve as supply for an eastern campaign (= in the direction of Zhangye, capital of Northern Liang).

Several comments on this paragraph are in order. First, by proclaiming his own era title, Li Hao not only definitely severed his links to his neighbours Duan Ye and Later Liang's Lü Zuan, but also jeopardised his relationship with other regimes further afield, Yao Xing's Later Qin as well as Eastern Jin under Sima Dezong 司馬德宗 (Emperor An 安帝, r. 397–418), since establishing one's own calendar was an imperial prerogative. Second, the list of appointees manifestly

---

4   Correcting Hehuang 河湟 to Huanghe, see *js* 87:2272 note 2.
5   Xi'an Commandery is first mentioned in 397 (*js* 122:3062), therefore no doubt established by Lü Guang, possibly southeast of Zhangye.
6   Yumen and Yangguan lay to the west of Dunhuang, whereas modern Yumen City lies east of Dunhuang. See Tan Qixiang, op. cit., Vol. IV map 15–16. Yumen, the "Jade Gateway," marked China's final western frontier, but in light of political reality, the toponym Yumen was movable: modern Yumen City is in retreat vs. Li Hao's Yumen. See also Demiéville, op. cit., pp. 365–366.

BUILDING A STATE, PART 1

shows that Li Hao counted on the support of a limited set of notable families, the Suo, Zhang and Linghu clans in particular, whom we can assume to be the local "Han elite."[7]

As for the titles that Li Hao himself agreed to espouse, one notes "Commandant Protector of the Qiang." It is possible, certainly, that this was a conscious throwback to the Former Liang rulers of the Zhang clan, who had combined their governorship with this ancient Han military responsibility. However, it perhaps also throws a certain light on how Western Liang viewed its relationship with the Qiang and, naturally, with the Lu River nomads as well. Neither Lü Guang nor, a fortiori, Duan Ye or Juqu Mengxun sported it; one would think that to them it sounded odious. Consequently, it is truly puzzling, to me, why in 411, Juqu Mengxun appointed a brother and later a cousin Commandant Protector of the Qiang (stationed in Guzang).[8]

As a fourth point, let us presume that the series of appointments made by Li Hao follows a significant order. First to be mentioned, singled out here for his special role in bringing Li Hao to power, is the Prefect of Jinchang. Tang Yao was rewarded not just with a generalship, but with a military title that expressed the ambition to vanquish Juqu Mengxun's polity to the east: "General of the Eastern Expeditionary Force." Next comes the Libationer of the Military Council. When in 417, under Li Hao's son Li Xin, the position of Libationer of the Military Council went to Li Hao's half-brother Song You, the text there specifies that the Libationer "oversaw the affairs of the Three Bureaus (*lu sanfu shi* 錄三府事)" that formed the government.[9] It therefore looks equivalent to a chief minister. In 400, the incumbent was given two Chief Clerks (Senior and Junior) and — traditionally subordinate to the Chief Clerks — two Majors (Senior and Junior). Of the Three Bureaus, two are named here: the Governor's Bureau and the Grand Bureau. The Governor's Bureau, which would have been Li Hao's civil administration, is headed by two Chief Clerks (Senior and Junior). The Grand Bureau would have brought together all of Li Hao's military staff. It was

---

7   As pointed out by 尤成民, "Han Jin shiqi Hexi daxing de tedian he lishi zuoyong 漢晉時期河西大姓的特點和歷史作用," in *Lanzhou daxue xuebao* (*Shehui kexue ban*) 蘭州大學學報 (社會科學版) 20 (1992).1, pp. 80–87 at p. 83.

8   *JS* 129:3195. Juqu Mengxun had just conquered Guzang (see hereunder) and had his family members Juqu Shu 沮渠挈 and Juqu Yizi 沮渠益子 in succession hold the place (bearing the title *hu Qiang xiaowei*) before he made Guzang his new capital and moved in himself.

9   According to Hu Sanxing's note on *ZZTJ* 116:3699, the Three Bureaus comprised the staffs of Li Hao [1] in his capacity as Area Commander-in-chief and General-in-chief (that is to say, his military staff) 大都府、大將軍府, [2] in his capacity as Duke of Liang (that is to say, his household staff) 涼公府, and [3] in his capacity as Provincial Governor (that is to say, his civil administration) 州牧府. [2] goes unmentioned in the text.

headed by a Recorder, and seconded by two Gentleman Retainers who concurrently held general's titles (Song You and Zhang Su), presumably also high up on the Grand Bureau's staff. What follows is a list of appointees on the Grand Bureau, many of whom combined military with civil administrative titles. (It is unclear why this ensemble includes a Junior Major in the Governor's Bureau, both because one would expect this office to follow directly upon those of the Governor's Bureau's two Chief Clerks, and because one would expect a "Senior" Major to be mentioned before this "Junior" one.)

In the fifth place, what further strikes one about the civil administrative titles is that none of the commanderies mentioned were actually under Li Hao's control: Xijun and Xi'an were in Northern Liang (the territory neighbouring Li Hao to his southeast), Jinxing, Huanghe, Xiping and Guangwu were in Tufa Lilugu's Southern Liang, and Wuwei and Wuxing were in Lü Zuan's Later Liang (to the southeast of Northern Liang), while Daxia was located even further away, in Yao Xing's Later Qin. Evidently, what these titles were meant to convey were Li Hao's territorial ambitions, harboured not for himself but ostensibly on behalf of, or in order "to conciliate (*zhaohuai* 招懷)," Eastern Jin. A more pedestrian reality reasserts itself in the military title "Vice Commandant of Xingma," for Xingma was held by Li Hao, although it could not as yet dispense with a commander charged to protect it (*hujun* 護軍) from seditious Qiang.

•••

In 399, as Duan Ye was forced to recognise Li Hao's de facto independence in Dunhuang, "a reddish vapour rose from Li Hao's back garden, and dragon paw traces appeared in the small enclosure," as we have read. It was believed that Heaven brought down signs, conspicuous or even supernatural phenomena, to warn a bad monarch to mend his ways, or lucky omens to endorse his good government.[10] Amongst many expositions of this theory, this one is as eloquent as any:

> The testimony afforded by Heaven-sent calamities, no less than the rejoinder implied by happy auguries, are — one could say — bestowed onto such a one who may *expect* to be requited accordingly, i.e. they befall a person in response to the particular kind of person that he is. Therefore, to someone who applies himself to doing good works, Heaven lends a helping hand through its favour, by means of an auspicious portent. The *Changes*

---

10   On this subject, cf. Tiziana Lippiello, *Auspicious Omens and Miracles in Ancient China: Han, Three Kingdoms, and Six Dynasties* (Sankt Augustin 2001).

BUILDING A STATE, PART 1

say: "From Heaven come his blessings; good fortune; all signs are favourable." But when someone does evil, Heaven requites him with misfortune, such as early death or calamity. The *Spring-and-Autumn Annals* say: "In response to this there were Heaven-sent calamities." Kings Wen 周文王 (r. 1099–1050 BCE) and Wu of the Zhou revered men of worth and accepted their remonstrances; unremittingly vigilant, their unalloyed virtue spread goodness up [to Heaven] above, and the gods blessed them. The *Odes* say: "That rich blessings may come down, /Mighty blessings come down."[11]

To rulers, auspicious portents conferred legitimacy, as inauspicious portents could be early signs that the dynasty was in danger of losing Heaven's Mandate. However hallowed their celestial origin, though, only earthlings were capable of decoding them. Sightings of such phenomena were therefore not the product of someone's fevered imagination; rather, they favoured observers with a prepared mind. Just as officials reported bad omens to the court to express criticism of its policies, especially in Eastern Han[12] — minimising the risk they took in doing so by invoking Heaven — so too could officials signal loyalty to the court by sending news of supernatural sightings. In a way, for the ruler and his entourage, signs therefore served as a gauge of public (or at least official) opinion. The court need not be passively at the mercy of public opinion, either, but could try to suppress, manipulate or exaggerate it for its own ends. For instance, in 178, the Han Emperor Ling professed not to understand what a series of portents reported to him were meant to convey, until Cai Yong 蔡邕 (133–192), at the emperor's urging, interpreted them for him and put the blame for each and every portent on the eunuch faction at court.[13] The Grand Astrologer's 太史令 duties included recording "all portents and calamities that regarded the state" for the use of future historians,[14] but one imagines that higher authority could apply a filter to this. This is what transpires from Li Hao's biography, too, when later on it says:

11 *Yantie lun* 54:111 (cf. transl. Levi pp. 271–272): "天菑之證，禎祥之應，猶施與之望報，各以其類及。故好行善者，天助以福，符瑞是也。易曰：自天祐之，吉無不利。好行惡者，天報以禍，妖菑是也。春秋曰：應是而有天菑。周文、武尊賢受諫，敬戒不殆，純德上休，神祇相況。詩云：降福穰穰，降福簡簡。" Huan Kuan quotes *Yijing* Hexagram 14 (Dayou 大有), Sixth Yang; the *Gongyang Commentary* 公羊傳 to *Chunqiu* Xuan 15; and *Mao Shi* #274 (Zhi jing 執兢), transl. Waley p. 230.

12 See H. Bielenstein, "Is There a Chinese Dynastic Cycle?," in *BMFEA* 50 (1978).

13 B.J. Mansvelt Beck, *The Treatises of Later Han. Their Author, Sources, Contents and Place in Chinese Historiography* (Leiden 1990), p. 43.

14 *HHS*, "Treatises 志 25," p. 3572.

At this time (ca. 410), a white wolf, a white hare, a white sparrow, a white pheasant and a white dove were all seen nesting in his enclosed garden. His subordinates were of the opinion that these white portents had been brought forth by the essence of [the phase element] Metal and had all appeared in response to the prevailing concord. There were other auspicious signs as well: a supernatural halo, sweet dew, a twin tree[15] and an auspicious ear of grain; the archivist (*shiguan* 史官) was requested to record these occurrences, and Li Hao allowed it.[16]

In this way, a dialectic between the ruler and his officialdom would prompt, block, or channel what, in Li Hao's case, were coded signs of approval bearing a supernatural stamp. "Li Hao allowed it": this is tantamount to saying that he was confident of his subjects' support. To be noted is that, in the theory of legitimate dynastic succession — in which successive dynasties rule under the dispensation of one of the Five Elements (or Phases) — the Jin dynasty stood under the aegis of the Metal element. Thus, in considering "white portents" auspicious — white being the colour associated with Metal — Li Hao also signalled at least the appearance of continuing loyalty towards Eastern Jin. Clearly these supernatural appearances also promoted the mystification of power, as we noted with respect to Zhang Jun and the jade seal that the Yellow River produced to acclaim him (p. 69 above). Li Hao likewise acquired jade seals (see hereunder) that were, it is true, procured commercially; but should they miraculously have entered Li Hao's treasury of their own volition, one would not be too surprised.[17]

In the same register of culturally significant steps towards nation-building fall the places of assembly whose construction Li Hao commissioned, namely an academy of learning and two "halls" decorated with Confucian model heroes:

> Earlier, when Lü Guang proclaimed himself king (389), he sent an envoy to purchase six blocks of jade, for royal seals, in Khotan, and by this time (400), the jade had arrived in Dunhuang and was entered into the commandery treasury. Meanwhile, outside the southern gate, overlooking the

---

15   Such a miraculous tree (a *lianli* 連理 tree) also sprouted in Juqu Mengxun's domain; vide infra.

16   *JS* 87:2264.

17   On this topic, see Anna Seidel, "Imperial Treasures and Taoist Sacraments — Taoist Roots in the Apocrypha," in *Tantric and Taoist Studies in honour of R.A. Stein* Vol. 2 (Brussels 1983), pp. 291–371.

BUILDING A STATE, PART 1   111

river, a hall was erected, called the Hall of Respectful Observance 靖恭堂, meant for deliberating court policies and reviewing military affairs. It was painted with portraits, accompanied by encomia, of sage emperors and wise kings from antiquity onward, of loyal ministers and filial sons, illustrious men and chaste women; Li Hao personally added eulogies to them in order to illustrate the incentive or cautionary lessons to be drawn from them, and the civil and military officials of the present time were all pictured in it as well. A white bird hovered over the Hall of Respectful Observance; Li Hao watched it and was overjoyed. He also established an academy (*pangong* 泮宮), to which he added five hundred students from eminent families. He had a Hall of Gracious Acceptance 嘉納堂 erected in the rear garden, where he had depicted, each with a laudatory verse, [the great men] whom he emulated.[18]

• • •

An interesting sidelight on the years 399 to 400 is thrown by the *śramaṇa* Faxian 法顯 (ca. 340–421) who, deploring that the Disciplinary Rules section of the Tripiṭaka 律藏 (*Vinayapiṭaka*) was incomplete, travelled from Yao Xing's Chang'an to India. Faxian's *Account of Buddhist Lands* (*Foguo ji* 佛國記) says that he set out from Chang'an in 399 and, having crossed southern Gansu, no doubt along the River Wei, "reached [Qifu] Qiangui's state 乾歸國 (Yuanchuan, just east of modern Lanzhou), where [he and his four fellow travellers] passed the [three-month Buddhist] summer retreat (*xiazuo* 夏坐). That completed, [they] proceeded onward (along a stretch of the Yellow River, then along the River Huang) to [Tufa] Rutan's state 傉檀國 (Ledu, in modern Qinghai), and crossed the Yanglou Mountains 養樓山," now called Daban Mountains 達坂山: a distance of 300 km as the crow flies, in a northwestern direction towards Zhangye. The chosen route, which must have been the safest available under the circumstances, deliberately skirts the Lü "Later Liang" state and its capital Guzang; indeed, the Lü polity was in its death throes, with Lü Guang's successor Lü Zuan being murdered in a palace brawl in 401, and Yao Xing of Later Qin forcing the surrender of the last Later Liang ruler, Lü Long 呂隆 (r. 401–403, d. 416), in 403. Qifu Qiangui of "Western Qin," like Tufa Rutan (365–415, r. 402–414) of "Southern Liang," had been careful not to antagonise the far greater power of Yao Xing of Later Qin.[19] Faxian thus passed through what were in essence

---

18   *JS* 87:2259.

19   *ZZTJ* 112:3541–3562, passim.

vassal states of his own native land.[20] In Zhangye, Duan Ye was then (late 399 to early 400) still, if barely, Prince of Liang. "Reaching the garrison of Zhangye, it turned out that Zhangye was in great turmoil and that the roads were impassable. The King of Zhangye, however, showed us his solicitude and kept us as his guests, acting as our benefactor 檀越 (*dānapati*)." Duan Ye, then, had Buddhist sympathies, and the city housed a Buddhist community, for "soon after, we made the acquaintance of (the *śramaṇas*) Zhiyan 智嚴, Huijian 慧簡, Sengshao 僧紹, Baoyun 寶雲 and Sengjing 僧景, and, glad to find them of the same disposition, we passed that summer retreat together." At the beginning of autumn, they "went on again, towards Dunhuang. There was a section of frontier fortifications (*sai* 塞), easily 80 *li* from east to west and 40 *li* from south to north, where we halted for a month and some more days. Then I and my four [original] companions, going along with an emissary [sent by Li Hao], departed first, having said goodbye to Baoyun and the others." Faxian may have arrived in Dunhuang before the end of the year, where "the Prefect of Dunhuang, Li Hao 李浩 (*sic*; read 暠), gave us provisions for crossing the desert."[21] By then, Dunhuang was a Buddhist centre of long standing. As the *Wei shu* says:

> From the time of Zhang Gui onwards, Liangzhou has adhered to the Buddhist creed for generations. The area of Dunhuang adjoins the Western Regions; monks and lay people, without much distinction between them, have acquired [the Western Regions'] age-old ways of life and their villages, neighbouring one another, often have a *stūpa* or a temple.[22]

Facheng 法乘, a pupil of Dharmarakṣa's (Zhu Fahu 竺法護, vide infra, p. 121; born in Dunhuang), had founded the first Buddhist monastery in Dunhuang around 280, and according to tradition, the first cenobite to occupy a cave in what would become the Mogao cave complex in Dunhuang was a *śramaṇa* named Lezun 樂僔 in 366.[23] No documentary evidence beyond his gifts to Faxian links Li Hao with Buddhist fervour of any kind, but the silence of our

---

20   ZZTJ 111:3512–3542, passim.

21   All quotations are from Faxian's *Foguo ji* (*T* 2085).

22   *Wei shu* 114:3032. I quote from my own translation, "*Wei shu* 魏書, chapter 114: Treatise on Buddhism and Taoism 釋老志," in Lalji 'Shravak' & Supriya Rai, eds., *Investigating Principles* (Hong Kong 2019), pp. 45–133 at p. 72.

23   On Facheng, see Zürcher, op. cit., pp. 67–68; on Lezun, see the rather more suspect "Stele Inscription by Li Kerang upon Restoring a Buddhist Shrine at the Mogao Caves 李克讓 修莫高窟佛龕碑," a Tang dynasty text from 689. Today, in fact, "of the 492 caves ... the Dunhuang Research Institute dates the site's earliest caves to the Northern Liang dynasty (422–439 [*sic*; should be 397–439])": Hansen, *The Silk Road*, Ch. 6, with references n. 9.

BUILDING A STATE, PART 1 113

sources does not preclude it. Li Hao's break with Duan Ye is dated to the eleventh month of the year 400 by Sima Guang, when, according to the *Jin shu*, he became Duke of Liang and governor of the two provinces of Qin[zhou] and Liang[zhou]. The *Zizhi tongjian*, in what seems to corroborate Faxian's account and imposes no strict deadline on the moment of his arrival there, instead says that from the eleventh month onward, Li Hao remained "concurrently Prefect of Dunhuang."[24]

---

24   *ZZTJ* 111:3515.

CHAPTER 8

Building a State, Part 2: Juqu Mengxun's Northern Liang

By 401, Juqu Mengxun must have been certain that the choice of Duan Ye as nominal sovereign of Northern Liang was a false start. Duan Ye was a weak leader: "His solemn prohibitions had no effect, and his underlings issued orders as they themselves saw fit. He put great belief in divination, prognostication, spirit mediums and omens, so he was inevitably hoodwinked by schemers and sycophants." He had no strategic insight. He unwisely tried to divide the Juqu tribal leaders, and wrongly took it for granted that leading Chinese families sided with him. When open conflict between the two broke out, and Duan Ye despatched a Chinese-led regiment to capture Juqu Mengxun in a fortress that he had occupied, the commander abruptly switched sides, and Duan Ye instead found himself besieged by Juqu Mengxun in Zhangye. A Chinese inhabitant decided the outcome by "breaking the [city] gate's crossbar and letting him in. [Duan] Ye's retinue had scattered in all directions. Mengxun shouted: 'Where is [the General] Defending the West (= Duan Ye)?' A soldier said, 'Here!' [Duan] Ye then spoke: 'Alone have I strayed here, all by myself, to be pushed forward by your noble house: now see me begging for dear life, that I may betake myself south of this mountain range and may find my way back east to meet my wife and children again.' Mengxun then beheaded him."[1]

The scenario that then unfolded greatly resembled Li Hao's anointment by the citizenry of Dunhuang: the leading gentry acclaimed Juqu Mengxun as Area Commander-in-chief and General-in-chief Commissioned with the Staff of Authority, Governor of Liangzhou and Duke of Zhangye, and like Li Hao, he instituted his own era title, Yong'an 永安. Appointments of family members to various military commands followed, as well as of Chinese notables to civilian posts; and as his biographer approvingly notes, "his selection and assignment to office of such able and talented persons pleased both the military and the civil [branches of government]." One of Juqu Mengxun's new appointees was a younger brother; in the entirety of *Jin shu* chapter 129, which concerns Juqu Mengxun, no fewer than fifteen male family members of his are mentioned,

---

1 *JS* 129:3192: "威禁不行，羣下擅命，尤信卜筮、讖記、巫覡、徵祥，故為姦佞所誤。" "[田承愛] 斬關內之，業左右皆散。蒙遜大呼曰：鎮西何在？軍人曰：在此。業曰：孤單飄一己，為貴門所推，可見匃餘命，投身嶺南，庶得束還，與妻子相見。蒙遜遂斬之。" And in the next paragraph, from *JS*, ibid.: "擢任賢才，文武咸悅。"

© DOMINIK DECLERCQ, 2025 | DOI:10.1163/9789004727380_009

BUILDING A STATE, PART 2   115

all of them in some capacity or other active in managing Northern Liang. This suggests a horizontal rather than a hierarchical power distribution amongst the Juqu ruling clan, with Juqu Mengxun rather a *primus inter pares* than an undisputed leader.

...

However, after the loss of six commanderies to Li Hao, Northern Liang consisted of merely a strip of land between Zhangye, the capital near its western border, and Xijun Commandery, near its eastern one. This land was surrounded not only by Western Liang and Later Liang, but also by Northern Wei to its northeast; further south, south of Later Liang (now under Lü Long, and tottering), by Southern Liang and Western Qin; and to the southeast, by Yao Xing's Later Qin. The situation called for deft diplomacy as much as military bravery. So, when Yao Xing ("Emperor Wenhuan 文桓皇帝" of Later Qin) launched an assault on Lü Long's Later Liang, Juqu Mengxun offered help to Later Qin and followed this up with a carefully worded letter that implied a degree of allegiance to Later Qin, a certain desire to be serviceable, and a determination to prioritise agriculture over warfare. That would help to advance amicable relations with Later Qin without cementing any sort of subservience. The letter reads:

LEGEND
28   Liangxing 涼興   Est. 400   *JS* 14:434

MAP 9   Later, Northern, Western & Southern Liang, 400 CE

I am a shallow nobody, basely unworthy of the favourable turn the times have thrown at me: for I have been incapable of gloriously expanding the grand scheme [of the Later Qin empire, to reunite China], and of suppressing or eliminating the many scourges [still afflicting it], so that peach vermin [still] flap their wings in the Eastern Capital (= Luoyang) and great swine [still] romp in herds in the western marches.[2] Although my war chariots were often mobilised, shield and halberd have [still] not been set aside; the peasantry have had to forgo their occupation in the three [agricultural] seasons, and amongst the population, not a household can feed itself on grain. It is imperative that I waive and revoke all corvée labour, apply my undivided attention to [cultivating] our south-facing fields, set clear rules and regulations, and devote all efforts to bringing out the productivity of our land.[3]

Elsewhere, one learns that Juqu Mengxun also "frequently sent envoys bringing tribute" to Northern Wei, then ruled by Tuoba Gui 拓跋珪 (Taizu 太祖, r. 386–409);[4] and of diplomatic overtures to Eastern Jin we shall read later. As for Later Qin, Yao Xing sent two envoys to Juqu Mengxun in acknowledgement of the bond that now existed between them, and to bestow honorary titles upon him that, if accepted, would inch Juqu Mengxun that much nearer to real vassalage. However, at about the same time that Yao Xing's envoys came solemnly to appoint Mengxun General-in-chief Defending the West, Governor of Shazhou and Marquis of Xihai, it transpired that he had also appointed

---

2   "Peach vermin 桃蟲" is another name for the wren 鷦鷯 (*Troglodytes sp.*), a proverbially small bird, as used in Ode #289 (Xiao bi 小毖), *ssj* p. 601a, where the commentator, Kong Yingda 孔穎達 (574–648), says that the birds stand for "Guan[shu Xian] 管叔鮮 and Cai[shu Du] 蔡叔度 and their ilk," rebels against the Duke of Zhou 周公 (trad. d. 1104 BCE), who began inconspicuously as petty slanderers but turned into very serious rivals for power. In 401, the "Eastern Capital," Luoyang (which lay in ruins at this time: see e.g. Dai Zuo's 戴祚 eyewitness *Account of* [Liu Yu's 劉裕 (356–422), 417 CE] *Western Campaign* (*Xizheng ji* 西征記), quoted in *Shuijing zhu jiao* 15:371), was in the hands of the Murongs' "Later Yan." "Great swine 封豕" (the term is from *Zuo zhuan* 左傳 [*Zuo Tradition*] Zhao 昭 28.2b) "[plunge] in a herd through the waves 烝涉波矣," in Waley's translation of this line from Ode #232 (Jianjian zhi shi 漸漸之石), *ssj* p. 500a; an image for "strongman leaders who, alike to swine [...], lead people away from the security of ritual and righteousness to land them into the perils of chaos and perdition" (Kong Yingda's commentary, ibid.).

3   *JS* 129:3193: "孤以虛薄，猥添時運，未能弘闡大猷，戡蕩群孽，使桃蟲鼓翼東京，封豕烝涉西裔，戎車屢動，干戈未戢，農失三時之業，百姓戶不粒食。可蠲省百徭，專攻南畝，明設科條，務盡地利。"

4   *Wei shu* 99:2204 ("頻遣使朝貢").

BUILDING A STATE, PART 2 117

Tufa Rutan of Southern Liang Chariot and Horse General and enfeoffed him as Duke of Guangwu.

> When Mengxun learnt of this, he was ill-pleased, and said to [Yao Xing's envoys]: "What does [your lord] mean, making Rutan a duke and me [only] a marquis?" [Zhang] Gou (the main envoy) replied: "Rutan is flighty and cunning, as well as heartless, and his sincerity is yet by no means proven. The reason why our imperial court has conferred an important nobility upon him is to commend his intention of mending his ways and stepping into line, and no more. As for you, general, your loyalty is clear like the light of day, your accomplishments stand aloft over the age; we expect you to join in consultations on 'the flavour of the cauldron' and to bring your aid and succour to the imperial house, so how could we treat you otherwise than with full confidence?"[5] [...] Mengxun then said: "But why does the court not enfeoff me with Zhangye right here, instead of enfeoffing me with Xihai far away?" [Zhang] Gou replied: "Zhangye is already part of our scheme, since by your own situation you already have it, general. The reason why faraway Xihai is conferred upon you is no doubt because we wish to see the General-in-chief's state become larger, that is all." At this Mengxun was much pleased: he accepted the appointments.[6]

Diplomacy was no doubt an area in which Chinese literati more naturally excelled than did the Qiang (or Lushui nomads), and one does not conceive that any but highly-educated literati fashioned the written documents that the *Jin shu* quotes *in extenso*, as issued on Juqu Mengxun's authority. One learns for instance that "Zhang Mu 張穆, from Dunhuang, had a comprehensive understanding of the classics and the histories, as well as a clear mind and an elegant

---

5 "Join in consultations on 'the flavour of the cauldron' 入諸鼎味," elsewhere (*JS* 35:1038) "help to adjust the flavour of the cauldron 助和鼎味," i.e. to deliberate on government policy; refers to Yi Yin 伊尹, who "took hold of a cauldron and a chopping board, and became (founding ruler of the Shang) Tang's 湯 (trad. r. 1766–1754 BCE) cook and butcher; and by dint of getting familiar with and accustomed to each other, Tang only then came to realise his wisdom, and so he employed him [as his Chief Minister]" (*Han Feizi* 韓非子 3, *Ershi'er zi* 二十二子 ed. [Shanghai 1986], p. 1120a).

6 *JS* 129:3193–3194: "蒙遜聞之，不悅，謂[使人]曰：傉檀上公之位，而身為侯者何也？[張]構對曰：傉檀輕狡不仁，款誠未著，聖朝所以加其重爵者，襃其歸善即敘之義耳。將軍忠貫白日，勳高一時，當入諸鼎味，匡贊帝室，安可以不信待也。[…] 蒙遜曰：朝廷何不即以張掖見封，乃更遠封溪海邪？構曰：張掖，規畫之內，將軍已有之。所以遠授西海者，蓋欲廣大將軍之國耳。蒙遜大悅，乃受拜。"

literary style, and was promoted and appointed Vice Director of the Central Secretariat (*zhongshu shilang* 中書侍郎) and entrusted with the charge over essential and confidential [affairs of state]."[7] Yet while naturally availing himself of Zhang Mu's services, Juqu Mengxun was also genuinely concerned about governing his Chinese subjects on terms that would agree with Chinese sensibilities. The following proclamation is a case in point:

> For nourishing the aged and humbly requesting them to speak [their wise counsels], [Lord] Wen of Jin 晉文公 (r. 636–628 BCE) reaped praise from his rank and file,[8] for it is by such means that one can attract and reverence men of brilliant and outstanding [talent] and bring about the blessings of a harmonious age. So much the more must I, bereft as I am of virtue and of a wit ill-suited to make farsighted arrangements, apply all my powers of thought and perception to [advisers'] forthright talk that gives me matter for reflection! Let my subordinate officials within and outside [my court] seek out and raise up [men of] worth and excellence, bring in great numbers of such 'gatherers of grass and firewood,' to assist me when I do not measure up.[9]

The response to this was gratifyingly positive, as when an auspicious omen was spotted (in the shape of a "twin tree") by the Magistrate of Yong'an, who reported the find in the following terms:

> "With different branches sharing one same trunk, it responds to the successful acculturation that these distant parts are witnessing; with separate stems joined to the same core, it affirms that between superiors and inferiors, there is not a trace of dissent. Truly it is a happy sign marking the coming of the highest way, a noble witness to our perfect union."

---

7 *JS* 129:3195: "以敦煌張穆博通經史，才藻清瞻，擢拜中書侍郎，委以機密之任。"

8 *Liji* 8 (Wen wang shizi 文王世子) 3 (*SSJ* p. 1405b, cf. transl. Legge p. 347) prescribes "nourishing the aged and humbly requesting them to speak [their wise counsels] 養老乞言," although Lord Wen of Jin has nothing to do with it. He appears, with his "rank and file 輿人," but in a different context, in *Zuo zhuan* Xi 28.3a (*SSJ* p. 1824b; transl. Stephen Durrant, Wai-yee Li and David Schaberg, *Zuo Tradition*: Zuo zhuan 左傳. *Commentary on the "Spring and Autumn Annals"* [Seattle 2016; hereafter *Zuo Tradition*], p. 411) — a *lapsus calami* by Juqu Mengxun's ghostwriter!

9 "To seek counsel from [people as lowly as] gatherers of grass and firewood 詢于芻蕘" is a line from Ode #254 (Ban 板), *SSJ* p. 549b. *JS* 129:3193: "養老乞言，晉文納輿人之誦，所以能招禮英奇，致時邕之美。況孤寡德，智不經遠，而可不思聞讜言以自境哉！內外羣僚，其各搜揚賢雋，廣進芻蕘，以匡孤不逮。"

BUILDING A STATE, PART 2

Mengxun reacted: "All this has been brought about by the selfless dedication of our two-thousand-bushel [prefects] and our magistrates, and hardly in response to my own feeble merits!"[10]

Promoting agriculture was of life-and-death importance, and Li Hao has been shown "[setting] up military colonies in Yumen and Yangguan, where he extended the lands under cultivation"; similarly, Juqu Mengxun is on record as having captured five hundred households during a raid on a local enemy east of Zhangye, in Fanhe 番禾 County (Wuwei Commandery), and relocating them as registered tax-paying peasants nearer to home.[11]

•••

After the fall of the Lüs' Later Liang to Later Qin in 403, Guzang was for a few years governed by a Yao Xing appointee, sent from Chang'an; between Later Qin and Juqu Mengxun's Northern Liang, relations were peaceful, if not cordial. This changed when, in 406, egged on by Yao Xing, Tufa Rutan of Southern Liang made a bid to take over Guzang — indeed, to buy it.[12] No love was lost between Tufa Rutan and Juqu Mengxun; war was inevitable. In 411, Juqu Mengxun went after Tufa Rutan and defeated him outside of Guzang's walls, chasing him back to his base of Ledu in Qinghai. In the confusion of the moment, the citizens of Guzang, smarting from the knowledge that Yao Xing had sold them to Tufa Rutan's tender mercies, had one of their own appeal to Li Hao, intimating that the oasis was ready to subject itself to Western Liang. That forced Juqu Mengxun to make a swift U-turn to conquer Guzang for himself. The city surrendered, and in 412, Juqu Mengxun made Guzang his new capital. Holding a victory ceremony in a grand hall constructed by Zhang Jun nearly a century earlier, "he feasted the civil and military commanders and officials in

10   *JS* 129:3194: "異枝同榦，遐方有齊化之應；殊本共心，上下有莫二之固。蓋至道之嘉祥，大同之美徵。蒙遜曰：此皆二千石令長匪躬濟時所致，豈吾薄德所能感之！"

11   *JS* 129:3193.

12   In 406, Tufa Rutan essentially bought Guzang from Yao Xing for 3000 horses and 30,000 sheep (*JS* 126:3149). The citizenry of Guzang sent an emissary to Chang'an to intercede with Yao Xing in a vain attempt to maintain the status quo. It is interesting how the emissary tries to convince Yao Xing with a counter-offer: "Would it not be wrong for you to hold people cheap and cattle dear? If the army and the state need horses, you have but to importune the Secretariat 尚書 with a single directive 符, and every one of the 3000 or so households in our province will contribute a horse; sent down at dawn, it shall be done by dusk — it is no trouble at all!" (*ZZTJ* 114:3590; not, apparently, in *JS* or *Shiliu guo chunqiu*).

120   CHAPTER 8

the Hall of Bright Reserve, and gave out gold and horses to them, each according to his rank."[13]

•••

In Guzang, Juqu Mengxun gave ample proof of his patronage of Confucian and Buddhist learning, which surely counts as a prominent nation-building gesture — although one would look for it in vain in his Documentary Record in the *Jin shu*. He held the well-known Confucian scholar Kan Yin 闞駰 "in high esteem" and assigned thirty clerks to his service, "whom [Kan Yin] supervised in collating texts and in establishing a [new] edition of the Philosophers in over 3000 scrolls (!)."[14] Buddhism, too, flourished under Northern Liang. As the *Wei shu* says:

> Before this, when Juqu Mengxun held Liangzhou, he too sympathised with the Law of the Buddha. There was a *śramaṇa* from Jibin 罽賓, Dharmarddhin 曇摩讖 (385–433), who was well versed in several *sūtras*. In Guzang, together with the *śramaṇa* Zhisong 智嵩 and others, he had translated more than ten *sūtras*, including the *Nirvāṇa-[sūtra]* 涅槃[經]. He also knew mantic arts and secret spells, and having successively spoken of the safety and danger of other states, his words had often proved true and on the mark. [Juqu] Mengxun frequently consulted him on affairs of state.[15]

The *sūtra* that the *Wei shu* singles out is the huge and very important *Mahāparinirvāṇa-sūtra* (*Daban niepanjing* 大般涅槃經, *T* 374), of which Dharmarddhin, who came from Kashmir, the Gandhāra cultural area, made the first Chinese translation in Guzang during his time there, from 414 to 421, "at the same time acting as a kind of court magician" in the service of Juqu Mengxun.[16] One recalls the seer Guo Nun at Lü Guang's court. The following anecdote is beneath the dignity of the *Jin shu*:

---

13   *JS* 129:3195 ("饗文武將士于謙光殿，班賜金馬有差。"). Further, *JS* 122:3069–3070,
      129:3193–3195; *Shiliu guo chunqiu* 93:1035, 95:1058–1061; *Song shu* 98:2413; Zhou Weizhou,
      Nan Liang yu Xi Qin, p. 324. For the Hall of Bright Reserve, see Ch. 11 note 20 below.
14   *Bei shi* 34:1267.
15   *Wei shu* 114:3032; for the translation, also of the *Chu sanzang jiji* anecdote hereunder, see
      my "Wei shu, chapter 114," pp. 70–71 and n. 63.
16   Erik Zürcher, "Tidings from the South: Chinese Court Buddhism and Overseas Relations
      in the Fifth Century AD," in Antonino Forte and Federico Masini, eds., *A Life Journey to*

Dharmarddhin once told Mengxun: "Ghosts are entering our emplacement (*juluo* 聚落, = Guzang?), and will no doubt bring much pestilence over us." [Juqu Meng]xun did not believe him, wanting to see them for himself to be convinced. Immediately Dharmarddhin worked his arts on [Juqu Meng]xun: [Juqu Meng]xun saw, and was terrified. Dharmarddhin said: "We must fast and purify ourselves in all sincerity, and with divine spells I will drive them off." He then read out spells for three days, and said to [Juqu Meng]xun: "The ghosts have gone north." Afterwards, across the border, tens of thousands died of pestilence. [Juqu Meng]xun came to treat [Dharmarddhin] with even more respect and paid him even greater honour. It happened that Tuoba Dao 拓跋燾 (408–452, Emp. Taiwu 太武皇帝 of Northern Wei, r. 423–452), lord of the savages of Wei, heard of his arts of the Dao; he sent an envoy (= Li Shun 李順, d. 442) to meet and invite him, and even to declare to [Juqu Meng]xun that "if he did not send Dharmarddhin away, there would be war." [Juqu Meng]xun judged that because his state was weak, he could not possibly resist [Wei's] order, but at the same time, he considered that with Dharmarddhin's many arts, he might plot against him to Wei's advantage; and, fearful and alarmed about either outcome, he thereupon secretly planned to eliminate him.[17]

Shilun 施崙, another Buddhist adept who produced one translation there in 373, was a Kuṣāṇa. These translation activities presuppose the presence of bilingual or multilingual interpreters, men of the calibre of, for instance, the prolific translator Zhu Fahu (Dharmarakṣa, fl. 265–313), from a Kushan family that had long settled in Dunhuang, or Zhu Fonian 竺佛念 from Liangzhou, a Chinese, of whom his biographer says that "as his family had lived west of the Yellow River for generations, he was well versed in foreign languages."[18] The fact that we have this remark about Zhu Fonian's multilingualism may well

---

the East: Sinological Studies in Memory of Giuliano Bertuccioli (1923–2001), Kyoto 2002, pp. 21–43 at p. 27.

17 Sengyou 僧祐 (445–518), comp., *Chu Sanzang jiji* 出三藏記集 (*Collected Notes on the Rendering of the Tripiṭaka*, T 2145; ed. Su Jinren 蘇晉仁 & Xiao Lianzi 蕭鍊子, Beijing 1995), 14:540.

18 See Paul Demiéville et al., eds., *Hôbôgirin: Dictionnaire encyclopédique du bouddhisme d'après les sources chinoises et japonaises — Fascicule annexe* (Tôkyô 1931), p. 132 (Dharmaṣena > Dharmarddhin), p. 149 (Shilun), p. 140 (Zhu Fahu = Dharmarakṣa). The correct Sanskrit equivalent of 曇摩讖/曇無讖, Dharmarddhin instead of Dharmaṣena (alt. Dharmakṣema), was established by Charles Willemen, *Buddhacarita. In Praise of Buddha's Acts* (Moraga, Calif. 2009), p. xv. Zhu Fonian: Zürcher, *Buddhist Conquest*, p. 202; *Chu Sanzang jiji* 13:524.

122   CHAPTER 8

imply that it was rare. With interaction between Chinese and non-Chinese communities in Liangzhou having developed for generations if not centuries, it seems safe to say that learning Chinese must always have looked like the way forward. What Juqu Mengxun himself spoke we can only guess at. It is plausible that he spoke Chinese with Chinese subjects, and a Qiang vernacular with his relatives, in the same way as Yu Huan, in his *Wei lüe*, says about the Di people: "Most of them know Chinese ('the language of our Central States 中國語') due to the fact that they live interspersed in our Central States. But when they return amidst their own tribe, then naturally [they use] their Di language 氐語."[19] "Acculturation," then, only went so far in either direction.

· · ·

How did Juqu Mengxun manage his own Lu River nomads or branch of the Qiang? He employed them in military posts in government, as has been mentioned. He harangued his tribal following on occasions — a community of over ten thousand menfolk, presumably, that made up the "various branches of his clan and of their relatives by marriage"; and when two of his uncles charged with administering the tribal heartland made themselves hated by their exactions, he did not hesitate to condemn them to death.[20]

Probably the glue that held his community of Lu River nomads together was of a ritual or religious nature. Twice Juqu Mengxun is shown at the head of his troops, leading them to make sacrifice to Lanmen Mountain 蘭門山 and Golden Mountain 金山; Golden Mountain was also where his followers gathered and ritually beheaded the magistrate of Linsong on the day Juqu Mengxun broke off his allegiance to Lü Guang. In all probability, the two mountains are the same: a Tang dynasty source leads one to identify it with present-day Dongdashan 東大山 some 30 km east of Zhangye City, 3616 m high at its highest point.[21]

---

19   Quoted in the commentary on *SGZ* 30:858. Another hint: the founder of Later Zhao, Shi Le, spoke Chinese but could not read or write it: Liu Yiqing 劉義慶 (403–444), *Shishuo xinyu* 世說新語 (*A New Account of Tales of the World*) 7.7. A son of Tufa Rutan, on the other hand, was capable, at the age of 13 *sui*, of writing a *fu* on the palaces of Gaochang: *Shiliu guo chunqiu* 90:1009 (from *Taiping yulan* ch. 600 f. 2a, 602 f. 6a [pp. 2701b, 2711b]).

20   *JS* 129:3189, 3193.

21   *JS* 129:3189, 3191, 3197. "Mount Lanmen" was also called Mount Heli 合黎山, or Mount Qiong(shi) 窮(石)山, in Zhangye (and more specifically, in Shandan County 山 [alt. 刪] 丹縣), according to Li Tai, *Kuodi zhi*, quoted in *Zhongwen da cidian* 中文大辭典 (Taipei 1973[1]) s.v. *heli* (11.3391–223). This mountain is today called Dongdashan.

After one of the mentioned sacrifices, "subsequently, [Juqu Mengxun] went along the western shores of [Western] Lake [西] 海 (= Qinghai Lake 青海湖) to the Salt Ponds and made sacrifice at the Temple to the Queen Mother of the West 西王母寺. In the temple, there is the Divine Diagram of the Dark Stone 玄石神圖, and having commanded his Vice Director of the Central Secretariat, Zhang Mu, to compose verses about it, the text was engraved in front of the temple. Thereupon he returned by way of Golden Mountain."[22] Both the *Han shu* and the *Shuijing zhu* mention a "cave 石室" of the Queen Mother of the West in Linqiang County (modern Huangyuan County 湟源縣, Qinghai, east of Qinghai Lake). One can only guess what the "Divine Diagram of the Dark Stone" may have been; the *Shuijing zhu* at this point mentions a "stone cauldron 石釜" — possibly the same object?[23]

Is it too far-fetched to deduce from this that the Lu River nomads, in sacrificing to a sacred mountain and to a sacred cave, venerated a "Mother Earth" deity in her womb-like cave, paired with a "Father Heaven" deity on Golden Mountain? One is reminded that the Tuoba ruling house of Northern Wei also had a sacred cave, now called Gaxian Grotto 嘎仙洞, in northeastern Inner Mongolia, some 1800 km northwest of their capital Pingcheng 平城 (= modern Datong 大同, Shanxi). It was supposed to be where "the Wei emperor's august ancestor and first ancestress" hailed from in long-past pre-dynastic times. In 443, the emperor Tuoba Dao sent his Vice Director of the Secretariat Li Chang 李敞 to the rock cavern to perform a sacrifice to Heaven and Earth and, "conjointly, to my august ancestor, the first *Qaghan* 可寒; and to my august ancestress, the first *Qatun* 可敦." The text of the invocation was carved on the cavern wall, to be rediscovered, perfectly intact, in 1980. In 443, after having solemnly read this prayer (which is in archaising Chinese) on the emperor's behalf, Li Chang and his retinue "cut off a birch tree and planted it upright to put the carcasses of the sacrificial animals on it; and then returned. Later on, the birch tree they had planted grew into a wood, so that the people there revered [the site] even more for its sanctity. Everyone said that it was a response by the numinous divinities (*lingqi* 靈祇), moved as they had been by [the prayer from] the State of Wei."[24]

---

22   *JS* 129:3198.

23   *HS* 28B:1611, *Shuijing zhu jiao* 2:47.

24   *Wei shu* 4B:95, 100:2224, 108A:2738–2739. The inscription recorded in *Wei shu* 108A.2738 is nearly identical to the one recovered in situ and first published by Mi Wenping 米文平, "Xianbei shishi de faxian yu chubu yanjiu 鮮卑石室的發現與初步研究," in *Wenwu* 文物 (1981) 2.

124 CHAPTER 8

There are other examples; as Denis Sinor remarks, "[there] are many references to caverns in which the Türks had lived prior to their obtaining political power [...; as the *Zhou shu* 周書 notes,] the kaghan of the Türks 'every year leads the nobles to the ancestral cavern to offer a sacrifice.' [...] This ancestral cavern was clearly a national shrine [...] centred on Tängri, the Sky (or Heaven), to which in the fifth month of the year the Türks were wont to offer sheep and horses in sacrifice."[25] Further, in the Qiang origin myth recorded in the *History of Later Han*, a cave also plays a role:[26]

> The Qiang Wuyi Yuanjian 無弋爰劍 was taken into custody by Qin in the time of Lord Li of Qin 秦厲公 (r. 476–443 BCE) and made a slave. To what division of the Rong [Wuyi] Yuanjian belonged is unknown. Later he managed to escape and, hard-pressed by the Qin men who pursued him, got rid of them by hiding in a cave in the rocks. The Qiang relate that when [Wuyi] Yuanjian had only just hid in the cave, his Qin pursuers set fire to it, but an apparition that looked like a tiger shielded him from the flames, so that he did not die. After he got out, he met a girl in the wilds whose nose had been cut off, and they became man and wife. The girl, ashamed of her appearance, covered her face with her loose-hanging hair, and the Qiang people have since adopted this as a custom. Subsequently, they both absconded into the area of the Three Rivers. The various Qiang tribes, seeing that [Wuyi] Yuanjian had not died despite being subjected to fire, marvelled at his supernatural powers, and all together served him with reverential fear, putting him forward as their leader. Since between the Yellow and the Huang rivers, the five field crops are in short supply, while birds and beasts abound, hunting used to be their main occupation. It was [Wuyi] Yuanjian who taught them farming and stock breeding, for which they revered him, and gave him their confidence, with ever-increasing numbers of tribal people in their simple huts attaching themselves to him. The Qiang call a slave a *wuyi*, and because Yuanjian was once a slave, they used this term in front of his name. His descendants have held the leader's position generation after generation. His great-grandson Ren 忍 [...] remained in Huangzhong 湟中 ...

... which is precisely where the misnamed "cave [temple] of the Queen Mother of the West" was to be found. More than this, it may not be prudent to

---

25 Denis Sinor, "The Establishment and Dissolution of the Türk Empire," in Sinor, *The Cambridge History of Early Inner Asia*, pp. 285–316 at pp. 296, 314.

26 *HHS* 87:2875.

BUILDING A STATE, PART 2

extrapolate from the few hints that *Jin shu*, ch. 129 contains concerning Juqu Mengxun's cultural appurtenance.

• • •

It remains to be noted that in Guzang (in 412), Juqu Mengxun "arrogated the position of Prince of Hexi 河西王 for himself. He declared an amnesty within his dominions and changed his era title (from Yong'an) to Xuanshi 玄始. He set up an official apparatus in accordance with the precedent set by Lü Guang when he became Prince of the Three Rivers 三河王 (in 389).[27] He had the palace halls repaired and various watchtowers erected atop the city wall's gates. He established his son, Zhengde 政德, as his heir, and conferred on him the positions of General-in-chief of the Defence Guard and Overseer of the Secretariat (*lu shangshu shi* 錄尚書事)."

Certainly, Lü Guang had done much the same twenty years earlier, ultimately with disastrous consequences, as the historian surely intends readers to recall. But Lü Guang, although he assumed imperial prerogatives by creating central government-style ministries and by setting his own calendar, did not appoint his son and heir effectively prime minister. Qifu Qiangui of Western Qin had done the same with his son in 409, but there was no precedent for it in the Han or Jin dynasties. The appointment is of a piece with the prominent role in government of so many of Juqu Mengxun's relatives, both in military and in civil positions.

---

27   At this point in time, *js* 122:3059 merely says that Lü Guang established his officialdom "from *chenglang* 丞郎 down." According to Hucker, *A Dictionary of Official Titles*, #501, *chenglang* was an unofficial reference to vice ministers, but only "from T'ang on." *Chenglang* could however be read as an abbreviation of the Han (and later) titles *zuo/you cheng* 左右丞 (Assistant Director of the Left/Right) and *shilang* 侍郎 (Vice Director). Possibly these were equivalent to a prime minister and his deputy, and a number of ministers. Seven years later, in 396, the titles were upgraded to precisely this (*js* 122:3060, and p. 86 above).

CHAPTER 9

Relations with Eastern Jin

Li Hao's *Jin shu* biography prominently features two memorials (*biao* 表) that he sent by special courier to the imperial court in Jiankang, one dated to 405, the second to 407, sent because the first one had remained unanswered and perhaps never reached its destination. These are quite elaborate documents. The great connoisseur of refined literature Liu Xie 劉勰 (ca. 465–522) says that "during the first years of the Jin dynasty, Zhang Hua 張華 (232–300) was the leader among writers of this genre" because his memorials were "comprehensive in reasoning and succinct in language" and because "in elaborating ideas and in comparing facts, he always succeeded in producing a matched pair." Indeed, the first formal characteristic, also of Li Hao's memorials, is that they are couched in parallel prose (*pianti* 駢體). The prime purpose of a *biao* was to "express one's own feelings," but with a particular audience, namely the emperor, in mind: "to lay bare one's innermost feelings into the full light of day, so as in this way to requite and extol [favours received from] the royal court."[1] In other words, deep gratitude for imperial kindnesses received moved the writer of a memorial to speak out with the greatest possible sincerity, in the confident hope that this would forge an even closer mutual bond between subject and sovereign; for as a proverb had it, "one who brings utter sincerity to bear upon a subject can dissolve even metal and stone."[2] Of course, such a prescription, if carried out literally, would make composing a memorial a very risky undertaking. Therefore, no doubt, it was not undertaken lightly. What purpose did it serve?

After Western Jin was lost, Li Hao writes, and Sima Rui chose to abandon the Central Plain, the Zhang clan's Former Liang had saved Chinese civilisation from going under in the north; eventually, however, "the Five Barbarians" had occupied northern territory, aided by an adverse turn of the wheel of fortune.

---

1   Liu Xie, *Wenxin diaolong* 文心雕龍 (*The Literary Mind and the Carving of Dragons*), ed. Zhou Zhenfu 周振甫, *Wenxin diaolong jinyi* 今譯 (Beijing 1986) 22.2–4, pp. 204–208 ("逮晉初筆札，則張華為偶 […] 理周辭要，引義比事，必得其偶"; "表以陳請" [V. Shih nonetheless translates as if the text read 陳情]; "原夫章表之為用也，所以對揚王庭，昭明心曲"); cf. transl. Vincent Yu-chung Shih, *The Literary Mind and the Carving of Dragons* (Hong Kong 1983), pp. 247–251.

2   Wang Chong 王充 (27–97 CE), *Lunheng* 論衡 (*Discourses Weighed in the Balance*) 5 (Ganxu pian 感虛篇), ed. Peking University (Beijing 1979) p. 301 ("精誠所加，金石為虧"); also, proverbially, in *HHS* 42:1447 ("精誠所加，金石為開").

© DOMINIK DECLERCQ, 2025 | DOI:10.1163/9789004727380_010

RELATIONS WITH EASTERN JIN

If Eastern Jin forces did not at once manage to oust them, that was not for lack of ambition on the part of the current emperor An; indeed, Li Hao's own clan, past as well as present, knew all too well how good the imperial house had been to them, and so Li Hao (though he had admittedly not waited for the emperor's permission) knew he did the right thing in doing his own bit for the reunification of the Jin realm. That said, without military action by Eastern Jin to seal the final victory, Li Hao's effort might as yet remain fruitless and, just as Liangzhou now had a "Western Liang" calendar of its own forced upon it by circumstances, Li Hao might in that eventuality quite irrevocably drift apart from the Jin. This sums up the first memorial. It runs in full:

> In the first year of the Yixi 義熙 era (of Eastern Jin = 405), Li Hao changed his own era title to Jianchu 簡初, and sent his chamberlains (*sheren* 舍人) Huang Shi 黃始 and Liang Xing 梁興 on an incognito mission to the [Eastern Jin] palace [in Jiankang], bearing this memorial with them:[3]

> In the past, when the Han's fortunes had come to an end, three states came to confront each other like a tripod's feet, until, in the predestined course of midmost Heaven, the numbers favoured August Jin 皇晉. Its Lofty Progenitor 高祖 (= Sima Yi 司馬懿, 179–251) having revealed [the nascent Jin empire's] grand foundations, the Effulgent 景 and Cultured 文 [Emperors] (= Sima Shi 師, 208–255, and Sima Zhao 昭, 211–265) added glory to the imperial enterprise. Their successor, the Martial 武 [Emperor] (= Sima Yan 炎, 236–290, r. 265–290), accepted the demise [of the Cao-Wei state, when its last emperor Cao Huan 曹奐 (246–302, r. 260–265) abdicated]; then, distant peoples who used to be kept at bay through sheer intimidation or had no discernible bond with us at all collectively submitted: all six directions shared in the same vivifying breeze, the whole universe being uniformly suffused by it. Yet when the Complaisant Emperor 惠皇 (= Sima Zhong, r. 290–307) lost the reins of government, and opportunistic ministers threw norm-abiding order into turmoil; when the Cordial 懷 and the Hapless Emperors (= Sima Chi 熾 [284–313, r. 307–311] and Sima Ye [r. 313–317]) found themselves in perilous and precarious circumstances, covered by dust [in exile] abroad: then did the suspended images [of sun and moon] come unstuck above, and the nine dependencies [constituting the realm and its borderlands] split

---

3 I give here and hereafter the Chinese text of the more literary sections of *Jin shu* 87, Li Hao's biography.

apart below. Full of longing, one looks back at [how things were before];[4] all under Heaven share in the regret.[5]

Let me now humbly consider how the Middle Ancestor, the August Inaugurating Emperor 中宗元皇帝 (= Sima Rui, r. 318–323), continuing the Mandate based on Heaven's support, moved his imperial person to the other side of the Yangtse river, so that Jing and Yang 荊揚 (provinces; from modern-day Hubei to Jiangsu) basked in all-encompassing solicitude while the five capitals turned into a weed-choked morass.[6] It was because of this that the Defender-in-chief, the Martial Duke of Xiping 西平武公 [Zhang] Gui (r. as Governor of Liangzhou, and eventually as Duke of Xiping, 301–314), at the beginning of the Yuankang 元康 era (291–299), at that juncture of tumult and turmoil, having duly received his charge from authoritative quarters [in Luoyang, capital of Western Jin], came forth to console this province of ours: it was succoured by his renown and strategy, so that his fame resounded all over the world. The Brilliant 明 [Duke] (= Zhang Shi, r. 314–320) and the Accomplished 成 [Duke] (= Zhang Mao, r. 320–325) succeeded him,[7] and did not neglect [Zhang Gui's] earlier ambition: guided by his long banner, they continued to open up Tripartite Qin 三秦 (= modern-day Shaanxi province) and, resolute of will and militarily strong, extended the borders of their domain ten thousand *li*. When the Cultured 文 [Duke] (= Zhang Jun, r. 324–346, as "Prince of Liang 涼王" from 345)[8] and the Mighty 桓 [Duke] (= Zhang Zhonghua, r. 346–353) acceded to the ruling position, there had been successive generations rich in virtue. They incorporated the area west of the Passes 關西 into their domain, and their civilising influence reached to the slopes of Kun[lun] 崑[崙]; far and near they had loyal vassals, who for ages were punctilious in offering tribute. The far-reaching sway of Jin power, it is true, has been what this province of ours has ultimately relied

---

4   A quote from *Shijing* #203 (Da dong 大東), *ssj* p. 460b; transl. Waley p. 318: "Full of longing I look for them 眷言顧之; In a flood my tears flow."

5   *js* 87:2259-2260: "昔漢運將終，三國鼎峙，鈞天之曆，數鍾皇晉。高祖闡鴻基，景文弘帝業，嗣武受終，要荒率服，六合同風，宇宙齊貫。而惠皇失馭，權臣亂紀，懷愍屯邅，蒙塵于外，懸象上分，九服下裂，眷言顧之，普天同憾。"

6   The five capitals: Chang'an, Qiao 譙, Xuchang 許昌, Ye 鄴 and Luoyang, all in the north. See Pei Songzhi's commentary on *sgz* 2:77, note 3.

7   "Brilliant and Accomplished 明盛": Zhang Shi's posthumous title was "Brilliant Duke 昭公," with the synonym *ming* 明 taking the place of *zhao* 昭 here to observe the taboo on Sima Zhao's personal name. For *sheng* 盛, read *cheng* 成, Zhang Mao's posthumous title "Accomplished Duke 成公." See *js* 87:2272 note 4.

8   *zztj* 97:3068.

RELATIONS WITH EASTERN JIN 129

upon.[9] The Area Commander-in-chief and General-in-chief [Zhang] Tianxi was possessed of a noble bearing and inherited a vocation [to rule] of seven generations' standing. He aspired to be of succour in the troubles of his time, and to outdo his meritorious predecessors in glorious achievements; but in mid-age, disaster struck, armed raiders invaded the borders, and however long [the Zhang clan's] awesome might may have lasted, [Zhang Tianxi] was finally unable to equal the praise that [his predecessors] had earned. Withstanding troops from seven provinces with an army raised from just one, his soldiers found themselves defenceless, their force spent, and his state was consequently lost.[10]

I have heard that as successive time spans supplant one another, their last remaining years get compressed towards the end, and the emergence of an emperor or a king invariably occurs in one such open position. It is for that reason that Gonggong 共工 muddled up the interpretable signs in the interval between the reigns of the Yellow [Emperor] 黃[帝] and [Shen]nong [神]農, or that Qin 秦, as well as Xiang [Yu] 項[羽], could usurp [a ruler's position] and encroach [upon the normal course of history] during the transition from Zhou to Han. In both cases, the opportunity did not come around a second time; and "when [the Cauldron] overturned its pottage," misfortune was [inevitably] the result.[11] It has already been a hundred years since Rong and Di people began to infringe upon Chinese territory, but the turning point at which the Five Barbarians came presumptuously to take over [formal power] from us has [so far] been only of minute duration: the whole world holds its breath, anxious

---

9   *JS* 87:2260: "伏惟中宗元皇帝基天紹命，遷幸江表，荊揚蒙弘覆之祚，吾都為荒榛之藪。故太尉、西平武公軌當元康之初，屬擾攘之際，受命典方，出撫此州，威略所振，聲蓋海內。明盛繼統，不損前志，長旌所指，仍闕三秦，義立兵強，拓境萬里。文桓嗣位，奕葉載德，囊括關西，化被崐裔，遐邇款藩，世修職貢。晉德之遠揚，繄此州是賴。"

10 *JS* 87:2260: "大都督、大將軍天錫以英挺之姿，承七世之業，志匡時難，剋隆先勳，而中年降災，兵寇侵境，皇威遐邈，同獎弗及，以一方之師抗七州之衆，兵孤力屈，社稷以喪。"

11 A quote from *Yijing* Hexagram 50, *Ding* 鼎 (The Cauldron), Fourth Yang; transl. Richard John Lynn, *The Classic of Changes* (New York 1994), p. 455. "As in a cauldron food is cooked to nourish people, so will a sage sovereign promote humane and righteous government to teach his realm by example," writes Zheng Xuan 鄭玄 (127–200), quoted in Li Daoping 李道平 (*juren* 舉人 1818), *Zhou Yi jijie zuanshu* 周易集解纂疏 (Beijing 1994), p. 444; and woe betide that sovereign if "[the] Cauldron breaks its legs and overturns all its pottage" (transl. Lynn), for, as Yu Fan 虞翻 (170–239) explains, "it means that he is incompetent" (*Zhou Yi jijie zuanshu*, p. 449).

about [what the Jin] court [intends to do].[12] Thus, when the [Jin] army encamped in Dongguan, there was not a man in Zhao or Wei who did not stand on tiptoe [hoping to be liberated];[13] at the time of the great triumph south of the River Huai, three sides (i.e. northern entities) joyfully craned their necks [in the expectation that the north would be recovered].[14]

I do believe Your Majesty's way of government is consonant with that of [the Xia ruler] Shaokang, and that your virtue is on a par with that of [the Han emperor] Guangwu;[15] you have succeeded to your position to

---

12   The "[Jin] court": literally, Xiangwei 象魏. In the Spring-and-Autumn period, "[the] Xiangwei were the twin towers of the Pheasant Gate (*zhi men* 雉門), which stood outside the Ancestral Temple [of Lu 魯]": see *Zuo Tradition*, p. 1850 note 72.

13   In 347, a Jin army commanded by Huan Wen conquered Li Shi's 李勢 (r. 344–347) state of Cheng Han 成漢 (304–347), centred on Chengdu 成都 (*ZZTJ* 97:3073–3075). On his way back into modern Hubei, Huan Wen passed through the territory of what is now Shiyan City 十堰市; there, "after Huan Wen had pacified Shu 蜀, Jinchang Commandery 晉昌郡 was created for refugees from (Li Shi's) Han [state] in Ba 巴漢, with jurisdiction over ten counties [including] Dongguan 東關" (*JS* 14:438). Dongguan corresponds to modern Zhuxi County 竹溪縣. This resounding exploit appeared to announce that Eastern Jin might reconquer all its lost territory in the north: that is no doubt how the people ruled by Shi Hu's Later Zhao (319–351) and by Ran Min's 冉閔 ephemeral state of Wei 魏 (350–352) saw it. As if to prove them right, in 351, Huan Wen marched north again in order, as he says himself, "to wipe out Zhao and Wei" (*JS* 98:2570), but this campaign was aborted (*ZZTJ* 99:3120, *JS* 8:198, 98:2569).

14   The "great triumph south of the River Huai 淮南大捷" is shorthand for the battle of the River Fei in 383. Among other examples of this circumlocution, see e.g. *ZZTJ* 108:3424: there, the *śramaṇa* Zhi Tanmeng 支曇猛 tries to dissuade Murong Lin 慕容麟 (d. 397) of Later Yan from battling Tuoba Gui, ruler of Northern Wei (r. 386–409), at Shenhebei 參合陂 in 395. "Fu [Jian] with an army a million strong was defeated *south of the River Huai*, precisely because he trusted in his numbers and underestimated the enemy, and failed to believe the signs from Heaven!" The "three sides" who hoped that the 383 victory would lead to the reunification of China by Eastern Jin would be Eastern Jin itself, the Chinese elites suffering under the "barbarian yoke" in Former Qin, and Liangzhou, at that point ruled by its governor Liang Xi, appointed by Fu Jian. *JS* 87:2260: "臣聞曆數相推，歸餘於終，帝王之興，必有閏位。是以共工亂象於黃農之間，秦項篡竊於周漢之際，皆機不轉踵，覆餗成凶。自戎狄陵華，已涉百齡，五胡僭襲，期運將杪，四海顒顒，懸心象魏。故師次東關，趙魏莫不企踵；淮南大捷，三方欣然引領。"

15   Sima Zhen 司馬貞 (fl. 713–742), in his commentary on *Shiji* 2:86, n. 1, quotes a passage of the *Zuo zhuan* that partially corresponds to Ai 1.2 in the received text (*Zuo Tradition*, p. 1835): "When [the Xia ruler] Xiang 相 was extinguished by Ao 澆, [his consort] Lady Min 后緡 returned to Reng 有仍, where she gave birth to Shaokang 少康. The Xia minister Mi 靡 [...] put Shaokang on the throne (trad. r. 1972–1912 BCE), and Shaokang extinguished Ao in Guo 過," thus restoring the Xia Dynasty. Liu Xiu, Emperor Guangwu of Later Han, similarly restored the Han Dynasty's fortunes after the interregnum of Wang Mang.

RELATIONS WITH EASTERN JIN 131

extend the [Mandate of] Heaven, and your one ambition is to free all of the lands of Xia 函夏 from anything that sullies it. As for this province, it has been staunchly loyal [to the Jin court] for generations. Because my great-great-grandfather Yong, Prefect of Dongguan 東莞, and my great-grandfather Rou, Prefect of Beidi, received honours from the previous [Western Jin] court, and had a part, however insignificant, in the great concerns of their time; because my great-uncle the Marquis of Changning 長寧侯, Zhuo, General of Dragon-like Cavalry and Prefect of Guangjin 廣晉, and my late grandfather the Marquis of Anshi Precinct, Yan, General of the Martial Guard and Prefect of Tianshui, supported and assisted Liangzhou, distinguished themselves in Qin and Long (= Shaanxi and Gansu), were raised up through signal favour and served the court 天府 assiduously; [because of all this,] the officials in my employ, irresponsible and useless as they are, on their own initiative, and following the precedent set by Dou Rong, forcibly elevated me, in the name of righteousness, to Area Commander-in-chief, General-in-chief, Duke of Liang and concurrently Governor of the two provinces of Qin and Liang, as well as Commandant Protector of the Qiang.[16]

I believe that because Jing-Chu 荊楚 abolished its tribute [due to the Zhou court], [Lord] Huan of Qi 齊桓[公] raised an army at Shaoling 召陵;[17] and because the feudal lords lacked respect [for him], [Lord] Wen of Jin 晉文[公] started the battle of Chengpu 城濮.[18] Whoever employs capable and meritorious people to give lustre to the land under our feet may count his achievement as high, as if he had buttressed the whole empire; all nine [of the empire's] divisions shall be beholden to his grandiose project, and the *Spring-and-Autumn Annals* [already] speaks with

---

16 *JS* 87:2260: "伏惟陛下道協少康，德侔光武，繼天統位，志清函夏。至如此州，世篤忠義，臣之羣僚以臣高祖東莞太守雍、曾祖北地太守柔荷寵前朝，參忝時務，伯祖龍驤將軍、廣晉太守、長寧侯卓，亡祖武衞將軍、天水太守、安世亭侯弇毗佐涼州，著功秦隴，殊寵之隆，勒于天府，妄臣無庸，輒依竇融故事，迫臣以義，上臣大都督、大將軍、涼公、領秦涼二州牧、護羌校尉。"

17 In 656 BCE, Lord Huan of Qi, the first hegemon, raised troops against the state of Chu (Jing-Chu is an alternative name for the state of Chu), ostensibly because its "tribute of bundled *mao* grass did not arrive" at the Zhou court. But the allies led by Lord Huan soon realised that Chu's armies were no match for them, and the same year a covenant was sworn between the two sides, at Shaoling. See *Zuo zhuan* Xi 4.1, *Zuo Tradition*, pp. 265–267.

18 In 632 BCE, Chong'er 重耳, Prince of Jin 晉侯 (posthumously Lord Wen of Jin) won a victory against the Chu army at Chengpu, and was subsequently recognised as hegemon. See *Zuo zhuan* Min 閔 28.3, *Zuo Tradition*, pp. 409–421.

indulgence [of such a one] issuing orders on his own authority.[19] His merit will crown his epoch and his fame will be transmitted for a thousand years. The more so at this time, when the imperial residence has not yet been recovered, and all of China is thrown into turmoil; when [the land] that Yu the Great 大禹 traversed has wholly turned into Rong barbarian wasteland; when of our holy mountains, the Five Sacred Peaks, three are defiled by Di barbarians, and when, of the famous capitals of our Nine Provinces, Yi 夷 barbarians have fouled seven of them. Truly what Xin You once predicted has now come to pass.[20]

That is why I, your insignificant subject, pound my breast and am short of breath, forget to sleep as well as to eat, in such anxiety that it tears at my liver, with no time to breathe peacefully. However distant the Yangtse and Liangzhou are from each other, my sense of righteousness and sincerity is all the more intimate; for it is enough that the same mores connect us, for us to be truly as close as lips and teeth. Although my name is not connected with the Celestial Terrace (= the central government) and my capabilities have not made their mark on the world, nonetheless, relying on the remnant glow of the aura won by a succession of ancestors, my sense of righteousness is not in the least less than theirs, and it serves me to examine the great tasks [that lie before us] and, always heeding collective advice, to take up these matters even unto the death. The shafts [of the cart I am now pushing], it is true, are weak, and the charge heavy, and I fear not to be adequate to the majestic duty. In the past, in the Spring-and-Autumn period, the feudal lords paid formal homage to the Zhou court, yet every state proclaimed its own era title according to which it issued its seasonal commands. Today, as the Celestial Terrace is

---

19 The *Zuo zhuan*, not properly speaking the *Chunqiu* 春秋 (*Spring-and-Autumn Annals*), does so at Min 2.7a: a general necessarily "issues orders on his own 專命," because "troops are in the keeping of the one who issues the orders 師在制命而已," and for that same reason, no heir apparent to the throne should be entrusted with command over an army, since "if the heir apparent requests orders from his father, then he will not be authoritative 禀命則不威," while "for him to issue orders on his own is to be unfilial 專命則不孝" (*Zuo Tradition*, p. 243).

20 *Zuo zhuan*, Xi 22.4: "Earlier, when King Ping had moved the capital to the east, Xin You 辛有 had gone to Yichuan and, upon seeing someone with unbound hair offering a sacrifice in the countryside, had said, 'Within one hundred years, this likely will be the Rong's! Ritual propriety has been lost here already!'" (*Zuo Tradition*, p. 353.) *Js* 87:2261: "臣以為荊楚替貢，齊桓興召陵之師，諸侯不恭，晉文起城濮之役，用能勳光踐土，業隆一匡，九域賴其弘猷，春秋恕其專命，功冠當時，美垂千祀。況今帝居未復，諸夏昏墊，大禹所經，奄為戎墟，五嶽神山，狄汙其三，九州名都，夷穢其七，辛有所言，於茲而驗。"

RELATIONS WITH EASTERN JIN

distant and remote, no official first day of the year has been assigned, and so for issuing orders and effecting commands, there has been no means to give them a date; hence, on my own initiative, I have let our year count begin from Jianchu, so as to show reverence to the standards set by the state. I hope for the support that the potency of [Your Majesty's] favour will bring me, so that I may exercise full authority over this one corner [of the empire]; so, also, that my righteousness and sincerity may make their mark on [Your Majesty,] whom I hold to be our Heaven, and so that [Your Majesty's] mysterious charisma may fan out on the Nine Regions [that constitute the empire]. If it costs me my life, if my body turns to ashes, passion shall move me even in death.[21]

The second memorial was sent in 407, since there was no reply to the first one. In 407, Li Hao sent the *śramaṇa* Faquan 法泉 incognito to Jiankang to deliver it. What else could possibly have happened, after three more years of being separated incommunicado, but that Li Hao had drifted further apart from Eastern Jin? Indeed, the memorial starts with that observation, urging Emperor An to peruse a copy of the earlier memorial (thoughtfully presented together with this one, in case it had been lost) so as to acquaint himself with background events of which he may have been unaware. The memorial also concludes with a promise to keep the emperor informed of future events. But between the exordium and the peroration, so to speak, it is hard to conceal that Li Hao really lords it over Liangzhou, and has even given two of his sons civil and military commands that were for a national government, and not for him to bestow. The way to render this palatable to the court in Jiankang was to emphasise that his objectives were aligned with those of the imperial state: he hoped to unseat Juqu Mengxun, he had grain reserves aplenty should hostilities commence, he propagated Confucian learning, and in any case, he would not take rash action unless the emperor told him to. This is the full text:

Distantly divided from you by rivers and mountains, I am denied the stairway I would climb to pay you homage; I can but crane my neck towards the skyline, or stand on tiptoe [peering] towards your remote region.

---

21 *JS* 87:2261: "微臣所以叩心絕氣，忘寢與食，雕肝焦慮，不遑寧息者也。江涼雖遠，義誠密邇，風雲苟通，實如脣齒。臣雖名未結于天臺，量未著于海內，然憑賴累祖寵光餘烈，義不細辭，以稽大務，輒順羣議，亡身即事。轅弱任重，懼忝威命。昔在春秋，諸侯宗周，國皆稱元，以布時令。今天臺邈遠，正朔未加，發號施令，無以紀數，輒年冠建初，以崇國憲。冀杖寵靈，全制一方，使義誠著于所天，玄風扇于九壤，殉命灰身，隕越慷慨。"

I humbly consider that as Your Majesty ascended the throne at the [predestined] moment, your immense good fortune hails from Heaven. In the past *yisi* 乙巳 year (= 405), I Your subject, yielding to the collective opinion [of my advisers], provisionally took to govern this peripheral enclosure; at the time, I dispatched my chamberlain Huang Shi bearing my memorial to communicate my sincere [devotion to the Jin court], but given the hazards and the barrenness of the lengthy road, I wonder if it arrived? Wu 吳 (= modern-day Jiangsu) and Liang 涼 being so far from each other, and with hornets and scorpions infesting the routes, there has been no way for a tribute envoy carrying local rarities to go and lay these at your feet; but I have respectfully made a copy of my previous memorial to you in the hope that it may be brought to [Your Majesty's] attention.

In the year in question, I made my army advance to Jiuquan to startle the Rong [barbarians] in Guangping 廣平[22] and perchance root out that evil growth of tackweed; but before my awe-inspiring teachings could be put to good effect, the wily savages, untameable as they are, had ensconced themselves in their nests and lairs and barred my road forward. I then bethought myself that all our affairs were only just getting underway and that the granaries and treasury were far from full; hence I ceased the military effort and put down my suit of armour, devoting myself henceforth to [promoting] agriculture and [by setting up an academy] to nurturing scholars. Time passes, the seasons speed by, and imperceptibly, three years are already behind us; the days I have been taking up my sword, sighing with exasperation, have turned into years. Today, however, there are sufficient reserve supplies and ample weaponry; from the west I am summoning soldiers from our walled city [of Dunhuang], from the north I am calling up Dingling troops, and I hope that [with my armies and] relying on the authority of the [Jin] state, I shall be able to roll up all of [the area west of the] Yellow River and Long 河隴 (= Western Gansu) as if into a mat, and raise our banner in Qin-Chuan 秦川 (= Shaanxi and Gansu). I do but await [Your Majesty's] directive by way of an edict to put all my loyalty and integrity at your disposal, should even death ensue.

I would further have Your Majesty know that the borders of this province are situated far away, and that as long as these powerful bandits are not eliminated, it is necessary that garrison deputy [commanders] be put in charge of the different detachments [of the army] that are either being dispatched or kept stationed at base. Each time, I engage my eldest son

---

22   Unidentified.

Li Xin to supervise all military affairs pertaining to the van (*jian qianfeng zhu junshi* 監前鋒諸軍事), overseeing and directing the front army as General of the Pacification Army and Commandant Protector of the Qiang and serving me as vanguard. As Dunhuang is moreover a large commandery — with a sizeable army needed to control the Western Regions and exercise administrative jurisdiction over myriad square miles, which is the fundamental [task] for the army and the state [government] — each time, I give my second son, Li Rang, the charge of General Pacifying the North, Commandant of Western Yi and Prefect of Dunhuang in order to govern and direct the slopes of Kun[lun] and bring peace to these alien regions. My other sons are all serving in the army, commanding soldiers. As for me, Your subject has the overall supervision of the whole organisation; I am fully dedicated to contributing my effort, and to giving my orders [to the army] as the situation demands. Of further developments, I shall keep Your Majesty informed.[23]

As a matter of fact, Juqu Mengxun likewise saw to it that a memorial of his reached Eastern Jin. In Juqu Mengxun's as well as in Li Hao's case, diplomatic protocol appears to have dictated that someone with the post of chamberlain deliver the message. Also similar to Li Hao is the way Juqu Mengxun renders the people of Zhangye responsible for the usurped position he now finds himself in *vis-à-vis* the court in Jiankang; he calls himself, interestingly, "leader of an alliance (*mengzhu* 盟主)" between different populations. As with Li Hao, this delicate admission is at once countered with a vow to come to the aid of Eastern Jin once Emperor An is ready to don the mantle of "restorer" of the Jin empire. Even the rhetorical flourish designating Emperor An as such is identical to that in Li Hao's first memorial.

---

23 *JS* 87:2263-2264: "江山悠隔，朝宗無階，延首雲極，翹企遐方。伏惟陛下應期踐位，景福自天。臣去乙巳歲順從羣議，假統方城，時遣舍人黃始奉表通誠，遙途嶮曠，未知達不？吳涼懸邈，蜂蠆充衢，方珍貢使，無由展御，謹副寫前章，或希簡達。臣以其歲進師酒泉，戒戎廣莽，庶攘茲穢，而點虜恣睢，未率威教，憑守巢穴，阻臣前路。竊以諸事草創，倉帑未盈，故息兵按甲，務農養士。時移節邁，荏苒三年，撫劍歎憤，以日成歲。今資諸己足，器械已充，西招城郭之兵，北引丁零之眾，冀憑國威，席卷河隴，揚旌秦川，承望詔旨，盡節竭誠，隕越為效。又臣州界迥遠，勍寇未除，當須鎮副為行留部分，輒假臣世子士業監前鋒諸軍事、撫軍將軍、護羌校尉，督攝前軍，為臣先驅。又敦煌郡大眾殷，制御西域，管轄萬里，為軍國之本，輒以次子讓為寧朔將軍、西夷校尉、敦煌太守，統攝崑裔，輯寧殊方。自餘諸子，皆在戎間，率先士伍。臣總督大綱，畢在輸力，臨機制命，動靖續聞。"

Since Heaven above brought down calamity and all [the Jin Empire] between the four seas was divided and collapsed, your numinous radiance has secluded itself upon the southern fringes [of the realm] while the common folk have been engulfed by unsightly savages. Your Majesty has the accumulated brightness of a run of sagely [predecessors]; your way [of government] surpasses that of Zhou and Han: whoever is attained by your blissful, [civilising] influence finds his heart's refuge in you, [should they even reside] on the furthest borders of [your realm's] eight sides. Although I, your subject, with my hair streaming down my back,[24] at the frontiers' edge, lack any gift that would make me stand out in our age, nonetheless, I have — undeservedly — been pushed forward by the remaining [Chinese] population right of the Yellow River to be the leader of our alliance. My forebears have for generations been blessed with [past emperors'] gracious favour, and though we have traversed both smooth and rugged terrain, we have unswervingly carried out our duty, our heads bowed towards the [imperial] sun and our heart loyal towards the ruling house.[25] Last winter, Zhu Lingshi 朱齡石, the (Eastern Jin) Governor of Yizhou (379–418), sent an envoy to present himself to me, and that is when, for the first time, I was made privy to tidings from [Your Majesty's] court. Having received [the news], then, that Chariot and Horse General Liu Yu 劉裕 (356–422) feeds his horse and brandishes his halberd [in preparation for battle], having taken [the fate of] the Central Plain to heart, truly one may say that Heaven seconds the Great Jin in having exceptionally brought forth this brilliant support [to the imperial cause]. I have learnt that when Shaokang uplifted [the fortunes of] the Great Xia [Dynasty],[26] and when [Emperor] Guangwu restored the Han's [dynastic] undertaking, both rose up, sword in hand, with less than a battalion for an army, yet were able to achieve exploits on a par with Heaven, such as celebrated in [the Ode] "Our chariots are strong."[27] Your

---

24 As in the Qiang foundation myth, p. 124 above: "the Qiang people have since adopted [loose-hanging hair] as a custom."

25 Loosely quoted from *Shangshu* Zhou 25 (Kang wang zhi gao 康王之誥), *SSJ* p. 244b: "Although your persons may be outside [in your fiefs], may your hearts be nowhere but in the royal house 雖爾身在外，乃心罔不在王室."

26 For Shaokang, the sixth ruler of the Xia, and the first to "restore [his dynasty] in mid-course 中興," see n. 355 *supra*. Li Hao also adduces the two "restorers" Shaokang and Emperor Guangwu.

27 *Mao Shi* Ode #179 (Che gong 車攻), which begins (transl. Waley): "Our chariots are strong, /Our horses well matched. /Team of stallions lusty /We yoke and go to the east 我車既攻，我馬既同，四牡龐龐，駕言徂東 …" — but to go hunting, not waging battle.

Majesty has seized hold of all the lands of Chu 楚, and has crack troops from Jing[zhou] to Yang[zhou] 荆揚 (= from Hubei down the Yangtse, up to Jiangsu) at Your disposal,[28] and yet, with trailing [robe] and folded [hands], You would abandon the twin capitals (Chang'an and Luoyang) just like that, as if to support the Rong savages (of Later Qin, holding both Chang'an and Luoyang)? Should [Liu Yu's] six army corps wheel north, the moment to overcome and recover it (= the north) will then have arrived: I hereby beg to command my Rong [soldiers] from west of the Yellow River to serve as the vanguard of the Jin [army's] right wing.[29]

Now, what we observe in these memorials is a tool of strategic communication. In terms of relative power, neither Li Hao nor Juqu Mengxun felt demeaned by posing as subjects of Eastern Jin: it was, after all, the largest empire in East Asia by far. They would have done the same towards Yao Xing's Later Qin or Tuoba Gui's Northern Wei without much hesitation, and perhaps they did; but the historical record of these two rival empires (substantial in the case of Northern Wei) contains no trace of it, and the *History of the Jin* is naturally partial. For, whereas Eastern Jin was recognised as a beacon of civilisation, it was by no means the only contender for legitimacy; as long as the Jin Emperor An, or any other regional ruler, remained "incapable of uniting the Nine Provinces into one integrated whole, they were each and all of them Sons of Heaven only in

---

28   Having reconquered Sichuan (ruled by Qiao Zong 譙縱, 405–413, as a vassal state of Yao Xing's Later Qin) for Eastern Jin in 413, Liu Yu wrested control over Xiangyang 襄陽 from its governor (and Jin prince) Sima Xiuzhi 司馬休之 (d. 417) in 415, and thus took charge of the military stronghold that was Jingzhou (= Hubei; "Chu"), and with it, easy access to the capital Jiankang in Yangzhou (= Jiangsu) across the Yangtse River. By this time, the Jin emperor was a mere puppet. Sima Xiuzhi fled to Yao Xing in Chang'an: see *Song shu* 2:31, 34. Juqu Mengxun urges the Southern Jin to push on with conquering the north, including Chang'an and Luoyang, since the Jin can count on his assistance to reunify the empire. Liu Yu was to force the abdication of the last Jin emperor five years later, founding his own Liu-Song Dynasty (420–479). Liu Yu was Chariot and Horse General from 407 (*Song shu* 1:13) to presumably 411 (*Song shu* 2:27), when his appointment as General-in-chief would have made the earlier title redundant.

29   *JS* 129:3196–3197: "上天降禍，四海分崩，靈耀擁于南裔，蒼生沒于醜虜。陛下累聖重光，道邁周漢，純風所被，八表宅心。臣雖被髮邊徼，才非時雋，謬為河右遺黎推為盟主。臣之先人，世荷恩寵，雖歷夷嶮，執義不回，傾首朝陽，乃心王室。去冬益州刺史朱齡石遣使詣臣，始具朝廷休問。承車騎將軍劉裕秣馬揮戈，以中原為事，可謂天贊大晉，篤生英輔。臣聞少康之興大夏，光武之復漢業，皆奮劍而起，眾無一旅，猶能成配天之功，著車攻之詠。陛下據全楚之地，擁荊揚之銳，而可垂拱晏然，棄二京以資戎虜！若六軍北軫，克復有期，臣請率河西戎［旅］為晉右翼前驅。" (For the addition of the word *lü* 旅 in the last sentence, see *JS* 129:3200 n. 2.)

name, and not in substance." Indeed, as Sima Guang writes further in a careful essay on the fraught issue of "legitimate succession (*zhengtong* 正統)," "if one understands legitimacy as meaning occupying Central China, the territories that were obtained by Former Zhao (304–329), Later Zhao (319–351), Former Yan (349–370), Former Qin (351–384), Later Qin (384–417) and Xia (407–431) were one and all coterminous with where the Five Thearchs and the Three Kings (who lay at the basis of Chinese civilisation) had their capitals of old."[30] So any of these, too, could a priori have been or as yet prove to be worthy to govern a reunited China. Thus, for Li Hao or Juqu Mengxun to express the pious wish that Eastern Jin reunify the empire and restore it to its Han-era grandeur was an *obiter dictum*, something that went without saying, irrespective of what Eastern Jin had achieved or failed to achieve in that regard. Yet saying it did provide a foil for saying something else as well, namely *for staking out a position*. This is what Li Hao and Juqu Mengxun effectively did within the boundaries of diplomatic norms. Precisely the specious protection afforded them by this diplomatic nicety allowed Li Hao and Juqu Mengxun to convey their true message, which was to indicate to which position of power they laid claim. Eastern Jin would have to frame its foreign policy towards them accordingly. If Li Hao or Juqu Mengxun did address similar missives to other major neighbour states, then by so doing, they were hedging their bets, and the overall result of this active communication would be, for whatever it was worth, a comforted sense of safety.

---

30   *ZZTJ* 69:2185–2188.

CHAPTER 10

Li Hao Moves to Jiuquan

Starting off from Guzang (modern Wuwei), one could reach Zhangye, 500 *li* to the west, in six stages by cart or horse, through sandy desert, from oasis to oasis. After Zhangye, the terrain turned into gravel and oases became scarce. To cover the next six stages towards Jiuquan, not only did one have to carry enough water reserves but (as a tenth-century traveller noted) horses had to be shod with wooden boots (*muse* 木澀) and camel hooves wrapped in yak leather for them to make it over the unforgiving terrain unharmed. Beyond Jiuquan, one passed the Shule River 疏勒河 (as it is known today); Dunhuang lay 200 *li* further west — still an eight-day journey, nevertheless. This is where the Richthofen Range ends and dunes begin, extending westward into the Kumtag and then the Taklamakan Desert. Up to 70 m high, the ridge of the dunes' summits and slopes changing shape with the prevailing winds, these sand hills sometimes produce a booming sound, "in winter and in summer, a sound rumbling like thunder"; this is why they have been called the Singing-Sand Hills (Mingsha shan 鳴沙山) since the tenth century, at the very latest. The large Dunhuang oasis, with what was once a double crenellated wall protecting the habitations and cultivated plots of land within, is also known to tourists today for Crescent Lake (*Yueya quan* 月牙泉) a few miles away, strangely not encountered in ancient sources, and of course for the nearby Caves of the Thousand Buddhas (*Qianfo dong* 千佛洞, or *Mogao ku* 莫高窟) already mentioned.[1]

It stretches one's credulity somewhat, but we have it on good authority that tigers roamed the countryside outside Dunhuang's city wall. In 405, "Li Hao the Governor of Liangzhou had gone out of the city wall incognito when he came across a tiger on the side of the road. The tiger, transforming itself into a human being, shouted to [Li] Hao from afar as 'Lord of Western Liang ...!' Thus called to attention, [Li] Hao flexed his bow, waiting. Again, the creature called for [Li] Hao from afar, adding, 'I have something to tell you, do not misapprehend me!' [Li] Hao now realised that here was something out of the ordinary, and as he threw his bow down on the ground, the man stepped forward and said: 'Dunhuang is an empty void, not a place of promise. Should your sons and

---

1   This description borrows from Gao Juhui's 高居誨 938 CE *Yudianguo xingcheng ji* 于闐國行程記 (*An Account of my Voyage to Khotan*), quoted in Ouyang Xiu, ed., *Xin wudai shi* 新五代史 (*A New History of the Five Dynasties*, 907–960), 74:917–918; Mildred Cable, with Francesca French, *The Gobi Desert* (London 1942), p. 43; and Mrs Howard Taylor, *The Call of China's Great North-West* (London 1923), "Map of Kansu" (for the stages).

© DOMINIK DECLERCQ, 2025 | DOI:10.1163/9789004727380_011

grandsons ever become princes of Western Liang, my lord, I would advise you to move to Jiuquan."[2]

The *Jin shu* ascribes to Li Hao another motive for moving his capital from Dunhuang to Jiuquan — namely, to threaten Juqu Mengxun in Zhangye — saying that Dunhuang notables (represented by Zhang Miao) acclaimed the idea, and that Li Hao left his most trusted lieutenants (his half-brother Song You and his son Li Rang) in charge of Dunhuang. Perhaps Juqu Mengxun's growing clout really did leave Li Hao little alternative but to mount an invasion of Northern Liang, lest his own Western Liang should face annihilation. And perhaps also he meant to keep open the option of returning to Dunhuang, for "[he] also had a double protective wall built from east to west [reinforcing] the previous defences of Dunhuang, to protect it from the danger posed by northern caitiffs, and a double protective wall built from west to south [reinforcing] the previous defences of Dunhuang, to intimidate the southern caitiffs." These "southern caitiffs" were no doubt Juqu Mengxun's Lushui nomads.[3]

In any case, Li Hao's speech to his subordinate officials in Dunhuang, and the pithy "instructions" that, as a caring father, he left for his sons, sound like a valedictory of sorts.

> Li Hao said to his subordinate officials: "Years ago, when this region west of the Yellow River split up and [power] disintegrated, a number of bold men vied with each other to rise to prominence. Though lacking in virtue, I was myself propelled to a position of power by a group of worthy people, and ever since, I have often forgotten to sleep or to eat, so bent I am on bringing help to the common people. That is why I previously sent my half-brother You to the east at the head of an army of horsemen packed dense like a cloud, to make an end with anyone refusing to bow to our authority. Wherever that army showed up, everyone submitted or was brought down. Today only [Juqu] Mengxun still rebelliously holds on to a single fortress. From Zhangye eastward, the remaining populace of Jin may be under the control of barbarian savages, but when it comes to how keen they are to see right prevail and how they miss our customs, they surpass the men of Yin 殷 in the hopes they entertained of Xibo 西伯 (= King Wen of the Zhou 周文王, trad. 1152–1056 BCE, who was to liberate them of the tyranny of the last Yin ruler, Zhou 紂, ca. 1105–1046? BCE).

---

2   Liu Bing 劉昞 (d. 440), *Dunhuang shilu* 燉煌實錄 (*Veritable Records of Dunhuang*), quoted in *Taiping yulan* 165 f. 4b (p. 804b). The dating there is wrong: the quote from Liu Bing places the encounter "in the first year of the Long'an era" (of Eastern Jin: 397), whereas "the first year of the Yixi era" (405) is called for.

3   *JS* 87:2265.

For our great enterprise [to restore the empire] to be settled, we cannot afford to rest in comfort: I intend to move our capital to Jiuquan, so as to push closer to that bandit's lair step by step. What do you gentlemen think?" When Zhang Miao acclaimed his proposal, Li Hao, overjoyed, said: "For two men to share mind and heart, such sharpness severs metal![4] Now that Administrator Zhang and I are on the same page, what further doubts can there be?" He then made Zhang Tishun General Pacifying Distant Regions and Prefect of Jiankang, stationed in Leguan; he summoned Song You to be General of the Right, taking command of the Dunhuang protecting army, stationed in Dunhuang together with his other son, Rang, Prefect of Dunhuang; and subsequently moved his own residence to Jiuquan. In instructions written in his own hand, he admonished his sons as follows:

Since I reached the age of discernment, I have never dealt with worldly gain. I have experienced several governments and better and worse times in office; I never cudgelled my brains over it, except for being strict with myself. I never had the ambition to be where I am today. But one thing led to another, and in due course I have found myself shouldering the burden of this province. It is no light responsibility, and a heavy obligation on our family. Although I carefully examine the affairs of men, it is not given to me to know the intentions of Heaven: when I mount my carriage and adjust the reins, a hundred worries choke my breast. What follows I impart to you in simple terms, as they occur to me — a number of rather obvious matters of daily occurrence that I want briefly to bring to your attention, in no particular order. As for the art of anticipation and the proactive strike, the sense of which way the wind blows, [both so vital to a politician,] this is something for which you will have to trust in your native intelligence, not something that my admonitions will help you to improve. Nevertheless, though you have not attained that great age, as long as you can overcome yourself and sort out and tend to [the issues at hand], you ought to be no less well equipped to face your challenges than the ancients were before you. Should that not be so, no mane of grey hair will help you to succeed! Now be you admonished and heed this.[5]

---

4 From *Yijing, Xici* 繫辭 (Attached Verbalisations) A.6, *SSJ* (*Zhou Yi zhengyi* 周易正義 [The Changes of the Zhou, with Orthodox Exegesis]) p. 79c, transl. Lynn p. 58. James Legge translates (*The I Ching* [Oxford 1899, reprint New York 1963[1]]), p. 362: "But when two men are one in heart,/Not iron bolts keep them apart."

5 *JS* 87:2262: "吾自立身，不營世利，經涉累朝，通否任時；初不役智，有所要求，今日之舉，非本願也。然事會相驅，遂荷州土，憂責不輕，門戶事重。雖詳人事，未知天心，登車理轡，百慮填胸。後事付汝等，粗舉旦夕近事數條，遣意便言，不能次比。至於杜漸防萌，深識情變，此當任汝所見深淺，非吾敕誡所

142   CHAPTER 10

Be sparing with alcohol and cautious in words; think before allowing joy or anger to show on your face. Take a liking to someone, but know his bad points; dislike someone, but know wherein he is good.[6] Always remind yourself to be tolerant and magnanimous, and act only when you have made sure you are. Do not lightly give credence to the populace when they hate something, but carefully examine witnesses, distinguish true from fake, keep flatterers and sycophants at a distance, and hold loyal and honest advisers close to you. Dispense with torture to produce a verdict; bear with the irksome entanglement [of legal proceedings]; spare people of old age; show compassion to the bereaved and the sick; diligently examine the files [of cases brought before you] and give ear to both claims and counterclaims. When corporal punishment must be applied, pronounce the sentence with a composed mien, letting the law take its course; take care not to allow any emotion to affect your voice and countenance. When distributing rewards, don't pass over people you don't know; when meting out penalties, don't pardon your own kinsmen. Being the ears and eyes of your community, make it your duty to know what its cares and hardships are out there; forbid your attendants from screening you off; don't act proud or overbearing. Never boast of your own goodness, nor ever talk up your own merits;[7] neither anticipate attempts at deception nor presume on another's trustworthiness[8] to show off how clever you are. Consult widely, do not act alone: go along with good advice as if swimming with the flow, shun bad advice as if jumping back from boiling water. It is very difficult not to be proud when one has wealth and prestige; be mindful of this, impress it on your heart, do not forget it for an instant. The functionaries on your staff were born and raised here: be courteous to them in everything, make them feel respected, banquet and feast them, and be attentive and solicitous to them in every respect. You must not remain ignorant of what, over the ages, has caused [men in our position] to succeed or to fail; to that end, in your moments of leisure, when you have withdrawn from court, concentrate on reading ancient

---

益也。汝等雖年未至大，若能克己纂修，比之古人，亦可以當事業矣。苟其不然，雖至白首，亦復何成！汝等其戒之慎之之。"

6   A quote from *Liji* 1 (Quli, shang 曲禮上, 1.3), *SSJ* p. 1230a (cf. transl. Legge p. 62).

7   A quote from *Lunyu* 5.26; cf. transl. Lau p. 80, who understands *shi lao* 施勞 as "imposing onerous tasks upon others." I follow Zhu Xi 朱熹 (1130–1200) and Liu Baonan 劉寶楠 (1791–1855); see Liu Baonan, *Lunyu zhengyi* 論語正義 (Beijing 1990) pp. 204–205.

8   A variation on *Lunyu* 14.31, transl. Lau p. 129: "Is a man not superior who, without anticipating attempts at deception 不逆詐 or presuming acts of bad faith 不億不信, is nevertheless the first to be aware of such behaviour?" Here "acts of bad faith" are replaced with their opposite, "trustworthiness 必."

books and records — for one who[, as the *Book of Documents* says,] just stands blinking at a wall will not become very accomplished.[9]

This commandery has been deeply attached [to the Jin court] for generations. Its people are honest and have dignity; even when the empire was at its most prosperous, they were universally praised for these qualities, all the more so now that [loyalty to the Jin] is the main state policy of this famed land.[10] This has come about through five hundred years of integration, the result of marriage links forged between village communities, ending up in a shared sense of what is right and proper that, to be sure, occasionally lapses a little, but in any case needs occasional calibration as new situations demand. It is five years since I assumed this office; as regards the tribulations of warfare, I have not yet been able to offer respite to the population, to bring about a cessation of hostilities, or to favour gentlefolk and commoners alike with a life of tranquil ease. As for [the charge that I] cover up my blemishes, conceal my defaults and wash away my stains: at dawn I'm considered an enemy,[11] to be made [the Jin court's] core ally by dusk, and although I may not quite aspire to fit the ancients' mould, neither have I irresponsibly repudiated old or new friends. Just and fair in discharging my duty, calm and evenhanded, I have never authorised my feelings to get the upper hand. Should there be quibbles about that, [I am confident that] a count of recent [occasions for complaint] yields but few, and should there come more as time goes by, I trust I will never disavow the ideals that have motivated me from the start.[12]

---

9 An expression from the *Shujing*, Zhou 周 22 (Zhouguan 周官), ssj p. 236a.

10 Taking *shishi* 實是 to mean, as suggested in *Hanyu da cidian* 漢語大詞典 (Shanghai 1997¹) s.v., *guoshi* 國是, "the main state business."

11 *Mencius* IVB.3 is apposite here: "If a prince treats his subjects as his hands and feet, they will treat him as their belly and heart. If he treats them as his horses and hounds, they will treat him as a stranger. If he treats them as mud and weeds, they will treat him as an enemy 寇讐" (transl. Lau p. 128).

12 *JS* 87:2261–2263: "節酒慎言，喜怒必思，愛而知惡，憎而知善，動念寬恕，審而後舉。眾之所惡，勿輕承信，詳審人，核真偽，遠佞諛，近忠正。蠲刑獄，忍煩擾，存高年，恤喪病，勤省案，聽訟訴。刑法所應，和顏任理，慎勿以情輕加聲色。賞勿漏疏，罰勿容親。耳目人間，知外患苦；禁禦左右，無作威福，勿伐善施勞，逆懷憶必，以示己明。廓布誠信，無自專用，從善如順流，去惡如探湯。富貴而不驕者至難也，念此貫心，勿忘須臾。僚佐邑宿，盡禮承敬，讌饗饌食，事事留懷。古今成敗，不可不知，退朝之暇，念觀典籍，面牆而立，不成人也。此郡世篤忠厚，人物敦雅，天下全盛時，海內猶稱之。況復今日，實事名邦。正為五百年鄉黨婚親相連，至于公理，時有小小頗迴，為當隨宜斟酌。吾臨苟五年，兵難騷動，未得休眾息役，惠康士庶。至于掩瑕藏疾，滌除寇讐，夕委心膂，雖未足希準古人，粗亦無負於新舊。事任公平，坦然無類，初不容懷，有所損益，計近便為少，經遠如有餘，亦無愧於前志也。"

When Li Hao had installed himself in Jiuquan, he was 54 years old, and when Juqu Mengxun did the same in Zhangye, 37. Li Hao's first concern was to solidify Jiuquan's economic basis, and this clearly at the expense of Dunhuang. In ca. 380, when Liangzhou was a province of Former Qin, 17,000 households had been relocated from southern and central China to Dunhuang to farm the land, and several thousand more joined them when, in 397 and 398, they fled west from Wuwei Commandery, where Guo Nun spread havoc in his failed coup against Lü Guang. These households were now all made to follow Li Hao to Jiuquan Commandery, where he created five new commanderies to administer the immigrant farmer population.[13]

The initiative paid off; "as, in successive years, the crop grew to full height and the people took pride in their work, his staff requested that a commemorative stele inscription be carved in Jiuquan, and Li Hao approved it. Thereupon the Chancellor of Confucian Education (*rulin jijiu* 儒林祭酒) Liu 劉 [Bing 昞, byname] Yanming 彥明 (d. 440) composed a text that was engraved on a stone to eulogise [Li Hao's] virtue.[14] But soon [Juqu] Mengxun started yearly incursions to raid, which wouldn't stop. Li Hao was keen to rule his territory through peaceful means, and just to entertain friendly relations [with Juqu Mengxun] and establish a covenant with him, not otherwise opposing him at all. At this time a white wolf, a white hare, a white sparrow, a white pheasant and a white dove were all seen nesting in his enclosed garden [...]"[15]

On the political stage, it would thus seem as if higher powers gave their blessing to a covenant of peace between Western and Northern Liang, as well as to

---

13   *JS* 87:2263; the new commanderies were Wuwei, Wuxing, Zhangye, Kuaiji 會稽 and Guangxia 廣夏. Wuwei, Wuxing and Zhangye Commanderies existed, of course: Tufa Rutan (Southern Liang) had expanded his territory from Ledu and taken Wuwei and Wuxing with the blessing of Later Qin's ruler Yao Xing (who appointed him Governor of Liangzhou, based in Guzang, Wuwei Commandery) in 406 (*ZZTJ* 114:3590), whereas Juqu Mengxun had his capital in Zhangye (Northern Liang). What Li Hao created on his own territory of Western Liang, therefore, were "shadow commanderies," so to speak, expressing an ambition to take over the real Wuwei, Wuxing and Zhangye when conditions would permit. For the southerners relocated to Dunhuang ca. 380, who could be expected to feel nostalgia for the real Kuaiji Commandery in Eastern Jin (modern-day Shaoxing 紹興), and for those who originated in the "Central Land" and thus in the ancient heartland of Chinese civilisation, Li Hao established his own Kuaiji and Guangxia ("Greater Xia") Commanderies. This is also how Tan Qixiang, op. cit., map 15–16, interprets this, without being able to pinpoint the exact location of these administrative units.

14   Liu Bing, who wrote down the tiger anecdote related above, has biographies in *Wei shu* 52:1160–1161 and *Bei shi* 34:1267–1269.

15   *JS* 87:2264.

Li Hao's state's prosperity. Yet relations with Juqu Mengxun were nonetheless bound to remain parlous. In a raid on Jiuquan in 406, Juqu Mengxun unsuccessfully attempted to make off with 3000 peasant households.[16] A second major attack followed in 410, but the *Jin shu* does not mention it. The *Annals of the Sixteen States* relate that in 410, "in the seventh month of autumn, Juqu Mengxun came attacking at the head of his horsemen, and [Li] Hao sent his son and designated heir [Li] Xin together with his Adjunct Commandant (*biejiang* 別將) Zhu Yuanhu 朱元虎 to keep him off. They battled at Mamiao 馬廟, [Li] Xin was defeated, and [Zhu] Yuanhu was captured. [Li] Hao then redeemed Yuanhu with 3000 catties of silver and 2000 ounces of gold; Mengxun returned him, and having entered into a covenant with Hao, subsequently withdrew."[17] The covenant mentioned in the *Jin shu* would therefore hardly have been Li Hao's initiative. Nor was it kept; when Juqu Mengxun again broke the peace in 411, Li Xin defeated Juqu Mengxun and captured one of his commanders.[18]

• • •

Once in Jiuquan, Li Hao was also reunited with a daughter, Li Jing'ai 敬愛. In the course of his biography, nine sons of Li Hao's are mentioned (Tan 譚 [d. 404],[19] Xin 歆 [designated heir in 404, d. 420],[20] his "second son" Rang 讓,[21] Fan 翻 and his younger brother Xun 恂 (d. 421) [who, thus mentioned together, probably had the same mother], Yu 預, Mi 密, Tiao 眺 and Liang 亮), as well as "several daughters."[22] Chances are that Li Jing'ai deserves to be mentioned because, possibly like Li Tan and certainly like Li Xin, her mother was Li Hao's principal wife at this time, *née* Yin.[23] If so, Li Jing'ai would have been the daughter who ended up married to Juqu Mengxun's son and heir Juqu Mujian in 420.[24] In his second memorial to the Eastern Jin, Li Hao mentioned that, in preparation for a grand offensive that would reconquer all of Gansu and Shaanxi for a restored Jin empire, he was "summoning soldiers from our walled city [of Dunhuang],

---

16   Southern Liang (Tufa Rutan et al.) is on record as having forcibly moved 57,500 households into their domain over a period of ten years, from 400 to 411; for Western Qin (Qifu Qiangui et al.) the figure is 185,000 over a thirty-seven-year period, from 388 to 425. See the tables in Zhou Weizhou, *Nan Liang yu xi Qin* pp. 120–121, 262–264.

17   *Shiliu guo chunqiu* 93:1035 = *ZZTJ* 115:3636.

18   *JS* 87:2264 = *ZZTJ* 116:3647–3648.

19   Li Tan's mother must have been Li Hao's first wife, "a daughter of Xin Na's."

20   *ZZTJ* 113:3570, 113:3574.

21   *JS* 87:2264.

22   *JS* 87:2270 (Li Fan and Li Xun), 2271 ("several daughters").

23   *JS* 87:2268, *ZZTJ* 118:3699.

24   *ZZTJ* 119:3738.

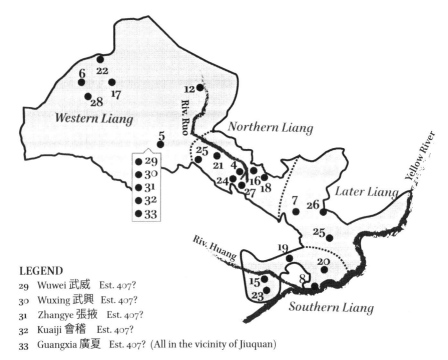

LEGEND
29 Wuwei 武威   Est. 407?
30 Wuxing 武興   Est. 407?
31 Zhangye 張掖   Est. 407?
32 Kuaiji 會稽   Est. 407?
33 Guangxia 廣夏   Est. 407? (All in the vicinity of Jiuquan)

MAP 10   Liangzhou in 410 CE

[and] from the north [...] calling up Dingling troops."[25] On the strength of what kind of relationship was Li Hao able to "call up Dingling troops"? A marriage bond is one possible answer. Evidence is lacking, but when, in a later document addressed to Li Hao's son and successor Li Xin, one reads of the latter's "concubines and consorts in the rear quarters of the palace, and sons and daughters of *various foreign blood*," this is certainly suggestive.[26]

Now, to come back to Li Jing'ai, before Li Hao's career took off in Xiaogu County in 397, he had lived in Guzang all his life. In 397, he moved away with his second wife, *née* Yin, but not before "entrusting his daughter Jing'ai to the care of her maternal grandfather Yin Wen." At this time, Guzang was in the hands of Lü Guang (Later Liang); in 403, it came into the hands of Yao Xing (Later Qin); and in 406, into the hands of Tufa Rutan (Southern Liang). "When [Yin] Wen moved east (to Later Qin's Chang'an, presumably), Liang Bao's 梁襃 (d. 407) mother, who was Li Hao's aunt on his father's side, took care of her."[27]

---

25   *JS* 87:2264.
26   *JS* 87:2269 ("後宮嬪妃，諸夷子女").
27   The editors of the *JS* (87:2272 note 5) identify this Liang Bao with Liang Pou 梁裒, who is mentioned in *JS* 126:3151 as Tufa Rutan's Libationer of the Military Council in Guzang, and was executed there for plotting treason at the end of 407.

Quite possibly, the enmity between Li Hao and Juqu Mengxun did not permit Li Jing'ai to cross Zhangye on her way from Guzang to Jiuquan to meet her father; thus, Tufa Rutan, "to establish amicable relations" with Li Hao, "gained permission [for Li Jing'ai] to pass through [the territory of] the Beishan Xianbei 北山鮮卑" north of Zhangye and dispatched Liang Bao with the girl to Jiuquan via that route. "Li Hao dispatched an envoy to reciprocate the gesture, and to present local products as gifts."[28]

•••

As for trade passing through Jiuquan, the record is unsurprisingly coy on the subject. The kings of Shanshan 鄯善 and of Qianbu 前部 dispatched envoys to present their local products as tribute.[29] One may take this to mean that they traversed Dunhuang, governed by Li Hao's son, but were hindered from travelling down from Jiuquan to Chang'an or to Jiankang, and of necessity traded their merchandise with Li Hao's agents. One can infer this from a statement in the *History of the (Liu-) Song Dynasty* that, in 422, "when the House of Li (= Western Liang) perished, Bilong 比龍 the King of Shanshan came on a visit to the (Liu-Song) court (in Jiankang), and all thirty-six oasis states of the Western Regions declared themselves our subjects and came to offer tribute."[30] They had manifestly been blocked from doing so during Li Hao's reign. This furnishes an indication of where the 3000 catties of silver and 2000 ounces of gold in ransom for Li Hao's commander Zhu Yuanhu may have come from.

•••

---

28   *JS* 87:2263. I adopt the suggestion of Zhou Weizhou, *Nan Liang yu Xi Qin* pp. 29–30, that there was a Xianbei tribe living in the "Northern Mountains" somewhere between Guzang and Jiuquan, e.g. in the Heli Mountains north of Zhangye, who were therefore known as Beishan Xianbei. "Northern Xianbei 北部鮮卑," in *JS* 117:2984, would refer to the same tribe. The punctuation of this sentence in *JS* 87:2263 has to be changed as a consequence.

29   *JS* 87:2263. "The kings of Shanshan and of Qianbu": in *JS* 95:2498, one reads: "Before the year was out, the kings of Shanshan as well as 及 Qianbu had presented themselves in audience before Fu Jian. On their return journey westward, the king of Shanshan died in Guzang." This makes it clear that *ji* 及 is not an interpolation and that Qianbu was an oasis city-state separate from Shanshan: namely, the abbreviated form of Jushi Qianbu 車師前部, or Nearer Jushi (see *HS* 96B:3921), on the northern Silk Roads. By contrast, Shanshan (alt. Loulan 樓蘭) corresponds to modern-day Ruoqiang County, or Qarkilik, under Lop Nur 羅布泊, on the section of the Silk Roads that skirts the Taklamakan Desert by a southern route (this historical Shanshan is therefore not at all identical with modern-day Shanshan County 鄯善縣, easily 500 km further north).

30   *Song shu* 98:2414.

Liu Bing was the most important scholar in Western Liang, on a par with Kan Yin at Juqu Mengxun's court. He studied with Guo Yu 郭瑀 (d. 386), a recluse who had "hollowed out a cave in the rock to live in, and ingested cypress seeds to lighten his body," but who was otherwise a scholarly Confucian with "more than a thousand disciples entered on his roll."[31] Liu Bing became his star student, and in his turn became a teacher as well as a recluse, in Jiuquan. He then entered Li Hao's service. He observed that Li Hao "loved and attached a special importance to the monuments of literature, and when the strings [holding the bamboo strips] of an [important] text or work of history 書史 [together] became unstuck, [Li Hao] would mend and repair it in person"; whereupon Liu Bing "begged to take over that task." As Li Hao's Chancellor of Confucian Education, Liu Bing wrote a *Digest* (*Lüeji* 略記) of the three major works of history that had appeared thus far (Sima Qian's *Shiji*, Ban Gu's *Han shu* and Ban Gu et al., *Dongguan Han ji* 東觀漢記 [*Han Records from the Eastern Lodge*]); a *History of [Former] Liang* 涼書, a *Veritable Records of Dunhuang* 敦煌實錄, a work on *Regional Expressions* 方言, and an *Inscription for the Hall of Respectful Observance* 靖恭堂銘, which could very well be the composition "that was engraved on a stone to eulogise [Li Hao's] virtue." He further wrote commentaries on the *Book of Changes, Han Feizi*, Liu Shao's 劉邵 (ca. 180–ca. 245) *Study of Human Abilities* 人物志 and the Han book on military strategy, *Master Yellowstone's Three Abstracts* 黃石公三略.[32]

---

31 *JS* 94:2454 ("鑿石窟而居，服柏實以輕身 [⋯] 弟子著錄千餘人。"). The tradition — which may or may not predate Zhong Gengqi's 鍾賡起 1744 *Ganzhou fuzhi* 甘州府志 — has it that the "Shallot Gully in Linsong, where [Guo Yu] hollowed out a cave in the rock to live in," stood at the origin of the Northern Wei and (later) Buddhist cave complex of Horseshoe Monastery 馬蹄寺, on the territory of Zhangye City, in Sunan Yuguzu Autonomous County 肅南裕固族自治縣.

32 *Wei shu* 52:1160 = *Bei shi* 34:1268. A short, fifth-century fragment of the last work (*Huangshi gong san lüe*) has turned up amongst the Dunhuang manuscripts held in St. Petersburg (Dx 17449); see Liu Jingyun 劉景允, "Xi Liang Liu Bing zhu '*Huangshi gong san lüe*' de faxian 西涼劉昞注《黃石公三略》的發現," in *Dunhuang yanjiu* 敦煌研究 2009.2, pp. 82–87. Of Liu Bing's *Zhou Yi* commentary, only one line subsists. Not much more (a dozen fragments collected by Tang Qiu, one of which I have quoted) has come down from his *Veritable Records of Dunhuang*, in spite of the high praise showered upon the work and its author by Liu Zhiji in his *Anatomy of Histories*, Outer Chapters 外篇 8 (Zashuo 雜說 C), *Shitong tongshi* 18:521: "an outstandingly impressive man of brilliant talent, as is immediately apparent; should this luminary never have been born and that region have gone without his record of it, how would the best men living in that far-off corner of the world ever have been heard of by posterity?"

CHAPTER 11

Li Hao's Last Years

Although the *Jin shu* does not say it, from the day that Juqu Mengxun drove Tufa Rutan out of Guzang and made it his own capital in 412, the budding alliance between Li Hao and Tufa Rutan that brought Li Jing'ai back to her father was suddenly no more. That is to say, Juqu Mengxun's Northern Liang in Zhangye was no longer sandwiched between Li Hao's Western Liang in Jiuquan (from 405) and Tufa Rutan's Southern Liang in Guzang (406–412). It was this, no doubt, that eventually decided Western Liang's fate. The shadow of Juqu Mengxun hangs over what remains to be told of Li Hao. An anecdote not given in the *Jin shu* vividly captures Li Hao's frustration. In 416,

> Major Suo Chengming submitted a letter urging [Li Hao] to attack [Juqu] Mengxun, Prince of Hexi; [Li] Hao invited him in for an audience, and said to him: "You know, it has hardly slipped my mind that Mengxun is a bane to our people![1] It is just that our current strength is not up to eliminating him. If you have a plan that will guarantee his capture, then lay it out for me; but if you would have me launch an eastern war merely with boastful talk, what's the difference with those who used to proclaim that 'Shi Hu, that dolt, should have his carcass end up on the market place!'?" Abashed and frightened, [Suo] Chengming took his leave.[2]

To take up Li Hao's *Jin shu* biography again, in Jiuquan:

> On the first *si* day 上巳 [of the third month of spring], Li Hao held a revel by a meandering stream and ordered his officials to compose poems, to which he added a postface himself.[3] He then copied Zhuge Liang's 諸葛亮

---

1 "Our people": *baixing* 百姓, the registered and taxed population whose grain crops Juqu Mengxun came every year to steal.
2 *ZZTJ* 117:3688. On Shi Hu, the Xiongnu ruler of Later Zhao, see Ch. 5 note 2 above.
3 Just as Wang Xizhi 王羲之 (303–361) did half a century earlier, when he composed his "Postface to a Collection [of Poems] from Orchid Pavilion 蘭亭集序" in 353, "on the occasion of the spring lustration festival 修禊事也." In fact, according to *JS* 51:1433, from Eastern Han times onward, the *xi* 禊 festival was always celebrated on the third day of the third month, irrespective of whether it was a *si* 巳 day or not (in 353, the fourth day of the third month was the first *si* day of that month.)

© DOMINIK DECLERCQ, 2025 | DOI:10.1163/9789004727380_012

(181–234) exhortations to urge his sons onward,[4] and said to them: "I shoulder a difficult responsibility, and have not yet accomplished the feat of bringing peace and relief. Although I have good and capable men assembled outside, and can rely on the ability of my ministers, the military concerns are so very many that I sit up [sleepless,] waiting for the dawn. I trust to the fastness of our string of fortresses, but in conjunction, I should also keep worthy people close by [to assist me]. So I have made each of you receive [official] appointments at a tender age, before you had even received instruction from a tutor or a preceptor. I live in constant fear that you will not be up to it, and will cause me repentance and self-reproach. It is not right that you should be unacquainted with [pertinent] events from antiquity to the present, but in case there are only recent events that you can draw lessons from, there is no point insisting on [the greater educational value of] events that happened long ago. Read, therefore, Zhuge Liang's exhortations and Ying Qu's 應璩 (190–252) memorial of warning,[5] and when you follow these from beginning to end, you will find that the teachings of the [Duke of] Zhou and of Confucius 周孔 are entirely contained therein. When having to rule a state, [these lessons] suffice to bring peace; when having to build character, they suffice to make one a reputation. Unaffected and brief, they are easy to comprehend and clear on the first reading; and though their words were addressed at men of the past, their message still teaches us today. Moreover, [detecting] the workings of the Way in the Classics and the histories is[, as the *Odes* say,] like gathering bean leaves in the middle

---

4 Zhuge Liang, the most famous general in Chinese history, left two letters of exhortation to his sons. They are short enough to be translated here: (1) "A truly great man in his conduct values calm, so as best to cultivate himself, and moderation, so as best to nurture his own virtue. If not tranquil and at rest, he cannot ascertain his own vocation; if not serene and calm, he cannot aim very far. To study, he needs calm; to develop his talents, he needs study. If he does not study, he cannot broaden his talents, and if he has no vocation, his study will come to nothing. He will fail to be inspired with enthusiasm if indolent, and fail to master his inner nature if agitated. As his years pass by, so will he become less determined by the day, [and] finally shrivel up and wither; and if, for the most part, he never had any real commerce with the world, and sadly kept to his poor hovel, all remedies will come too late." (2) "When setting out wine, do it wisely and to express true feeling, as agreeable to the body as welcome to the soul. [For host and guest] to retire after having made their mutual toasts is to have achieved harmony indeed; you may, as the host, if you feel particularly effusive and your guests don't look fatigued, go as far as to be flushed with wine, but never to the point that you lose control."

5 I find no hint as to this memorial in the one-line notice about Ying Qu in *SGZ* 21:604.

LI HAO'S LAST YEARS

of the plain: who works hardest at it will be most rewarded, so don't you be remiss at studying them!"[6]

•••

What follows then is Li Hao's "*Fu* Expressing my Aspirations (*Shu zhi fu* 述志賦)," which he wrote, as the historian prefaces the text, "in a forlorn mood (*gairan* 慨然)" some time shortly before 406. As suggested, the real date could rather be after 412, because Tufa Rutan's capture of Guzang opened diplomatic perspectives for Li Hao that vanished when Juqu Mengxun ousted Tufa Rutan from Guzang in 412. But that is a detail. More important are the few introductory lines in which the historian gives quite a summation of what Li Hao's undertaking might ideally have achieved: a near-bloodless, popularly acclaimed unification of Liangzhou "west of the Yellow River" that might have spearheaded even greater things should Eastern Jin have responded in kind. And indeed, Eastern Jin or its successor regime, Liu Yu's Southern Song (420–479), could in principle have done so: after Huan Wen's campaigns in Guanzhong (354) and through Henan to the Yellow River (369), Liu Yu recovered Shandong province in 410 and Guanzhong in 417 (though both were subsequently lost again).[7]

As it dawns on Li Hao as well as on the reader that this grand ambition will be frustrated, his *fu* takes on great importance. It stands as a noble testimony to the survival of Chinese civilisation in the last corner of Northern China not yet submerged by alien conquest or "barbarian" domination. Indeed, with its "unhurried, quiet and elegant diction (*wenci congrong danya* 文辭從容淡雅)," Li Hao's is the only *fu* that we have from Northern China in the century of the Sixteen Kingdoms.[8] It is a composition that stands with similar contemporary "rhapsodies" in which the author meditates on his own place in history: a thematic group that has Feng Yan's 馮衍 (fl. ca. 24–ca. 50) "*Fu* Revealing My Aspirations (*Xian zhi fu* 顯志賦)" as an influential precursor and Pan Yue's 潘岳 (247–300) "*Fu* on a Westward Journey (*Xi zheng fu* 西征賦)" as a famous anthology piece, and further includes Yang Gu's 陽固 (467–523) "*Fu* to Unveil

---

6 Loosely quoted from *Shijing* #196 (Xiaowan 小宛), *SSJ* p. 451c: "There are beans in the middle of the plain,/ People gather them."

7 See David A. Graff, "The Art of War," in *CHC* 2, pp. 275–295 at p. 277.

8 Ma Jigao 馬積高, *Fu shi* 賦史 (Shanghai 1987), pp. 234–235.

My Secret [Emotions] (*Yan ze fu* 演賾賦)" and Li Qian's 李騫 (508–549) "*Fu* Unbosoming My Feelings (*Shi qing fu* 釋情賦)."[9]

Because of his capacity to knit people and opinions together into one polity, at the end of the Lüs' time in power, Li Hao was held in the highest regard by all the region's strongmen. As a result, the design took hold in him to establish himself as their overlord. His soldiers did not have to besmear their sword blades with any blood; an area a thousand *li* in circumference settled into stable order without any effort. It was said that the [political] enterprise initiated by the Zhang rulers now reached its fruition at the time intended by fate, now that the ten commanderies west of the Yellow River had become unified over the years. But not long afterwards, Tufa Rutan invaded and seized Guzang (406), and the domain that Juqu Mengxun had established for himself was enlarged little by little; then, [Li Hao,] in a forlorn mood, wrote this "*Fu* Expressing My Aspirations," which reads:

Having forded the ultimate void in an unbridled equipage,
Driven that which carries being into original non-being,
Having a part in the mysterious prime, having all that I could wish for,
Sharing an invisible bond with the forces of sun and moon,
I was shaded at the dawn [of life] by wisps of cloud in great profusion,
And as I looked up, could bask in the brilliant sun's genial warmth.[10]

---

9   Cao Daoheng 曹道衡, *Han Wei Liuchao cifu* 漢魏六朝辭賦 (Shanghai 1989), pp. 182–184. Feng Yan's *fu* is in his biography, HHS 28B:985–1001; Pan Yue's *fu* is in *Wen xuan* 10, fols. 1a–12b, transl. Knechtges, *Wen xuan* Vol. Two, pp. 181–235; Yang Gu's *fu* is in his biography in *Wei shu* 72:1603 *sq.*, alternatively in Yan Kejun 嚴可均 (1762–1843), ed., *Quan shanggu sandai Qin Han Sanguo Liuchao wen* 全上古三代秦漢三國六朝文 (Beijing 1958¹): *Quan Hou Wei wen* 全後魏文 44, fols. 1b–4a (pp. 3731a–3732b); Li Qian's piece is in his biography in *Wei shu* 36:836 *sq.*, alternatively in Yan Kejun, op. cit., *Quan Hou Wei wen* 33, fols. 7a–9b (pp. 3680a–3681a).

10   The easiest way to understand this, I think, is this: in the unconscious state prior to his birth, Li Hao vacillated between being and non-being. About to be born, he was at one with the Dao at the origin of Heaven and Earth (the "mysterious prime 玄元") and contained in himself the dual forces of yin and yang (the "forces of sun and moon 景靈"). Once born, his high social status (his being "shaded 蔭") conferred on him social privilege, made more pronounced by his basking in his sovereign's favour (the "brilliant sun 朗日"). This sovereign, in Li Hao's birth year of 351, could either be the fifth governor of Liangzhou, Zhang Zhonghua (r. 346–353), or the Eastern Jin emperor at the time, Sima Dan 司馬聃 (343–361, Emperor Mu 穆帝, r. 345–361).

       I copy the text here stanza by stanza (as defined by the rhyme word). In this first stanza, the rhyme words are of the rhyme category *yú* 虞. JS 87:2265: "涉至虛以誕駕，乘有輿於本無，稟玄元而陶衍，承景靈之冥符。蔭朝雲之菴藹，仰朗日之照昫。"

Having been thus endowed, having thus embarked,
In such manner was I raised, in such manner brought up.
As a boy, I admired how noble was Yan Yuan to use his elbow for a pillow;[11]
I allowed my heart to roam amongst the works of past ages,
Pondered the rites, and was sedulous about the Classics.
I despised dark official caps at vermilion gates,
And envied [Zhuangzi in his] Lacquer Garden, disdaining ordinary
    mortals.
I exalted the fisherman in his watchet waves,
And approved of Chang Ju and Jie Ni tilling the fields, yoked together as
    a team.
Owls and harriers I thought vile, huffing in anger in their cages,
While I admired the flying phoenix in his heaven of great purity.[12]
I put a stop to worldly strife in my heart,
And cut myself off from the pleasing sound of praise by contemporaries.[13]

My chant on lofty heights would carry beyond the empyrean;
Men would wonder at me, a tree that thrives despite the frost;
I would stand upright, a lush and evergreen tall sapling,
Emitting a stronger scent at the coldest time of year.
In far-flung visions would I seek inspiration;
I'd see the Grizzled Foursome appear in brilliant light.[14]
I would keep clear of the bustle on ordinary thoroughfares
To prance high up, drawing my cloud-borne horse's reins.
Trees of carnelian I would climb in Kunlun's Hanging Garden;
Sip translucent nectar from its floreate springs;
Chime in with the ecstatic song of the fine-toned phoenix;
Answer the sweet-sounding simurgh on his southern ridge.[15]

---

11   Confucius' favourite disciple, Yan Yuan 顏淵, was poor (*Lunyu* 11.19). Praising principled
      poverty, the Master said (*Lunyu* 7.16, transl. Lau p. 88): "In the eating of coarse rice and the
      drinking of water, the using of one's elbow for a pillow, joy is to be found. Wealth and rank
      attained through immoral means have as much to do with me as passing clouds."
12   Images from *Zhuangzi* 17 (Autumn Floods 秋水), ed. Guo Qingfan 郭慶藩, *Zhuangzi jishi*
      莊子集釋(Beijing, 1961¹), 6B:605.
13   *JS* 87:2265 (rhyme: *gēng* 庚): "既敷既載，以育以成。幼希顏子曲肱之榮，游心上
      典，玩禮敦經。蔑玄冕于朱門，羨漆園之傲生；尚漁夫於滄浪，善沮溺之耦耕。歲
      鴞鳶之籠嚇，欽飛鳳于太清；杜世競於方寸，絕時譽之嘉聲。"
14   Four recluses who fled into the mountains of Shangluo 商洛, south of Luoyang, to escape
      the tyranny of Qin. See my *Writing Against the State* (Leiden 1998), pp. 357–359.
15   *JS* 87:2265 (rhyme: *yáng* 陽/*táng* 唐/*yáng* 陽/*táng* 唐): "超霄吟於崇領，奇秀木之陵
      霜；挺修幹之青蔥，經歲寒而彌芳。情遙遙以遠寄，想四老之暉光；將取繁

But quiet has eluded me in these times.
My heart yearned, but my mortal frame was stuck;
I dreamt of chasing my horse span through a sunny forest,
But as I turn my head, there's only a hillock.
Buffeted by winds, drenched by rain,
I barely manage not to be submerged.
Multiple interests are at loggerheads;
Joy comes on the heels of sorrow.
A window of opportunity has only just swung open, before it shuts again;
Heaven and earth are set apart by a navigable ford, but there is no ship.[16]
I lament how unsteadfast are probity and trust;
I leave those abashed at their own conduct amongst the rabble of the
  marketplace.[17]

And so, I took my leave of mystic contemplation,
And took my fellow travellers to heart.
I made my first mark in the Eastern Palace, as a callow youth, just
  capped;[18]
In my finery, I stood side by side with the best and brightest.
I stepped into that exclusive court, whence ruling power emanates,
Aiding an enlightened sovereign in his purple adyta.[19]

榮於常衢，控雲轡而高驤；攀瓊枝於玄圃，漱華泉之淥漿；和吟鳳之逸
響，應鳴鸞于南岡。”

16 "Window of opportunity": literally, "the door leaves of Qian 乾扉." As the Hexagram
Qian, in the first sentence of the *Book of Changes*, stands for "fundamentality, prevalence,
fitness, and constancy" (transl. Lynn p. 129), I think it is here a metonym for all that is
desirable — sc. "opportunity." Cf. *Yijing, Xici* A.6, transl. Lynn p. 58: "It is the opening of
this door 樞 or the release of this trigger 機 that controls the difference between honor
or disgrace," or *Xici* B.5, transl. Lynn p. 86: "*Qian* and *Kun*, do they not constitute the
two-leaved gate 門 into the *Changes*?" "Heaven and earth" is to be construed as "all that
conditions one's field of action." It matters little whether or not the "navigable ford 津" is
the Milky Way (銀河，天河，雲漢).

17 *JS* 87:2265 (rhyme: *yóu* 尤): "時弗獲彰，心往形留，眷駕陽林，宛首一丘；衝風沐
雨，載沈載浮。利害繽紛以交錯，歡感循環而相求。乾扉奄寂以重閉，天地
絕津而無舟；悼貞信之道薄，謝慚德於圜流。"

18 The "Eastern Palace 東宮" is traditionally the residence of the heir to the throne. "Just
capped": here we find *jin* 巾 instead of the normal *guan* 冠. Liu Xi's 劉熙 (early 3rd cent.)
Explanation of Names 釋名 (Ch. "Shi shoushi 釋首飾"), quoted in *Zhongwen da cidian*
s.v. *jin* (#8970), says that "when becoming adults at age 20, gentlemen are capped 冠 and
commoners don a headcloth 巾." Does this sentence mean that Li Hao served the heir to
Zhang Tianxi, Zhang Dayu, in 370 (see p. 85, above)? It seems probable.

19 *JS* 87:2265–2266 (rhyme: *zhēn* 真): "遂乃去玄覽，應世賓，肇弱巾於東宮，並羽儀
於英倫，踐宣德之祕庭，翼明后於紫宸。"

LI HAO'S LAST YEARS

Awe-inspiring, the Hall of Bright Reserve![20]
Great and grand, the [Hall of?] Sublime Brilliance!
Soaring high, the royal residence,
Teeming, all holders of high office.
The prince aspired to be a Shun or a Yu the Great,
His ministers resembled Kui and Boyi.[21]

Then the last Zhang prince collapsed like a wall of rock,
And Lord Liang fell to his death as if in a ravine.[22]

Uncorrupted morals became a fading memory, lost forever;
Officialdom was swept up as one, to be submerged and drowned.
When Lü [Guang] opened hostilities at the palace wall,
One push was enough to topple the structure.
Raging winds made tall trees sway,
Swirling geysers seethed in bottomless wells;
Flying dust entirely hid the sun from view,
While huge fires turned the parched plain into an inferno.
[Guzang,] a famed metropolis, was left a dismal shadow of itself;
A thousand villages turned desolate, not a kitchen stove still burning.

---

20 *JS* 86:2237–2238: "[Zhang Jun] further had a walled enclosure built to the south of the Guzang city wall, and there had the Hall of Bright Reserve 謙光殿 erected. It was painted in five colours and decorated with gold and jade, and all that was rare and ingenious was expended upon it. On each of the hall's four sides, a further hall was erected: to the east, the Green Hall of Genial Yang 宜陽青殿, for residing in during the three months of spring — the patterned robes, and ritual utensils, in each case matching the direction's colour. To the south, the Red Hall of Vermilion Yang 朱陽赤殿, for residing in during the three months of summer. To the west, the White Hall of Chastisement 政刑白殿, for residing in during the three months of autumn. And to the north, the Black Hall of the Dark Warrior 玄武黑殿, for residing in during the three months of winter. Adjacent to each of them were the offices of the court officials of the relevant secretariats, each in the colour of its given direction." It still existed in 412 (*JS* 129:3195 = *ZZTJ* 116:3644), when Juqu Mengxun "feasted his civil and military commanders and officials in the Hall of Bright Reserve and gave out gold and horses to them, each according to his rank" (*JS* 129:3195).

21 The legendary sage rulers Shun 舜 (here designated by the name of his hereditary domain of Yu 虞) and Yu the Great (here designated by the Xia 夏 Dynasty, of which he unwittingly became the founder); Shun appointed Kui 夔 his music master and Boyi 伯益 his game-keeper, according to the *Book of Documents*, Yu 2 (Shun dian), *SSJ* p. 131b. Text, *JS* 87:2266 (rhyme: *xī* 昔): "赫赫謙光，崇明奕奕，岌岌王居，詵詵百辟，君希虞夏，臣庶夔益。"

22 Zhang Tianxi was the last Zhang prince; he surrendered to Fu Jian of Former Qin in 376. Fu Jian appointed Liang Xi the new governor of Liangzhou; he was killed by Lü Guang when the latter took Guzang in 385. Text, *JS* 87:2266 (no rhyme): "張王頹巖，梁后墜壑。"

For the fatal number, 106, was then upon us;[23]
Ascent and destruction alternate, giving rise to one another.[24]

Thereupon, each man began to harbour thoughts of "chasing the deer";
Every family imagined itself bringing forth a strongman:
Ignorant of what a true king's mandate entails, they declined to find out,
Angling for what by rights was not theirs, in a world without interpretable signs.[25]
As a result, overturned carts piled up along the road;[26]
The flesh of living beings came to fertilise the soil.
I pitied the survivors, trembling and terrified,
So long bereft of all refuge and all hope;
The more ardently they desired [peace and order], the further they missed out on it,
And sought the dark pearl [of enlightenment] in vain illusions.[27]

Far into the distance lead the roads of Liang,
A hard-pressed land, a famished desolation.
And I, on my own, am but a mere speck
In the boundless expanse of this western realm.
It is not by design that I find myself here,

---

23   The number 106 is the ultimate yin number (as 101 is the ultimate yang number). Cf.
      HS 85:3468: "You have met with the bad fortune inherent in the Hexagram 'Pestilence,'
      and encountered the calamitous straits of 106." Or JS 105:2945: "Which era has been able
      to avoid the fate of 106! 百六之運何代無之！"

24   JS 87:2266 (rhyme: dàng 宕/yáng 陽/xiān 先/xiān 仙/yuán 元/xiān 先/xiān 仙/yǎng
      養): "淳風杪莽以永喪，搢紳淪胥而覆溺。呂發釁於閨牆，厥構摧以傾顛；疾
      風飄于高木，迴湯沸於重泉；飛塵翁以蔽日，大火炎其燎原；名都幽然影
      絕，千邑闃而無煙。斯乃百六之恒數，起滅相因而迭然。"

25   Zuo zhuan, Xiang 9.1b, Zuo Tradition, p. 953: "A domain in disorder has no interpretable
      signs, and the Way of Heaven can not be known." "Chasing the deer" means pursuing
      ambitions to create an empire.

26   "When the chariot in front overturns, the chariot behind should take heed 前車覆後車
      戒" (Liu Xiang, Shuoyuan 11.9 [ch. 4, fol. 10b]), so as not to stick to "the rut that overturns
      the chariot 覆車之軌." The latter expression, for a doomed enterprise, also occurs in a
      letter by Wang Bao 王豹 (d. 302), quoted in ZZTJ 84:2672, and is first attested in a text by
      Chen Zhong 陳忠 (d. 125), "Submission on Eliminating the Roots of Banditry 清盜源疏,"
      in HHS 46:1559.

27   JS 87:2266 (rhyme: yǎng 養. No change in rhyme, but "Thereupon 於是" marks a new turn):
      "於是人希逐鹿之圖，家有雄霸之想，闇王命而不尋，邀非分於無象。故覆車
      接路而繼軌，膏生靈於土壤。哀餘類之怵慓，邈靡依而靡仰；求欲專而失愈
      遠，寄玄珠於罔象。"

It will have been fated by a covert covenant.
In crossing the Weak Water I laid a foundation;
I stand by Kunlun's top, to build my ramparts here.[28]
I reined in my carriage's panicked four-horse span,
[And] rejoined its broken shafts on a steep-sided peak.[29]

Towering stand the mountain ridges,
Over a myriad spans stretch the double defiles:
Their dark recesses impenetrable to the eye,
Their boulders irregular, perilously peaked.
Hazelnut and jujube encroach on one another,
The river here is vast, its waters deep;
Foxes and raccoons lurk on both sides of the road,
Owls and kites screech in numbers.[30]

If not mine, then another man's talent would have found employ,
Although the position does fit me like a glove.
"One in heart" [with my subjects] is my principle in governing others;[31]
Impartial concern for all guides me as I keep things under control.
It's not that I affect these feelings and abandon [government] to neglect:
Instead, [me and my people,] in unspoken agreement, move in the same direction.
While civilised decorum is in evidence at audiences at the court,
Artless abandon is the norm when I fit my horse with its martingale.[32]

---

28 Through Fulu County 福祿縣, the administrative seat of Jiuquan Commandery, flowed (according to *HS* 28B:1614) the river Hucan 呼蠶水, better known as Taolai River 討賴河 and, nowadays, as Beida River 北大河. It is the largest affluent of the Hei River 黑河, better known in the past as the Weak Water (Ruoshui 弱水) because, after 950 km, it peters out in the Mongolian steppe. Li Hao uses "Kunlun" in a loose sense (for the Qilian Mountains), as also seen elsewhere: e.g., the Commander of Yihe 宜禾都尉, in the Han, was stationed in "Kunlun Fort 昆侖障," in Dunhuang Commandery (*HS*, ibid.).

29 *JS* 87:2266 (rhyme: *zhōng* 鍾/*jiāng* 江/*dōng* 東/*zhōng* 鍾/*zhōng* 鍾): "悠悠涼道，鞠焉荒凶，杪杪余躬，迢迢西邦，非相期之所會，諒冥契而來同。跨弱水以建基，躡崐墟以為墉，總奔駟之駭轡，接摧轅於峻峯。"

30 *JS* 87:2266 (rhyme: *qīn* 侵): "崇崖崨嶫，重嶮萬尋，玄邃窈窕，磐紆嶔岑，榛棘交橫，河廣水深，狐貍夾路，鴞鵄羣吟。"

31 From *Zhou Yi*, *Xici* A.6; see note 377, above.

32 *JS* 87:2266 (rhyme: *yǎng* 養): "挺非我以為用，任至當如影響；執同心以御物，懷自彼於握掌；匪矯情而任荒，乃冥合而一往，華德是用來庭，野逸所以就鞅。"

Of sterling quality are our epoch's men of promise;
Thriving, our people of eminent ability.
May they be caught in our net and trapped in our far-flung coop,
[to be appointed to office by us,]
For I will do better than just let bygones be bygones![33]
Some will be freed of their manacles, to be girded with the pendants [of
office];
Others will be late to arrive, to find they are the first to be lined up.
I shall pluck exceptional talent where the cliffs overlook dry land,[34]
[And] seize outstanding merit no matter where I find it.
I recall [Zhang Liang] Marquis of Liu and his supernatural encounter,
He who was to stir up high waves to sweep away all filth;[35]
I think of [Zhuge] Kongming in his thatched cottage,
Agitating abstruse stratagems that no one could obstruct.[36]
[Zang] Hong, holding the [oath's] tray in his hands, was earnestly indignant,

---

33　"The ancients shot at a belt buckle and cut off a sleeve, and yet it did not damage their prospects of becoming ministers," Liu Laozhi 劉牢之 (d. 402) is told (*ZZTJ* 112:3538). Hu Sanxing comments: "When Lord Huan of Qi 齊桓公 (d. 643 BCE, r. 685–643) vied for the state with [his elder brother] Gongzi Jiu 公子糾 (d. 685), Guan Zhong shot at Lord Huan and hit his belt buckle (see *Zuo zhuan* Xi 24.1b, *Zuo Tradition* p. 375); but after Zijiu had died, Lord Huan freed Guan Zhong from prison and made him his minister. Lord Xian of Jin 晉獻公 (d. 651, r. 677–651) had Eunuch Pi 寺人披 strike Chong'er 重耳 (697–628, later Lord Wen of Jin 晉文公) in Pucheng 蒲城, and when Chong'er fled by climbing over a wall, Pi cut off his sleeve (see *Zuo zhuan* Xi 5.2, *Zuo Tradition* p. 275); yet when Chong'er returned to take possession of his state, Pi on many occasions proved his loyalty." To "treat someone as if he had shot at a belt buckle or as if he had cut off a sleeve 射鉤斬袪" therefore means "to let bygones be bygones," "not to hold a grudge" (here, for reasons of rhyme, the synonymous *zhan mei* 斬袂 is substituted for *zhan qu* 斬袪).

34　An oblique reference to Fu Yue 傅說. The seventeenth Shang king Wuding 武丁 (trad. r. 1324–1266 BCE) dreamt that he had found a sage to help him with government. He had a likeness painted of the sage he had seen in his dream, and ordered his dominions searched: his emissaries finally discovered the man from the portrait, a convict labourer ramming earth under the Cliffs of Fu 傅巖. This was Fu Yue, "Yue of Fu." Wuding recognised him and made him his counsellor. See *Shiji* 3:102.

35　Without Zhang Liang (d. 186 BCE) as his adviser, Liu Bang (256/247–195 BCE, the first Han Emperor) would not have fulfilled the great task of founding the Han Dynasty. Li Hao hopes to identify a similar adviser for himself. Zhang Liang owed his uncanny insight in military strategy to "supernatural encounters 神遇" with Lord Yellowstone 黃石公, who bestowed the book *Taigong's Art of War* 太公兵法 upon him. See *Shiji* 55:2034–2035. The book *Master Yellowstone's Three Abstracts* (see p. 148, above) was also ascribed to him.

36　Zhuge Liang (Zhuge Kongming 孔明) was "visited three times in his thatched cottage [by Liu Bei 劉備, 161–223, the future emperor of Shu-Han, r. 221–223], who asked [his] advice on current affairs," i.e. on how to restore the Han Dynasty and reunify the empire (*SGZ* 35:920).

Raising three armies so as to incite [the realm's] best-trained soldiers to action.[37]

I sing the lofty standards of these assembled heroes,

Commend the soaring distinction of Guan [Yu] and Zhang [Fei];

I vow I shall take vengeance on Cao [Cao], and pledge allegiance to Liu [Bei]:

How did they all excel in rightfulness and courage!

[Zhang Fei,] brandishing his spear on a broken bridge,

Likewise showed a heroic bearing in valiant action.[38]

Splendid, these two treasures from southern lands:

Brilliant indeed were Zhou [Yu] and Lu [Su];

Outstandingly admirable there, in Jing and in Wu,

They shone amongst civil officials [and] sparkled amongst military officers,

Setting up that [celebrated] stratagem involving Crow Forest,

[And] galloping dragon-like along the Yangtse riverbank.[39]

They dashed a massive and formidable battle array to pieces,

Thronged like a storm soaring and clouds rising up;

They followed in the far-away steps of Fan [Kuai] and Han [Xin],

[And] matched [the Duke of] Shao and [King] Wu in their admirable scheme.

---

37   Zang Hong 臧洪 (160–196) swore an oath to rid the Han of Dong Zhuo and restore its greatness. To that purpose, "he stepped on the altar with the tray 操槃 for smearing blood [on the covenanters' lips] in his hands, and swore [...] The tone of his speech was earnestly indignant [...]" (*sGz* 7:232). "Three armies" presumably refers to the initial three conspirators, Zang Hong, Zhang Chao 張超 (d. 195) and the latter's brother Zhang Miao 張邈 (d. 195).

38   *JS* 87:2266 (rhyme: *xuē* 薛/*jì* 祭/*xuē* 薛/*jì* 祭/*fèi* 廢/*jì* 祭/*xuē* 薛/*shù* 術/*yuè* 月): "休矣時英，茂哉雋哲，庶罩綱以遠籠。豈徒射鉤與斬袂！或脫梏而纓蕤，或後至而先列，採殊才於巖陸，拔翹彥於無際。思留侯之神遇，振高浪以蕩礒；想孔明於草廬，運玄籌之罔滯；洪操槃而慷慨，起三軍以激銳。詠羣豪之高軌，嘉關張之飄傑，誓報曹而歸劉，何義勇之超出！據斷橋而橫矛，亦雄姿之壯發。"

39   It serves little purpose to detail the exploits of these Three States heroes — Guan Yu 關羽 (d. 220), Zhang Fei 張飛 (d. 221), Cao Cao, Liu Bei, Zhou Yu 周瑜 (175–210) and Lu Su 魯肅 (172–217). In 208, Cao Cao's flotilla sailed south on the Yangtse and moored at Red Cliff 赤壁 (in modern Hunan province) when Zhuge Liang and Zhou Yu, commanding armies for their respective lords Liu Bei and Sun Quan 孫權 (182–251), set fire to Crow Forest 烏林, on the riverbank, and so destroyed Cao Cao's fleet. They followed in the steps of Han and Zhou founding fathers Fan Kuai 樊噲 (d. 189 BCE), Han Xin 韓信 (d. 196 BCE), Ji Shi 姬奭 Duke of Shao 召公 (trad. d. 1053 BCE) and Ji Fa 姬發, much better known as King Wu of Zhou.

160   CHAPTER 11

Had it not been for Liu [Bei] and Sun [Quan's] magnanimity,
Who would have been capable of achieving such good fortune!
Truly [on that occasion] Qian and Kun complemented each other,
Like all sentient beings, yearning for the wind, are moistened by rain.[40]

Once they are scoured in Yizhou, flowing past Mount Min,
Cleansed, the Three Rivers continue on their course.[41]
Thus clement and placable an outcome may our great exploits bring;
Such merry and convivial times may prosperous peace usher in.
A band of dragons shall I lead to put my stratagem in motion;
Our glorious names shall be extolled for a myriad years to come.
Reverently regarding the traces left [by heroes] in times long past,
In their shadow I shall walk, looking up at these high mountains.
I shall plant a vermilion flag to point others the right way,
[And] chase my long carriage on its lightning expedition.
Blown back by the autumn storm, I shall nonetheless hold our banner
     aloft;[42]
I shall wave our floreate standard at the Brandishing Battler.[43]
Counting on a supernal sign emanating from the August Culmen,
I shall act in unison with the five weft stars in making equipoise return.[44]

---

40   *JS* 87:2266–2267 (rhyme: *mǔ* 姥/*yǔ* 麌/*mǔ* 姥/*yǔ* 麌/*mǔ* 姥/*yǔ* 麌): "輝輝南珍，英英周
     魯，挺奇荊吳，昭文烈武，建策烏林，龍驤江浦。摧堂堂之勁陣，鬱風翔而
     雲舉，紹樊韓之遠蹤，侔徽猷於召武，非劉孫之鴻度，孰能臻茲大祐！信乾
     坤之相成，庶物希風而潤雨。"

41   The Yellow River skirts Yizhou 益州 (at the northern border of modern-day Sichuan), and
     flows past the Min Mountains 岷山, 500 km long from northeast to southwest, that sepa-
     rate the Yellow River hydraulic system from that of the Yangtse. "Il n'y a pas 250 kilomètres
     à vol d'oiseau de l'un à l'autre, du sud-ouest au nord-est, mais une puissante barrière de
     monts neigeux les séparе," write Élisée & Onésime Reclus, *L'Empire du milieu* (Paris 1902),
     p. 278. Though Chang Qu's 常璩 (4th cent.) *Huayang guozhi* 華陽國志 (*Records of the
     States South of Mount Hua*) mentions "Three Rivers 三江" in Yizhou, here Li Hao means
     the Three Rivers 三河 of Liangzhou: Yellow River, Huang River and Cizhi River.

42   Literally, "*shang* storm 商風," *shang* being the name of a note on the pentatonic scale
     associated with autumn, the season for warfare.

43   The "Brandishing Battler 招搖," name of the last star in the Northern Dipper's 北斗
     handle, symbolic of warfare. "Floreate standard 華旌" — as in Hua-Xia 華夏, an ancient
     name for China's Central Plain — implies that Li Hao is a standard bearer for superior
     culture. In the next verse, "August Culmen 皇極" refers to the imperial house in Jiankang,
     whose support Li Hao is soliciting.

44   *JS* 87:2267 (rhyme: *qīng* 清/*gēng* 庚/*gēng* 庚/*gēng* 庚/*qīng* 清/*qīng* 清/*qīng* 青): "岷益
     既蕩，三江已清，穆穆盛勳，濟濟隆平，御羣龍而奮策，彌萬載以飛榮，仰
     遺塵於絕代，企高山而景行。將建朱旗以啟路，驅長轂而迅征，靡商風以抗
     斾，拂招搖之華旌，資神兆於皇極，協五緯之所寧。"

LI HAO'S LAST YEARS

Doughty and stalwart are our shields and ramparts;[45]
Placidly protecting us is the Upper Straightener in the sky.[46]
Without compunction, we shall cut the ears of the bolting culprits,[47]
[And] hew through that whole ill-favoured kind.
In so doing,
We shall scatter the spreading dust [raised in battle] so as to reach [the
    Jin emperor] facing south;
We shall save the valour of our land of Liang from [the humiliation to
    which] it had succumbed.
When Changyu is [the Yellow Emperor's] groom [again], I shall stand
    next to him,
And upon reaching Xiangcheng, take over the reins.[48]
I know the propitious time to get rid of this bane is here and now,
Now that I can re-enact what was narrated of that shepherd boy.
As I examine minute signs that a turning point is about to come,
I forego my meals and forget to sleep in my intense concentration.
Let this be my memorial, couched in clumsy rhyme on this piece of silk,
As I call on the bright sun itself to be witness to my sincerity.[49]

When Li Hao was bedridden with illness, he made this testamentary
command to Song You: "I have known bitterness when I was young, I have
tasted every hardship. In a time of destruction and chaos I was pushed

---

45 Loosely quoted from *Shijing* #7 (Tuju 兔罝), *SSJ* p. 281a, transl. Waley p. 110: "Stout-hearted
    are the warriors,/ Shield and rampart of our elder and lord."

46 The "Upper Straightener 上弼": a star in the constellation Draco, visible all year long in
    Northern China.

47 "Culprits 鯨," literally "whales," from *Zuo zhuan* Xuan 12.2i, *SSJ* p. 1883a, *Zuo Tradition*,
    p. 663: "In ancient times, when enlightened kings attacked the disrespectful, they took the
    greatest culprits 鯨鯢 among them and had them killed and sealed off in a mound as the
    most extreme punishment."

48 This refers to an anecdote in *Zhuangzi* 24 (Xu Wugui 徐无鬼), 8B:830–833: "The Yellow
    Emperor 黃帝 went to visit the Great God of Juci Mountain 具茨之山 [with six worthy
    attendants,] Changyu 昌寓 serving as his groom. [...] When they had arrived at the fields
    of Xiangcheng 襄城, all seven worthies were lost, and nowhere could they ask the way. By
    chance they came across a boy pasturing horses [... who not only knew the way, but also
    how to rule the world — in the same way as he pastured his horses]." Li Hao is like the
    "boy" (the "shepherd boy" in the next line) who would counsel the "Yellow Emperor," i.e.
    the Eastern Jin emperor.

49 *JS* 87:2267 (rhyme: *zhì* 質/*zhì* 至/*zhì* 至/*zhì* 至/*shù* 術/*zhì* 至/*zhì* 質): "赳赳干城，翼翼
    上弼，恣誠奔鯨，截彼醜類。且灑游塵於當陽，拯涼德於已墜。間昌寓之驂乘，暨
    襄城而按轡。知去害之在茲，體牧童之所述，審機動之至微，思遠餐而忘
    寐，表略韵於紈素，託精誠于白日。"

forward to run this place, but weak of talent and shallow of understanding as I am, I have not been capable of unifying all the lands west of the Yellow River under one rule. And now my energies are spent; I will no doubt not get up again. To die is the ultimate truth; it does not grieve me to die — I merely regret that my ambition has not been fulfilled. If one occupies the position of principal leader, one has to be much on guard for the first sign of danger. After I am no more, my successor ought to be like your own son to you: assist and guide him well, continue as I have been doing all my life, [and] don't let him place himself on a pedestal or be haughty and wilful. What is to be done with respect to the army and the state I entrust to you; don't contrive schemes that, in your heart, you don't feel to be right, lest you forfeit the one key to success and failure [namely, integrity]." In the thirteenth year (of the Jianchu era = 417), he passed away at the age of sixty-seven [*sui*]. His countrymen gave him the posthumous title Prince of Martial Splendour,[50] named his grave the Tomb of the Initiator of the Dynasty 建世陵, and gave him the temple name Grand Progenitor 太祖.[51]

Prior to this, west of the Yellow River there grew no catalpa trees, nor pagoda trees, cypresses or lacquer trees; in Zhang Jun's time, some had been planted, taken from Qin and Long (= Shaanxi and Gansu), but in the end they had all died. However, in the northwestern corner of the palace grounds in Jiuquan, a pagoda tree did grow, and Li Hao further composed a "*Fu* on a Pagoda Tree (*Huaishu fu* 槐樹賦)" in which he expressed his emotions — that is to say, lamented the fact that such an out-of-the-way, remote area was not the right place for him to establish merit. He likewise commanded his Recorder, Liang Zhongyong, as well as Liu [Bing, byname] Yanming, to write prose compositions. Upset by the military

---

50   No connection is to be sought between Li Hao's (not unusual) posthumous title "of Martial Splendour (Zhaowu 昭武)" and (1) the fact that there was a Zhaowu County in Zhangye Commandery, renamed Linze 臨澤 in early Western Jin (*JS* 14:433), and known for its strong Sogdian community; and (2) that Zhaowu also occurs as the Chinese transcription of a Sogdian noble title, as attested from Sui times onward. (See Yukata Yoshida, "On the Origin of the Sogdian Surname Zhaowu 昭武 and Related Problems," in *Journal Asiatique* 291.1–2 (2003), pp. 35–67.)

51   A tomb with a "truncated pyramid-shaped ceiling 覆斗頂," excavated in Dingjiazha 丁家閘, Suzhou District 肅州區, Jiuquan City, between 2000 and 2004, is presumed to be Li Hao's. It has a 70 m-long ramp descending towards a 90 m2 "underground home" for the deceased, 20 m underground. The tomb has long been robbed clean of its contents, but Dingjiazha Tomb 5 — a better-preserved tomb, nearby and of comparable date — contains murals that are illustrated in Wu Hung, *The Art of the Yellow Springs: Understanding Chinese Tombs* (Honolulu 2010), pp. 34–38.

troubles that so frequently flared up, and by the noisy contentiousness that was so commonplace at the time, he deliberately composed a "*Fu* on One Mightily Flushed with Wine 大酒容賦" to make a display of carefree and uninhibited feeling. Sharing the same ideals with Xin Jing 辛景 and Xin Gongjing 辛恭靖, these were his best friends; Jing and others sought refuge under the Jin, but were murdered south of the Yangtse, and Li Hao grieved for them when he heard the news. Li Hao's former wife was a daughter of Xin Na's, from the same commandery,[52] who in her loyalty and gentleness was of exemplary decorum; she died before him, and Li Hao wrote the funerary dirge for her in his own hand. Apart from these, he left ten books of poems and *fu*. His eldest son, Tan, died early (404); his second son, Xin, succeeded him.[53]

---

52 Xin Na is mentioned only this once in the *Jin shu*. Xin Jing and Xin Gongjing made their way to Eastern Jin, where Xin Jing became Prefect of Linhai 臨海太守 — he had this position in 402 (*JS* 10:255) — and Xin Gongjing became Administrative Advisor 諮議 參軍 (*JS* 89:2321). There is no mention other than here that they were murdered. The Xin clan was, like Li Hao's earliest-known ancestors, from Didao in Longxi.

53 *JS* 87:2267–2268.

CHAPTER 12

The Sequel: Li Hao's Son Loses Western Liang

In the first month of 417, Eastern Jin's Defender-in-chief (*taiwei* 太尉) Liu Yu set out with a naval force from Pengcheng 彭城 (modern-day Xuzhou, in Jiangsu) and reached the Yellow River four days later. By this time, the lower reaches of the Yellow River, from the seaboard up to Luoyang, marked the frontier between Eastern Jin and Northern Wei: "Those of Wei, with thousands of horsemen, followed [Liu] Yu's army on its westward course, along the Yellow River; his soldiers, on the southern bank, pulled [the barges onward] with ropes made of twisted bamboo strips, and whenever [a barge] drifted off towards the northern bank due to the strong wind, [its occupants] were at once killed or taken captive by the men of Wei."[1] One month and a half later, Liu Yu reached Luoyang; then, entering the Wei River, an advance corps set course for Chang'an while the main body of the army under Liu Yu's command followed over land, on the territory of Later Qin. By the ninth month, Chang'an had been taken and the last ruler of Later Qin, Yao Hong 姚泓 (388–417, r. 416–417), made prisoner. He was to be executed in Jiankang.[2]

Li Hao therefore did not live to see this Eastern Jin campaign, which not only stopped short of Liangzhou, but was abandoned altogether when it had served its political purpose to pave the way for Liu Yu's enthronement as the first emperor of Southern Song. Li Hao's son Li Xin gave the court in Jiankang formal notice of his father's death, and the court thereupon acknowledged Li Xin as the new Governor of Liangzhou and Duke of Liang.[3] To Juqu Mengxun, Liu Yu's impressively swift and forceful campaign came as a shock; Hu Sanxing conjectures that he was afraid his Chinese subjects ("notables and common people 士民" alike) would rally to Liu Yu, rising in revolt against him.[4] But nothing of the kind happened; Liu Yu retreated, and less than a year later, the Xiongnu Helian Qugai 赫連屈丐 (a.k.a. Helian Bobo 赫連勃勃, 381–425, r. 407–425), who from the north of modern Shaanxi already ruled his statelet of "Great Xia" 大夏 (407–431), descended upon Chang'an and proclaimed himself emperor of Xia in the last days of 418.[5]

---

1 *Song shu* 48:1425 = *ZZTJ* 118:3703.
2 *ZZTJ* 118:3704–3711.
3 *JS* 10:259, 262, 266.
4 *JS* 129:3198, *Shiliu guo chunqiu* 96:1070, *ZZTJ* 118:3711 (with Hu Sanxing's comment).
5 *ZZTJ* 118:3723.

THE SEQUEL: LI HAO'S SON LOSES WESTERN LIANG 165

Meanwhile, in Jiuquan, Li Xin had succeeded Li Hao as the ruler of Western Liang. His biography, appended to Li Hao's, begins:

> The Last Ruler of Liang had the personal name Xin and the byname Shiye (d. 420). When Li Hao passed away, the officers on his staff deferred to [Li Xin] as their Area Commander-in-chief, General-in-chief, Duke of Liang and concurrently Governor of Liangzhou, as well as Commandant Protector of the Qiang. He declared a general amnesty within the borders, and changed the era title to Jiaxing 嘉興 (417–420). His mother, *née* Yin, he honoured as Lady Dowager;[6] he made Song You General of the Martial Guard, Prefect of Guangxia and Libationer of the Military Council overseeing the Three Bureaus; Suo Xian he made General Conquering the Caitiffs and Prefect of Zhangye.

Juqu Mengxun challenged Li Xin to do battle, raided his territory and made off with the autumn harvest, and ruled his own state with commendable discipline — whereas Li Xin, though by no means lax at defending himself, unconscionably allowed Western Liang to become weakened from within. This reading of events is consonant with a general tendency amongst traditional historiographers to find character faults with the last rulers, but the *Jin shu* adduces contemporary documents to prove the point, as follows:

> Li Xin was unduly severe in his use of punishments, and undertook endless repair and construction projects. Palace Attendant Zhang Xian 張顯 submitted a remonstration to admonish him: "Since the beginning of this year, yin and yang have been out of kilter; there have been frequent treacherous storms and violent spells of rain that have violated and harmed the harmonious pneuma prevailing amongst us. Our domain (= Liangzhou) is at present separated into three parts which, due to circumstances beyond our control, have failed to stay permanently together; the fundamental way to merge and reunite them is to have a solid basis in farming as well as in warfare, just as the road towards conciliating [people] living far away comes down to treating them magnanimously and without excessive demands.[7] If, on the contrary, you subject them to

---

6 I render *wang* 王 as "prince," not "king," in Li Hao's posthumous title, and here give "Lady Dowager" for *taihou* 太后 (Hucker, op. cit., #6166, opts for "Consort Dowager") to underline that Western Liang did not officially proclaim itself independent of Eastern Jin.

7 As Southern Liang ceased to exist in 414, the "three parts" of "our domain 區域 (= Liangzhou)" cannot be Northern, Western, and Southern Liang, but rather correspond to Former Liang's

166   CHAPTER 12

frequent punishment and severe laws, and task them with [the construction of] palace halls, the people's forces will flag and wither away, [and]
the population will become plaintive and disheartened. Truly it is here
that the blame lies for the calamities that we have called upon ourselves!"

Assistant Magistrate 主簿 Fan Cheng 氾稱 submitted another remonstration to admonish him:

I have heard that Heaven cares about the successor to a ruler [whose
mandate came from Heaven itself] as if it were Heaven's own son, with
the utmost solicitude. That is why, if the government is not taken proper
care of, it rains down censure in the form of natural calamities, so as to
warn him. If he reforms, prosperity definitely will be his, however much
he courted danger before — as was the case with Duke Jing of Song.[8] If
he does not reform, he is bound to perish, however secure he seemed
before — as was the case with the Duke of Guo.[9] On the day *guimao* 癸卯,

---

division of the province into a Hezhou (east of the Yellow River), a Liangzhou proper (from the
Yellow River to the northwest, up to the Shule River), and Shazhou (further to the northwest,
past Dunhuang into Xinjiang) — in other words, a Liangzhou in its largest historical extent.

8   "In the thirty-seventh year [of Duke Jing of Song 宋景公, r. 516–451 BCE], [...] [the planet
    Mars, i.e.] the Sparkling Deluder 熒惑, stood in [the asterism] Heart 心. [The asterism] Heart
    is that to which [the state of] Song, on earth, corresponds. Duke Jing was troubled by it. His
    astrologer Ziwei 子韋 said, '[The looming disaster] can be deflected upon the prime minis-
    ter.' Duke Jing said, 'My prime minister is my indispensable support!' Ziwei said, 'It can be
    deflected onto the people.' Duke Jing said, 'A ruler depends on his people!' [Ziwei] said, 'It can
    be deflected upon the year's harvest.' Duke Jing said, 'If the harvest fails, the people will suf-
    fer; over whom then am I to rule?' Ziwei said, 'Although Heaven is high, it listens to [what is
    said] here below. You have said three things worthy of a true ruler, my Lord, and the Sparkling
    Deluder ought to move.' Thereupon he observed it, and indeed it moved three degrees away."
    See *Shiji* 38:1631. The "three degrees" meant that Duke Jing's lifespan was extended by 3 ×
    7 = 21 years, according to *Lüshi chunqiu*.

9   *Guoyu* 國語 8 (Jin yu 晉語), fols. 4b–5a (*Sibu beiyao* 四部備要 ed.): "[Chou] Duke of Guo 虢
    公醜 (d. 655 BC) dreamt, in his ancestral temple, that a god with human face, white hair and
    tiger claws stood by the western upturned eaves holding a battle-axe. Frightened, the Duke
    ran away. Said the god, 'Don't run! Heaven's command to you is to let Jin 晉 steal its way into
    your gate.' The Duke bowed and kowtowed, then woke up and summoned his astrologer Yin
    史嚚 to make divination. His reply was, 'The way you tell it, it must have been Rushou 蓐收,
    Heaven's punishing god. Its officers bring Heaven's affairs to completion (?天事官成).' The
    Duke had him imprisoned, and what is more, had his people congratulate him on his dream.
    Zhou Zhiqiao 舟之僑 declared to his family: 'Everyone says that the end of Guo cannot be
    far away, but now I know it for certain. Our lord unconscionably wants us to congratulate
    him because [Jin,] a large state, will steal its way in; he himself is beyond cure. I have heard
    it said that when a small state steals its way onto the roads of a large state, it is tantamount
    to submitting to it; but when a small state overreaches itself, and allows a large state to steal
    its way into it, it is tantamount to getting itself killed. [...] Within six years, Guo did indeed
    perish."

THE SEQUEL: LI HAO'S SON LOSES WESTERN LIANG 167

in the third month of the first year (of the Jiaxing era = 417),[10] the Hall of Self-effacing Virtue 謙德堂 in Dunhuang collapsed; in the eighth month, the earth split open in Xiaogu; on New Year's Day of the second year (418), gloomy fog blocked everything up; in the fourth month, the sun turned red and emitted no rays, and two weeks later it happened again; in the eleventh month, a fox climbed up the south gate; and now, this spring and summer, the earth has trembled no less than five times; while in the sixth month, a star fell in Jiankang. My studies may have stopped short of scrutinising antiquity, and in cleverness I must yield to [Dong] Zhongshu 董仲舒,[11] but I have nonetheless learnt much about the Way from my former teachers, and moreover I have fifty-nine years of age. I beg that I may briefly tell Your Highness what my own ears and eyes have heard and seen, since I am unable to discourse abstrusely of events that happened in [ancient] books and [old] traditions.

Well then, at the start of the Xian'an 咸安 era (371–372), the earth split open in Xiping and a fox entered the Hall of Self-effacing Virtue by the front; and erelong the Qin army arrived suddenly, and the capital city did not hold against them. When Liang Xi was then made to govern Liangzhou, alleging that the House of Qin was at war and, in turmoil, he set his sights on holding all the lands of Liang under his own control,[12] externally he did nothing to reconcile the people to his rule, while internally he raked in a maximum of taxes. In the nineteenth year of the Jianyuan era (= 383), the south gate of Guzang collapsed and a stone fell on the Hall of Leisured Ease 閑豫堂; in the twentieth year (= 384), Lü Guang rebelled in the east. First, [Liang Xi's] son was defeated; thereafter, he himself was slaughtered. Subsequently, Duan Ye, taking advantage of the fact that the barbarians created chaos, proclaimed himself in control of this area; over the next three years, however, the earth shook in over fifty places, and not long afterwards, our former prince rose up, dragon-like, in Guazhou 瓜州, while [Juqu] Mengxun killed [Duan Ye] in Zhangye. All these are facts that have happened before our own eyes, and Your Highness will also be aware of them. Xiaogu was where our former prince took the first steps of

---

10 There was no day *guimao* in that month (the second day of the fourth month was a *guimao* day: May 3, 417).

11 Dong Zhongshu (ca. 198–ca. 107 BCE), Academician 博士 under the Han Emperor Wu, specialised in the *Spring-and-Autumn Annals* with the *Gongyang Commentary* and had the reputation, for Ban Gu in HS 27A:1317, of having been "the founding father of the devotion to classical teachings and texts 為儒者宗."

12 The reader will remember that Liang Xi was appointed governor, in 376, by the (Former) Qin ruler Fu Jian; disaster struck in 383 at the battle at the River Fei, after which the Qin empire disintegrated.

his official career, while [the Hall of] Self-effacing Virtue was the very hall where he acceded to his exalted position; for [the hall] to collapse and the earth to split open [in Xiaogu] is a portent of the greatest misfortune. The sun is the essence of Great Yang, the emblem of the Central States: for it to turn red and emit no rays means that the Central States shall be overrun and destroyed by barbarians. As the adage has it, "When a wild beast enters the house, the master better leave." Now a fox climbed up the south gate: that too stands for a major calamity. Because *hu* 狐, "fox," equals *hu* 胡, "barbarian," it is as if Heaven had said that barbarians will take up residence in this city and will reside here as rulers. In the past, at the time of the Springs-and-Autumns, a star fell down in Song, and its Duke Xiang was eventually taken prisoner by Chu.[13] The earth is what is most yin in nature, and it is the emblem of the barbarians; it should be at rest, but if instead it moves and throws the normal order of Heaven into turmoil, it is as if Heaven said that the barbarians shall shake up the Central States — and that if the Central States fail to cultivate virtue, they will call the calamity of Duke Xiang upon themselves.

For a commoner clad in homespun, I have received signal munificence from the former court, always, as if self-evidently, being treated as familiarly as if I were a son or younger brother [of Li Hao's]; that is why I do not shirk from incurring punishment from you, presenting my ignorant yet earnest [advice] even at the risk of death. May Your Highness draw the noble in spirit near to yourself and treat your neighbours well;[14] conserve your power though looking for openings to use it; put a halt to efforts spent on [building] palatial halls; and end the pleasures of the hunt. Let the concubines and consorts in the rear quarters of the palace, and sons and daughters of foreign blood, each either receive his personal allotment of arable land or, as the case may be, the necessary encouragement to raise silkworms and spin silk; take pride in the simple virtues of honesty and thrift; [and] cease these extravagant and squanderous expenses. Let the tax you levy on the people be allocated exclusively to the needs of the army and the state. Treat subordinate officers with humility; welcome as many men of outstanding ability as you can; practice the same policies as the House of Qin in this regard, so as to strengthen the state and enrich its fabric. Once the state shall have accumulated several years

---

13   In 644 BCE, "stones fell from the sky in Song, five in number: they were meteorites" (*Zuo zhuan* Xi 16.1, *Zuo Tradition*, p. 331). In 639 BCE, in accordance with the predictions, Duke Xiang of Song 宋襄公 was taken prisoner by Chu (*Chunqiu* Xi 21.4, *Zuo zhuan* Xi 21.3; *Zuo Tradition* pp. 349, 351).

14   A quote, from *Zuo zhuan* Yin 6.4, *Zuo Tradition*, p. 41.

THE SEQUEL: LI HAO'S SON LOSES WESTERN LIANG

[of tax earnings] and the courts [of government] shall have filled up with officials civil and military, only then should [Your Highness] command a [new-found] Han [Xin] and Bai [Qi] to form the vanguard,[15] and take the marvellous stratagems of a [Zhang Liang, courtesy name] Zifang to heart; then with a single drumbeat shall Guzang be pacified, and in one long gallop, you may go drench your horse at the [Rivers] Jing and Wei. Just when, facing east, you contend for supremacy over the Empire, what cause for worry should [Juqu] Mengxun then still give you? But otherwise, I fear the peril that looms over your ancestral temple shall topple it within a decade.

But Li Xin did not adopt either remonstrance.[16]

And this, needless to say, was what doomed him. A Sogdian, no less, wearing the "conical hat (*qia* 帢)" typical of their costume, appeared in a dream to predict his end. Li Xin was killed in battle; Juqu Mengxun took Jiuquan, then marched upon Dunhuang, where another son of Li Hao's, Li Xun, was prefect. At first, Li Xun fled the city, and Juqu Mengxun installed, as his own new Prefect of Dunhuang, the son of the man whom Li Hao, at the dawn of his political rise, had rather deviously neutralised: Suo Si's son, Suo Yuanxu 索元緒. Some people of note in Dunhuang hankered after Li Xun's former leadership, however, and succeeded in engineering his return. Juqu Mengxun now besieged the city, and this, in 421, proved Western Liang's last stand. Dunhuang fell, the inhabitants were put to the sword, and although Li Xun's son somehow managed to escape, Li Xun himself, in one account, "requested [Juqu Mengxun] to surrender [honourably], but [Juqu Mengxun] would not allow it; the walled city fell, Xun committed suicide, and Mengxun then took Dunhuang."[17] Western Liang had lasted for twenty-two years (400–421).

---

15 *Renwu zhi* 人物志 A3 (Liuye 流業): "Leaving the common run of men behind them in terms of courage and strength; surpassing others in talent and strategic vision: that is what one calls valorous heroes, and Bai Qi 白起 (d. 257 BCE) and Han Xin 韓信 (ca. 231–196 BCE) fit that description" ("膽力絕衆，材略過人，是謂驍雄，白起、韓信是也。"). Cf. transl. John K. Shryock, *The Study of Human Abilities: The* jen wu chih *of Liu Shao* (New Haven 1937).

16 *JS* 87:2268–2270.

17 *Wei shu* 99:2203. According to *Song shu* 98:2414, Dunhuang surrendered in 422 (*sic*) through the initiative of two of Li Xun's subordinate officers, Song Cheng 宋承 and Zhang Hong 張弘, the same ones who, in 420, had brought Li Xun back to Dunhuang to chase away Suo Yuanxu after Juqu Mengxun first seized the city; that is the version of events adopted by *ZZTJ* 119:3737–3739. *Jin shu* 87 (see next page hereafter) fails to mention the role of Song Cheng and Zhang Hong as "capitulators" and does not say how Li Xun met his end.

CHAPTER 13

The Aftermath, and Conclusions

There is some confusion as to what happened to different members of the Li family after their state of Western Liang was lost. First, the version given in the *Jin shu*, chapter 87:

> [Li] Fan and his younger brother [Li] Xun, the Prefect of Dunhuang, together with [Li Hao's] other sons, now abandoned Dunhuang and fled to Beishan; Mengxun then made Suo Si's son, [Suo] Yuanxu, acting Prefect of Dunhuang. Yuanxu was a brutal and sinister character, much given to random killing, and utterly lost the people's support. Song Cheng and Zhang Hong, natives of the commandery, on account of the benevolent style of government [Li] Xun had evinced when he administered the commandery, invited Xun back in a secret letter. At the head of several dozen horsemen, Xun made his entry into Dunhuang, while Yuanxu fled east to Liangxing. Song Cheng and others publicly recognised Xun as their Army Commander and Governor of Liangzhou. Mengxun dispatched his chosen successor, Dezheng 德政,[1] with an army to attack Xun, but Xun locked the gates and would not engage in battle. Mengxun then personally led twenty thousand troops to attack him, and had a dam raised on three sides [of the walled city of Dunhuang] so as to flood it with water. Xun sent a thousand sturdy fellows out to make a bridge of planks bound together, intending stealthily to breach the dam; however, Mengxun directed his soldiers to confront them in battle and slaughter everyone in the walled city. Li Xin's son Chong'er 重耳 managed to escape south of the Yangtse and served in office under the Song; later, he took refuge in [Northern] Wei and became Prefect of Hengnong 恒農. Mengxun moved [Li] Fan's son [Li] Bao 寶 (d. 459) and others to Guzang, but before the year was out, [Li Bao] fled northwards to Yiwu 伊吾, and later took refuge in [Northern] Wei. Only [Li Xin's mother], *née* Yin, as well as his daughters died in Yiwu.[2]

---

1 Or Zhengde, according to *JS* 129:3198, *Song shu* 98:2413, *Shiliu guo chunqiu* 96:1071 (though 94:1047 has Dezheng), and *ZZTJ* 119:3738.

2 Yiwu corresponds to the modern city of Hami 哈密市 in Xinjiang, some 400 km north of Dunhuang. It was the last outpost on the northwestern fringe of Zhang Jun's territory during

THE AFTERMATH, AND CONCLUSIONS

Li Hao came to power in the fourth year of the Long'an era of [the Jin Emperor] An (= 400); by the first year of the Jingping 景平 era of Emperor Shao of the Song 宋少帝 (Liu Yifu 劉義符, 406–424, r. 423–424; = 423), when [his state] was destroyed, [the Li rulers] had held the territory west of the Yellow River for a total of twenty-four years.[3]

• • •

To start with, why "twenty-four years"? An honest mistake, induced by failing correctly to correlate the calendars of Eastern Jin and Southern Song with the events in Liangzhou, it appears.[4] This is, after all, a convoluted era in Chinese history.

Then, some loose ends. According to the *Wei shu*, when Juqu Mengxun entered Jiuquan in 420, he came upon the house inhabited by Li Hao's younger half-brother Song You, and instead of gold and silver, "he found only several thousand book scrolls and a few dozen jars with salt and rice, and said with a sigh, 'As little pleasure as I take in having vanquished Li Xin, so glad am I to have found Song You.' He appointed him Minister of Personnel in his Secretariat (*shangshu libu langzhong* 尚書吏部郎中), entrusting him with the responsibility to assess and select [candidates for office]."[5] His reputation for incorruptibility ensured that Song You continued to hold high office under Juqu Mengxun's son and successor, Juqu Maoqian (or Mujian, r. 433–439), until Northern Liang was finally overrun by Northern Wei in 439 and Song You followed Juqu Maoqian to the Northern Wei capital Pingcheng, where he died.[6]

To continue, according to the *Jin shu*, after the fall of Jiuquan, Juqu Mengxun "moved [Li] Fan's son [Li] Bao and others to Guzang" — these "others" including Li Hao's widow, *née* Yin, and her daughter Jing'ai. The *Wei shu* adds that in Guzang, Juqu Mengxun tried to console Li Hao's widow with the loss of her

---

the Former Liang, but by this time (421–422) it had fallen under the sway of the Rouran 柔然 qhaganate (ca. 394–552), known to the Romans as the Avars.

3   *JS* 87:2270–2271.

4   *Jin shu jiaozhu* 18:19b–20a.

5   *Wei shu* 52:1153. "Jars": *hu* 斛 in the text, a capacity measure equivalent to 30 litres at this time. Others besides Song You have been praised in similar terms for their incorruptibility: thus, in *SGZ* 12:347, Cao Cao, "inspecting [Wang] Xiu's 王脩 home, found less than ten jars of grain but several hundred book scrolls, and said with a sigh, 'His reputation is indeed far from baseless!' And with due courtesy, he appointed him Division Head of the Minister of Works, Acting Master of Metals — Leader of Court Gentlemen and, in a further promotion, Prefect of Wei Commandery."

6   *Wei shu*, ibid.

son Li Xin, but was haughtily told that "now that the House of Li has been destroyed by a barbarian, what more is there to say!" Yet, in what surely bears a charitable interpretation, Juqu Mengxun gave Li Jing'ai in marriage to his own son, Maoqian.[7] After Maoqian's death, says the *Wei shu*, "[Juqu Maoqian's] depraved wife, *née* Li, served his three older and younger brothers in succession as their paramour." This scurrilous formulation should perhaps not surprise us from a Chinese historian (Wei Shou), but it entirely misrepresents the institution of the levirate that is at issue here, and that was a cultural feature of the Qiang (and evidently also of the Northern Wei Xianbei).[8]

Another piece of information provided by the *Jin shu* and related at greater length in the *Wei shu* is that, in 423, Li Bao, his grandmother *née* Yin and other daughters of Li Hao's, in the company of an uncle, Tang Qi 唐契 (d. 442), fled from Guzang to Yiwu. This is the last one hears of Li Hao's widow *née* Yin. However, it bears mention that local traditions in Guzang (today's Wuwei City) are in disagreement with both the *Jin shu* and the *Wei shu* account. Indeed, until today, on Xinjian Street 新建路 in Wuwei's Liangzhou District, a Temple of [Lady] Yin's Terrace 尹臺寺 is reputed to be the place where Juqu Mengxun had a mansion built for Li Hao's widow to end her days (she reportedly died at the age of 75).[9] In the *Wei shu* account, on the other hand, Tang Qi, being the elder of the little band of refugees, not only found shelter in the Rouran qhaganate, but was allowed to call himself Prince of Yiwu 伊吾王. Upon Tang Qi's death in 442, Li Bao pledged allegiance to Northern Wei, returned to Dunhuang and had a further official career in Dunhuang and in Pingcheng under the Wei emperors Tuoba Dao 拓跋燾 (Emperor Taiwu 太武帝, Shizu 世祖, r. 424–452) and Tuoba Jun 拓跋濬 (Emperor Wencheng 文成帝, Gaozong 高宗, r. 452–465).[10] As we saw at the outset, the Tang imperial house claimed descent from the Li clan of Longxi (as well as, more abstrusely, from Laozi 老子, or Li Dan 李聃 — but of this claim we may make abstraction), and traced its ancestry more specifically to Li Chong'er, son of Li Xin and grandson of Li Hao. What appears from *Wei shu* 39, a chapter entirely devoted to the careers

---

7   *JS* 96:2527 = *ZZTJ* 119:3738.

8   *Wei shu* 99:2208; see also *HHS* 87 (Xi Qiang zhuan 西羌傳), p. 2869: "When the older brother dies, [his younger brother] takes in the widowed elder brother's wife 兄亡納釐娋 (*lisao*)."

9   This site, also called the Royal Lady's Terrace 皇娘娘臺, is in fact built upon the remnants of a Qijia Culture burial site, excavated in the years 1957 to 1975; it must have had cultic importance ever after, since it was also said to have been Dou Rong's headquarters early in the Eastern Han, as well as the site of a shrine erected to Dou Rong's memory that persisted into Tang times. See e.g. *Wuwei shi zhi* 武威市志 (Lanzhou 1998), p. 682.

10 *Wei shu* 39:885–886.

THE AFTERMATH, AND CONCLUSIONS   173

of Li Bao and his descendants, is that at least this branch of the Li clan from Didao in Longxi became incorporated into and indistinguishable from the Northern Wei elite. After a century of Northern Wei rule, and into the Sui, the Tang founder Li Yuan 李淵 (Gaozu 高祖, r. 618–626) claimed ancestry from this branch of the family. That is not necessarily in contradiction with the modern consensus that the Tang emperors were of mixed Chinese, Xianbei and proto-Turkish stock.[11]

• • •

Juqu Mengxun's Northern Liang proved to be the last of the Sixteen Kingdoms. After the conquest of Western Liang, it controlled all of the Hexi Corridor. Later Liang was gone (403), Southern Liang was gone (414), and so was Later Qin (417); that left the one small state still remaining in the larger Shaanxi-Gansu area, Western Qin, with its capital Jincheng, dangerously exposed to its western neighbour Northern Liang (as well as to the threat of Helian Bobo's Xia state to its northeast). In 431, Western Qin succumbed to Xia, which itself fell to Northern Wei only a few months later (431). As Northern Liang took on relatively greater importance, the two geopolitical giants Northern Wei and Liu-Song ("the Jiankang Empire," in Andrew Chittick's phrase) courted Juqu Mengxun with high-sounding titles (from Jiankang he received the nobility of "Duke" that Later Qin had not been ready to bestow upon him, and was made "Prince of Liang" by Tuoba Dao);[12] it would be equally true to say that Northern Liang was squeezed between the two. As a consequence, Juqu Mengxun sent submissive memorials in both directions and, interestingly, made a request to the emperor in Jiankang to be favoured with copies of the *Book of Changes*, "the philosophers (*ziji zhushu* 子集諸書)," and Gan Bao's 干寶 (ca. 285–ca. 350?) *In Search of the Supernatural* (*Soushen ji* 搜神記).[13] This evidence of Juqu Mengxun's more than superficial grounding in Chinese tradition is, again, strikingly absent from the *Jin shu*. His son and successor Maoqian reciprocated in 437, not only with another memorial, but with the gift of a treasure trove of writings emanating from Liangzhou:

---

11   *ZZTJ* 108:3429; D. Twitchett, ed., *The Cambridge History of China*, Volume 3: *Sui and T'ang China 581–906* (Cambridge 1979), pp. 150–151. Li Hao would have been Li Yuan's seventh-generation ancestor, says Liu Xu 劉昫 (888–947) et al., eds., *Jiu Tang shu* 舊唐書 (*Old History of the Tang*; Beijing 1975) 1:1, giving the full genealogy.

12   *Song shu* 98:2414, *Wei shu* 99:2205.

13   Memorial to the court in Pingcheng, in *Wei shu* 99:2204–2205; memorial to the court in Jiankang by Juqu Mengxun's designated heir mentioned, but not quoted, in *Song shu* 98:2415 together with the request for books.

- *Master Zhousheng* 周生子, in 13 scrolls: historical observations by Zhousheng Lie 周生烈 (3rd cent.) of Dunhuang;[14]
- *Treatise on the Trend of the Times* (*Shiwu lun* 時務論), in 12 scrolls, by Yang Wei 楊偉 (3rd cent.);[15]
- *Comprehensive Outline of the History of the Three States* (*Sanguo zonglüe* 三國總略), in 20 scrolls (anon.);
- *Common Questions* (*Su wen* 俗問), in 11 scrolls (anon.);
- *Treatise on the Thirteen Provinces* (*Shisan zhou zhi* 十三州志), in 10 scrolls, by Kan Yin 闞駰 (d. ca. 440) of Zhangye;[16]
- *Elegant Epistles* (*Wenjian* 文檢) (?), in 6 scrolls (anon.);
- *Lives Exemplifying [Confucius'] Four Headings* (*Si ke zhuan* 四科傳) (?), in 4 scrolls (anon.);
- *Veritable Records of Dunhuang* (*Dunhuang shilu* 燉煌實錄), in 10 scrolls, by Liu Bing 劉昞 (d. 440) of Dunhuang;
- *History of [Former] Liang* 涼書, in 10 scrolls, also by Liu Bing;[17]
- *Lives of Han [Emperors with] Imperial Charisma* (*Han huangde zhuan* 漢皇德傳), in 25 scrolls, by Hou Jin 侯瑾 (fl. ca. 190) of Dunhuang;[18]
- *Lost Statutes* (*Wang dian* 亡典) (?), in 7 scrolls (anon.);
- *Disputations from [the State of Cao-]Wei* (*Wei bo* 魏駁) (?), in 9 scrolls (anon.);

---

14 A digest of this work entitled *Zhousheng zi yaolun* 周生子要論 (in 1 scroll) is listed in *Sui shu* 34:998; it was lost in the infamous 555 burning of the imperial library in Jiangling 江陵 (mod. Jingzhou City 荊州市, Hubei). All that is known of Zhousheng Lie and his work comes from a few quotes in Ma Zong 馬總, comp., *Yilin* 意林 (*Forest of Opinions*; 787; *DZ* 1262) that goes back to Yu Zhongrong 庾仲容 (476–549), comp., *Zichao* 子鈔 (*Excerpts from the Masters*).

15 Listed in *Sui shu* 34:1006 (in 12 scrolls); still extant in the Tang, lost thereafter. For Yang Wei see *SGZ* 9:284 n. 2 (from Guo Ban 郭頒 [early 4th cent.], *Shiyu* 世語), and *JS* 17:503. He was from Pingyi (Shaanxi).

16 Of *Sanguo zonglüe* and *Su wen* nothing more appears to be known. Kan Yin's work is listed in *Sui shu* 33:985.

17 Of *Wen jian* and *Sike zhuan* nothing more is known; I guess the latter title refers to *Lunyu* 11.3, where the Master upholds "virtuous conduct 德行, speech 言語, government 政事, and culture and learning 文學" as the four noble aspirations 四科 of a gentleman. For the author of *Dunhuang shilu*, *Sui shu* 33:963 gives Liu Jing 劉景, but this is to avoid the Tang taboo on the character *bing* 昞 (says Pu Qilong in *Shitong tongshi* 4:84). Three works titled *Liang shu* (each consisting of 10 scrolls) are listed in *Sui shu* 33:963; the one authored by Liu Bing deals with the life and times of Zhang Gui, first potentate of Former Liang.

18 A variant title of *Han huangde ji* 漢皇德記 (in 30 scrolls), listed as Hou Jin's work in *Sui shu* 33:961; it recounted the reigns of eight Eastern Han emperors, from Emperor Guangwu to Chongdi 沖帝 (Liu Bing 劉炳, r. 145).

THE AFTERMATH, AND CONCLUSIONS   175

- *Collected Works of Xie Ai* (*Xie Ai ji* 謝艾集) (fl. mid 4th cent.) of Dunhuang, in 8 scrolls;[19]
- *Graphs Old and New* (*Gu jin zi* 古今字), in 2 scrolls, by Zhang Yi 張揖 (fl. early 3rd cent.);[20]
- *Writings by the Master of Mulberry Hill* (*Sangqiu xiansheng shu* 桑丘先生書), in 3 scrolls, by Yang Wei 楊偉;[21]
- *The Gnomon and the Circular Paths of Heaven* (*Zhou bi* 周髀), in 1 scroll (anon.);
- *A Triple Concordance of Imperial and Princely Calendars* (*Huangdi, wang li sanhe ji* 皇帝王歷三合紀), in 1 scroll (anon.);
- The *Life of Zhao Fei* (*Zhao Fei zhuan* 趙[匪 + 攴]傳) (early 5th cent.) of Dunhuang, together with his *Jiayin* (= 414) *Calendar* (*Jiayin yuanli* 甲寅元歷), in 1 scroll;[22] and
- *Eulogies of Confucius* (*Kongzi zan* 孔子讚), in 1 scroll (anon.).

Such a collection could only have been produced by a flourishing urban centre with leisure on its hands, and indeed, when Northern Liang fell to Northern Wei in 439, the capital Guzang, with a population of at least 200,000, was then one of the largest cities in the North.[23]

Just like Li Xin had his end predicted by a dream, so too did a hallucinating vision tell Juqu Mengxun that his death was imminent. He was sixty-five and had ruled for thirty-three years. In an extant fragment of the *Record of Retribution for Grievances* 還冤記, also known as the *Record of Wronged Souls* 冤魂記, by Yan Zhitui, one reads:

---

19   Of the *Wang dian* and the *Wei bo* nothing more appears to be known; Xie Ai, an official under Former Liang (see *Js* 86:2241–2243), has his works in 7 scrolls listed in *Sui shu* 35:1067.

20   I attribute the *Gujin zi* to the most famous lexicographer of his time, Zhang Yi, who was however not from Liangzhou; his *Gujin zigu* 古今字詁, in 3 scrolls, is listed in *Sui shu* 32:942.

21   Emending the *Song shu* reading *Chengqiu xiansheng* 乘丘先生 — as the *Song shu* editors do (98:2421 n. 30) — to *Sangqiu xiansheng shu*, by Yang Wei (in 2 scrolls), listed in *Sui shu* 34:1006 as lost in the 555 fire.

22   The *Zhou bi* (listed in *Sui shu* 34:1018), or *Zhou bi suanjing* 周髀算經 (*The Arithmetical Classic of the Gnomon and the Circular Paths of Heaven*) in full, could be as old as the fourth century BC, but in its present form, with its first commentary by Zhao Ying 趙嬰 (ca. 180), is an Eastern Han text. See Joseph Needham, with Wang Ling, *Science and Civilisation in China* Vol. 3: *Mathematics and the Sciences of the Heavens and the Earth* (Cambridge 1959), pp. 19–20. The *Huangdi wang li sanhe ji* appears not to be otherwise known. Zhao Fei was Northern Liang's Grand Astrologer, and his calendar was adopted by Northern Wei between 412 and 522. It is listed twice in *Sui shu* 34:1022, 1023 (1 scroll). The character *fei* in Zhao Fei's name is a *hapax legomenon*, occurring nowhere else but here.

23   *Wei shu* 4A:90; Victor Xiong, "The Northern Economy," pp. 326–327.

In Juqu Mengxun's time, there was a learned and wise *śramaṇa*, Dharmarddhin, with knowledge of many things, whom Mengxun confided in and valued highly. When the House of Wei sent Li Shun to confer upon Mengxun the title of Prince of Liang, it asked for Dharmarddhin in return, but Mengxun, embarrassed, did not give him away. Dharmarddhin, though, was intent on going to Wei. Several times he clung to Mengxun, begging to go, until Mengxun killed him in a bout of rage. Not long afterwards, his attendants, in the middle of the day, saw Dharmarddhin striking at Mengxun with a sword; following which, he took ill and died.[24]

The *Jin shu* does not record that, just like Li Hao, Juqu Mengxun was given a posthumous title (by Northern Wei), "Prince of Martial Renown 武宣王."[25] His tomb has not been found, although it must have been a conspicuous monument, as the Wei emperor Tuoba Dao "assigned thirty households to keep guard over it." When Northern Liang fell in 439, a younger son of Juqu Mengxun's, Juqu Wuhui 沮渠無諱 (d. 444), fled westward to the walled oasis city of Gaochang, and there continued precariously to rule as Liu-Song-appointed Governor of Liangzhou and Prince of Hexi, instituting his own era title Chengping 承平 in 443. This distant offshoot of Northern Liang was finally wiped out by the Rouran (Avars) in 460.[26] Amongst the refugees that Juqu Wuhui brought to Gaochang was one of his father's consorts, *née* Peng 彭, otherwise unknown to history, whose tomb (dated Chengping 18 = 458) was discovered in Turfan in 1994: curiously, hers was a Taoist burial that included a lead figurine (a "lead man 鉛人," as the accompanying tomb inventory says) to serve as a substitute for the body, should pestilential "infusions 注" try to harm it. The tomb inventory addresses these ghostly emanations: "If you need must stop here, pass on; do not tarry or harm. Make haste, in accordance with [Lord Lao's 老君] statutory command!"[27]

Northern Liang had been in existence for thirty-nine years.

---

24 This *Huanyuan ji* anecdote is in Li Fang et al., comp., *Taiping guangji* 太平廣記 (*Extensive Records for the Taiping* [*xingguo*] *Era*, Beijing 1981), 119:836–837.

25 *Song shu* 98:2414, *Shiliu guo chunqiu* 96:1075, *ZZTJ* 122:3848.

26 *Wei shu* 99:2208–2210, *Song shu* 98:2416–2418, *Shiliu guo chunqiu* 97:1081–1082.

27 Zhang Xunliao 張勳燎 & Bai Bin 白彬, *Zhongguo daojiao kaogu* 中國道教考古 (Beijing 2006), Vol. 2 ch. 3: "Zhongyuan he xibei diqu Wei Jin Beichao muzang de jiezhuwen yanjiu 中原和西北地區魏晉北朝墓葬的解注文研究," pp. 351–574 at pp. 562–563 ("所止經過，不得留難，急急如律令"); Bai Bin, "Religious Beliefs as Reflected in the Funerary Record," in John Lagerwey and Lü Pengzhi, eds., *Early Chinese Religion, Part Two: The Period of Division* (220–589 AD) (Leiden 2010), Vol. 2, pp. 989–1073 at pp. 1068–1069.

THE AFTERMATH, AND CONCLUSIONS

· · ·

As has been pointed out on several occasions, there is no good reason to think that the historiographical accounts of Li Hao and Juqu Mengxun — as they were written up prior to the Tang dynasty and found their way into Cui Hong's *Shiliu guo chunqiu* and similar works — differed substantially in their *parti pris*. On the contrary, evidence abounds that Fang Xuanling and his *Jin shu* co-editors doctored these accounts in such a way that Li Hao emerges as a more virtuous, exemplary leader than he probably was, and Juqu Mengxun a less polished leader, in terms of the extent of his adaptation to Chinese ways, than he would in fact have been.

That being said, Juqu Mengxun had two different people to manage, perhaps little distinguishable at a high social level, but culturally quite divergent at a more basic level: there, Chinese farmers stood apart from "Lu River nomads," and it was the equestrian mode of life and hardiness in battle of the latter that allowed Juqu Mengxun, in the final analysis, to subdue and govern the former. From the little evidence available, it would appear that the "Lu River nomads" (like "Lesser Yuezhi") were one particular "brand" of the Qiang, hence Northern Liang should, in my view, be classed together with Later Qin as a Qiang state. But Juqu Mengxun was more than a Qiang leader; he was the "leader of an alliance," and the weight of the Chinese component should not be minimised. His biography (or "documentary record") reproduces a remonstration that leading members of his civil administration addressed to him to point out shortcomings in the business of government; reading it, one is instead impressed by how sophisticated his civil government already was:

His subordinate officials submitted a letter that said:

Instituting offices and separating their obligations is how a state is run and how its timely needs are provided for. Carefully and assiduously fulfilling the duties of one's office is the way to gain enlightenment about all the different aspects of governance. Holders of office make it their business to be selfless; men entrusted with appointments make every effort to be oblivious of themselves. [However,] since [Your] sovereign order began to hold sway, "war horses breed on the border,"[28] and [rules for] public as well as individual [conduct] remain in an embryonic state, not having had the time to become established precedents. And so, most of [Your]

---

28   *Laozi* 46, transl. D.C. Lau p. 107: "[W]hen the way does not prevail in the empire, war-horses breed on the border."

court gentlemen disregard the hallowed institutions and fail to respect statutory rules: some have official documents presented to their desk but stay at home shunning the office; others do not care about things one way or another and let things pass, staring into the air. It has come so far that promotions and demotions have ceased altogether at [Your] imperial court; that critical discussion has been shelved away under [Your] sagely reign; that pure and impure [positions in the bureaucracy] intermingle,[29] and the capable and the incompetent intermix; that people have no sense of competition and, if anything, busy themselves to get through the day. Is that their way to serve Your Majesty, to concern themselves about public [affairs], to act selflessly? Now that [Your] imperial aura is still daily in the ascendant and calm and peace reign far and near, it behoves You to give a drastic pull to the rigging [that keeps the ship of state together], and to promote time-honoured norms [of conduct] to their full extent.

Juqu Mengxun took this advice to heart; he ordered Yao Ai 姚艾, [General] Campaigning in the South, as well as Fang Gui the Secretariat's Assistant Director of the Left, to write up Rules for the Halls of Court (*chaotang zhi* 朝堂制). After enforcing them for a mere ten days, all officialdom was jolted into order.[30]

The patronage of Confucianist learning and Buddhist piety completes the impression of a state on its way towards a reconciliation of Chinese and non-Chinese elements. The verse eulogy that concludes the account of Juqu Mengxun's career in the *Jin shu* therefore sounds rather more shrill than is warranted by the facts:

---

29   "Pure" positions in government were reserved for candidates from notable families with a long record of service; "impure" positions were for candidates of lesser background. Although in Northern Wei the system was adapted to give Tuoba nobles the same "pure" credentials as Chinese candidates, it seems very unlikely that the authors of this letter could have referred to non-Chinese officials. The classic study of the system is Miyazaki Ichisada 宮崎一定, *Kyūhin kanjinhō no kenkyū: kakyo zenshi* 九品官人法の研究：科擧前史 (*The Mechanism of the Aristocracy in China: Installation of Mandarins before the Establishment of the Competitive Examination System*), Kyoto 1956.

30   *JS* 129:3198. Yao Ai, incidentally, was a general in Later Qin who sought refuge from the fall of that state first with Western Qin's Qifu Chipan in 417 (he was made Governor of Qinzhou: *ZZTJ* 118:3712), then with Juqu Mengxun in 418 (118:3719–3720). In both cases, he was well received because he brought a substantial military force along with him. Like the Yao rulers of Later Qin, Yao Ai was most probably a Qiang, and in that case, Juqu Mengxun made a non-Chinese and a Chinese official jointly responsible for this assignment.

THE AFTERMATH, AND CONCLUSIONS

[Lü] Guang was wary of his eminence amongst men;
[Duan] Ye shunned this paragon of the age.
Off on drinking sprees to dissimulate who he was,
He hid his intelligence, intending to stay safe.
But once he did indulge his evil mind,
He was bound to rake up specious achievements.
Standing out, but now for acts of treachery,
He won what fame he had in his own time.[31]

...

As for Li Hao, before his verse eulogy (which we have already quoted on p. 92 above), the *Jin shu* historian presents a kind of moral based on his life and career in what feels to me like exceptionally intricate parallel prose. The historian does not doubt the personal qualities of the Prince of Martial Splendour, his virtue or his loyalty to Eastern Jin, but imputes the fall of Western Liang to the shakiness of its foundations:

The historian says: When a true king receives the charter [to rule], he owes it all to a store of virtue accumulated over generations. It is like what is confusedly formed preceding the advent of even the greatest thearch, or like a single pneuma giving rise to the two modes [of yin and yang].[32] By the same token, the fulgurant rise of [Liu Bang from] Zhongyang was due to the foundations laid by the Huanlong [or Dragon-feeding] lineage;[33] and [the ability of Tang the Victorious, from] Bo [by Mount] Jing, to pass

---

31   *JS* 129:3199: "贊曰：光猜人傑，業忌時賢。游飲自晦，晻智圖全。兇心既逞，偽績攸宜。挺茲姦數，馳兢當年。"

32   *Laozi* 25; cf. transl. Lau p. 82: "There is a shape confusedly formed, /Born before heaven and earth. [...] I know not its name/So I style it 'the way.' [...] Hence the way is great; heaven is great; earth is great; and the king is also great. Within the realm, there are four things that are great, and the king counts as one." To avoid repetition, "thearch 帝" is substituted here for "king 王." *Zhou Yi, Xici* A.11, transl. Lynn p. 65: "Therefore, in change there is the great ultimate. This is what generates the two modes [the yin and the yang]."

33   Liu Bang was born in Zhongyang hamlet 中陽里: *Shiji* 8:341. The link between Liu Bang and his putative ancestors of the Huanlong 豢龍 lineage, and their own ancestor, the sage-emperor Yao 堯, is tenuous. "The Taotang 陶唐 lineage branch [to which Yao belonged] had already fallen into decline, but among its descendants was a certain Liu Lei 劉累, who had studied dragon-taming with the Dragon-Feeding lineage [...]. The Fan 范 lineage are [Liu Lei's] descendants" (*Zuo zhuan* Zhao 29.4a, *Zuo Tradition* p. 1699). Of this Fan lineage, "those who stayed behind in Qin 秦 became the Liu line" (*Zuo zhuan* Wen 13.2, *Zuo Tradition* p. 533). These and other *Zuo zhuan* passages were adduced by e.g. Liu Xiang, quoted approvingly by Ban Gu in *HS* 1:81, to prove the theory that "Han is descended from Yao 漢為堯後"; see *Zuo Tradition* p. 1124 n. 721.

down his rulership [to his descendants] stemmed from the inaugural moment when [his mother] ingested a swallow's egg.[34] Of heroic bearing and outstanding talent, Liang's Prince of Martial Splendour, in patterning his military exploits, played yin against yang, almost uncanny was his way in adapting to ever-changing challenges; meanwhile, in adhering to Heaven's guidelines, he made abstraction of days and months, counting in years the merit that accrued to him from bringing other people's gifts to fruition.[35] That is why he was capable of placating people on the fringe of civilisation and of restraining them, given to violence as they are; of founding a state, and of inculcating high morals to his own family. Having made five commanderies his own demesne, he nonetheless proclaimed himself a vassal [of the Eastern Jin]; having been forced to bow to a tripartite division [of the original Liangzhou],[36] he nonetheless remained deferentially loyal [to the Jin]. Now the Odes praise Qin Zhong, whose later descendant [the First Emperor] constituted an empire by levelling [all differences];[37] they eulogise Liu the Duke, whose latter-day grandsons [Kings Wen and Wu of the Zhou] founded a throne matching Heaven in its greatness.[38] [The lords of Qin] made their first mark at the confluence of the Rivers Qian and Wei;[39] [the first lord of Zhou] spread his civilising

---

34 Tang the Victorious 成湯 (trad. r. ca. 1670–1587 BCE), founder of the Shang 商 dynasty, first resided in Bo 亳 (modern-day Shangqiu City 商丘市, Henan) in the vicinity of Mount Jing 景山 (*Shangshu*, Xia 夏 4 [Yin zheng 胤征], ssj p. 158c). His mother became pregnant after ingesting a swallow's egg: *Shiji* 3:91.

35 Alludes to *Liji* 28 (Zhong yong 中庸), transl. François Jullien, *Zhong yong: La Régulation à usage ordinaire* (Paris 1993), p. 109: "L'authenticité réalisante, ce n'est pas seulement se réaliser soi-même, c'est aussi ce par quoi réaliser autrui 成物."

36 *JS* 14:434 spells this out: the "five commanderies" together constituting Hexi were Zhangye, Jiuquan, Dunhuang, Wuwei and Jincheng; Liangzhou had for the last time been one under Lü Guang, "but then its land was split in three: the Prince of Martial Splendour governing Western Liang, having established his own era title in Dunhuang; Tufa Wugu governing Southern Liang, having established his own era title in Ledu; and Juqu Mengxun governing Northern Liang, having established his own era title in Zhangye."

37 *Shijing* #126 (Che lin 車鄰) "praises Qin Zhong 秦仲" (ssj p. 368c), the fourth lord of Qin (r. 844–822 BCE), who fell in battle against the Western Rong 西戎. The thirty-seventh lord of Qin was the First Emperor 秦始皇 (r. first as king, then as emperor, 246–210 BCE), who unified China, harmonised weights and measures, and thus "levelled [all differences] 削平."

38 *Shijing* #250 (Gong Liu 公劉) eulogises "Liu the Duke," who was an ancestor of the Zhou kings, the first of whom were King Wen and King Wu, who achieved the conquest of the previous Shang 商 Dynasty.

39 *Shiji* 28:1358: "Duke Wen of Qin 秦文公 (r. 765–716 BCE) went on an eastern hunt between the Rivers Qian 汧 and Wei 渭; he had divination performed as to whether to take up residence there, and the omens were favourable."

THE AFTERMATH, AND CONCLUSIONS

influence in [his land of] Bin and [near Mount] Qi;[40] at first, by tipping just a basketful of earth at a time,[41] they wrought a fundament worthy of mighty Heaven, and from dredging a rivulet, they proceeded to open up a realm bound only by the sea. As in their case progress was necessarily gradual, so we see the same inexorable law demonstrated here: one learns [from Western Liang] that from a single [successful] reign, it does not follow that [the ruling house] deserved [Heaven's] mighty Mandate, and that for such success to be repeated and for [Heavenly] favours to accumulate, the wellsprings of that fortune must lie deep in time.[42]

This highly allusive analysis nevertheless sounds about right. Li Hao had leadership qualities that enabled him to hold his own amongst the notable, long-established settler families in Dunhuang who initially considered him a malleable instrument in their hands. He proved to be made of stronger stuff; he nearly made true on his ambition to preserve the Zhang family's "Former Liang" Chinese enclave from being entirely submerged in an alien environment.

We do not know much about his early years, but Li Hao — a county magistrate in his 40s who, in 397, won much wider renown — was then already a skilled political operator. He maintained diplomatic relations with Eastern Jin and Southern Liang, and would have done so even with Juqu Mengxun himself had the struggle for survival not doomed such overtures from the start. How he handled relations with non-Chinese communities on Western Liang's own soil is unclear; one notes an appeal to military assistance from the Dingling people, suggesting that Li Hao might have had connections with them and been pragmatic in his approach; at the same time, however, virtually all civil appointments in his administration concurrently had military responsibilities, and nowhere in Li Hao's bureaucratic apparatus was there room for any

---

40   *Mencius* 1B.14, transl. Lau p. 71: "In antiquity [...] T'ai Wang 大王 was in Pin 邠. The Ti 狄 tribes invaded Pin and he left and went to settle at the foot of Mount Ch'i 岐山." Tai Wang, or "the Old Duke Danfu 古公亶父," was a descendant of Liu the Duke and the first to name his domain "Zhou 周," whence the name of the Zhou Dynasty (1045–771/770–256 BCE). See *Shiji* 4:112–114.

41   *Lunyu* 9.19, transl. Lau p. 99: "As in the case of levelling the ground, if, though tipping only one basketful 覆簣, I am going forward, then I shall be making progress."

42   *JS* 87:2271: "史臣曰：王者受圖，咸資世德，猶混成之先大帝，若一氣之生兩儀。是以中陽勃興，資豢龍之構趾；景亳垂統，本吞鷰之開基。涼武昭王英姿傑出，運陰陽而緯武，應變之道如神；吞日月以經天，成物之功若歲。故能懷荒弭暴，開國化家，宅五郡以稱藩，屈三分而舉順。若乃詩褒秦仲，後嗣建削平之業；頌美公劉，末孫興配天之祚。或發迹於汧渭，或布化於邠岐，覆簣創元天之基，疏涓開環海之宅。彼既有漸，此亦同符，是知景命攸歸，非一朝之可致，累功積慶，其所由來遠矣。"

non-Chinese. Consequently, there is no trace of a dual kind of administration as Juqu Mengxun practised.

He hoped against hope that Eastern Jin would find the momentum to strike out northward and reunify the empire to its Han dynasty extent, with the active help of northern supporters of such an enterprise, like himself. At the same time, he knew that his own position was vulnerable, that he could but "trust to the fastness of our string of fortresses" (p. 150 above); sure enough, his military might eventually proved no match for the mounted hordes of his Qiang and Xianbei neighbours. He may not have been lucky in his sons or in his heir Li Xin in particular, but no heir would have withstood the much larger force of Northern Wei that, watching from a distance how Juqu Mengxun swept Western Liang away, proceeded to destroy the last of the Sixteen Kingdoms and prepare the way for China's reunification.

Yet if his biography is to be believed, Li Hao on his own virtually personified Chinese civilisation in his beleaguered outpost of the empire. Author of an elegant and at times even moving rhapsody, the sole example of this genre that has come down to us from this troubled period in the North, as well as of one or two other literary artefacts that speak to righteousness and good Confucian sense, Li Hao succeeded in keeping the flame of Chinese civilisation alight in distant Liangzhou, where, needless to say, it is vibrant still.

Appendix 1: Commandant Protectors of the Qiang

Appointee and term of office	Based in	Source
Est. between 140–87 BCE?	?	*Hanguan yi* in *HHS* 1B:55
Xin Tang 辛湯 (ca. 60 BCE)	?	*HS* 69:2993
Xin Linzhong 辛臨眾 (ca. 60 BCE)	?	*HS* 69:2993
Xin Tong 辛通 (?–3 CE)	?	*HS* 69:2998
Dou Kuang 竇況 (ca. 7)	?	*HS* 99A:4087
Wen Xu 溫序 (30)	Intercepted *en route*	*HHS* 81:2672
Niu Han 牛邯 (33–34)	Lianju 令居	*HHS* 1B:55, 87:2878
Dou Lin 竇林 (58–59)	Didao 狄道	*HHS* 87:2880
Guo Xiang 郭襄 (59)	Resigned *en route*	*HHS* 87:2881
Wu Tang 吳棠 (76–77)	Anyi 安夷	*HHS* 87:2881
Fu Yu 傅育 (77–87)	Linqiang 臨羌	*HHS* 87:2881–2882
Zhang Yu 張紆 (87–89)[1]	Linqiang	*HHS* 87:2882–2883
Deng Xun 鄧訓 (89–92)	Linqiang	*HHS* 16:609
Nie Shang 聶尚 (92–93)	?	*HHS* 87:2883
Guan You 貫友 (93–96)	?	*HHS* 87:2883
Shi Chong 史充 (96–97)	?	*HHS* 87:2883
Wu Zhi 吳祉 (97–100)	?	*HHS* 87:2883–2884
Zhou Wei 周鮪 (100–101)	?	*HHS* 87:2884–2885
Hou Ba 侯霸 (101–108)	?	*HHS* 87:2885–2886
Duan Xi 段禧 (108–110)	?	*HHS* 87:2886–2887
Hou Ba (110–114)	Zhangye 張掖	*HHS* 87:2887, 2889
Pang Can 龐參 (114–115)	114: Zhangye, 115: Lianju	*HHS* 87:2889
Ma Xian 馬賢 (115–129)	Lianju	*HHS* 87:2889, 2894
Han Hao 韓皓 (129–130)	?	*HHS* 87:2894
Ma Xu 馬續 (130–136)	?	*HHS* 87:2894
Ma Xian (137–139)	?	*HHS* 87:2894–2895
Lai Ji 來機 & Liu Bing 劉秉 jointly (139)	?	*HHS* 87:2895

---

1 *HHS* 3:157 must be mistaken in attributing the title to Liu Xu 劉肝 in 87 CE. As Prefect of Longxi, Liu Xu did nevertheless have a role in fighting the Qiang in the years 56 to 57: *HHS* 87:2879.

184 APPENDIX 1: COMMANDANT PROTECTORS OF THE QIANG

(cont.)

Appointee and term of office	Based in	Source
Hu Chou 胡疇 (140–142)	?	*HHS* 60A:1971
Zhao Chong 趙沖 (142–144)[2]	?	*HHS* 87:2896–2897
Zhang Gong 張貢 (145–155)	?	*HHS* 87:2897
Diwu Fang 第五訪 (155–159)	?	*HHS* 87:2897
Duan Jiong 段熲 (159–161)	?	*HHS* 87:2897
Hu Hong 胡閎 (161–163)	?	*HHS* 87:2897–2898
Duan Jiong (163–165?)	?	*HHS* 87:2898
Huangfu Gui (170–172)	?	*HHS* 65:2137[3]
Ling Zheng 泠徵 (184)	Qianya 允吾?	*HHS* 87:2899
Xia Yu 夏育 (184)	Youfufeng 右扶風	*HHS* 58:1880
Yang Pei 楊沛 (210–213?)	?	*Wei lüe* in *SGZ* 15:486
Xu Miao 徐邈 (227–239?)	?	*SGZ* 27:739–740
Zhang Gui 張軌 (301–314)	Guzang 姑臧	*JS* 86:2221
Zhang Shi 張寔 (314–320)	Guzang	*JS* 86:2226
Zhang Jun 張駿 (324–345)	Guzang	*JS* 86:2233
Zhang Zhonghua 張重華 (346–353)[4]	Guzang	*JS* 86:2240
Zhang Yaoling 張耀靈 (353)	Guzang	*JS* 86:2245[5]

---

2 An "Acting 領" Commandant Protector is mentioned for the year 144, called Wei Ju 衛琚 in *HHS* 6:274 and Wei Yao 衛瑤 at 87:2897.

3 From the wording here (Huangfu Gui was "again transferred to [the position of] Commandant Protector of the Qiang 再轉護羌校尉"), Rafe de Crespigny (*A Biographical Dictionary*, p. 353) infers that in 162 and 163, he had been commandant a first time. He certainly fought the Qiang in those years; see *HHS* 65:2133 and particularly 87:2898, where it is however made clear that he was General of the Household (*zhonglang jiang* 中郎將) and of vital help to the clueless (*wu weilüe* 無威略) commandant at the time, Hu Hong — whom he did not however replace.

4 In 346, Zhang Zhonghua arrogated the title to himself upon succeeding his father Zhang Jun as Governor and Prince of Liang (*JS* 86:2240), but the Eastern Jin Emperor Mu 穆帝 (Sima Dan 司馬聃, r. 345–361) appointed him to the position, too, by an edict from Jiankang that arrived in Liangzhou in 352 (*JS* 86:2244).

5 Zhang Yaoling, upon succeeding Zhang Zhonghua in 353, inherited his titles, including that of Colonel Protector of the Qiang, abbreviated to *xiaowei* 校尉 in *JS* 86:2245. Yaoling was 10 *sui* at the time, and was murdered soon thereafter; his uncle and successor Zhang Zuo apparently did not declare himself Colonel Protector. After Zhang Zuo, Zhang Xuanjing and Zhang Tianxi again did (again, abbr. as "*xiaowei*").

APPENDIX 1: COMMANDANT PROTECTORS OF THE QIANG 185

(*cont.*)

Appointee and term of office	Based in	Source
Zhang Xuanjing 張玄靚 (355–362)	Guzang	*JS* 86:2248
Zhang Tianxi 張天錫 (363–376)	Guzang	*JS* 86:2250
Liang Xi 梁熙 (376–385)	Guzang	*JS* 113:2898
Li Hao 李暠 (400–405)	Dunhuang	*JS* 87:2259
Li Xin 李歆 (405–420)	Dunhuang	*JS* 87:2264

Appendix 2: Prefects of Wuwei, Zhangye, Jiuquan and Dunhuang

1 Wuwei 武威

Appointee and term of office	Source
Est. between 81 and 67 BCE	*CICA* p. 76 n. 40
Wang Han 王漢 (71 BCE)	*HS* 68:2952
Ma Qi 馬期 (?–25 CE)	*HHS* 23:796
Liang Tong 梁統 (25–32)[1]	*HHS* 23:797, 806
Ren Yan 任延 (ca. 40–50?)	*HHS* 66:2462
Fu Yu 傅育 (ca. 75–76)	*HHS* 87:2881, "Treatises" 11:3232
Lian Fan 廉范 (ca. 77–78?)	*HHS* 31:1103
Zheng Zhong 鄭衆 (ca. 79–80?)	*HHS* 36:1225
Meng Yun 孟雲 (84–85)	*HHS* 89:2950, 45:1518
Feng Bao 馮豹 (ca. 95?)	*HHS* 28B:1004
Li Xun 李恂 (after 95?)	*HHS* 51:1684
Ren Jia 任嘉 (126–128)	*HHS* 79:2564
Zhao Chong 趙沖 (131–141)	*HHS* 87:2896, 48:1409
Zhang Huan 張奐 (162)	*HHS* 65:2139
[No name given] (ca. 180)	*HHS* 58:1879
Zhang Meng 張猛 (194–210)[2]	*HHS* 9:384, *Dian lüe* in *SGZ* 18:548
Guanqiu Xing 毌丘興 (219)	*SGZ* 16:492
Fan Can 范粲 (240–?)	*JS* 94:2431
Ma Long 馬隆 (278–281?)	*JS* 57:1555
Zhang Dian 張琠 (ca. 301–ca. 314)	*JS* 86:2224
Zhang Jun 張駿 (320–323)	*JS* 86:2231
Dou Tao 竇濤 (326–?)	*JS* 86:2234
Suo Pan 索泮 (363–?)	*JS* 115:2954
Peng Ji 彭濟 (?–385)	*JS* 115:2943

---

1 *HHS* 23:796 says that an (unnamed) maternal cousin 從弟 of Dou Rong was Prefect of Wuwei. As 25 to 32 match the years of Dou Rong's satrapy of the region, and as the term for Liang Tong's tenure appears to have been particularly long, Liang Tong may well have been this cousin.

2 The dates for Zhang Meng's tenure seem fairly secure. Yet *JS* 14:434 mentions a certain Zhang Ya 張雅 as Prefect of Wuwei in 195; he cannot be identical to the Zhang Ya mentioned in *SGZ* 60:1377–78.

© DOMINIK DECLERCQ, 2025 | DOI:10.1163/9789004727380_016

APPENDIX 2: PREFECTS OF WUWEI, ZHANGYE, JIUQUAN AND DUNHUANG　187

(*cont.*)

Appointee and term of office	Source
Du Jin 杜進 (386–?)	*JS* 122:3058
Linghu He 令狐赫 (400–?)	*JS* 87:2259

2　Zhangye 張掖

Appointee and term of office	Source
Est. between 111 and 104 BCE	*Shiji* 37:1439 n. 2, *HS* 28B:1613
Dou [...?] 竇 [...?] (first appointee?)[3]	*HHS* 23:796
[No name given] (81 BCE)	*HS* 94A:3783
Xin Qingji 辛慶忌 (35–33 BCE?)	*HS* 69:2996
Niu Shang 牛商 (?–18 BCE)	*HS* 19B:833
Xiao Xian 蕭咸 (ca. 10 BCE?)	*HS* 78:3291
Ren Zhong 任仲 (?–25 CE)	*HHS* 23:797
Shi Bao 史苞 (25–?)	*HHS* 23:797
Deng Hong 鄧鴻 (?–82)	*HHS* 99:2950
Li Xun 李恂 (87–88)	*HHS* 51:1683
Deng Xun 鄧訓 (88–89)	*HHS* 16:609
Ma Xu 馬續 (130–?)	*HHS* 87:2894
Diwu Fang 第五訪 (ca. 145?)	*HHS* 76:2475
Du Tong 杜通 (219)	*SGZ* 16:492
Zhang Jin 張進 (self-proclaimed, 220)	*SGZ* 2:59, 15:474, 16:492
Jiao Sheng 焦勝 (ca. 267)	*JS* 3:55
Suo Fu 索孚 (354–355)	*JS* 86:2247
Peng Huang 彭晃 (386)	*JS* 122:3058
Juqu Mengxun 沮渠蒙遜 (397)	*JS* 129:3190
Ma Quan 馬權 (398)	*JS* 129:3192
Juqu Funu 沮渠伏奴 (401)	*JS* 129:3192
Zhang Qian (symbolic, 401)	*JS* 129:3192
Juqu Gouhule 沮渠句呼勒 (410)	*JS* 129:3194

3　According to *HHS* 23:796, Dou Rong's (unnamed) great-great-grandfather 高祖父 had been Prefect of Zhangye. He could have been the first appointee to the position.

188   APPENDIX 2: PREFECTS OF WUWEI, ZHANGYE, JIUQUAN AND DUNHUANG

(cont.)

Appointee and term of office	Source
Suo Xian 索仙 (420)	*JS* 87:2268
Juqu Guangzong 沮渠廣宗 (symbolic, 420)	*JS* 87:2268

3   Jiuquan 酒泉

Appointee and term of office	Source
Est. between 111 and 104 BCE	*Shiji* 37:1439 n. 2, *HS* 28B:1613
Xin Wuxian 辛武賢 (?–61 BCE)	*HS* 8:361
Xin Qingji 辛慶忌 (25–23 BCE?)	*HS* 69:2996
Zhai Wu 祭午 (ca. 20–24? CE)	*HHS* 20:744
Liang Tong 梁統 (24–25)	*HHS* 34:1165, 23:797
Zhu Zeng 竺曾 (25–31)	*HHS* 23:797, 805
Xin Tong 辛肜 (31–32)	*HHS* 23:805, 806
Duan Peng 段彭 (75–76)	*HHS* 3:130, 133
Geng Bing ("acting," 76)	*HHS* 19:722
Deng Xun 鄧訓 (86–?)	*HHS* 16:609
Zhai Pu 翟酺 (124–125)	*HHS* 48:1605
Dai Hong 戴宏 (ca. 140?)	*HHS* 64:2101
Huang Yan 黃衍 (ca. 150?)	*HHS* 58:1878
Su Ze 蘇則 (211?)	*SGZ* 16:490–491
Xin Ji 辛機 (219)	*SGZ* 16:492
Huang Hua 黃華 (self-proclaimed, 220)	*SGZ* 2:59, 15:474, 16:492
Wang Huiyang 王惠陽 (ca. 220–225?)	*SGZ* 23:676
Suo Jing 索靖 (288–290)	*JS* 60:1648
Zhang Zhen 張鎮 (312–314)	*JS* 86:2223
Xie Ai 謝艾 (346–349?)	*JS* 29:892, 86:2241
Ma Ji 馬岌 (350–353?)	*JS* 86:2240
Ma Ji 馬基 (ca. 355–360?)	*JS* 86:2248
Song Hao 宋皓 (?–385)	*JS* 115:2943
Lei Cheng 壘澄 (?–397)	*JS* 122:3061
Juqu Yisheng 沮渠益生 (397)	*JS* 129:3191
Li Fan 李翻 (420)	*JS* 87:2270
Juqu Maoqian 沮渠茂虔 (420–?)	*JS* 129:3199

APPENDIX 2: PREFECTS OF WUWEI, ZHANGYE, JIUQUAN AND DUNHUANG   189

4   Dunhuang 敦煌

Appointee and term of office	Source
Est. between 101 and 91 BCE	*CICA* p. 76 n. 40
[Surname unknown] Kuai 快 (61 BCE)	*HS* 69:2980
[No name given] (10 BCE?)	*HS* 70:3027
Xin Tong 辛彤 (24 CE)	*HHS* 23:796–797
Pei Zun 裴遵 (38–45?)	*HHS* 88:2924
[No name given] (75?)	*HHS* 19:722
Cao Zong 曹宗 (119)	*HHS* 47:1587, 88:2911
Zhang Dang 張瑻 (123)	*HHS* 88:2911
Zhang Lang 張朗 (127)	*HHS* 88:2928
Xu You (or Bai) 徐由/白 (129–132)	*HHS* 88:2915; *HHS* "Treatises" 11:3244
"Pei Tsen" (ca. 137)	Cable (1942) p. 149[4]
[Si?]ma Da [司?]馬達 (151–152)	*HHS* 88:2916, 2930
Song Liang 宋亮 (153)	*HHS* 88:2931
Zhao Zi 趙咨 (182)	*HHS* 39:1313
Zhao Qi 趙岐 (185)	*HHS* 64:2123
Left vacant for 20 years (185–205?)	*SGZ* 16:512
Ma Ai 馬艾 (218–220?)	*SGZ* 18:550
Yin Feng 尹奉 (220–230?)	*SGZ* 16:512
Cang Ci 倉慈 (227–232)	*SGZ* 16:512
Wang Yan 王延 (241–247)	*JS* 13:364
Wang Qian 王遷 (247–249)	*Wei lüe* in *SGZ* 16:513
Zhao Ji 趙基 (249–251)	*Wei lüe* in *SGZ* 16:513
Huangfu Long 皇甫隆 (251–253)	*Wei lüe* in *SGZ* 16:513
Yin Ju 尹璩 (?–272)	*JS* 3:66
Linghu Feng 令狐豐 (272–276)	*JS* 3:66
Linghu Hong 令狐宏 (276)	*JS* 3:66
Wu Yan 吾彥 (281?)	*JS* 57:1562
Yin Dan 陰澹 (ca. 320–ca. 325)	*JS* 94:2449
Huang Bin 黃斌 (ca. 324–ca. 346)	*JS* 86:2237
Yao Jing 姚靜 (?–385)	*JS* 115:2943
Suo Jia 索嘏 (386–?)	*JS* 122:3058

4   Cable & French, *The Gobi Desert*, p. 149, report that in Barkul they saw "an inscribed slab," recording "a victory gained by Pei Tsen, prefect of Tunhwang, over Hu Yan, king of the Northern Hsiung-nu in AD 137." Barkul was Pulei 蒲類 in the Han (*CICA* p. 180), now Barkol Township 巴里坤鎮 in Hami Prefecture 哈密地區; I have found nothing more about "Pei Tsen" (裴參?), but the report is credible.

(*cont.*)

Appointee and term of office	Source
Meng Min 孟敏 (?–397)	*JS* 87:2257
Li Hao 李暠 (398–405)	*JS* 87:2258
Suo Si 索嗣 (399 — killed before taking office)	*JS* 87:2258
Li Rang 李讓 (405)	*JS* 87:2261
Li Xun 李恂 (420)	*JS* 87:2270
Suo Yuanxu 索元緒 (acting, 421)	*JS* 87:2270

Abbreviations

CHC 1   Dennis Twitchett and Michael Loewe, eds., *The Cambridge History of China* Volume 1: *The Ch'in and Han Empires, 221 BC–AD 220*. Cambridge: Cambridge University Press, 1986.

CHC 2   Albert E. Dien and Keith N. Knapp, eds., *The Cambridge History of China* Volume 2: *The Six Dynasties, 220–589*. Cambridge: Cambridge University Press, 2019.

CICA   A.F.P. Hulsewé, with M.A.N. Loewe, *China in Central Asia. The Early Stage: 125 BC–AD 23*. Leiden: Brill, 1979.

DZ   *Daozang* 道藏 (*The Taoist Patrology*). Reduced-size photographic reprint of the *Zhengtong Daozang* 正統道藏 (1444–1445) with *Xu Daozangjing* 續道藏經 (1607), in 36 vols., Beijing: Wenwu chubanshe/Shanghai: Shanghai shudian/Tianjin: Guji chubanshe, 1988; with numbering following K.M. Schipper, *Concordance du Tao-tsang: Titres des ouvrages*, Paris: École française d'Extrême-Orient, 1975.

HHS   *Hou Han shu* 後漢書 (*History of the Later [or Eastern] Han Dynasty*), by Fan Ye 范曄 (398–446) et al. Beijing: Zhonghua shuju, 1965.

HS   *Han shu* 漢書 (*History of the [Western, Former] Han Dynasty*), by Ban Gu 班固 (32–92) et al. Beijing: Zhonghua shuju, 1962.

JS   Fang Xuanling 房玄齡 (578–648), ed., *Jin shu* 晉書 (*History of the Jin Dynasty*). Beijing: Zhonghua shuju, 1974.

SSJ   *Shisan jing* 十三經 (*The Thirteen Classics*). Ruan Yuan 阮元 (1764–1849), ed., *Shisan jing zhushu* (*fu jiaokan ji*) 注疏附校勘記 (1817); photomechanical reprint in 2 vols., with continuous pagination (1935[1]). Beijing: Zhonghua shuju, 1980.

T   *Taishō shinshū Daizōkyō* 大正新修大藏經 (*The Taishō edition of the Buddhist Canon*), ed. by Takakusu Junjirō 高楠順次郎 and Watanabe Kaigyoku 渡邊海旭 in 55 vols., Tokyo 1924–1929.

ZZTJ   *Zizhi tongjian* 資治通鑑 (*Comprehensive Mirror for Aid in Government*), comp. by Sima Guang 司馬光 (1019–1096) et al., annotated by Hu Sanxing 胡三省 (1230–1302). Beijing: Zhonghua shuju, 1959[1].

© DOMINIK DECLERCQ, 2025 | DOI:10.1163/9789004727380_017

Bibliography

Arakawa Masaharu, "The Transit Permit System System of the Tang Empire and the Passage of Merchants," in *Memoirs of the Toyo Bunko* 59 (2001), pp. 1–21.

Bagley, Robert, "Shang Archaeology," in Michael Loewe and Edward L. Shaughnessy, eds., *The Cambridge History of Ancient China: From the Origins of Civilization to 221 B.C.* (1999), pp. 124–231.

Bai Bin, "Religious Beliefs as Reflected in the Funerary Record," in John Lagerwey and Lü Pengzhi, eds., *Early Chinese Religion, Part Two: The Period of Division (220–589 AD)* (Leiden: E.J. Brill, 2010), Vol. 2, pp. 989–1073.

Bei shi 北史 (*History of the Northern Dynasties*, 386–618), ed. by Li Yanshou 李延壽 (fl. ca. 659). Beijing: Zhonghua shuju, 1974.

Bertrand, Arnaud, "Conquête et occupation de la frontière nord-ouest au temps des Han occidentaux (206 av. J.-C.–9 apr. J.-C.)," in Jean Baechler & Jérôme de Lespinois, eds., *La Guerre et les Eléments* (Paris: Hermann, 2019), pp. 211–246.

Bielenstein, Hans, "The Census of China during the Period 2–742 A.D.," in *Bulletin of the Museum of Far Eastern Antiquities* 19 (Stockholm 1947), pp. 125–163.

Bielenstein, Hans, "Is There a Chinese Dynastic Cycle?," in *Bulletin of the Museum of Far Eastern Antiquities* 50 (1978).

Bielenstein, Hans, *The Bureaucracy of Han Times*. Cambridge: Cambridge University Press, 1980.

Bielenstein, Hans, "Wang Mang, the Restoration of the Han Dynasty, and Later Han," in *CHC* 1, pp. 223–290.

Braudel, Fernand, *Civilisation matérielle, Economie et Capitalisme XVe–XVIIIe Siècle*, Tome 1: *Les Structures du Quotidien*. Paris: Librairie Armand Colin, 1979. Transl. by Siân Reynold as *Civilization and Capitalism, 15th–18th Century*, Vol. 1: *The Structures of Everyday Life*. Berkeley, Calif.: University of California Press, 1992.

Braudel, Fernand, *Civilisation matérielle, Economie et Capitalisme XVe–XVIIIe Siècle*, Tome 2: *Les Jeux de l'échange*. Paris: Librairie Armand Colin, 1979.

Cable, Mildred, with Francesca French, *The Gobi Desert*. London: Hodder and Stoughton Ltd., 1942.

Cao Daoheng 曹道衡, *Han Wei Liuchao cifu* 漢魏六朝辭賦. Shanghai: Guji chubanshe, 1989.

Chavannes, Édouard, *Le T'ai Chan: Essai de monographie d'un culte chinois*. Annales du Musée Guimet, Paris: Ernest Leroux, 1910.

Chen Jihong 陳繼宏, "'*Wei shu* Li Hao zhuan,' '*Jin shu* Li Xuansheng zhuan,' '*Shiliuguo chunqiu* Xi Liang lu' duidu zhaji 魏書李暠傳、晉書李玄盛傳、十六國春秋西涼錄對讀札記," in *Mingzuo xinshang* 名作欣賞 (Taiyuan, 2016.4), pp. 39–41.

BIBLIOGRAPHY

Chen, Sanping, *Multicultural China in the Early Middle Ages*. Philadelphia: University of Pennsylvania Press, 2012.

Chen Yinke 陳寅恪 (1890–1969), *Sui Tang zhidu yuanyuan lüelun gao* 隋唐制度淵源略論稿 (*A Draft Introduction to the Origins of Institutions of the Sui and Tang Dynasties*), Chongqing 1944¹, Beijing: Zhonghua shuju, 1963¹.

Chittick, Andrew, *The Jiankang Empire in Chinese and World History*. Oxford: Oxford University Press, 2020.

Chuci 楚辭 (*Elegies of Chu*). Ed. Chen Zizhan 陳子展, *Chuci zhijie* 楚辭直解; (Nanjing:) Jiangsu guji chubanshe, 1988. Transl. David Hawkes, *The Songs of the South*; Harmondsworth: Penguin, 1985.

Chu Sanzang jiji 出三藏記集 (*Collected Notes on the Rendering of the Tripiṭaka*), comp. by Sengyou 僧祐 (445–518). Ed. by Su Jinren 蘇晉仁 & Xiao Lianzi 蕭鍊子, Beijing: Guji chubanshe, 1995.

Crespigny, Rafe de, *A Biographical Dictionary of Later Han to the Three Kingdoms (23–220 AD)*. Handbuch der Orientalistik/Handbook of Oriental Studies IV (China), Vol. 19. Leiden: Brill, 2007.

Declercq, Dominik, "The Perils of Orthodoxy: A Western Jin 'Hypothetical Discourse,'" in *T'oung Pao* LXXX (1994), pp. 27–60.

Declercq, Dominik, *Writing Against the State. Political Rhetorics in Third and Fourth Century China*. Leiden: E.J. Brill, 1998.

Declercq, Dominik, "Wei shu 魏書, Chapter 114: Treatise on Buddhism and Taoism 釋老志," in Lalji 'Shravak' & Supriya Rai, eds., *Investigating Principles: International Aspects of Buddhist Culture. Essays in Honour of Professor Charles Willemen* (Hong Kong: The Buddha-Dharma Centre of Hong Kong, 2019), pp. 45–133.

Demiéville, Paul, et al., eds., *Hôbôgirin: Dictionnaire encyclopédique du bouddhisme d'après les sources chinoises et japonaises — Fascicule annexe*. Tokyo: Maison Franco-Japonaise, 1931.

Demiéville, Paul, *Le concile de Lhasa. Une controverse sur le quiétisme entre bouddhistes de l'Inde et de la Chine au VIIIième siècle de l'ère chrétienne*. Paris: Bibliothèque de l'Institut des Hautes Études chinoises, VII, 1952.

Di Cosmo, Nicola, "The Northern Frontier in Pre-Imperial China," in Michael Loewe and Edward L. Shaughnessy, eds., *The Cambridge History of Ancient China: From the Origins of Civilization to 221 B.C.* (1999), pp. 885–966.

Di Cosmo, Nicola, *Ancient China and Its Enemies: The Rise of Nomadic Power in East Asian History*. Cambridge: Cambridge University Press, 2002.

Di Cosmo, Nicola, & Michael Maas, eds., *Empires and Exchanges in Eurasian Late Antiquity: Rome, China, Iran, and the Steppe, ca. 250–750*. Cambridge: Cambridge University Press, 2018.

Di Cosmo, Nicola, "The Relations between China and the Steppe," in Nicola Di Cosmo & Michael Maas, eds., *Empires and Exchanges in Eurasian Late Antiquity* (2018), pp. 35–53.

Dien, Albert E. (丁愛博), *Six Dynasties Civilization*. New Haven: Yale University Press, 2007.

Dien, Albert E., and Keith N. Knapp, eds., *The Cambridge History of China* Volume 2: *The Six Dynasties, 220–589* (Cambridge: Cambridge University Press, 2019).

Egami Namio 江上波夫, *Yūrashia kodai hoppō bunka: Kyōdo bunka ronkō* ユーラシア古代北方文化: 匈奴文化論考 (*Ancient Northern Culture of Eurasia: Studies of Xiongnu Culture*). Tokyo: Yamakawa, 1948.

Farrer, Reginald, "My Second Year's Journey on the Tibetan Border of Kansu," in *The Geographical Journal* (London) Vol. LI (1918) No. 6, pp. 341–353.

Foguo ji 佛國記 (*Account of Buddhist Lands*), by Faxian 法顯 (ca. 340–421). *T* 2085. Transl. James Legge, *A Record of Buddhistic Kingdoms* (1886[1]). New York: Paragon Book Reprint Corp./Dover Publications, Inc., 1965[1]. Transl. Jean-Pierre Drège, *Faxian: Mémoire sur les pays bouddhiques*. Paris: Les Belles Lettres, 2013.

Ganzhou fuzhi 甘州府志 (*Gazetteer of Ganzhou* [= Zhangye] *Prefecture*), ed. by Zhong Gengqi 鍾賡起 (1744).

Gardiner, K.H.J., and Rafe de Crespigny, "T'an-shih-huai and the Hsien-pi tribes of the second century A.D.," in *Papers on Far Eastern History* 15 (Canberra, 1977), pp. 1–44.

Gibbon, Edward (1737–1794), *The Decline and Fall of the Roman Empire* (1776–1789[1]). New York: The Modern Library, 3 vols, n.d.

Graff, David A., "The Art of War," in *CHC* 2, pp. 275–295.

Grousset, René, *Histoire de la Chine*. Paris: Librairie Arthème Fayard, 1942.

Guang hongming ji 廣弘明記 (*Expanded Collection on the Propagation and Clarification* [*of Buddhism*]), ed. by Daoxuan 道宣 (596–667). *T* 2103.

Guanzi qingzhong pian xinquan 管子輕重篇新詮 (*The* Guanzi *"Qingzhong* 輕重 *Chapters* ['Striking the Balance']*" Newly Annotated*), ed. by Ma Feibai 馬非百 (1896–1984). Beijing: Zhonghua shuju, 1979.

Guoyu 國語 (*Conversations from the States*). *Sibu beiyao* 四部備要 ed.

Haloun, Gustav, "The Liang-chou Rebellion, 184–221 A.D.," in *Asia Major*, NS 1:1 (1949), pp. 119–132.

Han Feizi 韓非子 (*Master Han Fei, 280–233* BCE). Ed. *Ershi'er zi* 二十二子 (*Twenty-two Philosophers*), 1890[1]?, reprint Shanghai: Guji chubanshe, 1986.

Han shu 漢書 (*History of the* [*Western, Former*] *Han Dynasty*), by Ban Gu 班固 (32–92) et al. Beijing: Zhonghua shuju, 1962.

Holcombe, Charles, "The Sixteen Kingdoms," in *CHC* 2, pp. 119–144.

Honeychurch, William, *Inner Asia and the Spatial Politics of Empire. Archaeology, Mobility, and Culture Contact*. New York, Heidelberg, Dordrecht & London: Springer, 2015.

Hou Han shu 後漢書 (*History of the Later* [*or Eastern*] *Han Dynasty*), ed. by Fan Ye 范曄 (398–446) et al. Beijing: Zhonghua shuju, 1965.

Hucker, Charles O., *A Dictionary of Official Titles in Imperial China*. Stanford: Stanford University Press, 1985.

BIBLIOGRAPHY

Hulsewé, A.F.P., with M.A.N. Loewe, *China in Central Asia. The Early Stage: 125 B.C.– A.D. 23*. Leiden: Brill, 1979.

Jin shu 晉書 (*History of the Jin Dynasty*), ed. by Fang Xuanling 房玄齡 (578–648) et al. Beijing: Zhonghua shuju, 1974.

Jin shu jiaozhu 晉書斠注, ed. by Wu Shijian 吳士鑒 (1868–1933) and Liu Chenggan 劉承幹 (1882–1963). Facsimile edition of the 1919 ed.

Jiu Tang shu 舊唐書 (*Old History of the Tang*), ed. by Liu Xu 劉昫 (888–947) et al. Beijing: Zhonghua shuju, 1975.

Karlgren, Bernhard, *Grammata Serica*, reprint from the *Bulletin of the Museum of Far Eastern Antiquities* 12 (Stockholm 1940). Taipei: Ch'eng-wen Publishing Company, 1966.

Kleeman, Terry F., *Great Perfection. Religion and Ethnicity in a Chinese Millennial Kingdom*. Honolulu: University of Hawai'i Press, 1998.

Kleeman, Terry F., "Cheng-Han State," in CHC 2, pp. 145–154.

Laozi 老子. Ed. Zhu Qianzhi 朱謙之 (1899–1972), *Laozi jiaoshi* 老子校釋. Beijing: Zhonghua shuju, 1984. Transl. D.C. Lau, *Lao tzu: Tao te ching*. Harmondsworth: Penguin, 1963[1].

Lawergren, Bo, "Music," in CHC 2, pp. 698–720.

Lee, Jen-der (李貞德), "Women, Families, and Gendered Society," in CHC 2 pp. 443–459.

Lewis, Mark Edward, *The Early Chinese Empires: Qin and Han* (*History of Imperial China, Book 1*). Cambridge, Mass.: Harvard University Press, 2007.

Li ji 禮記 (*Record of Ritual*). Ed. *Liji zhengyi* 禮記正義, in SSJ. Transl. James Legge, *The Lǐ Kǐ*, in *The Sacred Books of the East*, Vols. 27–28. Oxford 1885[1], reprint Delhi: Motilal Banarsidass, 1964[1]. Transl. of *Li ji* ch. 28, *Zhong yong* 中庸: François Jullien, *Zhong yong: La Régulation à usage ordinaire*. Paris: Bibliothèque nationale, 1993.

Lippiello, Tiziana, *Auspicious Omens and Miracles in Ancient China: Han, Three Kingdoms, and Six Dynasties*. Sankt Augustin: Monumenta Serica Institute, 2001.

Liu Gang 劉剛 & Li Dongjun 李冬君, *Wenhua de jiangshan* 文化的江山, 01: *Wenhua Zhongguo de laiyuan* 文化中國的來源 (*Our Land of Culture*, 01: *The Origins of Cultural China*). Beijing: Zhongxin chuban jituan 中信出版集團, 2019.

Liu Jingyun 劉景允, "Xi Liang Liu Bing zhu '*Huangshi gong san lüe*' de faxian 西涼劉昞注《黃石公三略》的發現," in *Dunhuang yanjiu* 敦煌研究 2009.2, pp. 82–87.

Liu Shufen (劉淑芬), "The Southern Economy," in CHC 2 pp. 330–354.

Liu Wen 劉雯, "Longxi Lishi jiazu yanjiu 隴西李氏家族研究," in *Dunhuangxue jikan* 敦煌學輯刊, Lanzhou, 1996.2.

Loewe, Michael, *Crisis and Conflict in Han China, 104 BC to AD 9*. London: George Allen & Unwin Ltd., 1974.

Loewe, Michael, ed., *Early Chinese Texts: A Bibliographical Guide*. Berkeley, Calif.: The Society for the Study of Early China and the Institute of East Asian Studies, University of California, 1993.

Loewe, Michael, and Edward L. Shaughnessy, eds., *The Cambridge History of Ancient China: From the Origins of Civilization to 221 B.C.* Cambridge: Cambridge University Press, 1999.

Loewe, Michael, *A Biographical Dictionary of the Qin, Former Han and Xin Periods (221 BC–AD 24)*. Handbuch der Orientalistik/Handbook of Oriental Studies IV (China), Vol. 16. Leiden: Brill, 2000.

Lunheng 論衡 (*Discourses Weighed in the Balance*), by Wang Chong 王充 (27–97 CE). Ed. *Lunheng zhushi* 論衡注釋, by Peking University History Faculty Group for the Annotation of the *Lunheng* 北京大學歷史系《論衡》注釋小組, 4 vols., Beijing: Zhonghua shuju, 1979.

Lunyu 論語 (*The Analects*). Ed. *Lunyu zhengyi* 論語正義, in *SSJ*. Ed. *Lunyu zhengyi* 論語正義, by Liu Baonan 劉寶楠 (1791–1855), Beijing: Zhonghua shuju, 1990. Transl. D.C. Lau, *Confucius: The Analects*. Harmondsworth: Penguin, 1979.

Lüshi chunqiu 呂氏春秋 (The Spring-and-Autumn Annals of Master Lü [Buwei 呂不韋, d. 235 BCE]), in *Ershi'er zi* 二十二子 (*Twenty-two Philosophers*), 1890¹?, reprint Shanghai: Guji chubanshe, 1986. Transl. John Knoblock and Jeffrey Riegel, *The Annals of Lü Buwei*, Stanford, Calif.: Stanford University Press, 2000.

Ma Jigao 馬積高, *Fu shi* 賦史. Shanghai: Guji chubanshe, 1987.

Mair, Victor H., *Mei Cherng's 'Seven Stimuli' and Wang Bor's 'Pavilion of King Terng'*. Lewiston/Queenston: Edwin Mellen Press, 1988.

Mansvelt Beck, B.J., "The Fall of Han," in *CHC* 1, pp. 317–376.

Mansvelt Beck, B.J., *The Treatises of Later Han. Their Author, Sources, Contents and Place in Chinese Historiography*. Leiden: E.J. Brill, 1990.

Mather, Richard B., *Biography of Lü Kuang*. Chinese Dynastic Histories Translations No. 7. Berkeley and Los Angeles: University of California Press, 1959.

Meakin, Rachel, "Qiang 羌 References in the Book of Han 漢書, Part 1 (Chapter 1 to Chapter 78)," pp. 1–34 (2013). Accessible on www.qianghistory.co.uk.

Meakin, Rachel, "Qiang 羌 References in the Book of Han 漢書, Part 2 (Chapter 79 to Chapter 99)," pp. 1–51 (2013). Accessible on www.qianghistory.co.uk.

Meakin, Rachel, "Qiang 羌 References in the Book of the Later Han 後漢書," pp. 1–48 (2011). Accessible on www.qianghistory.co.uk.

Meakin, Rachel, "Qiang 羌 References in the Book of Later Han 後漢書 Chapter 117: The Biography of the Western Qiang," pp. 1–29 (2011). Accessible on www.qianghistory.co.uk.

Meakin, Rachel, "The Founding of the Qiang State of Later Qin: An Annotated Translation of *Jin shu* Chapter 116," pp. 1–31 (2012). Accessible on www.qianghistory .co.uk.

Mengzi 孟子 (*Mencius*). Transl. D.C. Lau, *Mencius*. Harmondsworth: Penguin, 1970.

Mi Wenping 米文平, "Xianbei shishi de faxian yu chubu yanjiu 鮮卑石室的發現與初步研究," in *Wenwu* 文物 (1981) 2.

BIBLIOGRAPHY

Misaki Yoshiaki 三崎良章, *Goko Jūrokkoku: Chūgoku shijō no minzoku dai-idō* 五胡十六国：中国史上の民族大移動 (2012), transl. by Liu Kewei 劉可維 as Wuhu Shiliuguo: Zhongguo shishang de minzu da qianxi 五胡十六國：中國史上的民族大遷徙. Beijing: Shangwu yinshuguan, 2019.

Miyazaki Ichisada 宮崎一定, *Kyūhin kanjinhō no kenkyū: kakyo zenshi* 九品官人法の研究：科擧前史 (*The Mechanism of the Aristocracy in China: Installation of Mandarins before the Establishment of the Competitive Examination System*), Kyoto 1956.

Momigliano, Arnaldo, *Claudius: The Emperor and his Achievement*. Cambridge: W. Heffer & Sons, 1961[2].

Mu Tianzi zhuan 穆天子傳 (*The Tradition of Mu, Son of Heaven*). *Sibu congkan* 四部叢刊 ed.

Müller, Shing, "Northern Material Culture," in CHC 2 pp. 384–417.

Needham, Joseph, and Wang Ling, *Science and Civilisation in China* Volume 3: *Mathematics and the Sciences of the Heavens and the Earth*. Cambridge: Cambridge University Press, 1959.

Pearce, Scott, Audrey Spiro, and Patricia Ebrey, eds., *Culture and Power in the Reconstitution of the Chinese Realm, 200–600*. Cambridge, Mass.: Harvard University Asia Center, 2001.

Qianfu lun 潛夫論 (*A Hermit's Disquisitions*), by Wang Fu 王符 (85–165). Wang Jipei 汪繼培 (1751–1819) & Peng Duo 彭鐸 (1913–1985), eds., *Qianfu lun jian jiaozheng* 潛夫論箋校正. Beijing: Zhonghua shuju, 1985. Transl. by Ivan P. Kamenarović: Wang Fu, *Propos d'un hermite* (Qianfu lun). Paris: Les Éditions du Cerf, 1992.

Quan shanggu sandai Qin Han Sanguo Liuchao wen 全上古三代秦漢三國六朝文. Ed. by Yan Kejun 嚴可均 (1762–1843). Reduced size photographic of the Guangxu 光緒 (1875–1908) era original edition, in 4 vols. with continuous pagination. Beijing: Zhonghua shuju, 1958[1].

Reclus, Élisée & Onésime, *L'Empire du milieu. Le climat, le sol, les races, la richesse de la Chine*. Paris: Hachette, 1902.

Renwu zhi 人物志 (*Treatise on Personalities*), by Liu Shao 劉邵 (ca. 180–ca. 245). Ed. *Renwu zhi*, with a running commentary by Liu Junzu 劉君祖, Taipei: Jinfeng chubanshe 金楓出版社, 1986. Transl. John K. Shryock, *The Study of Human Abilities: The jen wu chih of Liu Shao*. New Haven: American Oriental Society, 1937.

Rogers, Michael C., "The Myth of the Fei River," in *T'oung Pao* LIV (1968), pp. 50–72.

Rogers, Michael C., *The Chronicle of Fu Chien: A Case of Exemplar History*. Chinese dynastic histories project no. 10. Berkeley: University of California Press, 1968.

Sanguo zhi 三國志 (*Record of the Three States*), by Chen Shou 陳壽 (233–297) et al. Beijing: Zhonghua shuju, 1959.

Seidel, Anna, "Imperial Treasures and Taoist Sacraments — Taoist Roots in the Apocrypha," in Michel Strickmann, ed., *Tantric and Taoist Studies in Honour of R.A. Stein*, Volume Two, pp. 291–371. *Mélanges chinois et bouddhiques* Volume XXI, Brussels: Institut Belge des Hautes Études Chinoises, 1983.

Shatzman Steinhardt, Nancy, *Chinese Architecture in an Age of Turmoil, 200–600*. Honolulu/Hong Kong: University of Hawai'i Press/Hong Kong University Press, 2014.

Shiji 史記 (*Records of the Historian*), by Sima Qian 司馬遷 (ca. 145–ca. 86 BC) et al. Beijing: Zhonghua shuju, 1959.

Shijing 詩經 (*Book of Odes*). *Mao Shi zhengyi* 毛詩正義 (*The Mao Heng* 毛亨 *Version of the Book of Odes, with Orthodox Exegesis*), in *ssj*. Transl. Arthur Waley, *The Book of Songs* (London: George Allen and Unwin 1937[1], 1969[3]).

Shiliu guo chunqiu 十六國春秋 (*Annals of the Sixteen States*), ed. by Cui Hong 崔鴻 (d. ca. 525). Tang Qiu 湯球 (1804–1881), ed., *Shiliu guo chunqiu jibu* 輯補 (—, *Reconstituted, with Additions*), punctuated and collated by Nie Weimeng 聶溦萌, Luo Xin 羅新 and Hua Zhe 華喆, Beijing: Zhonghua shuju, 2020.

Shimunek, Andrew, *Languages of Ancient Southern Mongolia and North China: A Historical-Comparative Study of the Serbi-Mongolic Language Family, with an Analysis of Northeastern Frontier Chinese and Old Tibetan Phonology*. Wiesbaden: Harrassowitz Verlag, 2017.

Shiratori Kurakichi 白鳥庫吉, "A Study on Su-t'ê (粟特) or Sogdiana," in *Memoirs of the Research Department of the Toyo Bunko* 2 (1928), pp. 81–145.

Shisan jing 十三經 (*The Thirteen Classics*). Ruan Yuan 阮元 (1764–1849), ed., *Shisan jing zhushu (fu jiaokan ji)* 注疏附校勘記 (1817); photomechanical reprint in 2 vols., with continuous pagination (1935[1]). Beijing: Zhonghua shuju, 1980.

Shishuo xinyu 世說新語 (*A New Account of Tales of the World*), by Liu Yiqing 劉義慶 (403–444). Ed. Yang Yong 楊勇, *Shishuo xinyu jiaojian* 世說新語校箋. Taipei: Hongwen shuju, 1969[1]. Transl. Richard B. Mather, *Shih-shuo Hsin-yü. A New Account of Tales of the World* (1976[1]). Second edition, Ann Arbor: Center for Chinese Studies, The University of Michigan, 2002.

Shi tong 史通 (*Anatomy of Histories*), by Liu Zhiji 劉知幾 (661–721). Ed. Pu Qilong 浦起龍 (1679–1762), *Shitong tongshi* 史通通釋. 2 vols., Shanghai: Guji chubanshe, 1978.

Shuijing zhu 水經注 (*Itineraries of Rivers, with a Commentary*), by Li Daoyuan 酈道元 (d. 527). Ed. collated by Wang Guowei 王國維 (1877–1927): *Shuijing zhu jiao* 校, arranged and punctuated by Yuan Yingguang 袁英光 & Liu Yinsheng 劉寅生. Shanghai: Renmin chubanshe, 1984.

Shuijing zhu 水經注. Ed. by Chen Qiaoyi 陳橋驛, *Shuijing zhu jiaozheng* 校證. Beijing: Zhonghua shuju, 2007.

Shujing 書經 (*Book of Documents*). Ed. *Shangshu zhengyi* 尚書正義 (*The Hallowed Documents, with Orthodox Exegesis*), in *ssj*.

Shuoyuan 說苑 (Garden of Eloquence), ed. by Liu Xiang 劉向 (79–8 BCE). *Sibu congkan* ed. Translated and introduced by Eric Henry, *Garden of Eloquence. Shuoyuan* 說苑. Seattle: University of Washington Press, 2021.

Sinor, Denis, ed., *The Cambridge History of Early Inner Asia*. Cambridge: Cambridge University Press, 1990.

BIBLIOGRAPHY

Song shu 宋書 (*History of the [Liu* 劉*] Song Dynasty,* 420–479), ed. by Shen Yue 沈約 (441–513). Beijing: Zhonghua shuju, 1974.

Sui shu 隋書 (*History of the Sui Dynasty,* 581–618), by Wei Zheng 魏徵 (580–643), Linghu Defen 令狐德棻 (583–661) et al. Beijing: Zhonghua shuju, 1973.

Tackett, Nicolas, *The Destruction of the Medieval Chinese Aristocracy.* Cambridge, Mass., and London: Harvard University Press, 2014.

Taiping guangji 太平廣記 (*Extensive Records for the Taiping [xingguo* 興國*] Era,* 976–984), comp. by Li Fang 李昉 (925–996) et al. Beijing: Zhonghua shuju, 1981.

Taiping yulan 太平御覽 (*Imperial Digest for the Taiping [xingguo* 興國*] Era,* 976–984), comp. by Li Fang 李昉 (925–996) et al. Photographic reprint of the 984 ed., in 4 vols. with continuous pagination. Kyoto: Chūbun shuppansha, 1980.

Tan Qixiang 譚其驤, chief editor, *Zhongguo lishi ditu ji* 中國歷史地圖集 (*The Historical Atlas of China*). Shanghai: Cartographic Publishing House, 1982.

Tan Qixiang, Volume I: The Primitive Society, Xia, Shang, Western Zhou, the Spring and Autumn, Warring States Period 原始社會、夏、商、西周、春秋、戰國時期.

Tan Qixiang, Volume II: Qin Dynasty Period, Western Han and Eastern Han Period 秦、西漢、東漢時期.

Tan Qixiang, Volume III: The Three Kingdoms Period, the Western Jin Dynasty Period 三國、西晉時期.

Tan Qixiang, Volume IV: The Eastern Jin Dynasty and Sixteen Kingdoms Period, the Southern and Northern Dynasties Period 東晉十六國、南北朝時期.

Tang Zhangru 唐長孺, "Wei Jin zahu kao 魏晉雜胡考" (1955), reprinted in *Tang Zhangru wenji* 文集 (Beijing: Zhonghua shuju, 2011), pp. 369–435.

Taylor, Mrs. Howard, *The Call of China's Great North-West, or Kansu and Beyond.* London, Philadelphia, Toronto, Melbourne, and Shanghai: The China Inland Mission, 1923.

Thierry, François, "Yuezhi et Kouchans: Pièges et dangers des sources chinoises," in Osmund Bopearachchi and Marie-Françoise Boussac, eds., *Afghanistan, Ancien carrefour entre l'est et l'ouest,* pp. 421–539. Coll. "Indicopleustoi," Turnhout: Brepols, 2005.

Tian Yuqing 田餘慶, *Dong Jin menfa zhengzhi* 東晉門閥政治. Beijing: Beijing daxue chubanshe, 2005.

Tse, Wicky W.K., "Fabricating Legitimacy in a Peripheral Regime: Imperial Loyalism and Regionalism in the Northwestern Borderlands Under the Rule of the Former Liang (301–376)," in *Early Medieval China* 24 (2018), pp. 108–130.

Twitchett, Dennis, ed., *The Cambridge History of China* Volume 3: *Sui and T'ang China 581–906.* Cambridge: Cambridge University Press, 1979.

Twitchett, Dennis, and Michael Loewe, eds., *The Cambridge History of China* Volume 1: *The Ch'in and Han Empires, 221 B.C.–A.D. 220.* Cambridge: Cambridge University Press, 1986.

Vaissière, Étienne de la, *Histoire des marchands sogdiens.* Paris: Collège de France — Institut des hautes études chinoises (2002[1]), 2016[3].

Wang Zhongluo 王仲犖, *Wei Jin Nanbeichao shi* 魏晉南北朝史. 2 vols., Shanghai: Shanghai renmin chubanshe, 1979.

Wei shu 魏書 (*History of the [Northern] Wei* [386–534]), ed. by Wei Shou 魏收 (505–572). Beijing: Zhonghua shuju, 1974.

Wenxin diaolong 文心雕龍 (*The Literary Mind and the Carving of Dragons*), by Liu Xie 劉勰 (ca. 465–522). Ed. Zhou Zhenfu 周振甫 (1911–2000), *Wenxin diaolong jinyi* 文心雕龍今譯. Beijing: Zhonghua shuju, 1986. Transl. Vincent Yu-chung Shih, *The Literary Mind and the Carving of Dragons*. Hong Kong: The Chinese University Press, 1983.

Wen xuan 文選. Xiao Tong 蕭統 (501–531), ed., *Fang Song Hu ke Wen xuan* 仿宋胡刻文選 (*Selections of Refined Literature, in Hu* [*Kejia's* 胡克家, 1757–1816] woodblock print after the [1181] *Song* [*edition by You Mao* 尤袤, 1127–1194]). S.l., s.d. (1809?).

Wen xuan, or Selections of Refined Literature, Volume One: *Rhapsodies on Metropolises and Capitals*. Translated, with Annotations by David R. Knechtges. Princeton: Princeton University Press, 1982.

Wen xuan, or Selections of Refined Literature, Volume Two: *Rhapsodies on Sacrifices, Hunting, Travel, Sightseeing, Palaces and Halls, Rivers and Seas*. Translated, with Annotations by David R. Knechtges. Princeton: Princeton University Press, 1987.

Willemen, Charles, *Buddhacarita. In Praise of Buddha's Acts*. Moraga, Calif., 2009.

Wu Hung, *The Art of the Yellow Springs: Understanding Chinese Tombs*. Honolulu: University of Hawai'i Press, 2010.

Wu Jinhua 吳金華 (1943–2013), *Gu wenxian yanjiu conggao* 古文獻研究叢稿. Nanjing: Jiangsu jiaoyu chubanshe, 1995.

Wuwei Shi zhi 武威市志 (*Wuwei Municipality Gazetteer*). Comp. by the Editorial Committee for the Gansu Province, Wuwei Municipality, City Gazetteer 甘肅省武威市市志編纂委員會, for the series *Zhonghua renmin gongheguo difangzhi congshu* 中華人民共和國地方志叢書. Lanzhou: Lanzhou daxue chubanshe, 1998.

Xin Tang shu 新唐書 (*New History of the Tang Dynasty*, 618–907), by Ouyang Xiu 歐陽修 (1007–1072) and Song Qi 宋祁 (998–1061). Beijing: Zhonghua shuju, 1975.

Xin wudai shi 新五代史 (*A New History of the Five Dynasties*, 907–960), by Ouyang Xiu. Beijing: Zhonghua shuju, 1975.

Xiong, Victor Cunrui, "The Northern Economy," in CHC 2, pp. 309–329.

Yanshi jiaxun 顏氏家訓, by Yan Zhitui 顏之推 (531–591). Ed. Wang Liqi 王利器, *Yanshi jiaxun jijie* 集解; Shanghai: Guji chubanshe, 1980. Transl. Teng Ssu-yü 鄧嗣禹, *Family Instructions for the Yan Clan*. Leiden: Brill, 1968.

Yantie lun 鹽鐵論 (*Discussions on Salt and Iron*), ed. by Huan Kuan 桓寬 (2nd half 1st cent. BCE). Shanghai: Renmin chubanshe, 1974. Translation by Jean Levi, *La Dispute sur le sel et le fer*. Paris: Les Belles Lettres, 2010.

Yijing 易經 (*Book of Changes*). Ed. *Zhou Yi zhengyi* 周易正義, in SSJ. Ed. *Zhou Yi jijie zuanshu* 周易集解纂疏, ed. by Li Daoping 李道平 (*juren* 舉人 1818). Beijing:

BIBLIOGRAPHY

Zhonghua shuju, 1994. Transl. James Legge, *The I Ching* (Oxford 1899), reprint New York: Dover Publications, Inc., 1963[1]. Transl. Richard John Lynn, *The Classic of Changes*. New York: Columbia University Press, 1994.

Yi Zhou shu 逸周書 (*Remnant Zhou Documents*).

Yoshida, Yutaka, "On the Origin of the Sogdian Surname Zhaowu 昭武 and Related Problems," in *Journal Asiatique* 291.1–2 (2003), pp. 35–67.

You Chengmin 尤成民, "Han Jin shiqi Hexi daxing de tedian he lishi zuoyong 漢晉時期河西大姓的特點和歷史作用," in *Lanzhou daxue xuebao* (*Shehui kexue ban*) 蘭州大學學報 (社會科學版) 20 (1992).1, pp. 80–87.

Yu Taishan 余太山, "Daxia he Da Yuezhi zongkao 大夏和大月氏綜考," in *Zhong Ya xuekan* 中亞學刊 III (Beijing 1990), pp. 17–46.

Yü Ying-shih, "Han Foreign Relations," in *CHC* 1 pp. 377–462.

Yü, Ying-shih, "The Hsiung-nu," in Denis Sinor, ed., *The Cambridge History of Early Inner Asia* (1990), pp. 118–149.

Zhang Xunliao 張勳燎 & Bai Bin 白彬, "Zhongyuan he xibei diqu Wei Jin Beichao muzang de jiezhuwen yanjiu 中原和西北地區魏晉北朝墓葬的解注文研究," in Zhang Xunliao & Bai Bin, *Zhongguo daojiao kaogu* 中國道教考古 (Beijing 2006), Volume 2 ch. 3, pp. 351–574.

Zhou Weizhou 周偉洲, *Nan Liang yu Xi Qin* 南涼與西秦. Beijing: Shehui kexue wenxian chubanshe, 2021.

Zhou Yiliang 周一良, "Beichao de minzu wenti yu minzu zhengce 北朝的民族問題與民族政策" (1948), reprinted in *Zhou Yiliang ji* 集 (Shenyang 1998), Vol. 1 pp. 149–223.

Zhuangzi 莊子. Ed. Guo Qingfan 郭慶藩 (1844–1896), *Zhuangzi jishi* 莊子集釋, 4 vols. Beijing: Zhonghua shuju, 1961[1].

Zizhi tongjian 資治通鑑 (*Comprehensive Mirror for Aid in Government*), comp. by Sima Guang 司馬光 (1019–1096) et al., annotated by Hu Sanxing 胡三省 (1230–1302), 20 vols. Beijing: Zhonghua shuju, 1959[1].

Zuo zhuan 左傳 (*Zuo Tradition*). Ed. *Chunqiu Zuo zhuan zhengyi* 春秋左傳正義, in *SSJ*. Translation by Stephen Durrant, Wai-yee Li, and David Schaberg, *Zuo Tradition*: Zuo zhuan 左傳. *Commentary on the "Spring and Autumn Annals."* Seattle: University of Washington Press, 2016.

Zürcher, E., *The Buddhist Conquest of China. The Spread and Adaptation of Buddhism in Early Medieval China* (2nd ed.). 2 vols., Leiden: Brill, 1972.

Zürcher, Erik, "Tidings from the South: Chinese Court Buddhism and Overseas Relations in the Fifth Century AD," in Antonino Forte and Federico Masini, eds., *A Life Journey to the East: Sinological Studies in Memory of Giuliano Bertuccioli (1923–2001)*, Kyoto: Scuola Italiana di Studi sull'Asia Orientale, 2002, pp. 21–43.

Index

Anding 安定　12, 13, 14, 20–24, 27, 32, 37–38, 51, 71

Anyi 安夷　34

Bai Qi 白起 (d. 257 BCE)　169

Ban Biao 班彪 (3–54 CE)　32

Ban Chao 班超 (32–102)　36

Ban Gu 班固 (32–92)　3, 51, 70–71, 91

Baoyun 寶雲　112

Beidi 北地　12, 13, 14, 32, 37–39, 51, 71

Beigong Boyu 北宮伯玉 (d. 186)　39, 41

Bi 比 (*chanyu*, r. 48–56)　5

Bian Yun 邊允 (a.k.a. Zhang 章, d. 186)　40–41

Bilong 比龍　147

Braudel, Fernand　3

Cai Yong 蔡邕 (133–192)　109

Cang Ci 倉慈　58–59, 101–102

Cao Cao 曹操 (155–220)　9, 11, 14, 42, 53, 159

Cao Huan 曹奐 (246–302)　127

Cao Pi 曹丕 (187–226, Emp. Wen of Wei 魏文帝, r. 220–226)　54, 56

Cao Rui 曹叡 (204–239, Emp. Ming of Wei 魏明帝, r. 227–239)　56

Changsong 昌松　18

Cheng-Han 成漢 (state)　69, 130

Chen Yi 陳懿　40–41

Chen Zhong 陳忠 (d. 125)　156

Chittick, Andrew　173

Chuoqiang 婼羌 (tribe)　27

Commandant for the Southern Division 南部都尉　37

Commandant of the Western Qiang 西羌校尉　62

Commandant Protector of the Qiang 護羌校尉　29, 30–42, 63, 107, 165

Commandant Protector of the Western Nomads 護西胡校尉　101, 103

Commandant Protector of the Wuhuan 護烏桓都尉　8

Cui Hong 崔鴻 (d. ca. 525)　1, 75, 92

Dahu 大胡 (tribe)　9

Dao'an 道安 (312–385)　89

Daoxuan 道宣 (596–667)　7

Deng Ai 鄧艾 (ca. 197–264)　61

Deng Sui 鄧綏 (Empr. Dowager Deng 鄧太后 81–121)　36

Deng Xun 鄧訓 (36–92)　34–35

Dependent States 屬國　4, 17, 30, 51, 59

Dianlian 滇零 (d. 112)　35–36

Di Cosmo, Nicola　24

Dingling 丁零　9–11, 55, 134, 146

Discussions on Salt and Iron 鹽鐵輪　45–49

Diwu Fang 第五訪 (d. 159)　49

Dong Zhuo 董卓 (d. 192)　41–42, 53, 159

Dou Kuang 竇況　32

Dou Lin 竇林 (d. 59 CE)　34

Dou Rong 竇融 (15 BCE–62 CE)　31–32, 95, 131

Dou Xian 竇憲 (d. 92 CE)　5

Duan 段 (tribe)　8

Duan Jiong 段熲 (d. 179)　33

Duan Ye 段業 (d. 401)　86, 98, 99–104, 105–106, 111–112, 114, 167

Duke of Shao 召公 (trad. d. 1053 BCE)　159

Duke of Zhou 周公 (trad. d. 1104 BCE)　116, 159

Dunhuang 敦煌　4, 19, 22, 29, 43, 57, 112 and *passim*

Dunqiu 頓丘　14

Facheng 法乘　112

Fan Can 范粲 (fl. ca. 240)　59

Fan Cheng 氾稱　166

Fan Deyu 氾德瑜　106

Fang Xuanling 房玄齡 (578–648)　2, 75, 93

Fan Kuai 樊噲 (d. 189 BCE)　159

Faquan 法泉　133

Faxian 法顯 (ca. 340–421)　111

Feng Yan 馮衍 (fl. ca. 24–ca. 50)　151

Feng Zong 馮宗 (fl. ca. 60 CE)　31

Fotudeng 佛圖澄 (d. 349)　90

Fu Deng 符登 (343–394)　79, 81, 82

Fufeng 扶風　14, 33, 36, 38

Fuhan 枹罕　39, 42, 79

Fu Hong 符洪 (285–350)　76

Fu Jian 符健 (317–355)　76

Fu Jian 符堅 (338–385)　76–80, 83, 89, 130

INDEX

203

Funan 傅難 (tribe/clan)   37
Fu Qian 服虔 (ca. 125–195)   27
Fu Yu 傅育 (d. 87)   34
Fu Yue 傅說   158

Gan Bao 干寶 (ca. 285–ca. 350?)   173
Gaochang 高昌   56, 67, 83, 175
Geng Yan 耿弇 (3–58 CE)   73
Gibbon, Edward   58
Gonggong 共工   129
Great Proscription 黨錮   40
Grousset, René   52
Guangwei 廣魏   10
Guangwu 廣武   66, 90, 108
Guan Lu 管輅 (209–262)   91
Guan You 貫友 (fl. 93–96)   35
Guan Yu 關羽 (d. 220)   159
Guan Zhong 管仲 (ca. 723–ca. 645 BCE)
    15, 21, 94, 158
Guanzhong 關中   12, 13, 14, 17, 33, 39
Guide 歸德   35, 39
Guo Nun 郭黁 (363?–403)   88, 90, 91, 101,
    120, 144
Guo Pu 郭璞 (276–324)   20
Guo Qian 郭謙   100, 106
Guo Qin 郭欽   11
Guo Yu 郭瑀 (d. 386)   148
Guo Zhong 郭忠 (d. 71 BCE)   31
Guzang 姑臧   28, 32, 43, 83, 90, 97, 119, 175
    (and *passim*)

Han 罕 (tribe/clan)   27, 38
Han Xin 韓信 (d. 196 BCE)   159, 169
Hanyang 漢陽   51
Han Yue 韓約 (a.k.a. Sui 遂, d. 215)   40–42
Hao Duyuan 郝度元   12
Hedong 河東   13, 14, 36
Heguan 河關   39
He Jin 何進 (d. 189)   40
Helian Qugai 赫連屈丐 (Helian Bobo
    勃勃 381–425)   164
Henan 河南   14
Henei 河內   14, 36
heqin 和親 policy   4
Hezhou 河州   67, 79, 80, 166
Holcombe, Charles   2
Hongnong 弘農   14
Hou Jin 侯瑾 (fl. ca. 190)   174

Huangfu Long 皇甫隆   56
Huangfu Song 皇甫嵩 (d. ca. 195)   41
Huanghe 湟河   90, 108
Huang Shi 黃始   127, 134
Huan Kuan 桓寬 (2nd half 1st cent. BCE)
    46
Huan Wen 桓溫 (312–373)   77, 130, 151
Huhanye 呼韓邪 (r. 58–31 BCE)   4, 28
Huijian 慧簡   112
Hunye 渾邪 king (d. 116 BCE)   4
Huo Qubing 霍去病 (ca. 140–117 BCE)   4, 48

Jade Gateway Pass 玉門關   19, 22, 67, 106
Ji Commandery 汲郡   14
Jiayuguan 嘉峪關   19
Jian 幵 (tribe/clan)   27
Jiang Tong 江統 (d. 310)   12–17, 33
Jiaohe 澆河   90
Jinchang 晉昌   59, 67, 105
Jincheng 金城   9, 29, 33, 37, 40, 51, 53, 59, 66
Jing Fang 京房 (77–36 BCE)   90
Jingyang 涇陽   12
Jingzhao 京兆   14, 33
Jinxing 晉興   65, 108
Jiuquan 酒泉   9, 19, 43, 45, 48, 59
Judong 且凍 (tribe/clan)   37
Juqu Fahong 沮渠法弘 (d. ca. 400?)   96–97
Juqu Luochou 沮渠羅仇 (d. 397)   86, 97–98
Juqu Mengxun 沮渠蒙遜 (368–433)   92, 95
    sq. passim
Juqu Mujian 沮渠牧犍 (alt. Maoqian 茂虔,
    r. 433–439)   145, 171–173
Juqu Nancheng 沮渠南城   98, 99, 103
Juqu Qifuyan 沮渠祁復延 (fl. ca. 340–370)
    96
Juqu Quzhou 沮渠麴粥   97–98
Juqu Shu 沮渠挐   107
Juqu Wuhui 沮渠無諱 (d. 444)   176
Juqu Yizi 沮渠益子   107
Juqu Zhengde 沮渠政德 (alt. Dezheng
    德政)   125, 170

Kangju 康居   9
Kan Yin 闞駰 (d. ca. 440)   23, 120, 174
Kayue 卡約 (culture)   19
Khotan 和田   19, 110
King Mu of Zhou 周穆王 (r. 956–918 BCE)
    20

King Wen of Zhou 周文王 (r. 1099–1050 BCE) 109, 140, 180

King Wuding of Shang 商武丁王 (trad. r. 1324–1266 BCE) 158

King Wu of Zhou 周武王 (r. 1049/1045–1043 BCE) 62, 94, 109, 180

Kumārajīva 鳩摩羅什 (350–409) 83, 90

Kushan Empire 24, 57

Lai Ji 來機 37

Ledu 樂都 18, 90–91, 119

Lezun 樂傳 112

Liang Bao 梁襃 146

Liang Xi 梁熙 (d. 385) 77–78, 81, 83, 89, 97, 155, 167

Liangxing 涼興 103

Liang Xing 梁興 127

Liang Zhongyong 梁中庸 102, 162

Liangzhou 涼州 9, 28, 37, 43, 48, 54, 59, 67, and *passim*

Liangzhou Rebellion 39–42, 53

Liangzhu 良渚 (culture) 19

Lianju 令居 10, 28–29, 32–33, 45

Li Bao 李寶 170, 172

Li Bian 李辯 (fl. 376–380?) 80

Li Bokao 李伯考 87

Li Chang 李昶 (334–351) 75, 88, 105

Li Chang 李敞 123

Li Chong'er 李重耳 170, 172

Li Daoyuan 酈道元 (d. 527) 14

Li Fan 李翻 145, 170

Li Guang 李廣 (d. 119 BCE) 25–26, 71, 87

Li Guangli 李廣利 (d. 89 BCE) 44, 48

Li Hao 李暠 (351–417) 2, 31, 70, 87 *sq. passim*

Li Jing'ai 李敬愛 145, 146–147, 171–172

Li Liang 李亮 145

Li Ling 李陵 (1st cent. BCE) 26, 47, 75

Linghu Feng 令狐豐 (d. 276) 61

Lingu He 令狐赫 106

Linghu Hong 令狐宏 (d. 276) 61

Linghu Qian 令狐遷 106

Lingyu Yi 令狐溢 106

Ling Zheng 冷徵 40

Linqiang 臨羌 34, 123

Li Qian 李騫 (508–549) 152

Li Rang 李讓 103, 135, 140–141, 145

Li Rou 李柔 71–72, 88, 131

Li Shimin 李世民 (598–649, Emp. Taizong of Tang 唐太宗, r. 626–649) 75

Li Shun 李順 (d. 442) 121, 176

Li Tai 李泰 (Tang dyn.) 21, 23, 122

Li Tan 李譚 (d. 404) 145, 163

Li Te 李特 (ca. 250–303) 64

Li Tiao 李眺 145

Liu Bang 劉邦 (256/247–195, Emp. Gaozu of W. Han 漢高祖, r. 202–195) 158, 179

Liu Bao 劉保 (115–144, Emp. Shun of E. Han 漢順帝, r. 125–144) 49

Liu Bei 劉備 (161–223) 158, 159, 160

Liu Bian 劉辯 (173/174–190, Emp. Shao of E. Han 漢少帝, r. 189) 42, 53

Liu Biao 劉表 (144–208) 53

Liu Bing 劉秉 37

Liu Bing 劉昞 (d. 440) 140, 144, 148, 162, 174

Liu Che 劉徹 (156–87, Emp. Wu of W. Han 漢武帝, r. 141–87 BCE) 4, 23, 28, 44, 47, 51

Liu Heng 劉恒 (Emp. Wen of W. Han 漢文帝, r. 179–157 BCE) 4

Liu Hong 劉宏 (157–189, Emp. Ling of E. Han 漢靈帝, r. 168–189) 40, 109

Liu Laozhi 劉牢之 (d. 402) 158

Liu Qi 劉啟 (Emp. Jing of W. Han 漢景帝, r. 157–141 BCE) 5

Liu Shao 劉邵 (ca. 180–ca. 245) 148

Liu Xiang 劉向 (79–8 BCE) 62

Liu Xie 劉協 (181–234, Emp. Xian of E. Han 漢獻帝, r. 189–220) 42, 53

Liu Xie 劉勰 (ca. 465–522) 126

Liu Xiu 劉秀 (Emp. Guangwu of E. Han 漢光武帝, r. 25–57) 5, 6, 32, 96, 130, 136

Liu Yifu 劉義符 (406–424) 171

Liu Yu 劉裕 (356–422) 116, 136, 137, 151, 164

Liu Zhang 劉章 (d. ca. 223) 53

Liu Zhiji 劉知幾 (661–721) 91, 93, 148

Liwei 力微 (d. 277) 8

Li Wenhou 李文侯 (d. 186) 39, 41

Li Xian 李賢 (651–684) 53

Li Xin 李歆 103, 107, 135, 145, 164–169 *passim*

Li Xun 李恂 (fl. ca. 85–100) 49

Li Xun 李恂 (son of Li Hao) 145, 169, 170

Li Yan 李弇 71–73, 74, 88, 105, 131

Li Yanshou 李延壽 (fl. ca. 659) 72

Li Yi 李毅 (d. 306) 64

INDEX

Li Yu 李預 145

Li Yong 李雍 71–72, 88, 131

Li Yuan 李淵 (Emp. Gaozu of Tang 唐高祖, r. 618–626) 173

Li Zhongxiang 李仲翔 (fl. ca. 200 BCE) 27, 87

Li Zhuo 李卓 73, 74, 131

Longguan 龍關 (pass) 37

Longxi 隴西 26, 36, 39, 51, 70, 74

Lord Huan of Qi 齊桓公 (r. 685–643 BCE) 131, 158

Lord Li of Qin 秦厲公 (r. 476–443 BCE) 124

Lord Wen of Jin 晉文公 (r. 636–628 BCE) 118, 131, 158

Loyal Nomad Auxiliary 義從胡 25, 35, 39, 42

Luoyang 洛陽 2

Lushui nomads 盧水胡 12, 54–55, 62, 95, 122–125

Lu Su 魯肅 (172–217) 159

Lü Guang 呂光 (338–399) 83–86, 88–91, 97–104, 110, 125

Lü Fu 呂覆 84

Lü Hong 呂弘 84

Lü Long 呂隆 (d. 416) 111, 115

Lü Shao 呂紹 84, 91

Lü Zuan 呂纂 84, 90, 91, 98, 106, 111

Malan Qiang 馬蘭羌 (tribe) 12

Ma Long 馬隆 (fl. 278–281?) 61, 63

Mao Xing 毛興 80

Ma Teng 馬騰 (d. 212) 42

Ma Wu 馬武 (d. 61) 34

Ma Xian 馬賢 (d. 141) 36, 38

Ma Yuan 馬援 (14 BCE–49 CE) 33, 80

Mengjin 孟津 12

Meng Kang 孟康 (fl. 180–260) 10

Meng Min 孟敏 99–100

Meng Tian 蒙恬 (d. 210 BCE) 3

Mitang 迷唐 (d. ca. 105) 34–35

Miwu 迷吾 (d. 87) 34

Modun 冒頓 (r. 209–174 BCE) 3, 23

Murong 慕容 (tribe) 8

Murong Chui 慕容垂 (326–396) 79

Murong Lin 慕容麟 (d. 397) 130

Niu Han 牛邯 (fl. 33 CE) 32–33

Pan Yue 潘岳 (247–300) 151

parallel prose 駢體 126

Peng Yue 彭越 80

Pingyang 平陽 12

Pingyi 馮翊 12, 13, 14, 33, 36, 38

Protector-General of Western Regions 西域都護 4, 36, 67

Qiang 羌 9, 26–42, 48, 55, 62, 71, 124, 177 (and *passim*)

Qian Hong 牽弘 (d. 271) 61

Qiao Zong 譙縱 (fl. 405–413) 137

Qifu 乞伏 (tribe/lineage) 8, 80, 81–82

Qifu Chipan 乞伏

Qifu Guoren 乞伏國仁 (d. 388) 80

Qifu Qiangui 乞伏乾歸 (d. 412) 80, 82, 90, 111, 125

Qifu Sifan 乞伏思繁 (d. 376) 80

Qijia 齊家 (culture) 19, 26

Qilian 祁連 (commandery) 105

Qilian Mountains 祁連山 18

Qin Shi Huangdi 秦始皇帝 20

Qi Wannian 齊萬年 (d. 295) 12, 15, 62

Queen Mother of the West 西王母 123, 124

Ran Min 冉閔 130

Ren Shang 任尚 (d. 118) 36

Ren Yan 任延 (5–68) 49

Sang Hongyang 桑弘羊 (152–80 BCE) 45–47

Sanhe 三河 97

Sengjing 僧景 112

Sengshao 僧紹 112

Shangdang 上黨 12, 62

Shangjun 上郡 12, 29, 32, 37–39

Shaodang 燒當 (tribe/clan) 34, 62, 81

Shaohe 燒何 (tribe/clan) 38

Shaoti 邵提 10

Shazhou 沙州 23, 67, 100, 166

Shengle 盛樂 8

Shi Cong 石聰 84

Shi Hu 石虎 (295–349) 76, 130, 149

Shi Le 石勒 (274–333) 76, 122

Shilun 施崙 121

Shimao 石峁 (culture) 11

Shiping 始平 14

Shiratori Kurakichi 24
Shun 舜 (trad r. 2255–2206 BCE) 81, 155
Shu Xi 束皙 (ca. 264–ca. 303) 14–16, 33
Sima Bao 司馬保 (296–320) 66, 72–73
Sima Chi 司馬熾 (284–313, Emp. Huai of
 W. Jin 晉懷帝, r. 307–311) 127
Sima Dan 司馬聃 (343–361, Emp. Mu of
 E. Jin 晉穆帝, r. 345–361) 152
Sima Dezong 司馬德宗 (Emp. An of E. Jin
 晉安帝, r. 397–418) 106, 135, 137, 171
Sima Guang 司馬光 138
Sima Jiong 司馬冏 (d. 302) 64
Sima Lun 司馬倫 (d. 301) 63–64
Sima Qian 司馬遷 (ca. 145–ca. 80 BCE) 3,
 26, 91
Sima Rui 司馬睿 (276–323, Emp. Yuan of
 E. Jin 晉元帝, r. 318–323) 65–66, 126, 128
Sima Shi 司馬師 (208–255) 127
Sima Xin 司馬歆 (d. 303) 64
Sima Xiuzhi 司馬休之 (d. 417) 137
Sima Yan 司馬炎 (236–290, Emp. Wu of
 W. Jin 晉武帝, r. 265–290) 1, 11, 62
Sima Ye 司馬鄴 (300–318, Emp. Min of W. Jin
 晉愍帝, r. 313–317) 64, 68, 72
Sima Yi 司馬乂 (277–304) 64
Sima Yi 司馬懿 (179–251) 127
Sima Ying 司馬穎 (279–306) 64
Sima Yong 司馬顒 (d. 307) 64
Sima Zang 司馬臧 (297–301) 64
Sima Zhao 司馬昭 (211–265) 127
Sima Zhen 司馬貞 (fl. 713–742) 130
Sima Zhong 司馬衷 (259–306, Emp. Hui of
 W. Jin 晉惠帝, r. 290–306) 1, 63
Sinor, Denis 124
Siwa 寺洼 (culture) 19, 26
Sizhou 司州 14
Sogdians 57, 169
Song Cheng 宋承 169, 170
Song Jian 宋建 (d. 214) 40, 42
Song Liao 宋寮 (d. 361) 87
Song You 宋繇 (361–439?) 87, 88, 100, 106,
 107, 108, 140–141, 165, 171
Stein, Aurel 57
Sun Ce 孫策 (175–200) 53
Sun Quan 孫權 (182–251) 159–160
Suo Ban 索班 101
Suo Chengming 索承明 106, 149
Suo Ci 索慈 106
Suo Fu 索輔 65

Suo Jing 索靖 (239–303) 101
Suo Mai 索勱 101
Suo Pan 索泮 78
Suo Shu 索術 106
Suo Si 索嗣 101–103, 169
Suo Xian 索仙 100, 106, 165
Suo Xun 索訓 106
Suo Yuanxu 索元緒 169, 170
Su Qin 蘇秦 (d. 284 BCE?) 91
Sushen 肅慎 (tribe) 61
Su Yu 蘇愉 (d. 270?) 61
Su Ze 蘇則 (d. 223) 55

Taiyuan 太原 12
Tang (the Victorious 成湯, trad.
 r. 1761–1754 BCE) 117, 179–180
Tang Qi 唐契 (d. 442) 172
Tang Xi 唐熙 105
Tang Yao 唐瑤 105, 106, 107
Tanmochen 曇摩讖 (Dharmarddhin
 385–433) 120–121, 176
Tanshihuai 檀石槐 (ca. 136–181) 8, 9
Tianshui 天水 27, 36, 51, 71, 73
Tanzhe 檀柘 10
Tufa 禿髮 (tribe/lineage) 8, 61, 86
Tufa Rutan 禿髮傉檀 (365–415) 111, 117, 119,
 146–147, 149, 151
Tufa Shujineng 禿髮樹機能 (d. 279) 61, 86
Tufa Sifujian 禿髮思復鞬 (d. ca. 390) 85
Tufa Wugu 禿髮烏孤 (d. 399) 86, 90
Tuguilai 禿瑰來 10
Tuoba 拓跋 (lineage) 123
Tuoba Dao 拓跋燾 (408–452, Emp. Taiwu of
 N. Wei 魏太武皇帝, r. 423–452) 121,
 172–173, 176
Tuoba Gui 拓跋珪 (Emp. Taizu of N. Wei
 魏太祖, r. 386–409) 116, 130
Tuoba Jun 拓跋濬 (Emp. Wencheng of
 N. Wei 魏文成帝, r. 452–465) 172
Tuyuhun 吐谷渾 (tribe) 8

Wang Bao 王豹 (d. 302) 156
Wang Chong 王充 (27–97) 126
Wang Fu 王符 (85–165) 37
Wang Guo 王國 (d. 189) 40–41
Wang Jia 王嘉 (d. ca. 390) 89
Wang Mang 王莽 (r. 9–23 CE) 5, 14, 21,
 31–32, 75
Wang Meng 王猛 (325–375) 78

INDEX

Wang Xiang 王詳　90, 99
Wang Xiu 王脩　171
Wang Xizhi 王羲之 (303–361)　149
Wang Yan 王彥　64
Wang Yin 王隱 (4th cent.)　25
Wei Ao 隗囂 (d. 33)　96
Wei Commandery 魏郡　14
Wei Ping 衛平　81
Wei Shou 魏收 (505–572)　57, 75
Wei You 尉祐　84
Wen Xu 溫序 (d. 30 CE)　32
wu Hu luan Hua 五胡亂華　2
Wuhuan 烏桓　6–9
Wulei 烏壘　4
Wusun 烏孫　22
Wu Tang 吳棠 (fl. 65–77)　34
Wuwei 武威　9, 18, 28, 29, 48, 108 and *passim*
Wuxing 武興　65, 66, 108
Wuyi Yuanjian 無弋爰劍　124

Xiahou Yuan 夏侯淵 (d. 219)　42
Xiang Yu 項羽　129
Xi'an 西安　108
Xianbei 鮮卑　6, 7–8, 9, 59, 61
Xianlian 先零 (tribe/clan)　30, 33, 35, 39, 41
Xiao Fangdeng 蕭方等　92–93
Xie Ai 謝艾 (fl. mid 4th cent.)　175
Xie Xuan 謝玄 (343–388)　79
Xihai 西海　31, 67
Xihe 西河　12, 29, 39
Xijun 西郡　100, 108, 115
Xindian 新店 (culture)　19, 26
Xining 西寧　18, 23
Xin Gongjing 辛恭靖　163
Xin Jing 辛景　163
Xin Na 辛納　74, 163
Xinping 新平　14
Xin Qingji 辛慶忌 (d. 18 BCE)　31, 75
Xin Tang 辛湯 (fl. ca. 6 BCE)　29
Xin Tong 辛通 (d. 3 CE)　31, 75
Xin Wuxian 辛武賢　31, 75
Xingma 騂馬　106, 108
Xiongnu 匈奴　3–6, 22, 32, 38–39, 47, 93, 95–96
Xiping 西平　23, 66, 90, 108
Xiuli 休利 (*chanyu*, r. 128–140)　38
Xu Miao 徐邈 (172–249)　56–57

Yang Gu 陽固 (467–523)　151
Yangping 陽平　14
Yang Wei 楊偉 (3rd cent.)　174, 175
Yang Xin 楊欣　61
Yan Shigu 顏師古 (581–645)　22
Yangguan 陽關　106, 119
Yang Gui 楊軌 (d. 400)　90
Yan Zhitui 顏之推　87, 175
Yao Ai 姚艾　178
Yao Chang 姚萇 (329–393)　79
Yao Hong 姚泓 (388–417)　164
Yao Xing 姚興 (366–416)　80, 82, 90, 106, 111, 115, 116, 146
Yao Yizhong 姚弋仲 (280–352)　62–63
Yellow Turbans 黃巾　40
Yijian Jiqie 伊健妓妾　54
Yin Feng 尹奉　102
Yin Hua 殷華 (d. 178)　40
Ying Qu 應璩 (190–252)　150
Ying Shao 應邵 (ca. 140–before 204)　29, 40
Yin Jianxing 尹建興　103, 106
Yin Mountains 陰山　8
Yin Wen 尹文　87, 146
Yiwu 伊吾　101, 170
Yi Yin 伊尹　117
Yongzhou 雍州　53–54, 59
Yuan Shao 袁紹 (d. 202)　53
Yuan Shu 袁術 (d. 199)　53
Yu Huan 魚豢 (3rd cent.)　9, 10, 40, 122
Yue Chan 樂產 (n.d.)　12
Yuezhi 月氏　3, 20–24, 27, 35, 47, 96, 177
Yumen 玉門　119
Yu the Great 大禹　132, 155
Yuwen 宇文 (tribe)　8
Yu Xu 虞詡 (d. 137)　38

Zang Hong 臧洪 (160–196)　158–159
Zhang Chao 張超 (d. 195)　159
Zhang Dayu 張大豫 (d. 386)　85, 154
Zhang Fang 張魴 (fl. ca. 70 CE)　31
Zhang Fei 張飛 (d. 221)　159
Zhang Gong 張恭 (fl. 221–230?)　67
Zhang Gui 張軌 (255–314)　63–65, 72–73, 105, 128, 174
Zhang Hong 張弘　169, 170
Zhang Hua 張華 (232–300)　126
Zhang Ji 張既 (d. 223)　53
Zhang Jing 張靖　106

Zhang Jue 張角 (d. 184)   40
Zhang Liang 張良 (d. 186 BCE)   158, 169
Zhang Jun 張駿 (307–346)   66, 68, 77, 97, 119, 128, 155, 162
Zhang Lin 張林   106
Zhang Lu 張魯 (fl. 190–215)   53
Zhang Mao 張茂 (278–325)   66, 128
Zhang Meng 張猛 (d. 210?)   53
Zhang Miao 張邈   103, 106, 141
Zhang Miao 張邈 (d. 195)   159
Zhang Mu 張穆   117–118, 123
Zhang Qian 張騫 (ca. 164–113 BCE)   22–27, 28, 44
Zhang Shi 張寔 (271–320)   65–66, 72–73, 128
Zhang Shoujie 張守節 (fl. ca. 737)   21
Zhang Su 張譏   106, 108
Zhang Tianxi 張天錫 (346–406)   77–78, 84, 85, 89, 129, 155
Zhang Tiao 張條   106
Zhang Tishun 張體順   106, 141
Zhang Xian 張顯   165
Zhang Xuanjing 張玄靚 (350–363)   70, 105
Zhangye 張掖   10, 19, 29, 43, 45, 48, 51
Zhang Yi 張儀 (d. 309 BCE?)   91
Zhang Yi 張揖 (fl. early 3rd cent.)   175
Zhang Yu 張紆 (fl. 86–88)   34

Zhang Zhonghua 張重華 (327–353)   69, 128, 152
Zhang Zuo 張祚 (d. 355)   69–70, 71, 73, 75, 96
Zhao Chong 趙沖 (d. 144)   38
Zhao Chongguo 趙充國 (ca. 137–51 BCE)   11
Zhao Kai 趙開   106
Zhao Xin 趙廞 (d. 301)   64
Zhao Zhen 趙貞 (fl. ca. 315–327?)   67
Zhao Zhen 趙振   86
Zhen Kan 甄侃   106
Zhisong 智嵩   120
Zhi Tanmeng 支曇猛   130
Zhiyan 智嚴   112
Zhiyuanduo 治元多   54
Zhongshan 中山   79
Zhousheng Lie 周生烈 (3rd cent.)   174
Zhou Yu 周瑜 (175–210)   159
Zhuangzi 莊子 (ca. 360–ca. 300 BCE)   89
Zhu Fahu 竺法護 (Dharmarakṣa, fl. 265–313)   112, 121
Zhu Fonian 竺佛念   121–122
Zhuge Liang 諸葛亮 (181–234)   149–150, 158
Zhu Lingshi 朱齡石   136
Zhu Yuanhu 朱元虎   145
Zou Qi 鄒岐   55

Printed in the United States
by Baker & Taylor Publisher Services